Facing Florida

Facing Florida: Essays on Culture and Religion in Early Modern Southeastern America

Edited by
Timothy J. Johnson and Jeffrey M. Burns

Essays from a Conference Hosted by
Flagler College
St. Augustine, Florida

The Academy of American Franciscan History
Oceanside, California
2021

Table of Contents

Foreword

On October 26th and 27th of 2018, Flagler College hosted the Colloquium on Culture and Religion in La Florida. This conference was the third in a series of gatherings on Franciscans in the Spanish Borderlands sponsored by Flagler College in association with the Academy of American Franciscan History (AAFH). This latest conference invited archaeologists, anthropologists, historians, linguists and theologians to focus primarily on St. Augustine and northeast Florida. Dr. John Worth of the University of West Florida set the tone with his keynote address, "Exploring the Franciscan Legacy in Spanish Florida: Historical and Archaeological Evidence." His Friday evening address, known as the Tibesar Lecture, was possible due to the generous funding of AAFH and the assiduous assistance of Dr. Jeffrey Burns, the co-editor of this volume.

The following day was filled with engaging, well attended presentations. Flagler College, and indeed the city of Saint Augustine, once again·provided the perfect setting for scholarly interaction with an informed and, indeed, enthusiastic general public. The timing of the conference proved to be serendipitous as Dr. Kathleen Deagan, who is the Lockwood Professor of Florida and Caribbean Archaeology Emeritus of the University of Florida, had recently reopened the archaeological site at Nombre de Dios. Conference attendees were not only able to visit the site, but thanks to the gracious hospitality of Joanna Stark and her staff at the Our Lady of Leche National Shrine, conference participants enjoyed a wonderful lunch on the lovely mission grounds.

As during previous conferences in this series dedicated to Franciscans in the Spanish Borderlands, the Flagler College community worked tirelessly to organize and manage the event with aplomb and graciousness. Thanks are due to President Joseph Joyner and Vice President of Academic Affairs, Alan Woolfolk. Their commitment to academic integrity and the promotion of high-level academic exchanges was crucial from the conception to the completion of this conference. Ms. Laura Stevenson Dumas and William Jackson played crucial roles in the practical organization of the gathering and ensuring the necessary technical assistance. Ms. Jan Cheney, Faculty Coordinator for Special Projects, displayed her well-known organizational expertise once again, and was assisted by two Flagler College alumnae, Jenna Hardin and Hannah Simmons. Another gifted alumna, Abby Richardson, designed the poster that now graces the cover of our volume. Of course, the magical presence of the Franciscan extraordinaire, Agnieszka Johnson, was everywhere to be seen, ". . . for those who have eyes to see."

DR. TIMOTHY J. JOHNSON
Craig and Audrey Thorn Distinguished Professor of Religion
Flagler College

Introduction

KATHLEEN DEAGAN

The contributors to this volume, *Facing Florida: Essays on Culture and Religion in Early Modern Southeastern America*, came together at Flagler College in St. Augustine during October of 2018 for the third conference held by Flagler College in collaboration with the Academy of American Franciscan History to examine and understand the Franciscan mission experience and its legacy throughout the North American Spanish borderlands and frontier. Each conference resulted in a book that explored multiple perspectives on that experience, with new multivalent scholarship that often challenged prevailing assumptions about motives, social relations and power structures in the mission systems.

The first volume, *From La Florida to La California*,[1] addressed the medieval foundations of the missionary traditions and religious zeal the Franciscan friars brought to the Americas. It additionally offered an exceptionally broad treatment of Franciscan activity throughout the American "borderland" regions—La Florida, the Southwest and Alta California. This regional breadth was paralleled by disciplinary breadth, incorporating perspectives from history and ethnohistory, religious studies, archaeology, linguistics, literary analysis, architecture and art.

The volume resulting from the second conference, *Franciscans and American Indians in Pan-Borderlands Perspective*[2] maintained and built upon this inclusive approach, focusing a lens on the circumstances and experiences of the Native American recipients of Franciscan missionary attention. As David Thomas noted in his introduction to that volume, the contributors included an unusually diverse group of voices including scholars from Europe and throughout the Americas, some of whom were of American Indian heritage and others who were Franciscans. The multi-vocal, multi-regional and multi-disciplinary examination of the world created jointly by Franciscan Friars and

1. *From La Florida to La California: Franciscan Evangelization in the Spanish Borderlands, eds.* Timothy J. Johnson and Gert Melville (Berkeley, California: Academy of American Franciscan History Press, 2013).

2. *Franciscans and American Indians in Pan-Borderlands Perspective: Adaptation, Negotiation and Resistance, eds.* Jeffrey M. Burns and Timothy J. Johnson (Berkeley, California: Academy of American Franciscan History Press, 2018).

American Indians represents what Thomas famously called a "cubist" perspective.[3] That is, a perspective recognizing that no single positioned observer, discipline or point of view can capture (or even express) past experience. Depending on perspective, there were multiple realities of experience and meaning operating at any given moment.

The volume I have the pleasure of introducing here acknowledges both the essential multivocality of the past and the potential perils of trying to condense it. The authors explore a wide range of issues at a series of scales, all of which inform our understanding of the Franciscan-Indian experience in La Florida in different ways. The geographic focus of the volume is the southeastern United States (La Florida), contextualized in the larger circum-Caribbean Franciscan world. In general, these authors tend to focus their inquiry at a fine-grained human scale, often emphasizing individual events, people and ideas that illustrate just how complex and distinct the various perspectives in the past were (and equally how diverse present perspectives of the past are).

Despite the diversity of topics in the volume, several thematic threads run through the essays, and I have chosen to address three of these by way of introduction. One is a concern with locating belief, motive and intention in past actors. Eliciting thought and belief in the past is a notoriously murky undertaking, but one that is directly relevant to understanding the legacy of the Franciscan project in America. Another thread in the volume is a concern with language and meaning, particularly in the ways language has conditioned how we understand the past from written and iconographic sources. A third is what I call "exemplars," with a meaning similar to that used by Franciscan friars in conversion. Many of the essays in the volume incorporate historical anecdote, but some of the contributors highlight the ways that foregrounding a particular individual or event can bring important but under-represented issues into sharper focus.

Belief, Motive and Intention

John Worth's essay—the Academy of American Franciscan History sponsored Tibesar lecture—sets the stage for the volume. With the challenging charge of providing an overview of the Franciscan Legacy in Spanish Florida, Worth emphasizes the impossibility of doing so without a multi-scalar approach. He characterizes the mission communities of La Florida as part-

---

3. David H. Thomas, "Cubist Perspectives on the Spanish Borderlands: Past, Present and Future" in *Columbian Consequences Volume 3. The Spanish Borderlands in Pan-American Perspective*, ed. David H. Thomas (Washington, D.C.: Smithsonian Institution Press, 1991), xii–xx.

nerships between Franciscan and (elite) Natives. At a systemic scale there was always an interplay between pragmatic economic-defensive motives and spiritual motives on both sides of the partnership. He argues, however, that the balance was different in each community, pointing out that engagements and social transformation in the missions can only be interrogated in local geographic and social contexts.

Worth suggests that eliciting intention or belief can be possible at an individual scale through first person accounts, anecdotal evidence, and martyrdoms, but admits that there is no reason to believe that Native mission populations were any more uniform and homogenous in their religious belief and practice than contemporaneous Catholic populations in Spain or the Spanish New World.

Denise Bossy approaches the question of belief head on, asking what conversion meant from the perspectives of the Native communities who engaged with, rejected, and reformulated Catholicism within their own cultural frameworks. She examines Yamasee-Spanish negotiations in eighteenth century Florida, a time during which conflict with the English and their Native allies had reduced the frontier mission communities and Native refugees from the 1715 Yamasee war to the immediate vicinity of St. Augustine. Like Worth, she characterizes the mission experience as an alliance between Spanish and Native players, predicated on both spiritual and tangible returns. This is revealed starkly in the Spanish anxiety to provide Yamasees with the guns they demanded, largely in the interest of mutual defense. Some of the Yamasee in these encounters accepted baptism, but in the documentary words of both the Franciscans and the Indians themselves, the Yamasee who converted to Catholicism continued to live and believe as they had before, largely without censure. Bossy underscores the necessity of seeking out accounts by or on behalf of Native people to counter long-held assumptions about what conversion meant.

Insights into the long-term impact on belief brought about through conversion are addressed by Lisa Marie Noetzel in her comparison of the 1612 and 1627 versions of Fr. Francisco Pareja's Spanish-Timucuan catechism. In the 14 years between the editions, Pareja and his coworkers made editorial decisions about what should be added and deleted, and Noetzel examines these changes as a reflection of what the conversion process may and may not have altered in Timucua notions of sin and belief. Her analysis indicates that additions were made to accommodate Timucuan notions of sinful behavior (such as marrying into the wrong lineage). It also showed that the Timucua were still adhering to sexual practices contrary to Christian teaching. Noetzel concludes that Franciscan proselytizing was productive in terms of spiritual conversion, but perhaps, not as "genuinely successful as one would like to believe."

Native spiritual belief is approached in a very different way by archaeologists Keith Ashley and Buzz Thunen. Like most archaeologists, they rely primarily on material by-products of past behavior and the integration of these data with available ethnohistorical data. Ashley and Thunen approach the question of Mocama religion and beliefs through mortuary behavior, documenting a series of sites in which early contact period (ca. 1500–1600) burials were made in burial mounds from much earlier precontact dates. The internments were accompanied by rich burial goods, suggesting that the appropriation of earlier burial mounds was a claim on and a connection to the past, reflecting a vital role played by ancestors in the cosmological world-view of the Mocama.

They also argue in the essay that a genuine grasp of the consequences of the encounters between Native people and European newcomers can only be attained through research firmly anchored in a rich and nuanced understanding of a region's precontact indigenous culture and society. To that end, they outline the precontact history and archaeology of the Mocama people of northeast Florida, which included several encounters with other intrusive Native groups entering their region. Patterns of adjustment and engagement developed during those encounters conditioned subsequent interactions with the later European arrivals.

Archaeologist David H. Thomas also addresses motive and mentalité in his examination of the Jesuit and Franciscan mission projects among the Guale of the lower southeastern Atlantic coast. He turns his attention to the Spanish missionaries themselves, asking why Jesuit efforts ended in failure, and Franciscan efforts flourished in the same region, for the same purpose and among essentially the same people. Thomas points to the very different theo-visions of the two missionary orders. The Jesuit approach emphasized the individual missionary as the spiritual voice that both brought about evangelization and enforced uncompromising adherence to the rules of Christian life. The Franciscan theo-vision in contrast, developed over centuries of prior mission activity, emphasized construction of a community of conversion that practiced a flexible accommodation to existing structures in the Native communities. Thomas, like Worth, Ashley and Thunen, acknowledged the importance of pre-contact Native political organization in shaping the process of conversion in La Florida.

Thomas also makes two other important points in his discussion. He reminds us that the natural world cannot be ignored in understanding historical outcomes, noting that a period of severe drought and environmental disruption corresponded to the years of Jesuit missionary effort, and undoubtedly affected the Jesuits and the Guale's mutual (mis)understanding of each other. He also notes the importance of understanding gendered roles and politics in all sides of cultural encounter, citing responses to polygamy, the work of women and notions of masculinity as misunderstood elements leading to conflict.

Language and Meaning

Linguist George Aaron Broadwell's groundbreaking work on the Timucua language is concerned with meaning and belief at the most basic level of the very words used to express them. In previous work, Broadwell and colleagues Timothy Johnson and Alejandra Dubcovsky revealed the multi-authored nature of Spanish-Timucua texts published by Fr. Francisco Pareja[4] and the significant degree to which the Native authors shaped the Timucuan translations to fit their own belief systems. In Chapter 4, Broadwell extends these efforts to elicit the meaning of certain untranslated Timucua words that refer to objects of veneration in the 1627 version of Fr. Pareja's Catechism. Using a most original integration of linguistic and archaeological contexts, Broadwell is able to convincingly suggest that one of the revered animals was the manatee. His analysis further suggests that one of the words poses a puzzling confluence of meaning between a guiding spirit or soul, and a physical "idol" in Timucua belief. This interestingly mirrors the union of the physical and spiritual in the *cemi* concept that is central to the belief system of the Caribbean Taíno people.[5]

Historians have always been acutely aware of the perils of transcription and translation in creating what we know about the past. The epistemological centrality of language and image in creating understanding and misunderstanding is considered by several authors in the volume. Timothy Johnson examines *reducción* (reduction of souls), as a word and concept both in the seventeenth century missionary effort in La Florida, and by those studying it. He notes that it is a problematic word to translate in that it has a much more expansive meaning in Spanish than in English, pointing out that translation is in itself a reduction of language into a different system of meaning. Many of those who write about the missions use the term to denote a physical consolidation of Native people to a central location, or a gathering of souls through baptism so that salvation might be possible. Johnson argues, however, that *reducción*, as used by Fr. Pareja and other friars, was grounded in Franciscan theology, referring to a dynamic ordering from mundane and imperfect to God and perfection; in other words, bringing the souls of Native converts closer to spiritual perfection. He further argues that baptism and the

---

4. George Aaron Broadwell, "Shadow authors: The texts of the earliest indigenous Florida writers" in *Franciscans and American Indians in Pan-Borderlands Perspective*, 139–152; Alejandra Dubcovsky and George Aaron Broadwell, "Writing Timucua: Recovering and Interrogating Indigenous Authorship" in *Early American Studies: An Interdisciplinary Journal* 15 (2017):409–441.

5. See for example, José Oliver, *Caciques and Cemí Idols: The Web Spun by Taíno Rulers Between Hispaniola and Puerto Rico* (Tuscaloosa: University of Alabama Press, 2009).

sacraments were not necessarily essential for salvation, given the Franciscan understanding of natural law and God's grace at work in native cultures. Acknowledging that this was not the only meaning of *reducción* in Spanish colonial culture, Johnson considers that the religious dimensions of the term in the Franciscan world view are essential to an understanding of the Franciscan mission effort.

Consideration of language is embedded in Noble David Cook's critical analysis of Luis Gerónimo de Oré's seventeenth century report, *Verdadera relación de la Florida*, which has been a standard and much-cited source on both the Native people and the missionaries of La Florida. In the Spanish language of Oré's time, there were often multiple meanings of the same word, and in Cook's comparisons of the various transcriptions and translations of the document he notes a number of variations that potentially lead to confusion. He also comments on the number of chronological and other errors in Oré's report itself that could exacerbate difficulties in interpretation of the text. Cook is also concerned with the larger context of Oré's production of the report, detailing Oré's own background as well as his sources, collegial interactions and writing chronology, providing a rich contextualization of an important source.

Helmut Flachenecker, too, is interested in the production of information. He investigates 16th century travel accounts and imagery, and their role in shaping European understanding of the Americas. Like many authors before him, he questions the veracity of the engraved images depicting America in Theodore de Bry's massive 13-volume *Les Grandes Voyages*, which were compiled from numerous sources between 1590 and 1634. In Chapter 9 Flachenecker focuses on the images of Florida based on the lost paintings and a descriptive account of Jacques Le Moyne de Morgues, the French painter who accompanied René de Laudonnière to Florida in 1564 as an expedition artist. Earlier studies of the Florida images addressed inconsistencies between plants and animals represented in de Bry's engravings and those indigenous to Florida.[6] Flachenecker expands this with a detailed comparison between the images and Le Moyne's written account, concluding that the two sources tell quite different stories. He agrees that De Bry adapted, combined and adjusted images and used his own imagination to provide exciting and exotic adventure tales for sixteenth century European audiences.

---

6. See, for example William Sturtevant, "The Ethnological Evaluation of the Le Moyne-De Bry Illustrations" in *The Work of Jacques Le Moyne de Morgues, a Huguenot Artist in France, Florida and England*, vol. 1, ed. Paul Hulton (London: British Museum Publications Ltd. in association with the Huguenot Society of London, 1977), 69–74. Jerald Milanich, "The Devil in the Details" in *Archaeology Magazine* 58:3 (2005): 26–31.

Exemplars

Timothy Johnson discusses Franciscan exemplars—stories—that were used to communicate and underscore specific principles of Christian belief. Likewise, several authors in this volume show how a particular individual or event can bring important but underrepresented issues into sharper focus. Noble David Cook's contextualization of Oré's work, discussed above, is an example.

In my own contribution to this volume, I take a biographical approach to a single mission to consider how modern assumptions of place can distort our understanding of the actual circumstances of evangelization. Mission Nombre de Dios in St. Augustine was the first and last Franciscan mission in La Florida, and the only one in continuous proximity to the Spanish town. From at least the early seventeenth century onward the Franciscan Shrine of Nuestra Señora de la Leche y Buen Parto, a devotion important to Spanish and Native families, was also at the mission.

Long-standing assumptions about the primacy of Nombre de Dios appear to have dampened systematic scholarship on the site and shrine. Using largely unpublished archaeological and documentary information, the essay documents the shifting locales, populations and built landscapes of Nombre de Dios in an effort to untangle some assumptions about place, context and circumstance.

Alejandra Dubcovsky is concerned with bringing Native American actors into the foreground of colonial-era studies, noting that most historiography has focused on interaction between Europeans and Native Americans, to the exclusion of interaction between different Indian groups. In colonial La Florida, Dubcovsky points out, Native people continued to engage in exchange, war and diplomacy with one another, and these kinds of engagements were probably more influential in shaping their everyday lives than were European-Native interactions.

In Chapter 6, she concentrates on the trial of a Timucua man accused of murder in 1697. The trial was overseen by a Spanish official in the accused's town, which was near the boundary with Apalachee territory. The proceedings were complex and lengthy, with no clear outcome, but Dubcovsky's analysis of it reveals tensions and rivalries between Timucua groups, as well as between Timucuas and Apalachees. As Dubcovsky shows, foregrounding engagements between and within Indian groups reveals largely neglected but powerful forces that shaped the colonial world in critical ways.

Leonardo Falcón's essay on Franciscan Friar Francisco Carranco also addresses largely neglected but powerful forces. Falcón writes about processes and machinations related to the Inquisition that have, as he notes, been largely neglected by historians studying Cuba, and we might add, Florida as well.

Carranco was the Commissary of the Inquisition in Havana during the early years of the seventeenth century, with responsibility for forwarding names of suspected heretics in Florida and the Caribbean to the Inquisition Tribunals. Through Carranco's story, Falcón reveals some of the inner working and politics of the Franciscan hierarchy in the region, as well as a case of what readers today might regard as abuse of office and power.

Friar Carranco worked under Bishop Juan de las Cabezas Altamirano, known in La Florida for his visitations and very useful accounts of the missions. Fr. Carranco, however, was ambitious and wanted the establishment of an Inquisition Tribunal in Cuba, imagining himself as its head. Apparently to that end, he pushed the limits of his own power, and stretched the Church's determination of what constituted a religious crime. Fr. Carranco targeted people of social and economic importance as subjects of his investigation "manufacturing sin" to implicate them, including Governor Ybarra of Florida, and Bishop Altamirano himself. This, Falcón argues, was done to advance his cause and establish himself as a powerful figure in the region. Falcón acknowledges that Carranco's mission was to safeguard the Catholicity of the King's subjects and prevent heretics from infiltrating the colonies, leaving open the question of whether this was a case of overzealous protection of the people and church, or an ambitious Friar who manipulated and sometimes abused the system for his own ends.

The thematic threads used to organize this discussion overlap in these essays, and readers will undoubtedly see others not mentioned here. The overarching theme, however, is that regardless of our viewpoint, the notion of past experience and meaning is multi-faceted, multi-vocal and multi-scalar, a position shared widely and generally today in the social sciences, history and the humanities. It assumes a fragmented past, but one that might be more fully articulated at very specific scales. The essays in this volume offer readers a rich array of perspectives that may inspire such efforts.

Chapter 1

Exploring the Franciscan Legacy on Spanish Florida: Historical and Archaeological Evidence

JOHN E. WORTH

The connection between Spanish Florida and its Franciscan missions has long been recognized by scholars and the general public alike. From their early description as Spain's "peculiar frontier institution . . . to realize the ideal of conversion, protection, and civilization" of Native American groups confronting colonial expansion, to the more recent assertion that because of their truly pivotal role in colonial strategies, "missions *were* colonialism," Florida's Franciscan missions have always figured prominently in its Spanish colonial history.[1] Evaluating the legacy of those missions, however, is somewhat more challenging, since with only a single exception, every Native American culture originally assimilated within Florida's mission system has been effectively extinct since the eighteenth century, and because virtually no physical traces of these missions remain above ground today. While individual biological descendants of many or most of Florida's mission Indians likely exist among modern populations in Cuba, Mexico, and the United States, only one group, the Talimali Band of Apalachee in Louisiana, is known to have preserved its social and cultural identity to the present day. And only the early eighteenth-century Franciscan convent building still stands in St. Augustine, repurposed as the St. Francis Barracks of the Florida National Guard. Beyond these examples, the only direct traces of Florida's Franciscan missions are to be found below ground in the archaeological record, or in archives and libraries in the documentary record, both within the domain of ongoing modern scholarship. Even beyond the frequently arcane academic pursuit of pure knowledge about the past, however, the living memory of these missions and the friars and Native Americans who lived in them still plays a role not just in the shared heritage and historical identity of Florida

1. Herbert E. Bolton, "The Mission as a Frontier Institution in the Spanish-American Colonies," *American Historical Review* 23, no. 1 (1917): 42–61; Jerald T. Milanich, *Laboring in the Fields of the Lord: Spanish Missions and Southeastern Indians* (Washington, DC: Smithsonian Institution Press, 1999), xiii.

and the United States in general, but also as a formal and informal component of present-day Catholic spirituality.

Before proceeding with an assessment of the Franciscan legacy, it is important to keep in mind the scale of analysis for any such evaluation, including not just temporal and geographic scales, but also social scales. If we consider the fate of all Native societies ultimately assimilated within the entirety of Florida's mission system at the broadest possible scale, extending from the moment of first European contact to their status today, then we must of course recognize that nearly total extinction (cultural, social, and biological) was the rule rather than the exception, even though one might argue this was more in spite of the missions than because of them. But if we narrow our focus to the individual scale over the course of single lifetimes, then we must also acknowledge that individual Franciscan missionaries provided aid and comfort for many thousands of Native congregants within their own indigenous communities, in many cases as protection both individually and collectively from some of the worst abuses of Spanish colonialism, and even against direct external threats from both competing European powers and other Native groups. In between these extremes of scale lie many examples of consequences and impacts of the Franciscan presence in Spanish Florida, some positive and some negative, some intentional and some unintentional. Ultimately, when we assess the legacy of Franciscan activity during the sixteenth through seventeenth centuries in Florida, we must consider this legacy at multiple scales of analysis, partly in order to understand the motivations, intentions, actions, and reactions of many different agents situated within multiple factions with entangled and overlapping spheres of influence and jurisdiction, and partly in order to situate short-term and long-term impacts and transformations within their original social and geographical contexts.

A substantial part of the Franciscan legacy in Spanish Florida lies in what we can learn from the historical and archaeological record of their missionary activities during the more than two centuries that they interacted with Native Americans in the southeastern United States. After more than a century of historical investigations and well over half a century of archaeological research, we are now in a better position than ever before to understand the nature of these interactions and their impact on the indigenous groups that lived across this region as competing European powers vied for colonial dominance. The documentary record of the Franciscan missions and missionaries has always loomed large in historical research and exposition regarding Spanish Florida, and the academic literature on this subject is correspondingly large. Apart from a handful of contemporaneous colonial-era works regarding the Florida missions,[2] early

2. Notable examples include Alonso Gregorio de Escobedo, *La Florida*, MSS/187, Biblioteca Nacional, Madrid, http://bdh-rd.bne.es/viewer.vm?id=0000013549&page=1;

modern compilations and publications of documents with general and specific relevance to Florida mission studies include late nineteenth-century and early twentieth-century work by Buckingham Smith, Woodbury Lowery, Jeannette Thurber Connor, and Irene Wright (who assembled the massive John B. Stetson collection).[3] More synthetic overviews and analyses were conducted by a number of historians between the 1920s and 1960s focusing on many of the basic questions regarding the Florida missions.[4] Recent historical analyses of

---

Luís Hierónimo de Oré, *Relación de los mártires que a avido en las provincias de la Florida* (Madrid, ca. 1619), http://iberian.ucd.ie/view/iberian:55282; and Andrés González de Barcía [under pseudonym Gabriel de Cárdenas Cano], *Ensayo cronologico para la historia general de la Florida* (Madrid: Oficina Real, 1723), https://books.google.com/books?id=dNREAAAAcAAJ&pg=PP5#v=onepage&q&f=false.

3. Apart from their published documents, these researchers compiled important collections of copies, transcripts, and translations of primary source material that bear on Franciscan missionary activity in Florida. In addition to Buckingham Smith's papers at the New York Historical Society (http://dlib.nyu.edu/findingaids/html/nyhs/smithbuckingham/bioghist.html), several bound collections of original manuscripts assembled by Smith are found in the Biblioteca Nacional de España in Madrid. The US Library of Congress houses the papers of Woodbury Lowery (https://catalog.loc.gov/vwebv/search?searchCode=LCCN&searchArg=mm%2082030676&searchType=1&permalink=y), Jeannette Thurber Connor (https://catalog.loc.gov/vwebv/search?searchCode=LCCN&searchArg=mm%2082016642&searchType=1&permalink=y), and Irene Wright (https://catalog.loc.gov/vwebv/search?searchCode=LCCN&searchArg=mm%2082048272&searchType=1&permalink=y), as well as the original John B. Stetson Collection, although a detailed calendar of the collection is found at the P.K. Yonge Library of Florida History at the University of Florida in Gainesville (https://ufdc.ufl.edu/contains/?t=%22John+B.+Stetson+Jr.+Card+Calendar%22&f=TI).

4. Published works include Herbert E. Bolton and Mary Ross, *The Debatable Land: A Sketch of the Anglo-Spanish Contest for the Georgia Country* (Berkeley: University of California Press, 1925); John Tate Lanning, *The Spanish Missions of Georgia* (Chapel Hill: University of North Carolina Press, 1935); Maynard Geiger, *The Martyrs of Florida (1513–1616)*, by Luis Gerónimo de Oré (New York: J. F. Wagner, Inc., 1936); *The Franciscan Conquest of Florida (1573–1618)* (Washington, DC: Catholic University of America, 1937); *Biographical Dictionary of the Franciscans in Spanish Florida and Cuba (1528–1841)* (Paterson, NJ: St. Anthony Guild Press, 1960); Charles W. Spellman, "The Spanish Missions of Florida, 1618–1763" (master's thesis, University of California, 1947; "The 'Golden Age' of the Florida Missions, 1632–1674," *The Catholic Historical Review* 51, no. 3 (1965): 354–372; Mark F. Boyd, Hale G. Smith, and John W. Griffin, *Here They Once Stood: The Tragic End of the Apalachee Missions* (Gainesville: University of Florida Press, 1951); Gregory Joseph Keegan and Leandro Tormo Sanz, *Experiencia misionera en la Florida, siglos XVI y XVII* (Madrid: Consejo Superior de Investigaciones Cientificas, Instituto Santo Toribio de Mogrovejo, 1957); Michael V. Gannon, *The Cross in the Sand: The Early Catholic Church in Florida, 1513–1870* (Gainesville: University Press of Florida, 1965). Documentary collections and research papers include those of Herbert E. Bolton at the Bancroft Library at the University of California, Berkeley (https://oac.cdlib.org/findaid/ark:/13030/kt9z09s1s7/), Mary Letitia Ross at the Georgia Department of Archives and History (https://galileo-usg-archives-primo.hosted.exlibrisgroup.com/permalink/f/ff4mml/ARCHIVES_ALMA21524609000296 3), Mark F. Boyd (https://atom.library.miami.edu/asm0037), John Tate Lanning (https://library.duke.edu/rubenstein/findingaids/

Florida's Franciscan missions carried out during the half century since the 1970s encompass research by a wider range of scholars including historians and archaeologists whose investigations took place concurrent to ongoing archaeological work, and which thus incorporated new types of data and addressed many new questions and topics.[5]

Archaeological research into Florida's Franciscan missions began more recently in the second quarter of the twentieth century, and includes early work by Hale Smith, John Griffin, John Goggin, and Sheila Caldwell,[6] but a fluorescence of Florida mission archaeology from the 1970s through the

---

ualanning/), and Charles W. Spellman (http://www.library.ufl.edu/spec/pkyonge/spellman.htm).

5. A sampling of works includes Robert Allen Matter, "Economic Basis of the Seventeenth-Century Florida Missions," *The Florida Historical Quarterly* 52, no. 1 (1973): 18–38; Matter, "Missions in the Defense of Spanish Florida, 1566–1710," *The Florida Historical Quarterly* 54, no. 1 (1975): 18–38; Fred Lamar Pearson Jr., "Spanish–Indian Relations in Florida 1602–1675: Some Aspects of Selected Visitas," *The Florida Historical Quarterly* 52, no. 3 (1974): 261–273; Pearson, "Timucuan Rebellion of 1656: The Rebolledo Investigation and the Civil–Religious Controversy," *The Florida Historical Quarterly* 61, no. 3 (1983), 260–280; John H. Hann, *Apalachee: The Land Between the Rivers* (Gainesville: University of Florida Press, 1988); Hann, *Missions to the Calusa* (Gainesville: University Press of Florida, 1991); Hann, *A History of the Timucua Indians and Missions* (Gainesville: University Press of Florida, 1996); Isabel Arenas Frutos, "Los Franciscanos en Florida (1573–1763)," in *Actas del I Congreso Internacional sobre Los Franciscanos en el Nuevo Mundo* (Madrid: Editorial Deimos, 1987), 809–822; Amy Turner Bushnell, "Ruling the 'Republic of Indians' in Seventeenth-Century Florida," in *Powhatan's Mantle: Indians in the Colonial Southeast*, eds. Peter H. Wood, Gregory A. Waselkov, and M. Thomas Hatley (Lincoln: University of Nebraska Press, 1989), 134–150; "The Sacramental Imperative: Catholic Ritual and Indian Sedentism in the Provinces of Florida," in *Columbian Consequences, Vol. 2: Archaeological and Historical Perspectives on the Spanish Borderlands East*, ed. David Hurst Thomas (Washington, DC: Smithsonian Institution Press, 1990), 475–490; *Situado and Sabana: Spain's Support System for the Mission Provinces of Florida*, Anthropological Papers of the AMNH, 73 (New York: American Museum of Natural History, 1994); John E. Worth, *The Struggle for the Georgia Coast: An Eighteenth-Century Spanish Retrospective on Guale and Mocama*, Anthropological Papers of the AMNH 74 (New York: American Museum of Natural History, 1995); *The Timucuan Chiefdoms of Spanish Florida*, 2 vols. (Gainesville: University Press of Florida, 1998); "Catalysts of Assimilation: The Role of Franciscan Missionaries in the Colonial System of Spanish Florida," in *From La Florida to La California: Franciscan Evangelization in the Spanish Borderlands*, eds. Timothy J. Johnson and Gert Melville (Berkeley, CA: Academy of American Franciscan History, 2013), 131–142; Paul E. Hoffman, *Florida's Frontiers* (Bloomington: Indiana University Press, 2002); J. Michael Francis and Kathleen M. Kole, *Murder and Martyrdom in Spanish Florida: Don Juan and the Guale Uprising of 1597* (New York: American Museum of Natural History, 2011).

6. For example, Boyd, et al., *Here They Once Stood*; John M. Goggin, "An Introductory Outline of Timucua Archeology," *Southeastern Archeological Conference Newsletter* 3, no. 3 (1953), 4–17; Sheila K. Caldwell, "Excavations at a Spanish Mission Site in Georgia," *Southeastern Archaeological Conference Newsletter* 3, no. 3 (1953), 31–32; "A Spanish Mission Site near Darien," Early Georgia 1, no. 3 (1954), 13–17.

1990s resulted in a considerable body of published research by a long list of professors and their students, often conducted and analyzed in direct consultation with historians using primary documentary sources.[7] Florida mission archaeology has continued since that time, including newer fieldwork at less well-known eighteenth-century refugee missions, as well as continuing or returning fieldwork at many earlier sites.

Franciscan missionary activities in Spanish Florida were part of an evolutionary process that spanned more than two and a half centuries, and thus characterizing the role and impact of the Florida mission system must necessarily take changes over time into account. To this end, elsewhere I have proposed a three-phase chronology of all Florida mission activity that separates early missionary participation in predominantly military expeditions and fortified garrisons (1513–1573) from the primary period of Franciscan-led

7. For example, Lana Jill Loucks, "Political and Economic Interactions between Spaniards and Indians: Archaeological and Ethnohistorical Perspectives of the Mission System in Florida" PhD diss., University of Florida, 1979); Rochelle A. Marrinan, "The Archaeology of the Spanish Missions of Florida: 1565–1704," in *Indians, Colonists, and Slaves: Essays in Honor of Charles H. Fairbanks*, edited by K.W. Johnson, J.M. Leader, and R.C. Wilson, *Florida Journal of Anthropology*, Special Publication, no. 4, 1985), 241–252; David Hurst Thomas, ed., *The Archaeology of Mission Santa Catalina de Guale: 1. Search and Discovery*, Anthropological Papers of the AMNH, 63, pt. 2 (New York: American Museum of Natural History, 1987); *Columbian Consequences: Archaeological and Historical Perspectives on the Spanish Borderlands East* (Washington, DC: Smithsonian Institution Press, 1990); B. Calvin Jones, John Hann, and John F. Scarry, "San Pedro y San Pablo de Patale: A Seventeenth-Century Spanish Mission in Leon County, Florida," *Florida Archaeology* (Tallahassee) 5 (1991); Brent R. Weisman, *Excavations on the Franciscan Frontier: Archaeology at the Fig Springs Mission* (Gainesville: University of Florida Press, 1992); Bonnie G. McEwan, ed., *The Spanish Missions of La Florida* (Gainesville: University of Florida Press, 1993); Bonnie G. McEwan and John H. Hann, *The Apalachee Indians and Mission San Luis* (Gainesville: University of Florida Press, 1998); Rochelle A. Marrinan, J.A. Halpern, G.M. Heide, and C. Blackmore, "An Overview of Findings from the O'Connell Mission Site, Leon County, Florida," *Florida Anthropologist* 53, nos. 2–3 (2000), 224–249; Jerald T. Milanich, *Laboring in the Fields of the Lord: Spanish Missions and Southeastern Indians* (Washington, DC: Smithsonian Institution Press, 1999); "A Century of Research on the Franciscan Missions of Spanish Florida," and "Archaeological Evidence of Colonialism: Franciscan Spanish Missions in La Florida," *Missionalia* 32, no. 3 (2004), 313–356; Andrea P. White, "Living on the Periphery: A Study of an Eighteenth-Century Yamasee Mission Community in Colonial St. Augustine" (master's thesis, College of William and Mary, 2002); Willet T. Boyer III, "Nuestra Senora del Rosario de la Punta: Lifeways of an Eighteenth-Century Colonial Spanish Refugee Mission Community, St. Augustine, Florida" (master's thesis, University of Florida, 2005); Gifford Waters, "Maintenance and Change in 18th-Century Mission Indian Identity: A Multi-Ethnic Contact Situation" (PhD diss., University of Florida, 2005); Alyssa M. Slade, "An Analysis of Artifacts and Archaeology at 8JE106, a Spanish Mission Site in Florida" (master's thesis, Florida State University, 2006); Kathleen Deagan and David Hurst Thomas, eds., *From Santa Elena to St. Augustine: Indigenous Ceramic Variability (A.D. 1400–1700)*, Anthropological Papers of the AMNH, 90 (New York: American Museum of Natural History, 2009).

expansion into Native provinces across the upper Florida peninsula and extending from the Atlantic to Gulf coastlines of Georgia and Florida (1573–1706), and from the final period of refugee missions during which surviving indigenous communities, both converted and unconverted, relocated near remaining Spanish ports at St. Augustine, Pensacola, and St. Marks (1706–1763).[8] Even though Franciscan missionaries only played a comparatively minor role during the first phase as part of the early expeditions of Pánfilo de Narváez (1528) and Hernando de Soto (1539–1543), it was ultimately under the Franciscan Order's guidance that the Florida's mission system experienced substantial grown and tragic decline during the next two phases. In fact, it was after the collapse of Pedro Menéndez de Avilés' short-lived attempt to establish military control of an area extending from the southern tip of Florida to the Appalachian summit and beyond, that Franciscan missionaries gradually and sustainably pushed Spanish Florida's reach to its maximal extent by the last quarter of the seventeenth century, ultimately ministering to the survivors of epidemic depopulation and English-sponsored slave-raiding as Native provinces collapsed and withdrew to the outskirts of Spanish settlements.[9]

What exactly were missions, and how were they established? Though fully entrenched in popular mentality and academic literature, the term "missions" might actually be considered something of a misnomer, since the religious function of these communities was only secondary. In contrast to some other regions and times within the broader Spanish colonial world, Florida's "missions" were actually pre-existing Native American communities with indigenous leadership, albeit nominally under colonial Spanish political and military jurisdiction. What made them "missions" was the fact that their Native leaders had accepted formal political subordination to the Spanish Crown through a process called "rendering obedience," and had concurrently agreed to convert to Christianity as administered through Spain for the Catholic Church in Rome through the institution called the Patronato Real. At the local level, this meant that multi-community indigenous chiefdoms within Florida's expanding colonial mission system were typically characterized at least by a handful of Christian churches located near the central plazas of the most populous Native communities, with the most formalized mission compound consisting of a church (*iglesia*), a friary (*convento*), and a detached kitchen (*cocina*) situated at the chiefly administrative center. Most such mission chiefdoms

8. John E. Worth, "Missions and Colonialism: The View from Spanish Florida, 1513–1763," in *Fine-Tuning the "Big Picture" in the Archaeology of Florida and Beyond*, edited by Ann Cordell (Gainesville: University Press of Florida, in press).

9. John E. Worth, "Inventing Florida: Constructing a Colonial Society in an Indigenous Landscape," in *Native and Imperial Transformations: Sixteenth-Century Entradas in the American Southwest and Southeast*, eds. Clay Mathers, Jeffrey M. Mitchem, and Charles M. Haecker (Tucson: University of Arizona Press, 2013), 189–201.

would normally have housed no more than one resident Franciscan missionary at this central *doctrina*, while subordinate communities without a resident friar would form *visitas* within the itinerant circuit of the priest. Contemporaneous Spaniards most commonly called all such communities *pueblos* (towns) or simply *lugares* (literally "places," which I have normally translated as "villages"), and the term *misiones* was virtually never used in reference to the physical places we now call missions.

Assimilation into the Franciscan mission system of Spanish Florida as vassals of the Spanish Crown was normally a voluntary act on the part of Native leaders, at least within the context of the broader historical circumstances that placed Spanish colonial settlements and Native American communities in geographic proximity to one another, either directly or indirectly through allies and proxies. This is not to say that there was ever complete Native unanimity in such alliances, because there is ample evidence for individual and factional resistance, including at least low levels of routine fugitivism as well as occasional armed rebellions by entire provinces. And not all Native leaders and groups responded to Spanish entreaties in the same manner, as witnessed by the inability of the Franciscan missionaries ever to gain more than temporary footholds among any of the nonagricultural societies of central and south Florida, whose steadfast resistance to Spanish subordination or alliance was matched by a persistent aversion to either religious conversion or the adoption of farming. But within the region that ultimately formed the durable core of the primary mission provinces comprising greater Spanish Florida, the Native–Spanish partnership that manifested as what we call missions was one that offered at least perceived benefits to both sides, as illustrated not just by the voluntary nature of their original establishment, but by the multi-generational persistence of this particular type of relationship throughout the turbulent decades of the seventeenth and early eighteenth centuries, even as refugee communities that chose to relocate closer and closer to remaining Spanish settlements, up to and including voluntary expatriation with the Spanish to both Cuba and Mexico.

What exactly were the perceived benefits of Florida's mission system? From the perspective of the Spanish, Florida's Franciscan missions represented not just a fulfilment of their own moral and legal imperative to spread the Christian gospel by extending the Catholic Church to include the Southeastern Indians, but also a fundamental component of their overarching colonial strategy to assimilate functioning Native societies into the political and economic fabric of the broader Spanish empire. In contrast to other European colonial strategies that prioritized the acquisition of increasing swaths of unoccupied land for settlement by colonists, Spain's approach was instead predicated on the incorporation of indigenous populations as vassals of the Spanish Crown, enforcing religious conversion while still leaving many political and social institutions intact under traditional leadership. Even though Florida's Natives were explicitly exempt from tributary obligations arising from vassalage, they were nonetheless subject to an obligatory labor draft called the *repartimiento* throughout most of the seventeenth century. On a practical level, in Florida this made the inhabitants of its mission provinces a pivotal pool of inexpensive wage labor that formed the backbone of local corn production for the Spanish garrison for many decades, providing a much-needed buffer against shortages or interruptions in external supply lines. However, this broader colonial strategy also meant that greater Spanish Florida was a truly multi-ethnic colonial society with just a few hundred Spanish soldiers and officials along with families, servants, slaves, and other support personnel of many different backgrounds and ethnicities residing amid literally tens of thousands of Native American inhabitants across a broad region extending from the interior from the Atlantic coast to the Gulf of Mexico.

And from the perspective of the Southeastern Indians who lived in them for so many generations, even to the point of following the Spanish as they evacuated across the sea, what was it about Florida's mission system that proved so persistently attractive? The initial impetus for Native leaders across much of the region surrounding St. Augustine to request Franciscan missionaries during the late sixteenth and early seventeenth centuries seems to have been related to the perceived benefits of political and military alliance with the Spanish. After the collapse of Pedro Menéndez de Avilés' short-lived attempt to maintain a string of Spanish forts and garrisons within indigenous chiefly centers extending from the coast to the Appalachian summit, Franciscan friars ultimately became the principal vanguards of prospective alliances with the Spanish, in effect offering themselves as resident intermediaries and cultural brokers. In exchange for accepting a resident missionary and initiating the process of religious conversion, and professing vassalage to the Spanish king through the Florida governor as his local representative, Native leaders not only received diplomatic gifts of sumptuary exotica ranging from fancy Spanish clothing to strings of colored glass beads, but also gained a powerful military ally against which no regional indigenous enemies could hope to stand. Moreover, missionized chiefdoms also gained access to a growing market for the direct products of their own labor, especially surplus staple foods such as corn, the production of which was concurrently boosted by access to iron tools and other imported technology. Indigenous products were ultimately supplemented by many introduced species of domesticated animals and plants suitable for consumption or sale and increasing participation in Florida's growing colonial economy thus resulting in even more access to Spanish goods. Ultimately, the perceived benefits of assimilation into Florida's expanding mission system led more than a few Native leaders to request Franciscan missionaries repeatedly for their own provinces, even to the extent that demand far outstripped the Spanish ability to supply additional friars to more distant locations for many years.

Beyond this, while the origin of the Native–Spanish partnership embodied by Florida missions seems to have been predicated substantially on the opportunity for political and military alliances, combined with access to and participation in the expanding colonial economy with connections to both Europe and Asia, over time the religious component of this relationship clearly grew in both depth and importance. The root impetus for missions and missionary work was, after all, conversion, and there is ample evidence that over the course of multiple generations, this resulted in a fundamental and lasting shift in religious identity and practice among the Native inhabitants of the Florida missions, specifically toward Spanish Catholicism. And as will be discussed below, maintaining access to the sacraments was unquestionably perceived by indigenous Catholics as a significant benefit that grew increasingly important as new generations were enculturated into mission life.

So what does historical and archaeological research tell us about the extent to which these perceived benefits actually materialized, or perhaps even more importantly, about the broader consequences of the mission system, whether anticipated or not? As noted above, this is a question that must be considered at different temporal, social, and geographic scales, accommodating and reconciling (to the extent possible) the inherent differences between documentary and archaeological data sets. While this is of course a tall order, and far more than can be explored in this essay, some general statements can be offered based on available research to date.

As noted above, the religious impact of the missions was substantial and long-lasting, extending even to the present day among the few descendants who remain. In broad perspective, Florida's Franciscan mission system ultimately led to a wholesale transformation in the professed religious identity and practice of hundreds of Native communities originally comprising tens of thousands of individuals within dozens of local chiefdoms within several regional provinces. On an individual scale, this was manifested in both belief and day-to-day practice, including devotions and rituals both public and private.[10] Documentary evidence provides abundant attestation of the reality of both initial conversions as well as ongoing Catholic practice, though obviously it is difficult to quantify the extent of its impact among and between communities, and virtually impossible to assess the depth of individual belief except through anecdotal evidence such as eyewitness testimony, particularly martyrdom events.[11] In this connection, there is no reason to believe that Native

10. For example: Bushnell, "Sacramental Imperative"; Bushnell, *Situado and Sabana*, 95–103.

11. For example: Boyd et al., *Here They Once Stood*, 74–82.

mission populations were any more uniform and homogenous in their religious belief and practice than contemporaneous Catholic populations in Spain or the Spanish New World, and at least some of the documented fugitives from Florida's mission system seem indeed to have had religious motivations in addition to the more common complaints about the demands of the colonial labor system.[12]

But despite our inability to assess the exact degree of acceptance or resistance to Christianity among missionized Native groups, the archaeological record of the Florida missions nonetheless provides robust material evidence for the pervasiveness and persistence of Catholic practice at the community and individual level.[13] This evidence includes surviving traces of numerous rectangular wooden church foundations, normally situated (along with associated friaries and kitchens) adjacent to the village plaza, as were indigenous public structures such as the Native council house.[14] Apart from being places of community worship, mission churches were normally underlain by many hundreds of Native burials interred in colonial-era Catholic fashion (fully extended, arms folded, feet toward the altar).[15] Only those in full communion

---

12. For example: John H. Hann, "Heathen Acuera, Murder, and a Potano Cimarrona: The St. Johns River and the Alachua Prairie in the 1670s," *Florida Historical Quarterly* 70, no. 4 (1992): 451–474; Willet A. Boyer III, "Missions to the Acuera: An Analysis of the Historic and Archaeological Evidence for European Interaction with a Timucuan Chiefdom," *Florida Anthropologist* 62, nos. 1–2 (2009): 45–56; "Missionization, Negotiation and Belief: The Role of the Acuera Chiefdom in Colonial Seventeenth-Century Florida," in *Indigenous Landscapes and Spanish Missions: New Perspectives from Archaeology and Ethnohistory*, edited by Lee Panich and Tsim Schneider, 53–72 (Tucson: University of Arizona Press, 2014).

13. Bonnie G. McEwan, "The Spiritual Conquest of La Florida," *American Anthropologist*, n.s. 103, no. 3 (2001), 633–644.

14. For example: B. Calvin Jones and Gary N. Shapiro, "Nine Mission Sites in Apalachee," in *Columbian Consequences: Archaeological and Historical Perspectives on the Spanish Borderlands East*, edited by David Hurst Thomas (Washington, DC: Smithsonian Institution Press, 1990), 491–509; Gary Shapiro and John Hann, "Documentary Image of the Council Houses of Spanish Florida Tested by Excavations at the San Luis de Talimali Mission," in *Columbian Consequences: Archaeological and Historical Perspectives on the Spanish Borderlands East*, edited by David Hurst Thomas (Washington, DC: Smithsonian Institution Press, 1990), 477–490; Rebecca Saunders, "Ideal and Innovation: Spanish Mission Architecture in the Southeast," in *Columbian Consequences: Archaeological and Historical Perspectives on the Spanish Borderlands East*, edited by David Hurst Thomas (Washington, DC: Smithsonian Institution Press, 1990), 527–542; Bonnie G. McEwan," San Luis de Talimali: The Archaeology of Spanish–Indian Relations at a Florida Mission, *Historical Archaeology* 25, no. 3 (1991): 36–60; David Hurst Thomas, "The Archaeology of Mission Santa Catalina de Guale: Our First 15 Years," in *The Spanish Missions of La Florida*, edited by Bonnie G. McEwan (Gainesville: University of Florida Press, 1993), 1–34.

15. The practice of church-floor burials was normal throughout most of the colonial era, and was not prohibited in Spain and its colonial empire until April 3, 1787; *Real Cédula de S.M. y Señores del Consejo, en que por punto general se manda restablecer el uso de*

with the Catholic Church would have been allowed burial in the church floor, and it is important to remember that in the longer-lived missions, most of these were likely second-, third-, and even fourth-generation Christians who grew up in these mission communities, and who collectively could be considered "old Christians."[16] Normally, at least a portion of these burials were accompanied by Catholic devotional objects such as crosses, crucifixes, religious medallions, and rosaries, along with other non-religious objects of both Native and Spanish origin.[17] However, despite the widespread assumption among archaeologists that grave goods would have been prohibited among Christian converts, and that such practices represented a persistence of non-Christian beliefs that were either covert or simply "overlooked" and tolerated by Franciscan missionaries, there does not actually seem to have been a formal ecclesiastical rule against the inclusion of ordinary personal possessions, beyond the principle that expensive clothing and other valuable items were to be allowed only for those of high social status buried "according to the custom of the land."[18] Church-floor cemeteries in Florida missions may well have been a local adaptation of that broader policy to accommodate practices reflecting Native social structure within a Catholic religious framework.

Such accommodations clearly extended to many other areas of indigenous culture and society as well, and indeed many were not so much accommodations as simply reflections of the Spanish colonial policy not to interfere with local practices that did not directly conflict with Spanish law or the precepts of the Catholic Church, reinforcing a conditional degree of local autonomy and

---

Cementerios ventilados para sepultar los Cadáveres de los Fieles, y que se observe la ley 11, tit. 13 de la Partida primera, que trata de los que podrán enterrarse en las Iglesias; con las adicciones y declaraciones que se expresan (Madrid: Imprenta de Don Pedro Marin, 1787), https://books.google.com/books?id=NBSDD5Q9gV8C&pg=PP1#v=onepage&q&f=false.

16. In 1724, for example, Florida's Franciscan provincial commissioner emphasized the distinction between ongoing conversions and the remnants of the earlier missions, lamenting that "of the old Christians, there have remained five little towns"; Francisco Doblado to the Bishop of Cuba, April 29, 1724, Archivo General de Indias, Santo Domingo 513B. Mission lists from 1726 make the same distinction: John E. Worth, *The Timucuan Chiefdoms of Spanish Florida*, vol. 2: *Resistance and Destruction* (Gainesville: University of Florida Press, 1998), 149–151.

17. For example: McEwan, *Spiritual Conquest*, 640; Katherine Brewer, "Engendered Death: A Comprehensive Analysis of Identity in the Mission System of 17th-Century Spanish Florida" (master's thesis, University of West Florida, 2014), http://etd.fcla.edu/WF/WFE0000474/Brewer_Katherine_Louise_201506_MA.pdf.

18. In the seminal thirteenth-century legal tract attributed to Alfonso X of Castile, exceptions to the prohibition against the burial of valuables included "certain persons, like a king or queen, or one of their children, or another honored person or knight, whom they inter according to the custom of the land." Gregorio Lopez, *Las Siete Partidas del Sabio Rey don Alonso el nono* (Andrea de Portonaris, Salamanca, 1555), Primera Partida, Title XIII, Law XIII, ff. 108v–109r, https://books.google.com/books?id=M7MMAAAAYAAJ&pg=PA108-IA1#v=onepage&q&f=false.

self-governance. While on the surface this policy meant that traditional matrilineal-chiefly sociopolitical organization was actually reinforced and bolstered by Spanish authorities in Florida,[19] elsewhere I have argued that in the face of steep population decline within the mission provinces during the seventeenth century, the persistence of this hereditary system based on the chiefly management of land and labor ultimately proved to be more of a liability than an advantage, since it literally left too many chiefs with too few vassals (to use the Spanish term).[20] Even though Spanish officials seem not to have interfered with matrilineal succession as a general rule, they did so within the context of strict adherence to Catholic norms regarding marriage and the nuclear family, routinely bringing absent husbands and fathers back to their home villages upon requests by Franciscan missionaries, for example.[21] However, in some instances certain aspects of Native social structure were inherently incompatible with Catholic and Spanish law, and one of the more infamous examples of the tragic consequences of this conflict is the 1597 Guale rebellion during which five Franciscans were murdered, sparked by the interference of Franciscan missionaries in chiefly inheritance due to the heir's refusal to reject polygamy.[22]

To say that many other traditional Native practices persisted within the Florida missions is perhaps misleading, since this implies that Franciscan friars or Spanish military or civilian authorities actually had an active, vested interest in the rapid and wholesale transformation of most or all aspects of Native cultures to match European Spanish norms. To the contrary, most aspects of daily life in missionized Native villages seem to have been left alone or largely ignored, particularly as regards ordinary material culture. For exam-

---

19. For example, Worth, *Timucuan Chiefdoms*, vol. 2: 122–124, 192–197.

20. John E. Worth, "Spanish Missions and the Persistence of Chiefly Power," in *The Transformation of the Southeastern Indians, 1540–1760*, edited by Robbie Ethridge and Charles Hudson (Jackson: University Press of Mississippi, 2002), 39–64.

21. Several examples can be found in visitation records translated by John H. Hann, "Visitations and Revolts in Florida, 1656–1695," *Florida Archaeology* (Tallahassee) 7 (1993).

22. Of seven captured Guale Indians who testified in July 1598, six provided testimony about the reason for the murders of the Franciscans, all specifying that the Franciscans had prohibited traditional Guale customs, with five singling out polygamy. From Gonzalo Méndez de Canço, Official investigation into the Guale rebellion, July 1–28, 1598, Archivo General de Indias, patronato 19, ramo 28. While contemporary Franciscan chronicler Luis Jerónimo de Oré emphasized this as the origin of the 1597 uprising in his book published two decades later, recent analysis of many additional contemporary documents by historians J. Michael Francis and Kathleen M. Kole provides additional context for internecine conflict among Native chieftains at the time. See Luis Jerónimo de Oré, *Account of the Martyrs in the Provinces of La Florida*, edited and translated by Raquel Chang-Rodríguez and Nancy Vogeley (Albuquerque: University of New Mexico Press, 2017); and J. Michael Francis and Kathleen M. Kole, "Murder and Martyrdom in Spanish Florida: Don Juan and the Guale Uprising of 1597," Anthropological Papers of the AMNH, 95 (New York: American Museum of Natural History, 2011).

ple, one area of Native material culture that seems to have witnessed comparatively little change as a result of missionization is domestic and public architecture. The immense Apalachee council house constructed at Mission San Luis de Talimali bears no evidence of European architectural influence, a pattern presumably repeated at corresponding public structures across the Florida mission provinces, and Native residences at mission-era sites also seem to have retained traditional forms.[23] In fact, it was the European-style Spanish structures built at mission communities that show the greatest degree of architectural adaptation to local materials, labor, and environmental conditions, a fact that Franciscans alternatively were proud of but nonetheless lamented for their "poverty."[24]

From an archaeological perspective, nowhere is the persistence of Native material culture more obvious than with regard to household pottery production and use, which continued largely unabated through the collapse and withdrawal of the mission communities toward remaining Spanish settlements by the first two decades of the eighteenth century, and even to the very end of the First Spanish Period in 1763. While the establishment of new patterns of interaction between and among Native groups, including short- and long-distance moves within and from beyond the mission system, did result in Native-driven transformations in the broader landscape of their own ceramic practice,[25] Spanish-style tablewares, cookwares, and storage wares never evidenced widespread adoption by Florida's mission Indians. Sherds from such tin-enameled and lead-glazed ceramics generally appear only in comparatively small numbers on mission sites, along with even lower percentages of Native-

23. John F. Scarry and Bonnie G. McEwan, "Domestic Architecture in Apalachee Province: Apalachee and Spanish Residential Styles in the Late Prehistoric and Early Historic Period Southeast," *American Antiquity* 60, no. 3 (1995), 482–495; Shapiro and Hann, "Documentary Image."

24. See John H. Hann, "1630 Memorial of Fray Francisco Alonso de Jesus on Spanish Florida's Missions and Natives," *The Americas* 50, no. 1 (1993), 93–94; see also letter and attached testimony in Dionisio Martínez de la Vega, Letter to the Spanish Crown regarding the state of the Florida missions, August 27, 1728, Archivo General de Indias, Santo Domingo 866, ff. 83r–114r.

25. For example, John E. Worth, "Ethnicity and Ceramics on the Southeastern Atlantic Coast: An Ethnohistorical Analysis," in *From Santa Elena to St. Augustine: Indigenous Ceramic Variability (A.D. 1400–1700)*, edited by Kathleen Deagan and David Hurst Thomas, Anthropological Papers of the AMNH, 90 (New York: American Museum of Natural History, 1990), 179–207, http://digitallibrary.amnh.org/handle/2246/5987; "What's in a Phase? Disentangling Communities of Practice from Communities of Identity in Southeastern North America," in *Forging Southeastern Identities: Social Archaeology, Ethnohistory, and Folklore of the Mississippian to Early Historic South*, edited by Gregory A. Waselkov and Marvin T. Smith (Tuscaloosa: University of Alabama Press, 2017), 117–156; Michelle Pigott, "The Apalachee after San Luís: Exploring Cultural Hybridization through Ceramic Practice" (master's thesis, University of West Florida, 2015), http://etd.fcla.edu/WF/WFE0000518/Pigott_Michelle_Marie_201508_MA.pdf.

made copies (called colono-wares), both of which appear to have been more a product for consumption by resident Spaniards.[26]

One reason for this persistence of Native household pottery is likely the fact that the basic roster of most commonly prepared foods in the Native diet does not seem to have changed substantially for residents of Florida missions, except as a result of increased reliance on agricultural products as a natural by-product of increased staple crop production (particularly corn and beans) for sale to Spanish St. Augustine, along with the addition of a number of Old World foods to the dietary range of the mission inhabitants, including domesticated livestock such as cattle, pigs, and chickens, both from privately operated Spanish ranching operations within and near the mission provinces, and some probably also from the mission communities themselves.[27] Dietary changes appear to have been far more substantial for resident Spaniards than Native Floridians during the mission period, and thus it is not surprising that Spaniards seem to have made use of more Native-made ceramics than Natives did Spanish ceramics.

What dietary changes did occur were part of a broader suite of changes that ultimately resulted in rather profound effects on individual and community health among Native inhabitants of the Florida missions. Assimilation of indigenous communities and chiefdoms into the geographically extensive mission system of Spanish Florida meant more than just religious conversion; as discussed above, the missions were a fundamental source of both labor and

---

26. For example, Jennifer Melcher, "More Than Just Copies: Colono Ware as a Reflection of Multiethnic Interaction on the 18th-Century Spanish Frontier of West Florida" (master's thesis, University of West Florida, 2011), http://etd.fcla.edu/WF/WFE0000265/Melcher_Jennifer_Ann_201104_MA.pdf.

27. For example, Elizabeth J. Reitz, "Zooarchaeological Evidence for Subsistence at La Florida Missions," in *Columbian Consequences: Archaeological and Historical Perspectives on the Spanish Borderlands East*, edited by David Hurst Thomas (Washington, DC: Smithsonian Institution Press, 1990), 543–554; "Evidence for Animal Use at the Missions of Spanish Florida," in *The Spanish Missions of La Florida*, edited by B.G. McEwan (Gainesville: University of Florida Press, 1993), 376–398; Donna L. Ruhl, "Spanish Mission Paleoethnobotany and Culture Change: A Survey of the Archaeobotanical Data and Some Speculations on Aboriginal and Spanish Agrarian Interactions in La Florida," in *Columbian Consequences: Archaeological and Historical Perspectives on the Spanish Borderlands East*, edited by David Hurst Thomas (Washington, DC: Smithsonian Institution Press, 1990), 555–580; "Customs and Traditions in New Terrain: Sixteenth and Seventeenth-Century Archaeobotanical Data from La Florida," *Foraging and Farming in the Eastern Woodlands* (Gainesville: University of Florida Press, 1993), 255–283; C. Margaret Scarry, "Plant Production and Procurement in Apalachee Province," in *The Spanish Missions of La Florida*, edited by Bonnie G. McEwan (Gainesville: University Press of Florida, 1993), 357–375; Elizabeth J. Reitz, Barnet Pavao-Zuckerman, Daniel C. Weinand, and Gwyneth A. Duncan, *Mission and Pueblo Santa Catalina de Guale, St. Catherines Island, Georgia: A Comparative Zooarchaeological Analysis*, Anthropological Papers of the AMNH, 91 (New York: American Museum of Natural History, 2010), http://digitallibrary.amnh.org/handle/2246/6036.

staple foods for the Spanish garrison town of St. Augustine, and not only was agricultural production increased on a local level in response to higher demand, but also in fields around St. Augustine itself through the mechanism of the annual *repartimiento* labor draft. Each year, some three hundred young, unmarried Native males from all provinces, constituting an estimated average of about 3 percent of the total mission population, were selected by their chiefs in response to a Spanish gubernatorial order to be escorted to St. Augustine to serve as wage labor on farms for periods of between four and seven months.[28] Not even counting documented abuses to this system, the ripple effect of not just the increased labor demand, but also the diminished pool of available marriage partners in each mission community, combined with the increased frequency and intensity of face-to-face contacts between Spaniards and Indians that served as a potential vector for disease spread, resulted not just in negative effects to community health, but also increased mortality and decreased fertility, all of which can be documented through bioarchaeological studies of skeletal remains in mission cemeteries.[29] Moreover, as initially dispersed mission populations declined and were successively aggregated together into centralized communities, not only would disease transmission have increased and overall community health have declined, but there is also evidence for biological mixing between previously distinctive and diverse Native populations.[30]

Even though the long-term effect of declining health and population loss exacted a very harsh toll on Native residents of the mission communities, resulting in many unintentional and unanticipated consequences to conversion and assimilation within the colonial system of Florida, Spanish authorities of both

---

28. Worth, *Timucuan Chiefdoms*, vol. 1, 190–197.

29. For example, Clark Spencer Larsen, *The Archaeology of Mission Santa Catalina de Guale: 2. Biocultural Interpretations of a Population in Transition*, Anthropological Papers of the AMNH 68 (New York: American Museum of Natural History, 1990); "On the Frontier of Contact: Mission Bioarchaeology in La Florida," in *The Spanish Missions of La Florida*, edited by Bonnie G. McEwan (Gainesville: University Press of Florida, 1993), 322–356; Clark Spencer Larsen, Margaret J. Shoeninger, Dale L. Hutchinson, Katherine F. Russell, and Christopher B. Ruff, "Beyond Demographic Collapse: Biological Adaptation and Change in Native Populations of La Florida," in *Columbian Consequences: Archaeological and Historical Perspectives on the Spanish Borderlands East*, edited by David Hurst Thomas (Washington, DC: Smithsonian Institution Press, 1990), 409–428; Clark Spencer Larsen, Christopher B. Ruff, and M.C. Griffin, "Implications of Changing Biomechanical and Nutritional Environments for Activity and Lifeway in the Eastern Spanish Borderlands, in *Bioarchaeology of Native American Adaptation in the Spanish Borderlands*, edited by B.J. Baker and L. Kealhofer (Gainesville: University of Florida Press, 1996), 95–125.

30. Christopher M. Stojanowski, *Biocultural Histories in La Florida: A Bioarchaeological Perspective* (Tuscaloosa: University of Alabama Press, 2005); "The Bioarchaeology of Identity in Spanish Colonial Florida: Social and Evolutionary Transformation Before, During, and After Demographic Collapse," *American Anthropologist* 107, no. 3 (2005), 417–431.

ecclesiastical and military jurisdictions expended considerable attention, effort, and cash in repeated and ongoing attempts to support, protect, and ultimately shelter its mission Indians from threats both internal and external. While the practice of *congregación* was one of the early solutions to depopulation in geographically dispersed chiefdoms when individual communities no longer contained enough people to be viable, and for mutual support, it was external threats that prompted increasingly more direct assistance from the Spanish military. The establishment of the Indian militia during the late 1640s and 1650s was in large part a response to the threat posed by hostile anti-Spanish Native forces during the 1647 Apalachee revolt, and resulted in the distribution of a small number of firearms and military training by a handful of resident Spanish soldiers.[31] Franciscans generally opposed the military presence in Apalachee that began in the 1640s not long after the port at St. Marks was established, but did an about-face after the 1659 arrival of English-backed Chichimeco (Erie) slave-raiders in the interior Southeast, followed by their 1661 attack on the southernmost Guale mission on the Georgia coast, and other raids in subsequent years.[32] From that point onward, direct protection of the mission provinces became an increasing concern of Spanish military officials in St. Augustine, and small resident garrisons were ultimately placed in both Apalachee and Guale at the western and northern ends of Florida's mission system, with soldiers also stationed at river crossings and other locations. And as the English-sponsored Indian slave raids increased during the closing decades of the seventeenth century and the first years of the eighteenth, Spanish soldiers played an increasingly important defensive role alongside the Native militia.[33]

As mission populations declined and regional hostility increased, Spanish governors even allowed refugee Native groups such as the Yamasee to relocate within depopulated mission territory, though they were exempted from converting to Christianity in exchange for their inclusion in the labor draft.[34] And even despite the flight of the Yamasee away from the missions and into English Carolina as slave raiders themselves between 1683 and 1715, when they finally returned, they were once again assimilated into the remnants of the mission system around St. Augustine, to which were added other as-yet unconverted refugees from the central and southern Florida peninsula.[35] Apalachee who had

31. Worth, *Timucuan Chiefdoms*, vol. 1, 120–125.

32. Worth, *Struggle*, 15–18; and *Timucuan Chiefdoms*, vol. 1, 112–113.

33. John E. Worth, "Razing Florida: The Indian Slave Trade and the Devastation of Spanish Florida, 1659–1715," in *Mapping the Mississippian Shatter Zone: The Colonial Indian Slave Trade and Regional Instability in the American South*, edited by Robbie Ethridge and Sheri Shuck-Hall (Lincoln: University of Nebraska Press, Lincoln, 2009), 295–311.

34. Worth, *Struggle*, 18–22, 34–36.

35. John H. Hann, "St. Augustine's Fallout from the Yamasee War," *The Florida Historical Quarterly* 68, no. 2 (1989), 180–200.

been living among the Creeks since 1704 settled around the Pensacola presidio of Santa María de Galve in 1718, as did Yamasee around the newly re-established San Marcos de Apalache the next year.[36] And starting in 1716 with a royal decree increasing the annual expenditures of Florida's "Indian fund" to nearly four times its earlier amount, St. Augustine effectively reversed its previous dependence on agricultural surplus from the mission provinces, instead actually providing staple foods, clothing, trade goods, guns and ammunition, and other in-kind aid to the Native inhabitants of the refugee missions huddling around the military protection of Florida's three remaining garrisons.[37]

During the final decades of Spain's first colonial era in Florida, Spaniards and mission Indians frequently fought alongside each other in defense of the missions and nearby presidios, and when Spain officially evacuated Florida in advance of the British takeover resulting from the 1763 Treaty of Paris ending the Seven Years War, just over two hundred mostly "old Christian" Florida Indians chose to exile themselves as well, instead of remaining within British Florida.[38] Settling in communities near both Havana and Veracruz, they were able to continue their lives as part of the Spanish Catholic world, perhaps leaving descendants still alive today. And even the Christian Apalachee who had settled in French territory after the 1704 destruction of their homeland also relocated out of British Florida and moved west into Spanish Louisiana, where their descendants still maintain their Catholic identity despite a long history of marginalization after the end of the Spanish and French colonial eras.

Returning to my original question—what is the legacy of Florida's Franciscan missions?—there are of course multiple answers, much depending on our perspective and scale of analysis. If we view the cumulative fate of the Native individuals and groups within the mission system in direct comparison to what might have happened in the absence of any European colonial presence at all, then of course the near total extinction of these indigenous populations in both a biological and cultural sense represents an almost immeasurable human tragedy. Or if we consider that fate in comparison to what would have happened had a different European nation first colonized Florida,

---

36. For example, James Covington, "Apalachee Indians: 1704–1763," *The Florida Historical Quarterly* 50, no. 4 (1972), 366–384; John E. Worth, "The Yamasee in West Florida," in *The Yamasee Indians from Florida to South Carolina*, edited by Denise I. Bossy (Lincoln: University of Nebraska Press, 2018), 309–338; "Exploring an 18th-Century Refugee Mission in West Florida: Archaeological Investigations at Mission San Joseph de Escambe," in *Unearthing the Missions of Spanish Florida*, edited by Tanya M. Peres and Rochelle A. Marrinan (Gainesville: University Press of Florida, in review).

37. Worth, "Missions and Colonialism."

38. Robert L. Gold, "The Settlement of the Pensacola Indians in New Spain, 1763–1770," *Hispanic American Historical Review* 45, no. 4 (1965), 567–576; *Borderland Empires in Transition: The Triple-Nation Transfer of Florida* (Carbondale: Southern Illinois University Press, 1969).

or had Spain not incorporated Franciscan missionaries so integrally into its colonial model, then we would be obliged to assess the extent to which Florida's missions provided a counterbalance to purely commercial or military interests that might have resulted in very different outcomes. There are many other "what-if" questions that could be asked in evaluating the impact and legacy of the Florida missions. What if European plague diseases had not ravaged Spanish Florida and the rest of the Spanish New World empire so frequently, perhaps leaving Native populations far more robust and sustainable within Florida? What if English settlements along the Atlantic coast had not been so close to Florida, and had not spurred their Native allies to conduct the slave raids against the Spanish missions as a devastating and effective tool for geopolitical supremacy? We can of course only speculate about answers to all of these questions.

However, in the context of the lived experience of the Native inhabitants of Florida's Franciscan mission communities, taking for granted that Spain had already established a colonial presence on the mainland of southeastern North America as an outguard to its more productive colonies in Central and South America, the mission system clearly provided substantially positive benefits for many Native individuals who were born into and grew up inside Florida during the European colonial era, and for the communities in which they lived. In practice, Franciscan missionaries formed a sort of "Peace Corps" in concert with their conversion and ministry efforts, acting as cultural brokers, advocates, defenders, facilitators, and general guides to navigating the complexities of the new, multicultural landscape that was continually in the process of emerging. As part of an emerging global system of interconnected peoples and cultures, linked by vast and expanding maritime networks of travel and trade, mission communities were also able to access a wider range of foods, materials, tools, techniques, ideas, and even people than would otherwise have been the case. And since the Florida missions fell under the protection of the Spanish Crown, they were afforded at least a measure of coordinated defense against external threats, however ineffectual it ultimately proved to be. In the final analysis, however, what is perhaps most telling is that mission communities and the majority of their inhabitants chose again and again to remain associated with the Spanish, or at the very least with the Catholic Church, even after years of absence in some cases, and even to the point of leaving their homes on ships to travel to unknown lands across the ocean. And that legacy continues to inspire today, not just among their living descendants and others who share the faith that they adopted, but among a wide range of scholars who dig into dusty archives and sandy ground in search of answers regarding the Franciscan missions of Spanish Florida, and the Native peoples whose lives were played out on that landscape.

Chapter 2

Are They Damned? Timucuans, Theology, and the Necessity of the Sacraments

TIMOTHY J. JOHNSON

On October 12, 1599, Fray Francisco Pareja wrote to Philip III, King of Spain from Mission San Juan del Puerto, and recounted how, in an earlier letter, he arrived in Florida with eleven other Franciscans "to work for the conversion and teaching of doctrine to these natives, and when we arrived, we were divided among different places, where each one of us would do whatever could be done for the reduction of these souls."[1] Later in the same letter, he notes that his confrere, Fray Baltasar Lopez, had already sought to convert the Timucua for more than ten years. In this period, Fray Lopez "learned the language of the Indians in which he preached with the assistance of the Indians who took part in the sacraments of confession and communion."[2] Fray Pareja evinced a similar interest in language and sacramental ministry and subsequently devoted himself to the study of the Timucua language and, together with select Timucua co-authors, composed several Spanish–Timucua texts on questions of conversion, confession, and communion. These sources reveal an intrinsic link between the "reduction of souls" and reception of the sacraments. In this paper, I examine the concept of the "reduction of souls" from a theological perspective in light of what has been termed the "sacramental imperative."[3] I argue here that the root understanding of "reduction" as used by Pareja is grounded in the theology of the friars and that the current articulation of the "sacramental imperative" needs to be nuanced in accord with the friars' perception of indigenous Floridians as "natives" or *naturales*, and their corresponding necessity of the sacraments

1. "Quatro Cartas sobre Las Misiones de la Florida," ed. Fr. Atanasio López, in *Archivo Iberio-Americano* 1 (1914), 360. All translations are by the author unless otherwise noted.

2. Ibid., 360.

3. On this theme, see Amy Turner Bushnell, "The Sacramental Imperative: Catholic Ritual and Indian Sedentism in the Provinces of Florida," in *Columbian Consequences*, vol. 2, *Archaeological and Historical Perspectives on the Spanish Borderlands East*, ed. David Hurst Thomas (Washington, DC: Smithsonian Institution Press, 1990), 475–490.

in the economy of salvation. While the friars viewed sacraments as a most fitting medium of grace in the economy of salvation, their absence did not restrict the divine ability or desire to redeem humanity, and other activities such as prayer and preaching also served as crucial mediums to that end. All three realities—sacraments, preaching, and prayer—fostered a life of grace and communion with God often within the context of a local church.

Reducción as a Cultural–Theological Concept

In the 2017 translation of the *Account of the Martyrs in the Provinces of La Florida* by Luis Gerónimo de Oré, Raquel Chang-Rodríquez and Nancy Vogeley note the problematic nature of the Spanish verb, *reducir* when it is translated into English. They write, "English cognates of these words—such as *reduce* or *submit*—introduce connotations of Spanish superiority and Indian inferiority and forced change."[4] Nevertheless, these two translators employ *reduce* since the term has a much broader meaning in Spanish that includes notions common to missionary activities such as persuading or attracting some to embrace a view through rational argumentation.[5] This assessment resonates well with early modern Franciscan views of American Indians, in that the friars insisted the *naturales* were created in the image of God, and thus by definition, rational human beings.[6]

William F. Hanks moves us even further beyond any simplistic English connotation by delineating three interwoven aspects of *reducción* in his book, *Converting Words: Maya in the Age of the Cross*, that revolve around another Spanish term, *policía cristiana*.[7] Hanks reminds us that the *policía cristiana* concerns the everyday conduct, both spiritual and temporal, of individuals within the Spanish social world, which they understood, of course, as a thoroughly Christian world. In the Yucatan—and I would maintain in La Florida with some reservations—the *policía cristiana* is inseparable from the *reducción* of "social space, human conduct, and language. . . ."[8] Social space can refer to numerous areas of human activity, but Hanks's definition focuses on built space, that is, sites like missions and towns, old and new, where indigenous people were first relocated through a *reducción*. This principle of missionization is not evident in the early 1599 sources from La Florida, in which the

4. *Account of the Martyrs in the Provinces of La Florida*, ed. and trans. Raquel Chang-Rodríquez and Nancy Vogeley (Albuquerque: University of New Mexico Press, 2017), 62.

5. Ibid., 62.

6. Edwin Edward Sylvest, Jr., *Motifs of Franciscan Mission Theory in Sixteenth-Century New Spain* (Washington, DC: Academy of American Franciscan History, 1975), 44.

7. William F. Hanks, *Converting Words: Maya in the Age of the Cross* (Berkeley: University of California Press, 2010), 1–9.

8. Ibid., 7.

friars describe their original arrival vis-à-vis how they were embedded in specific villages and speak in general terms of their effort to "reduce" the inhabitants to Christianity through preaching and the sacraments.[9]

Hanks's first manner of *reducción* is mirrored in Fray Pedro Vermejo's 1602 statement found in Fernando de Valdés's *Inquiry into the Viability of the Saint Augustine Settlement and the Florida Missions.*[10] Fernando, son of the governor of Cuba, Pedro de Valdés, was to investigate the ongoing situation and future prospects of the colonial effort in Florida in general, and Saint Augustine, in particular. The list of questions prepared by Fernando de Valdés for those to be interviewed underscores Spanish interest in Indian conversions and the potential for their long-term persistence in the faith. Like Fray Baltasar Lopez and Fray Francisco Pareja, Fray Vermejo also gave witness to the inquest, but is the only one who suggests the geographical *reducción* of selected Indian villages outside of Saint Augustine into what is often termed a *congregación* centered on Nombre de Dios. Pareja suggested that instead of a *reducción* of natives to the city of Saint Augustine, the presidio in Saint Augustine should be transferred north to the territory of the Guale because the land was more fertile and the territory more favorable for the conversion and instruction of the natives.[11]

Fray Vermejo's proposition is motivated by what Hanks classifies as the second meaning of *reducción*—that is, the intention of promoting civility proper to the *policía cristiana.* As Vermejo suggests, this gathering of Indians into closer proximity with each other is intended to create a community of compassion in which individuals can comfort each other in their everyday struggles and allow the friars to offer solace to them in times of sickness, provide for their needs, and further instruct the natives in the faith.[12] John Hann observes that Vermejo's proposal was motivated as well by the shrinking native population and the small number of friars, and that there is no evidence of

9. On various scholarly views regarding *reducción* in Spanish Florida, see Eliot H. Blair, "Beyond *Reduccíon* and Coalescence: Population Aggregation and the Spanish Missions of La Florida," in *Franciscans and American Indians in Pan-Borderlands Perspective: Adaptation, Negotiation, and Resistance*, ed. Jeffrey Burns and Timothy Johnson (Oceanside, CA: Academy of American Franciscan History, 2018), 153–168.

10. John H. Hann, trans., *The 1602 Fernando de Valdés Inquiry into the Viability of the St. Augustine Settlement and the Florida Missions*, rev. and exp. version (Tallahassee: Florida Bureau of Archaeological Research; Gainesville: John H. Hann Collection at University of Florida, 1996), available at http://ufdc.ufl.edu/AA00038864/00001. In 1630, Fray Alonso de Jesus also speaks of the benefits of geographical "reduction" of potential Christian Indians south of Saint Augustine. See "1630 Memorial of Fray Francisco Alonso de Jesus on Spanish Florida's Missions and Natives," trans. John H. Hann, *The Americas* 50, no. 1 (1993), 100.

11. Hann, *The 1602 Fernando de Valdés Inquiry*, 147.

12. Ibid., 144–145.

the early friars practicing a forceful *reducción* of natives in their first missions among the Timucua.[13] Quite the contrary, as Pareja wrote earlier in 1599, "we were divided among different places," which were typically the existing villages of the head chiefs of the area. Pareja himself does speak of *reducción* with regard to those Indians who became Christian but returned to the hinterland and had not attended mass for years. He argued in 1602 that if the governor would threaten them in words, they would make their way back to the Christian villages.[14]

Hanks acknowledges that the first two understandings of *reducción* are well accepted by scholars, and then introduces a third aspect linked to linguistics. The importance of language in the conversion process is obvious in the areas of preaching, praying, singing, catechesis, and celebrating the sacraments. Hann perceives that the dynamic of *reducción* in missionary efforts to "reduce" indigenous languages through grammar and rules constitutes one aspect of the *policía cristiana* along with regulations for proper conduct, speech, and even the systematic layout of quadrilateral towns like Saint Augustine.[15] Linguistic *reducción* maintains that language is not simply an instrument used in the process of spiritual transformation, but is itself the object of conversion. Those who were to be reordered into some level of *policía cristiana,* such as the Timucua, required a language suitable to civil discourse. It should be both indigenous and transformed, marked by a certain level of continuity within the changing context of conversion. The grammars and dictionaries produced by the missionaries evince linguistic *reducción*, according to Hann, but he is cautious in his claim due to the multiple roles these texts played. Indeed, Fray Pareja reminds readers of his 1614 *Arte de la lengua Timuquana* that his own efforts to *ordenar y reduzir* the language are driven by the material and spiritual injuries inflicted on the natives by missionaries who were unable to understand and preach in indigenous languages.[16] It is incumbent upon them to learn these languages well, since even native interpreters, often referred to as *atequi*, are unaware of the secrets of the Spanish language and mysteries of the Christian faith.

Moving beyond Hann, we encounter a fourth aspect of *reducción* that derives from the highly influential Franciscan theologian, Bonaventure of Bagnoregio: "All creatures are defective and are led back to God, who is the principle and end of all things, and without whom there is neither perfect rest nor

13. John H. Hann, *A History of the Timucua Indians and Missions* (Gainesville: University of Florida Press, 1996), 168–169.

14. Ibid.

15. Hanks, *Converting Words*, 4–6.

16. Francisco Pareja, *Arte de la lengua Timuquana*, ed. Lucien Adam and Julien Vinson (Paris: Maisonneuve Frères et Leclerq, 1884), 1–2.

perfect position."[17] Bonaventure's theological vocabulary reveals that *reducción* or *reductio*[18] in Latin denotes a dynamic ordering of the imperfect to the perfect, the mutable to the immutable, the visible to the invisible, and the good to the best.[19] In summary, it explicitly concerns the return of creation to God through Christ, who is the *medium reducens*, who comes forth from the Father in the Incarnation and through his death and resurrection, leads all of creation back to the Father in the power of the Holy Spirit. This overarching salvific reality of the *reductio* shapes how men and women consider the physical, political, social, and ethical aspects of life; it fosters ordered thinking and ordered living. In this light, we best understand what Francisco Pareja intends in 1559 when he says the friars "would do whatever could be done for the reduction of these souls."[20] While *reducción* in La Florida is rightly interpreted via the *policía cristiana* as an ordering of spatial relationships, the promotion of proper social conduct, and linguistic adaptation and construction, we cannot dismiss the theological significance of *reductio* since it serves as the fundamental framework for the Franciscan interpretation of not only the term itself, but of the very meaning of their labors in the New World. Since the friars were well practiced in the spirituality of Bonaventure by the pattern of their well-ordered cloister *horarium* and immersed in his writing during their theological studies, the salvific dynamic of the *reductio* was something they were called to embody in the missions, and impelled to announce to others through their preaching, praying, and celebration of the sacraments.

Revisiting the Sacramental Imperative

In his letter of 1595, Pareja also mentioned that his confrere Fray Lopez "preached with the assistance of the Indians who took part in the sacraments of confession and communion."[21] This statement confirms that there were Indians who had already been baptized, although numbers are

---

17. *Doctoris Seraphici S. Bonaventurae opera omnia*, 10 vols. (Quaracchi: Collegii S. Bonaventurae, 1882–1902), 2: 2 Sent, art 3, q 1, resp ad 3, 346.

18. The Spanish translation of Bonaventure's *Reductio artes ad theologiam*, *Reducción de las ciencias a la teología*, thus demonstrates the linguistic affinity of the two terms. See San Buenaventura, *Obras de San Buenaventura*, vol. 1, *Breviloquio, —Itinerario de la mente a Dios, —Reducción de las ciencias a la teología, —Cristo, maestro único de todos, —Excelencia del magisterio de Cristo*, Texto bilingüe latín-castellano (Madrid: B.A.C., 1945).

19. Guy-H. Allard, *La technique de la «reductio» chez Bonaventure in vol 2 of S. Bonaventura 1274–1974* (Grottaferrata: Collegio S. Bonaventura, 1973), 399–400. On the *reductio* in Bonaventure's theology, see also J.A. Wayne Hellmann, *Divine and Created Order in Bonaventure's Theology*, trans. with app. Jay M. Hammond (St. Bonaventure, NY: The Franciscan Institute, St. Bonaventure University, 2001), 18–25.

20. "Quatro Cartas sobre Las Misiones de la Florida," 360.

21. Ibid.

not known. The Roman Catholic sacramental system stretching from baptism to the last rites before death was deeply integrated into early modern Spanish culture and deemed necessary for indigenous Christians throughout the realm.

As Amy Turner Bushnell points out, this reality created what she calls "the sacramental imperative." This imperative is "the obligation to be present in church on set days to observe set rituals, and the related obligation to stay within the beat of an itinerant priest. These two unyielding, enforceable obligations prescribed fixed settlement to the Indian convert. The importance of this imperative in shaping the course of Spanish and Indian interaction has not been widely appreciated."[22] Bushnell argues that rigid liturgical prescriptions and anthropological presumptions of the friars regarding the natives created a spatial dialectic within which the power of the sacraments was inextricably bound to specific sedentary sites of habitation. Since many Indians were nomadic at various times of the year, they were by nature difficult, if not impossible, to evangelize. At this juncture, we can understand why frustrated friars sometimes urged representatives of the Spanish Crown to institute a geographical *reducción* to promote the theological *reducción*.

While the friars were eager to "reduce" the Indians they encountered in a theological sense by leading them back to God through the sacraments, the sacramental imperative was not driven primarily at the theological level by the Franciscans or by the doctrine that salvation was impossible without baptism. The unbaptized were not believed to be "barred from the presence of God forever"[23] by all theological schools in Spain. Indeed, the issue of the state and fate of the *naturales* was fiercely debated.[24] From their arrival in 1492 throughout what is called the Spanish colonial period, Spanish theologians offered conflicting views of the indigenous capability for rational thought, but never doubted that they were created by God and were human beings. Hence, according to Roman Catholic theology, the *naturales* were created in the image and likeness of God. Unlike numerous Protestant theologians of the period, Catholic theologians argued that people everywhere retained the divine image after the sin of Adam and Eve yet were bereft of

22. Bushnell, "The Sacramental Imperative," 475–490.

23. Ibid., 484.

24. Elsa Cecilia Frost, "Indians and Theologians: Sixteenth-Century Spanish Theologians and Their Concept of the Indigenous Soul," in *South and Meso-American Native Spirituality: From the Cult of the Feathered Serpent to the Theology of Liberation*, ed. Gary H. Gossen in collaboration with Miguel León-Portilla (New York: Crossroad Publishing, 1993), 119–139. The question of salvation outside of Christianity emerged in the popular religious culture of this same period; see Stuart B. Schwartz, *All Can Be Saved: Religious Tolerance and Salvation in the Atlantic Iberian World* (New Haven, CT: Yale University Press, 2008), especially 134–137 regarding Franciscans.

the grace necessary for salvation. If the Indians were creatures of God, how then could they be condemned to eternal punishment if, by no fault of their own, they had not been afforded the very means of salvation? This question provoked varied responses that were problematic and plagued by inconsistencies. With regard to baptism in particular, the Council of Trent (1545–1563) decreed that baptism was essential, but we must remember that the thrust of this and other doctrinal statements of the council was against the Reformers, and in this case, those who considered sacraments to be meaningless. When the council was convened, it intended to formulate a response to the many doctrinal challenges posed by reformers; yet, there was a clear understanding that within the ecclesiastical community debates regarding the nature of sacraments could continue within the various Roman Catholic schools of thought.[25]

The Franciscan position on the necessity of the sacraments developed in the high Middle Ages at the University of Paris. The first friar theologian to articulate this perspective was Alexander of Hales (1185–1245), who wrote, "God sanctifies as the first efficient cause; grace as the efficient proximate and necessary cause, since this cause is always joined with what is caused; and sacrament as the material cause within which is grace, and it is not necessary."[26] The key concept here is that God alone is the source of sanctification, whose grace is necessary and works through material realities (bread, oil, water, wine) of the sacrament, which in themselves are not necessary for salvation. Bonaventure of Bagnoregio nuanced his professor's view in the *Commentary on the Book of Sentences*, where he wrote, "It was necessary, therefore, to institute the sacraments by the necessity of congruity but not of inevitability, because 'God did not bind his power to the sacraments,' as the Master [Peter Lombard] says in one place."[27] Dun Scotus (1266–1308), whose theology, along with that of Alexander of Hales and Bonaventure, was studied by Franciscans in the sixteenth through eighteenth centuries, concurred with his confreres. He argued that the need for the sacraments was not so pressing that people could not attain salvation without it. He based this conclusion on the conviction that divine wisdom provides innumerable ways to bring those who stray back into the dynamic of sanctification.[28]

---

25. Peter Walter, "The Council of Trent," in *The Oxford Handbook of Sacramental Theology*, ed. Hans Boersma and Matthew Levering (New York: Oxford University Press, 2018), 315.

26. Alexander of Hales, *Glossa in quatuor libros sententiarum petri lombardi*, vol. 4 (Quaracchi: College of Saint Bonaventure, 1957), Dis. 1, n. 7, 15.

27. Ibid., Sent. 4, d. 1, p. 1, art unicus, resp. (4:12).

28. The Franciscan reception of Scotus's views in the seventeenth and eighteenth centuries is evident in Jeromo of Montefortino, *Johannis Duns Scoti Doctoris Subtilis Summa Theologica* (Rome: Sallustiana, 1903), 569.

So, if the sacraments were not absolutely necessary for salvation, why did so many friars undertake long voyages, face innumerable hardships and, at times, suffer death in order to introduce indigenous peoples like the Timucua to them? We could, no doubt, seek out an answer in many academic disciplines such as history and psychology, to name only two. From a theological perspective, however, the answer lies in Bonaventure's distinction between the necessity of congruity and the necessity of inevitability. The former term, *congruitas*, means "fittingness," while *inevitabilitatis* means "unavoidable." While sacraments are not the unavoidable, mandatory way to encounter the salvific power of the divine, they are undoubtedly the most fitting manner according to God. This insight advocates for a broader interpretation of Fray Vermejo's motivations for requesting the *reducción* of Indians in the vicinity of Nombre de Dios, since he writes, "[B]ecause . . . [they are] Christians, it is appropriate that his majesty should order that they be amalgamated with the other settlements, for they would have the same comfort in them and even better comfort by way of being helped with their labors. And the aforesaid would be better instructed, because in the areas where they are, there are poor conditions for the religious who have responsibility for them to visit them in their illness and need."[29] The friars certainly understood "illness and need" more broadly than simply bodily ailments and corporal deprivation.[30] Within a long tradition of interpreting Christ as an holistic healer, Christians conceived of the sacraments as medicinal and claimed a link between spiritual and physical disease.[31]

As one of their most revered theologians, Dun Scotus, observed, "[M]edicine is necessary for any state where there is sickness; and [in] any state of life after the fall there is sickness and nature; so for the whole of that state it was fitting for some sacrament to be instituted."[32]

There are other avenues of salvation, of course, that were also fitting and employed by Franciscans in La Florida. The *Summa Alexandri*, initi-

---

29. Hann, *The 1602 Fernando de Valdés Inquiry*, 144–145.

30. On the question of physical and spiritual care, see Timothy J. Johnson, "Franciscan Bodies and Souls: Bonaventure and Bacon on Scripture, Preaching and the Cura vita," in *Franciscans Preaching*, ed. Timothy J. Johnson (Leiden: Brill, 2013), 73–89.

31. On Christ as physician, see Gerhard Fichtner, "Christus als Artz: Ursprünge und Wirkungen eines Motivs," in *Frühmittelalterliche Studien* 16 (1982): 1–18. On the continuation of this theme into the Reformation period, see Johann Anselm Steiger, *Medizinische Theologie: Christus medicus und Theologia medicinalis bei Martin Luther und im Luthertum der Barockzeit* (Leiden and Boston: Brill Academic Publishers, 2005).

32. This English translation of *The Ordinatio of Blessed John Duns Scotus*, p. 48 (http://www.aristotelophile.com/Books/Translations/Scotus%20Ordinatio%20I%20dd.1-2.pdf) by Peter L.P. Simpson is based on *Ordinatio*, Liber Quartus, Distinctiones 1–7, vol. XI (Vatican City: Typis Polyglottis Vaticanis, 2008), dis 1, pars secunda, q. 2, c. 246.

ated by Alexander of Hales and completed by Bonaventure and other theologians in Paris in the 1250s reveals the friars' understanding of how the divine invites humanity into a salvific relationship.[33] It is noteworthy that friars in La Florida were well acquainted with the works of their earlier colleagues such as Alexander of Hales, Bonaventure, and Scotus, and in the case of Bonaventure, a vernacular text of his teachings was prepared for novices, as the 1612 chronicle from Fray Francisco Pareja's native Province of Castile indicates.[34] When the authors of the *Summa Alexandri* discuss whether it is fitting or appropriate (*convenit*) for the minister to give the gift of grace, they argue in the negative and maintain that ministers can only cooperate with the Holy Spirit by preparing themselves to receive the gift within and without. Regarding the sacraments such as baptism, they must properly dispose themselves outwardly for their dispensation. Two other exterior actions are also linked to receiving grace: praying and preaching. Petitioning God's grace for others by ministers in prayer is confirmed by scripture. According to Acts 8:15, Peter and John "prayed for them, that they might receive the holy Spirit." As Saint Paul, the undisputed Apostle to the Gentiles, wrote in Romans 10:17, "Thus faith comes from what is heard. . . ." For our purposes, this treatment of grace and ministry in the *Summa Alexandri* illustrates that ministers, and Franciscans in particular, were not restricted to sacramental categories when pondering how God's salvific grace might be dispensed among the indigenous peoples they encountered in La Florida.

Sacraments and Sermon Exempla

The nexus of grace, conveyed through the sacraments, prayer, and preaching, is the liturgy. While the celebration of the eucharist and other sacraments such as baptism and marriage undoubtedly claimed pride of place in early modern Franciscan–Spanish spiritual theory and practice, a recognition of the significance of a variety of liturgical celebrations such as the celebration of the liturgical hours and various communal devotions is crucial for understanding the religious life of the friars and those they considered in their pastoral care. Franciscan textual witnesses in La Florida speak time and time again of the broad, wide-ranging liturgical activities of friars and Native Americans alike. The threefold disposition for the reception of grace noted by the *Summa*

33. Alexander of Hales, *Summa universis theologiae*, ed. Bernardini Klumper and the Quaracchi Fathers, 4 vols. (Rome: Collegii S. Bonaventurae, 1924–1948), 1: pars secunda, sect. 2, q. 2. C. 4, 712.

34. *Coronica y historia de la fundacion y progreso de la provincia de Castilla de la Orden del bienauenturado padre san Francisco* (Madrid: En la Imprenta Real, 1612), 131.

Alexandri coalesced in a liturgical performance comprised of ritual gestures, recited prayers, and participative preaching.[35]

Franciscan friars in La Florida employed stories in their sermons that they hoped would engage listeners and draw them into a grace-filled dynamic of preaching. Known as *exempla*,[36] these narrative tales of salvation are characterized by their brevity and elasticity. They are often found in sermon collections as a record of the oral nature of the original sermon, yet given their elasticity, they frequently appear in other texts such as doctrinal and hagiographical works where the appeal to an illustrative story would underscore the teaching in question. *Exempla* proper to the friars' efforts in La Florida appear in the catechetical-doctrinal works of Fray Francisco Pareja[37] and Fray Gregorio di Movilla.[38] While the theology of the friars rejected the arbitrary nature of the sacramental imperative inasmuch as it restricted the salvific power of God to participation in transitory rites, they turned at times to *exempla* to demonstrate the necessity of the sacraments understood as the most fitting means by which men and women are healed from the ravages of sin and participate in the graced *reductio* of salvation.

Gregorio di Movilla's *exempla* collection in his *Doctrina* contains twenty-six stories, both in Spanish and Timucua, highlights the importance of the sacraments of the eucharist, confession, and extreme unction, and sacramentals such as the cross and devotional images of Jesus and the Virgin Mary in the life of Floridian Christians. While the dangers of clerical and marital infidelity are mentioned, the sacraments of marriage and ordination are not examined in any detail nor is the sacrament of baptism. The absence of a concerted emphasis on baptism suggests that the intended audience comprises almost exclusively Spanish

35. On liturgical celebration and textual performance, see *The Prayed Francis: Liturgical Vitae and Franciscan Identity in the Thirteenth Century*, ed. Marco Bartoli, Jacques Dalarun, Timothy J. Johnson, and Filippo Sedda (Saint Bonaventure, NY: Franciscan Institute Publications, 2019). The recent discovery of a text by Francisco Pareja will provide scholars with insights into the Spanish-Timucua understanding of liturgical celebration, see https://www.flagler.edu/campus-community/news/flagler-professor-discovers-unknown-spanish-timucua-book-while-on-sabbatical.php. This text, Francisco Pareja, *IIII. parte de catechismo en lengua Timuquana y castellana: En que se trata el modo de oyr Missa, y sus ceremonias* (Mexico: Iuan Ruiz, 1628), was unknown at the time this article was written.

36. Jean-Claude Schmitt, "Conclusion générale," in *Le Tonnerre des exemples: Exempla et médiation culturelle dans l'Occident médiéval*, ed. Marie Anne Polo de Beauliey, Pascal Collomb, and Jacques Berlioz (Rennes: Presses Universitaires de Rennes, 2010), 368–369.

37. Francisco de Pareja, *Confessionario en lengua castellana y timuquana con algunos consejos para animar al penitente* (Mexico City: Diego López Dávalos, 1613).

38. *Explicacion de la Doctrina que compuso el cardenal Belarmino, por mandado del Señor Papa Clemente 8, Traducida en Lengua Floridana por el Padre Fr. Gregorio de Movilla. . .* (Mexico City: Imprenta de Iuan Ruyz, 1635). I would like to thank Jenna Hardin and Daniella Tichenor from Flagler College for their assistance in transcribing, classifying, and translating selected *exempla* from Movilla's *Doctrina* in the spring semester of 2019.

and Timucua Christians. At the same time, Movilla's pastoral commitment to these Christians is evident in his *Brief Form of Administering the Sacraments*[39] that depicts the cycle of Christian life as experienced through the sacraments. To assist both the presiding minister and congregation, Movilla presents the liturgical formulas for baptism, marriage, extreme unction, and burial in Latin, Spanish, and Timucua with occasional rubrics in Spanish. The celebration of these crucial rites of passage comes full circle in the final ritual, where the community welcomes women back into the church after they have given birth.[40] With baby in arm and lit candle in her right hand, the kneeling mother is met at the church door by the priest who, blessing mother and child with holy water, invites her to enter with these words in Latin, "Handmaiden of God, enter into the temple of God, and adore the son of the Blessed Virgin Mary, who grants you the offspring of fruitfulness." Mother, child, and minister move in a procession to the middle of the church or the main chapel, where the priest turns toward the mother, who is on her knees, and repeats the opening of John's gospel, "In the beginning was the Word." After the "Our Father" and a short responsorial, the priest ends the ritual with the prayer, "God, you who granted the gift of eternal salvation through the fruitfulness of the Blessed Virgin Mary, grant that we may experience her interceding for us, and thus merit to receive the author of life, your Son, Our Lord Jesus Christ."

The locus of the church, essential to the ritual of welcoming mother and child into the life of the Christian community, is center stage for numerous *exempla* in Movilla's corpus. One that reinforces the cycle of life and the mother and child relationship is *Exemplum Four*, entitled, "Concerning a little boy who pulled his mother out of Purgatory."[41] Here we learn of a bishop, who while praying, saw a vision of a boy fishing in a well with a thread of silver and a hook of gold. Within a short time, the bishop was delighted to see the boy pull out a beautiful, richly dressed woman. The bishop then went to the church and saw the boy in front of an image of the Virgin, praying over the grave of his mother. When asked what he was doing, the boy recounted he was collecting "Our Fathers" and "Hail Marys" as his mother taught him. She had begged and commanded him to pray them every day for her after her death. And thus, the bishop knew that the boy was able to pull his mother out of Purgatory with the prayers. This story ends with a telling admonition, "And so let fathers and mothers learn to teach their sons and daughters as well to go each day to the church to pray for them and put holy water on their graves."[42]

---

39. Gregorio de Movilla, *Forma breue de administrar los sacramentos a los Indios, y Españoles que viuen entre ellos* (Mexico City: Por Iuan Ruyz, 1635).
40. Ibid., f. 32r.–v.
41. Ibid., f. 156r.–v. (Spanish version).
42. Ibid., f. 156v. (Spanish version).

Another story of an image of Mary, childhood devotion, and a church appears in the very next *Exemplum Five*, "Concerning a poor, young girl who was very devoted to Our Lady."[43] In this case, the church is a tiny hermitage chapel, built by her father and adorned with a simple, poorly dressed image of the Virgin Mary. Here, as the *exemplum* recounts, the girl prayed before the image as if it were living. When the girl's parents died, she erected a simple hut so that she and her younger brother could remain close to the chapel. When she died, her soul returned to heaven, and a great church was erected on that very same site.

Conclusion

Gregorio di Movilla's texts (like those of his colleague Francisco Pareja) no doubt were often co-authored with unknown Timucua authors.[44] Movilla's two known works appeared in print only a few years after Fray Francisco Alonso de Jesus, the custos of the Santa Helena Province, submitted a report to the Spanish Crown. With the hope of securing more missionaries, he provided an overview of the pastoral situation in La Florida.[45] In what may be considered the peak period of mission expansion, one resident friar served in each *doctrina* that included at least one outlying *visita*, both of which included churches. With the mission *doctrina* as the pastoral center, each Franciscan, together with indigenous sacristans and catechists, would serve between 1,500 to 2,100 Indians of whom perhaps 600 were baptized.[46]

The churches, as Fray Alonso stated, were sites of intense liturgical devotion throughout the liturgical year marked by singing and frequent services, which culminated in feasts such as the Easter Triduum.[47] It was in this particular period that they embodied through worship the grandest narrative of *reducción*; that is, the death and resurrection of Jesus. This central mystery of the Christian faith celebrated in the sacraments throughout the life cycle of indigenous Indians and colonial Spaniards alike—and likewise prayed and preached in Timucua and Spanish—evokes the memory of Jesus's own return or *reductio* to God and likewise invites others to follow him. When considered from this theological perspective, sacraments, together with the preaching and

43. Ibid., f. 157r.–159v. (Spanish version).

44. On Pareja's texts, see George Aaron Broadwell, "Shadow Authors: The Texts of the Earliest Indigenous Florida Writer," in *Franciscans and American Indians in Pan-Borderlands Perspective: Adaptation, Negotiation, and Resistance*, ed. Jeffrey Burns and Timothy Johnson (Oceanside, CA: Academy of American Franciscan History, 2018), 139–152.

45. John H. Hahn, "1630 Memorial of Fray Francisco Alonso de Jesus on Spanish Florida's Missions and Natives," in *The Americas* 50, no. 1 (1993), 88–105.

46. John E. Worth, *Timucuan Chiefdoms of Spanish Florida*, vol. 1, *Assimilation* (Gainesville: University of Florida Press, 1998), 110–111.

47. Hahn, "Natives," 100–101.

praying that accompany them, are not compulsory requirements for eternal salvation, whose absence arbitrarily ensures damnation. They are, of course, "necessary" in Franciscan sacramental theology since they are the most fitting way in this life to encounter the divine invitation to enter into the *reductio* of faith. It would be foolish to claim that the term *reducción* in Spanish colonial culture refers exclusively or even primarily to the theological definition offered in this essay; nevertheless, a critical study of the term goes amiss if it ignores the religious dimensions of the term proper to the Franciscan worldview.

The significance of the sacraments, praying, and preaching found a specific locus in the local mission churches of La Florida. While many indigenous natives refused to gather into communities under the bells of the church or yearned to escape their influence, others sought them out for reasons ranging across a broad spectrum of economic, political, and religious motivations. For many, their ties to the faith, grounded literally and figuratively in their local churches, was so profound they died protecting them—even when they were given a chance to escape with their lives.[48] Drawing to the close of this essay, the question arises: Why such devotion to a place, albeit a sacred place? According to friars such as Fray Francisco Pareja, the Christian *reductio* finds a specific locus in a church, where the beauty of the transcendent comingles within the intimate interactions between a wounded humanity and a crucified God, who like a divine physician, graciously heals those in need and offers them sanctuary. In the *Catechism and Examination in the Castilian and Timucua languages for those whose receive Communion*[49] in 1627, he clarifies why a church—even a simple hermitage—could mean so much to so many:

> Explanation of the Respect, Veneration, and Reverence that One should have for the House and Temple of God[50]
>
> > *My eyes are always open, and my ears very attentive, to see and hear the prayer from him who in this place prays, because I chose this place so my name may always be magnified and praised in it (2 Chron 7: 15–16).*
>
> This material sun shows its virtue more (according to Ptolemy) when it is in his [zodiac] house of the Lion as takes place in the scorching days of Summer. So, too, Our Lord I E S V Christ, Sun of Justice in the Church, wanted to choose here his own house to honor his own Majesty,

48. See, for example, Timothy J. Johnson, "Florida's Martyrs," in *The St. Augustine Catholic* (March/April 2017), 18–19.

49. Francisco Pareja, *Cathecismo y Examen para los qve comvlgan, en lengua Castellana y Timuquana* (Mexico City: Iuan Ruyz, 1627), 7v.–9r. I would like to thank Sarahi Monjaras, Michelle Henning, and Prof. Aggie Johnson at Flagler College for their assistance in transcribing and translating this text during the spring semester of 2016.

50. Ibid.

[a place] where his piety and immense charity appears greatest. For among the many names that are given to this holy place due to the properties bestowed in this place, here one only speaks of this name *Domus Dei* (house of God). It is called the house of God because this physical Church is according to the likeness of the Triumphant [Church] since it is beautified by a diversity of offices, dignitaries, and ministers.

Because to the house of God, *decet sanctitudo* (sanctity is fitting), all holiness is fitting to the house of God, and as this place was made in peace, for this reason it holds peaceful worship. And therefore, the Christian, when he enters in the Church, the house of God, he ought to enter with great humility and profound devotion since this holy church is an apothecary of diverse medicines that cure the spiritual wounds of the soul. Likewise, this house of God is a house of spiritual treasures of the celestial King, for in her the richest treasures of the body and blood of our Lord IESV Christ are found [along with] other sacraments, indulgences, gratitudes, and jubilees that Saint Peter and his successors, the supreme pontiffs, bestow on us, which they dispense and give in the Church. Likewise, the Church is a school of morals and Christian documents, and in her the word of God is preached, and the sacred mystery of the Mass is celebrated, and the other divine offices, and prayers with which we please God. The Prophet Ezekiel saw the house of God, full of clouds, so one knows of the healthy doctrines and devotion with which dry hearts are watered.

The reasons why the Church should be revered are (1) respect of the divine Majesty; (2) our benefit, because in her we revere the abundant, beneficial salt of Baptism with the rest of the holy sacraments; (3) we are buried in her, or in her cemetery, taking ground like our own house, until the day of judgment and resurrection, and we receive many other favors in the Church, so we can say with the Royal Prophet David, *We receive Lord God your mercy in the middle of your Temple* (Ps 47:9); and (4) we are granted from the Church temporal goods, such as the fruits of health, life, and spiritual goods, the grace of God, the remission of sins, and the gift of the holy virtues. Therefore, considering all of these things, the Christian is moved to go [to church] with devotion, and tears, ashamed to raise the eyes to that King of high Majesty that we have offended so many times; having done this, he prays humbly to the Lord, and definitely he will not be disappointed by his good desire. And so to achieve this, we have to ask this from God with cleanliness of soul, and this is signified for us in the command of the Church to place holy water at its doors, which gives us an understanding of the cleanliness of the soul with which we should enter the Church, Temple, and the house of God. And if it is done like this with cleanliness, our spirit will be the true house and Temple of God. *Ut Templum Dei efficiaris* (*So you may become a Temple of God*). One should have reverence for the Temple like I E S V Christ Our Lord, who left it when they tried to stone him, so that they do not violate or desecrate it.

Chapter 3

Additions, Corrections, and Deletions: A Comparison of the 1612 and 1627 Spanish–Timucuan Catechisms

LISA MARIE NOETZEL

Those who are specialists in Spanish colonial Florida know that the earliest and the best attested indigenous language from that period is Timucuan. This tongue, spoken in all its variations by natives belonging to distinct chiefdoms living in a large area stretching from present-day southeast Georgia (St. Simons, Jekyll, and Cumberland Islands) past St. Augustine, Florida and to the central hinterlands of that state, was and still is preserved in a small number of bilingual texts and letters *credited* to a handful of authors and/or translators.[1] Among these men, one stands out: Friar Francisco Pareja, OFM, whose works comprise most of the Timucuan language corpus (TLC).

The objective of the present article is to compare Father Pareja's very first and penultimate works, which will be referred to by their sobriquets as *Baptism* and *Catechism Vol. 2.* Although both works share numerous similarities—their didactic nature, the common title of "catechism," and subject matter—there are, in fact, significant differences between the two editions that are worthy of analysis. While presenting every single variation between the texts is beyond the scope of this essay, I discuss the most significant dissimilarities, which offer insight regarding publication of the aforementioned works, the ongoing Christian conversion of Timucuan speakers, and the challenges or concerns of the Franciscan spiritual guides.

1. The word *credited* is emphasized for I agree with G. Aaron Broadwell and Timothy Johnson (personal communications) that Pareja's texts are the product of a collaboration among multiple Franciscans and their indigenous interpreters and translators. While it will be shown that the friar later acknowledges help from specific fellow missionaries, he never mentions nor identifies any native Timucuan speaker who could have assisted him and his peers in the production of those texts.

The Timucuan Texts of Fray Francisco Pareja

As alluded to previously, the TLC is a very limited collection of ten printed texts and two handwritten letters.[2] Despite the best efforts of, primarily, two individuals—Buckingham Smith and James Reed Stanton—who tried to concentrate all existing works in a single location, the original copies are spread out over three countries (US, Great Britain, and Italy) and seven repositories (New York Historical Society, New York Public Library, John Carter Brown Library, Library of Congress, British Library, All Souls College in Oxford, and the Biblioteca Nazionale Centrale di Roma).

Of the nine printed texts currently identified, seven are attributed to Father Pareja. His name *alone* appears on the title page of each of the books and, where there are authorizations (*licencias*) of the civil and religious authorities, they affirm that the friar *composed*, *ordered*, *declared*, and/or *translated* the texts.[3] These works, which are listed in Table 1 with their publication dates, location, access, and *sobriquets*, indicate a literary process that can be best described as fervent and frenetic. Details from the first *licencia* in the *1613 Confessionario* given by the president and judges (*oydores*) of the Royal Audience (Audiencia Real) in New Spain reveal that Father Pareja arrived in Mexico with "the Christian Doctrine, three Catechisms, the Confessionary, the Grammar [*Arte*], the Dictionary [*Vocabulario*], a Treatise on the Sorrows of Purgatory and Hell and the Joys of the Glory, and (another Treatise) on

2. There are two original copies of the *1627a Catecismo en Lengva Timvqvana y Castellana*, one of which is archived in the Library of Congress as part of the Jay I. Kislak Collection, and the other is held by the Biblioteca Nazionale Centrale di Roma, which is also known as the Biblioteca Nazionale Centrale di Vittorio Emanuele II. According to Google's digital records, Pareja's text was a part of the original collection from the Collegio Romano, the seat of the Jesuits' ancient Bibliotheca Secreta/Bibliotheca Major. Thus, counting the two copies of the 1627a Catechism as one and the same text, the TLC is composed of ten *unique* works.

3. Francisco Pareja, *Confessionario* (Mexico City: En la imprenta de la Viuda de Diego Lopez Daualos, 1613), 7, available at http://dcmny.org/islandora/object/nyhs%3A3281#page/7/mode/1up NB. Page numbers refer to the *digitized pages*, not the hard copy. The original text is as follows (italics are mine): "Porquanto Fr. Francisco Pareja de la Orden de san Francisco Padre de la Custodia de santa Elena de la Florida, nos ha hecho relacion, que a el, y a los demas Religiosos de la dicha orden que assisten en la conuersion de los naturales de aquellas prouincias, para cuya enseñança y saluacion de sus animas, *el de su parte a compuesto, traduzido y declarado la doctrina Christiana, tres Cathecismos, confessionario, Arte, y Vocabulario, y otro tratado de las penas del Purgatorio, y de las penas del infierno: y gozos de la Gloria, y el Rosario de la Virgen con otras cosas de deuociõ, en lẽgua Castellana y Floridana y gastado en esto mas de diez y seys años. . . .*" This source was used because the John Carter Brown Library's digitized version (https://archive.org/details/confessionarioen00pare) is inferior because words along the right-hand margin on the verso of numerous pages are cut off due to the book binding.

TABLE 1. Francisco Pareja's Works

Year	Title	Location and Access	Sobriquet
1612(a)	Cathecismo en Lengva Castellana, y Timuquana. En el qual se contiene lo que se les puede enseñar a los adultos que ande ser baptizados.	New York Historical Society *Digitized	Baptism
1612(b)	Cathecismo y Breve Exposicion de la Doctrina Christiana. Muy util y necessaria, assi para los Españoles, como para los Naturales, en Lengua Castellana, y Timuquana	New York Historical Society *Digitized	Doctrine
1613	Confessionario en Lengua Castellana, y Timuquana Con algunos consejos para animar al penitente.	John Carter Brown Library *Digitized	Confessionary
1614	Arte y pronunciacion en Lengva Timvqvana y Castellana.	New York Public Library *Digitized (Google Books)	Arte
1627(a)	Catecismo en Lengva Timvqvana y Castellana, en el qual se instruyen y cathequisan los adultos infieles que an de ser christianos. Y no serà menos vtil para los ya christianos. (Pt.1) Segunda Parte del Cathecismo. (...) en el qual se instruye el Cathecumeno, como à de receuir el Sancto Sacramento de el Bautismo, y de algunos de sus effectos, y se informa en las cosas de la Fè (Pt. 2)	Library of Congress *Paper and Biblioteca Nazionale Centrale di Roma *Digitized (Google Books)	Catechism Pt. 1, 2
1627(b)	Cathecismo y Examen para los qve comvlgan, en lengua Castellana y Timuquana	British Library *Paper Codrington Library All Souls Oxford *Paper	Examen
1628	IIII. parte de catechismo en lengua Timuquana y castellana: En que se trata el modo de oyr Missa, y sus ceremonias	Codrington Library All Souls Oxford *Paper	Catechism

the Rosary of the Virgen, and other things of devotion," which he had created during slightly more than a sixteen-year period.[4]

Undoubtedly, the period of Father Pareja's most intense literary endeavor is 1595–1614, from when he arrived in Florida to the year when the *Arte* was finally published. This burst of activity is understandable considering that having arrived in a province lacking any religious texts translated into the indigenous language meant that Father Pareja and others engaged in the campaign to transmit the Christian faith to the native population had to prioritize the elements of Christianity that would be taught and translated first. Given that Christian proselytization in Europe and other world regions had been underway for over a millennium, the Roman Catholic Church already had numerous models of successes and failures from which it could and would ultimately synthesize into a standard practice following the Council of Trent (1545–1563). Thus, Father Pareja did not work in a vacuum; he had models to follow.[5] Moreover, observing the titles and publication dates of his works in Table 1, one clearly notes the prioritization of topics to be taught during the conversion of the Timucuan-speaking natives. What is particularly interesting, however, is that given a lull of fifteen years before producing second editions of the earlier works, one will observe that these later texts are not simple cut-and-paste duplications of the first editions. Father Pareja and those religious who approved the publication of the second editions made decisions about what information should be added and deleted. It is these editorial decisions that I will now analyze.

4. Ibid. The phrasal segment "y otro tratado de las penas del Purgatorio, y de las penas del infierno: y gozos de la Gloria, y el Rosario de la Virgen con otras cosas de deuociõ, en lẽgua Castellana y Floridana" is misleading. One interpretation is that there is a single treatise because the adjective and noun (*otro tratado*) are clearly singular; a second and more accurate interpretation is that there are multiple treatises because there is an ellipsis following the antecedent (*otro tratado*). This latter interpretation is proven to be correct in later statements in the *licencias* section by Fr. Ioseph Sanchez: ". . . and another (treatise) on the Fifteen Mysteries of the Rosary of Our Lady," ". . . y otro de los quinze Mysterios del Rosario de nuestra señora." Ibid., 14.

5. The most influential catechisms among Hispanics in the sixteenth and seventeenth centuries (and in modern times) were the *1591 Catecismo y Exposición Breve de la Doctrina Cristiana* by Jerónimo Martínez de Ripalda, S.J., and the *1599 Catecismo de la Doctrina Cristiana* by Gaspar de Astete, S.J. These two texts were often combined in subsequent centuries, such as the *Catecismos de Ripalda, Astete, Reinoso, Fleuri, de la Primera Comunion y de lo que precisamente ha de saber el cristiano para salvarse*, and the *Catecismo de la doctrina cristiana explicado o explicaciones del Astete que convienen tambien al Ripalda.*

Comparing the 1612(a) Catechism "Baptism" to the 1627(a) Catechism Pt. 2

The two works to be compared in this section are the *1612(a) Cathecismo en Lengva Castellana, y Timuquana: En el qual se contiene lo que se les puede enseñar a los adultos que ande ser baptizados*, henceforth referred to by its sobriquet, the *1612 Baptism*, and the *1627(a) Catecismo en Lengva Timvqvana y Castellana: Segunda Parte del Cathecismo . . . en el qual se instruye el Cathecumeno, como à de receuir el Sancto Sacramento de el Bautismo, y de algunos de sus effectos, y se informa en las cosas de la Fè*, henceforth referred to as the *1627 Catechism Pt. 2*. While both editions can be read as independent works, they are the only texts in the Pareja collection that are physically bound to other catechisms. Thus, the *1612 Baptism* and the *1612 Doctrine* comprise one volume just as *1627(a) Catechism* with two parts is another. Interestingly, despite the *1627 Catechism Pt. 2* being a second edition of the 1612 *Baptism*, which is obvious with the words *aora de nueuo corregido en esta segunda impreßion* (now again corrected in this second printing) on its title page, it does not precede its companion text (the *1627 Catechism Pt. 1*) like the first edition counterpart.[6] Perhaps this ordering sequence is different, in part, due to the slight change in audience: the 1612 text is directed at adult pagans (*infieles*), presumably the caciques and other adults with whom the Franciscan missionaries would have had initial contact, while the 1627(a) edition addresses the catechumen (*Cathecumeno*), an individual of any age group.

Despite these external variations, the core of both texts—their content and structure—is almost identical as presented in Table 2. Indeed, sections within each book, marked with a bullet (•), indicate that there are no significant changes regarding content. One may certainly find superficial alterations on the orthographic and diacritic levels, but the purpose and meaning are the same across both texts. Taking a quick glance at the orthographic level, for example, one finds the same large numbers of misspellings in both works: given that all of Father Pareja's works were printed in Mexico by individuals with no knowledge of Timucuan or, perhaps, possessing a low level of literacy themselves, or the fact that there was still no imposed standardization of writing conventions, one can reasonably assume that the errors are those of the typesetter. This is not to say that Father Pareja was perfect and never made mistakes; his errors, one would assume, would occur at a more sophisticated level and, indeed, misspellings and grammar problems appear in all three languages (Spanish, Timucuan, and Latin) appearing throughout the texts.

6. It is unknown whether Father Pareja intended the two 1612 texts and those of the 1627(a) text to be joined or separated.

TABLE 2. Comparative Organization of Texts

1612 Baptism	1627 Catechism Pt. 2
Title Page	•
x	Prologue*
Poem	•
Introduction*	x
• Declaration of Christian Doctrine by Q&A	•
• Identity	•
• Creed	•
• Trinity	•
• Incarnation of God	•
• Resurrection	•
• Seven Sacraments	•
• Fourteen Articles of Faith	•
• Ten Commandments*	•
x	Five Church Commandments*
Man Is the Slave of the Devil	•
• Renunciation of Prior Religion	•
Goodness of God	•
• Sign of the Christian	•
Sacrament of Baptism	•
• Ceremonies and Effects	•
• Exorcism	Exorcism*
• Anointing with Holy Oil	•
• Significance of the Veil	•
• Significance of the Candle	Significance of the Candle*
• Properties of Baptismal Water	Properties of Baptismal Water*
• Declaration of Spiritual Relationship	Declaration of Spiritual Relationship*
• Questions at Church Entrance	Questions at Church Entrance*
Warnings and Denunciations	Warnings and Denunciations*
• Public Impediments to Marriage	•
• Questions to Marrying Couple	•
• Document after the blessings	•
Benefits of Baptism and Other Sacraments	•
• Dispensation	•
Relationship Words	Relationship Words*
• Words Only Men Use	•
• Words Only Women Use	•
• Words used by everyone	Words used by everyone*
Notes on the Sacrament of Baptism	Notes on the Sacrament of Baptism*
• Impediments to Baptism	Impediments to Baptism*
The Four Qualities of Godparents	•
• Two Spiritual Relationships*	x
Sacrament of Confirmation	Sacrament of Confirmation*
• The Chrism	The Chrism*
Papal Concessions	•,

Notes: Bullet (•) = no significant change in content or meaning. Asterisk (*) = change in content and meaning. Cross-out (x) = absence of content appearing in previous or subsequent edition.

Table 3. Fifth Catechistic Lesson

1612 Baptism	English	1627 Catechism Pt. 2
Lo quinto se les enseñara los siete pecados mortals y el daño y estrago que haze en el anima, para queassi sepan huir dellos, y como en grande manera an de ser aborrecidos, particularmente el de la carne sodomia y adulterio, y como an de tener grã dolor, ypessar de los passados, para receuir este sancto Sacramento, y proponer de alli adelãte, no tornar a incurrir en ellos.	The fifth thing they (the catechumens) will be taught are the seven mortal sins and the damage and ravage they do to the soul; so that (the catechumens) will know how to flee from them and how, to a large extent, those sins must be abhorred, particularly that of the flesh—sodomy, adultery, and larceny—and how (the catechumens) must have great pain and sorrow for the past (sins) in order to receive this holy Sacrament and to resolve henceforth to not return and to fall into those sins.	Loquinto se les enseñara los siete pecados mortals y el daño y estrago que hazen en el anima, pera queassì sepan huir dellos, y como en grande manera an de ser aborrecidos, particularmente el de la carne sodomia y adulterio, y hurtos, y como an de tener grã dolor, y pessar de los passados, para recebir este sancto Sacramento, y proponer de alli adelante, notornar a incurrir en ellos.

Besides the spelling mistakes, other common errors that fit a pattern suggesting the Mexican typesetters are to blame are missing letters (e.g., *parntesco* for *parentesco*) or entire words (e.g., *No soy christiano* vs. *No soy christiano, Padre*); upside-down characters (e.g., ɘ vs. *e*, *p* vs. *b*, *n* vs. *u*); incorrect selections for similarly shaped characters (e.g., *f* vs. *ſ*, *r* vs. *t*, *h* vs. *b*, *o* vs. *c*), likely due to worn print blocks; and word boundary errors (e.g., àde vs. à de, caquiDiosi vs. caqui Diosi). Additional superficial changes that do not significantly affect content but are indicative of patterns originating from the author or, possibly, his editors are spelling changes to indicate stress (e.g., *y* vs. *i* to designate a tonic vowel as in *cuydado* or initial word position as in *Yglesia*), Latin- and Greek-type spellings or abbreviations (e.g., *sancta* vs. *santa*, *Xpo* for *Christo/Cristo*), diacritical marks (e.g., sharp, grave, and circumflex accents) used indiscriminately to designate parts of speech (à = verb *ha* vs. à = preposition *a*) and or verb tense/stress (e.g., *mando* vs. *mandó*).

Infinitely more interesting are the sections marked by an asterisk (*) or an (x), which denote additions or deletions, respectively. Oftentimes the change can be limited to a word or two as exemplified in Tables 3 and 4.[7,8]

7. Francisco Pareja, *Cathecismo en Lengva Castellana, y Timuquana* (Mexico City: En la Empre[n]ta de la Viuda de Pedro Balli, 1612), 20–21, available at http://dcmny.org/islandora/object/nyhs%3A2261#page/1/mode/2up; Pareja, *Catecismo en Lengva Timvqvana y Castellana* (Mexico City: En la Emprenta de Iuan Ruyz, 1627), 9; available at

TABLE 4. Family Lineage

1612 Baptism	English	1627 Catechism Pt. 2
Otro linaje particular, que es de auras Apohola deíte deciende, nuculaha, nuculahaquo, nucula haruqui chorofa vsinaca, Ayahanisino, napoya, amacahuri; hauenayo Amusaya. Todos estos-linajes salen de aquel Apohola: nose casan vnos cõ otros los destos linajes.	Another particular lineage that is from the Elk, Apohola, from this descends nuculaha, nuculahaqûo, nucula haruqui, chorofa vsinaca, Ayahanisino, napoya, amacahurì; hauenayo White Fox Amusaya. All these lineages come from that Apohola: those (people) from these lineages do not marry one another.	Otro linaje particular, que es de antas Apohola deíte deciende, nuculaha, nuculahaqûo, nucula haruqui, chorofa vsinaca, Ayahanisino, napoya, amacahurì; hauenayo çorra blanca Amusaya. Todos estos linajes salen de aquel Apohola: nose casan vnos cõ otros los destos linajes.

While these particular passages may not seem to reveal earth-shattering news by modern standards, they do demonstrate that Father Pareja and/or his content editors carefully reviewed the original 1612 work and, conscientiously, updated missing information. Further, in each of these cases, there is insight as to what the seventeenth-century Church and Timucuan speakers considered important. For the former, theft was as sinful as homosexuality and adultery; for the latter, an important family line, the Elk, was the source of other lineal offshoots of which one was the White Fox. Also, for unknown and unexplained reasons, relatives from within that family would not marry one another *even if*, presumably, the Church were to permit it, that is, a union that fit the Catholic criteria related to consanguinity and affinity.[9]

https://books.google.com/books?id=ykx-MMdohTAC&printsec=frontcover&dq=editions: UEHaxC1nFwoC&hl=en&sa=X&ved=0ahUKEwj4-P3xgujgAhXvzVkKHZ4JAK4Q6AEIMTAB NB. To obtain the correct page number in Google, access via Read eBook.

8. Pareja, *Cathecismo* (1612), 137, and Pareja, *Catecismo* (1627), 102. The word "*anta*" has changed meaning. In the early eighteenth century it meant "a type of buffalo," cf. Capt. John Stevens, *A New Dictionary: Spanish and English, English and Spanish* (London: J. Darby, 1726), 62; available at https://books.google.com/books?id=9q56ebQJf7sC&printsec=frontcover&authuser=0&source=gbs_ge_summary_r&cad=0. In modern times, it seems to mean "elk, moose, or tapir," cf. "Anta," WordReference.com, accessed March 2, 2019, at https://www.wordreference.com/es/en/translation.asp?spen=anta. The Real Academia Española similarly defines "anta" as "alce," which is a "Mamífero rumiante, parecido al ciervo y tan corpulento como el caballo, de cuello corto, cabeza grande, pelo oscuro y astas en forma de pala con recortaduras profundas en los bordes," and originating from Latin *alce*. "Anta," Real Academia Española, *Diccionario de la lengua española*, accessed March 2, 2019, available at https://dle.rae.es/?id=2lHM86O|2lHlpJa.

9. In both editions, Father Pareja, as would any religious, objected to Timucuan relationships that violated Christian ideas regarding consanguinity, affinity, and monogamy.

TABLE 5. Four Types of Relationships

English	1627 Catechism Pt. 2
1. There are four types of relationships. The first is called consanguinity, which the Christian Indian has with his parents, grandparents, children, grandchildren, first cousins, siblings, and nieces/nephews. What is between a stepfather/stepmother and stepchildren will be called affinity rather than consanguinity.	1 Quatro maneras ay de parenteʃcos. El primero ʃe llama conʃanguinidad, la qual tiene el indio Chriʃtiano con ʃus padres, abuelos, hijos nietos, primos hermanos, y ʃobrinos. La que ʃe pone entre padraʃtro, y entenados, mas propriamente ʃe dirà, affinidad que conʃanguinidad.
2. The second is called affinity, which the married Indian has with his wife's parents, grandparents, children, grand-children, aunts/uncles, first cousins, siblings, and nieces/nephews, up to the second degree.	2 La 2. ʃe llama affinidad, la qual tiene el Indio, caʃado cõ los padres, y abuelos, hijos, y nietos, tios, y primos hermanos, y ʃobrinos de ʃu muger, haʃta el ʃegundo grado.
3. The third affinity [is] illicit excopula when one is single or married and a relative of his wife's relatives with whom he committed the sin up to the second degree. . . . The fourth is spiritual kindred through Baptism or Confirmation as already mentioned.	3 La tercera affinidad excopula illicita, ora ʃea ʃoltero, ora caʃado, que da el que cometio el pecado hecho pariente delos parientes de la muger con quiʃ pecò haʃta el 2 grado, (...) El quatro es Cognacion eʃpiritual, por el Baptiʃmo, ò Confirmacion, que ya queda dicho.

A recurring theme stressed throughout the first and second editions of these texts is relationships a Christian forms and cultivates with others. The relationships can be sublime and spiritual as one may have with God, base and mundane as one may have with the Devil, and close as one may have with family members and so on. Although Timucuan-speaking natives had familial and social units, some aspects of which were shared cultural practices observed by the Spanish, there still, apparently, was a significant amount of misunderstanding or, perhaps,

This is observed, for example in the section regarding the secret impediments of marriage: "Therefore, the man ought to report whether he has secretly copulated with the mother of the woman he wants to marry, or with her grandmother, or her aunt, or her sister, or her cousin, or her niece; he cannot marry her and, even if it is a secret, there is the obligation to tell this to the priest who is to marry you. The same is said to the woman: she ought to consider whether she has copulated with the father, or grandfather, or brother [or nephew, or cousin] of the man whom she wants to marry; even if it has been hidden, she must declare it to the one [the priest] who is to marry them." Por tanto el hombre aduierta, que si secretamente à tenido copula con la madre de aquella con quien se quiere casar, ô con su abuela, ò cõ su tia, ò cõ su hermana, ô prima, ò sobrina, no puede casarse con ella, y aunque sea secreto, ay obligacion de dezirlo al Sacerdote que te à de casar. Lo mesmo se le dize à la muger, que mire si à tenido copula con ella el padre, ò abuelo, ò hermano del con que se quiere desposar, ô sobrino, ò primo, aunque aya sido oculto lo à de declarar al que à de casarlos. Ibid., *1612 Cathecismo*, 91, and Ibid., *1627 Catecismo*, 71.

resistance on the part of the Indians to renouncing their practices and to embrace those of the Christian faith. A perfect example of this, which is part of one of the longest and most detailed additions to the 1627(a) Catechism, concerns the idea of Christian sexual relationships, shown in Table 5.[10]

The above passage, which has no exact equivalent in the *1612 Baptism*, is significant: it reflects two cultural practices and values at odds, even after thirty-plus years of contact between Franciscan missionaries and natives in Florida. While Father Pareja acknowledges in an earlier passage that some of the Indians did observe ideas concerning consanguinity, he also says that many did not pay any attention to the impediment of affinity. Further, he classifies the Indians' rejection of it as a type of malice, which appears to be one of the reasons he purposefully added the above passage in the second edition.[11] Certainly Father Pareja was not alone in this battle of wills: he also acknowledges the help of his colleague, Father Gregorio Movilla, who helped him with the Timucuan hinterland dialects. Importantly, this collegiality between Pareja and Movilla seems to have contributed to Movilla's later publication of two Timucuan–Spanish texts in the following decade, texts which made him the second-most important author/contributor to the TLC.

Conclusions

There are various conclusions that one can draw from comparing the *1612 Catechism aka "Baptism"* and the 1627 edition. First, with regard to the literary output of Father Pareja, it further attests to the zeal, energy, and resolute nature noted by other famous accounts such as Luís Jerónimo de Oré's noted. The publication dates of Father Pareja's works along with their accompanying *licencias* also provide insight on the inter-order (Franciscan, Jesuit, and Dominican) bureaucracy that Pareja successfully navigated to publish four texts in four years (and possibly more that may someday be discovered).

The fifteen-year gap between the 1612 and 1627 editions also provides insight on the conversion process in Florida. It suggests that Franciscan proselytizing was productive but, perhaps, not as successful as many would like to believe. The *1627(a) Catechism* clearly attests that, after approximately thirty years or more than a generation, the Florida natives had not completely embraced Christianity in all its aspects. A significant number still observed indigenous cultural/sexual practices that were contrary to Church teachings and were considered by Pareja to be spiteful behavior. Nevertheless, it is also clear that by publishing up to the year of his death in 1628, Father Pareja was tenacious and dedicated to his flock to the end.

10. Pareja, *1627(a) Catechism*, 66–67.

11. Ibid., 62: "[Y] assi por esta parte de affinidad, ay toda via alguna rotura, y aun malicia, por lo qual deuen vigilar sus ministros."

Chapter 4

The Things They Formerly Worshipped: Timucua Christian Texts on Native Worship

George Aaron Broadwell

The Timucua People and Their Language

At the time of Spanish contact, the Timucua were the original people of northern central Florida, and lived in an area from the Atlantic coast to the Gulf of Mexico as far north as southeast Georgia and south to around Ocala, Florida.[1] They were first contacted by Europeans in 1513, but intensive contact came in 1565 with the establishment of the Spanish colony at St. Augustine, Florida. In 1595, the Franciscans established missions to convert the Timucua to Christianity. With the assistance of Timucua converts, the Franciscans produced a large number of Timucua language documents.

The primary person responsible for introducing literacy to the Timucua was Friar Francisco Pareja. Pareja's work was continued by Gregorio de Movilla, another Spanish friar, who oversaw the production of other religious documents in Timucua. Although the religious documents have only the names of the Franciscan friars attached to them—effectively giving the friars sole credit for their production—a closer look reveals that the Timucua portions of documents are more likely to have been written by Timucua writers themselves, under the direction of Pareja and Movilla.[2] In the course of two centuries after Spanish contact, the Timucua faced warfare and epidemic disease, until the recorded number of Timucua people associated with these missions was reduced from an estimated 200,000 persons at the time of contact to less than a hundred in the mid-eighteenth century. In 1763, as the Spanish ceded La Florida to the English, Timucua people at the missions, some of them converts, and other Indigenous refugees, left Florida for Cuba. Their language, Timucua, has not been spoken since around the middle of the eighteenth century.

1. See Jerald Milanich, *The Timucua* (Oxford: Blackwell, 1996).
2. See Alejandra Dubcovsky and George Aaron Broadwell, "Writing Timucua: Recovering and Interrogating Indigenous Authorship," *Early American Studies: An Interdisciplinary Journal* 15 (2017): 409–441.

Our knowledge of Timucua comes almost entirely from seventeenth-century Spanish colonial documents, which include multiple works authored or edited by Pareja and Movilla.[3]

There are explorations of a few areas of Timucua grammar in nineteenth-century works by Gatschet, De la Grasserie, and Adam and Vinson.[4] The only twentieth-century treatment of Timucua grammar is by Julian Granberry, but more recent work has proposed extensive revisions to his account of the language.[5]

A fortunate result of a new understanding of the Timucua grammar and lexicon is the possibility of translating Timucua texts that were previously unreadable. This chapter focuses on the translation and interpretation of one such long passage dealing with objects of worship in traditional Timucua religion.

---

3. Francisco Pareja, *Catechismo y breve exposición de la doctrina christiana* (Mexico City: Casa de la viuda de Pedro Balli, 1612a); Pareja, *Cathecismo en lengua castellana, y Timuquana: En el qual se contiene lo que se les puede enseñar a los adultos que an de ser baptizados* (Mexico City: Impresa de la Viuda de Pedro Balli, 1612b); Pareja, *Confessionario en lengua castellana y timuquana con unos consejos para animar al penitente* (Mexico City: Emprenta de la viuda de Diego Lopez Daualos, 1613); Pareja, *Arte y Pronunciacion de la Lengua Timucvana y Castellana* (Mexico City: Emprenta de Ioan Ruyz, 1614); Pareja, *Catecismo en lengua timuquana y castellana en el qual se instruyen y cathequizan los adultos infieles que an de ser Christianos* (Mexico City: Emprenta de Ioan Ruyz, 1627a); Pareja, *Cathecismo y Examen para los que comulgan. En lengua castellana y timuquana* (Mexico City: Imprenta de Iuan Ruyz, 1627b); Gregorio de Movilla, *Explicacion de la Doctrina que compuso el cardenal Belarmino, por mandado del Señor Papa Clemente 8, Traducida en Lengua Floridana: por el Padre Fr. Gregorio de Movilla* (Mexico City: Imprenta de Iuan Ruyz, 1635a); and Movilla, *Forma breve de administrar los sacramentos a los indios y españoles que viven entre ellos* (Mexico City: Imprenta de Iuan Ruyz, 1635b).

4. See Raoul de la Grasserie, *Esquisse d'une grammaire du Timucua* (Orleans: G Jacob, 1893); Gatschet, Albert, "The Timucua language," *Proceedings of the American Philosophical Society* 16 (1877): 1–17; Albert Gatschet, "The Timucua language," *Proceedings of the American Philosophical Society* 17 (1878): 490–504; and Albert Gatschet, "The Timucua language," *Proceedings of the American Philosophical Society* 18 (1880): 465–502; Lucien Adam and Julien Vinson, eds. *Arte de la lengua timuquana, compuesto en 1614 por el padre Francisco Pareja, y publicado conforme al ejemplar original único* (Paris: Maisonneuve Frères, 1886).

5. See Julian Granberry, *A Grammar and Dictionary of the Timucua Language* (Tuscaloosa: University of Alabama Press, 1993), and contrary analyses in George Aaron Broadwell, "Timucua -ta: Muskogean Parallels," in *New Perspectives on Language Variety in the South: Historical and Contemporary Approaches*, ed. Michael D. Picone and Catherine Evans Davies, 72–81 (Tuscaloosa: University of Alabama, 2015); George Aaron Broadwell, "Shadow Authors: The Texts of the Earliest Indigenous Florida Writers," in *Franciscans and American Indians in Pan-Borderlands Perspective*, ed. Jeffrey Burns and Timothy Johnson, 139–152 (Oceanside, CA: Academy of American Franciscan History, 2017); and George Aaron Broadwell, "Honorific Usage in Timucua Exempla," in *Preaching and New Worlds: Sermons as Mirrors of Realms Near and Far*, ed. Timothy Johnson, Katherine Wrisbey Shelby, and John D. Young. 280-294 (New York: Routledge, 2019). The Web edition of George Aaron Broadwell, *Timucua–English Dictionary* (Gainesville: University of Florida, 2018), at http://timucua.webonary.org/ is a new lexicon of Timucua.

The 1627 Pareja *Catecismo* and Objects of Worship

The 1627 *Catechism* focuses on the creation of the world and on the passion of Christ. It has some of the longest connected passages of Timucua with no clear Spanish translations. In previous work, I have described the account of creation in this work and its long lists of birds, fish, and animals.[6] In this chapter, I focus on items that the text identifies as objects of reverence for non-Christian Timucua people. Since the text is written from a Christian perspective, these are described as "idols."

The most enlightening text is the account of the fall of Lucifer described in folia 13r–15v of the 1627 *Catechism*. As seen here, the Spanish account is very short—about ten lines. In contrast, the Timucua version is about five pages (2.5 folia) long. Although it covers some of the same topics as the Spanish account, the Timucua version adds many details. The Spanish account is given below.

> *LA CAYDA DE LVCIFER, Y sus sequaces, y como fueron alançados del Cielo, y desterrados al infierno: y como por embidia que no vamos à gozar lo que el dexò. Y por eso enseñò auer muchos Dioses, aßi en la Florida como en todas partes de la gentilidad, y para esto embia Lucifer desde el infierno Demonios hechos Capitanes para esto, diziendo, Bien veis que estoy en estas penas preso, y pues yo no puedo yr, yd vosostros à hazer gente, y con engaños traedmelos aqui, q<ue> no es justo que vayan allà de donde yo cay, pues son miseros, y yo tan noble. etc. aßi lo dize S<an> Vicente Ferrer en la D<ue>ña.*
>
> The fall of Lucifer and his minions and how they were thrown from Heaven and landed in hell, and how through envy we will not enjoy what he left. And so one taught that there were many Gods here in Florida, as in other parts of the heathen world, and because of this, Lucifer sent demons from hell who were made captains for this [task], saying, "Look well, you see that I am have been sentenced to [eternal] imprisonment, so I cannot leave; go work on people and with trickery bring them to me here, for it is not just that they [may] go there to the place from which I fell, since they are so wretched and I so noble" (thus says Saint Vincent Ferrer en La Dueña).

The Timucua version along with its English translation is shown in (1). Because our knowledge of Timucua is imperfect, some parts are currently untranslated, shown by the ellipses in the English.

(1) a. ***Caqi abo, ano eatema, chi abodelesibotanchu, nana, ocorosota, Dios areconima, yanqua Capitani chieta ano, yayileta, aricoqe virosa***

6. My work relies on a transcription made by Lisa Noetzel. I thank her for her generosity in sharing this with me.

teracocoleta, minesimi eneqe anoterunumate naquenta, yayiletenomate naquenta mosota mine, yayi, nechenomaqua, ano, aneqetileta, ano, acochatileta.
I previously told you about the ones who lived in heaven. . . . [W]hen God made them all together, he made one Captain, who was a strong person, a very handsome and good man. . . . [H]e looked at himself [?] as good and strong . . . and he was a proud and haughty person.
b. ***hachibueno, caretera, naquanimaqua, naquenihabela manda, Diosimaquì nimositiacu, manda mine acatala hibuantanima, hote naqua, chinaquale, hibuahalecu, maniqe Diosi utina napirasota minequa, naihiribososiro manda.***
[H]e thought, "I want good things and I want to be like God; he is sitting on his throne, and I want to live in similar honor. God Utina has not done enough [lit. caused to be insufficient] (for me). I want to stand(?) with him." [H]e wanted. . . .
c. ***cumepaliqe Diosimano, caqi yayi, ano aneqetileta, ocochatiletàquene, nahiabota enetaqere, ya, nanacu naqueniheleqete, ho, vtina chiarecota, honihe chi yayisota, mosotanchu, hachaquenta ninamorosinta, taninaquale chimoheti, hochiequa ygiriboso siro mantachiqe cumepalichiqe honihe, charicota, anochiyayisota, virosa aco, chisiqisotana, honihenìntela, hachquenta, taninamorosinta taninaquale lehero, mantecho?***
[A]nd God saw and knew this strong, proud, haughty person and said, "No, it is not at all like this. I, Utina, made you, and I made you strong. Why do you insist to me that you will be equal to me? You want and desire to stand next to me. I . . . made you strong and I [am the one who?] created you as a very beautiful man. Why do you insist to me that you want to be like me?"
d. ***hochiequa, nayhiribososiro, chi maniheleqete, quentetiacu, mandaqere. Naquana Arcangel San Miguel monoma, hasala Capitanileta, Lucifer norocomichu emoqua ecata, naputysinihabeleta, ista, yqua yquamota. Quis sicut Deus noster, qui in altis habitat, monoma, Diosi eyotorola, vtinaeyotorono, taco, Diosi anocomile naquale, moheti, maninolebiti, monolebiti motaqere. San Miguelino, Angeli eyopuqua puqua mota, Diosibohota, nacobosota, eatema epabota, Onate Lucifer, ano puquaebelecaco, metenolehety, naquata, yrileta, naputisisinimoqe.***
"Surely you do not at all want [him?] to stand next to you." Without delay the Archangel St. Michael said that a captain, the powerful Lucifer . . . had sinned long ago and to fight against . . . [Lucifer and others] Who [say they are] . . . like our God, who lives on high[?]. . . . [St. Michael?] called, saying, "There is no other God, . . . [such as] Utina. No one must want to be the equal of God our Lord." St. Michael and the other angels spoke together and gathered [the ones who] believed in God and . . . said, "Indeed, Lucifer's group is great beyond counting, [and so we must?] fight a war.
e. ***San Miguel [f. 14r.] yayitocòta Luciferimate, yioquacare naurute atimoma, pataquilosobota numa abo, carema narutuquasota, hiti hica carema, nacalubosota, intamale hochoso, mitequa, puqua puquamota numota eata abosintamale, yàno puqua, inibiti, caqua, vtireqema,***

qebeta, maninoreqe ano, chalasosiromanda, abosinte, yano inibiti metonolehèti, hitìhicama nanemitacata, nahachinaramino nanemima, nafuina hachinaramita, eatamale.
St. Michael was stronger than Lucifer and the others and made them . . . miserable, and [they were] exiled from the heavens, and caused them to be punished in the hells and . . . to lose [all?] . . . and [they live there?]. And a huge group of them want to tempt every nation; furthermore an uncountable number of them live in the eternally burning hell, where they continue in this state of mind forever.
f. ***Yano, caqi abosininteno, abosinta anochalasosiba, yayicocoleta, abosinte quenteno.***
Naquenemano, hachaquenenco, ano, nochalososiba tariabosinte? chi manibohabele. Caqi Luciferino, hiticare holataleta, hibuatema, mine nalimo aboma.
Also, those living in this way are powerful tempters . . . "So why are they strong tempters?" You (pl) will think, "This Lucifer remains chief of the demons, [and] the Lord [is chief] in heaven.
g. ***Diosi vtina, hibuantemaqua, anoyayileta nihibuabilechu, aye hibuano, care terarabama, eneta, Acu ysaco manino, care machino, nanemimate, orabono, toomamate qebeta, naqua, homoqe, enèta, melachita, mosotequa, cha manta yquatubuota, hila hila, mota, hibuataqe mine cumeleno, isticobi maqua, inecalubosoqe, vti horobani, hochota, qebeta hity inibiti, eata, Christiano vti caremate, anopira, vticaremate, qebeta, maninoreqe quenequa nahimesotequa.***
I said that God Utina remains powerful. He [Lucifer] sees his excellent seats and all the happiness and eternal rest and eternal joy for that one and [he is angry?] and [fails to show contrition?] and disobeys and speaks. . . . [A]nd he is punished for the evil his soul committed, and because of the . . . lands that were lost, many demons exist in Christian countries and Indian countries and they want to blow [insert?] themselves into each one [person?].
h. ***Ca, motele honihe, nalimo abo, niánola, chinahiabobotele, ho, niyayila, ho, nicho corila, queniqe, hachaquentana, vtipichiquilàno, mosima, nanemi hachinarachiqequa, nihibatela, anochequa, hachequamota, anofaramiti, niacoleta, ninte, aboma, hachibueno, careteraco, hanta, melachita, himenimichu, Christiano homohàbemanda, chimasiboqiti, honihe, cumeletanincoqua, niquasimohero, manda, anotoomanco, namoquareqe, chicumelesobohalecu, manda.***
Saying "I am [worthy of?] heaven, you all know. I am strong, I am powerful, and why do I remain eternally . . . [in] the [wet?] earth? I continue miserable and despised . . . lacking the good things above; [misery?] has come . . . wanting Christians to come to an end, I say to you, wanting to counsel you [wanting you to counsel them?] [that] if I act wickedly, all people will want to do the same.
i. ***Dios vtina, aro aromota, nahicareqema, namòquareqema, Diosima, nahisota, nacumelesibota hebuano ecasta, naquosomaca, Diosi vtina, patucusi yayima, cano cantele, motachicaqe, ybaha vtima, Diosi utina, yaqe anocumetotaqe.***

There are many Gods that exist in each village and on every side. You must prepare them and teach that they create [these] God[s] [themselves]. If you say God Utina is a great war chief, alone [?] on the earth, you honor your God Utina with devotion.

j. ***Apalachico, vtina, eyo, oca, cantela anoquayaqe nante Timuquaco, anocomitotate, naquostaqe, vtireqema hicareqema vtina eyocote, naquosotaqe, mosonoletemano, Diosi vtina yaha, nahiabota cumeletanima, vquatequa hachibuenotera, ysaco homama, hanta, himenchu nabeta, homohabe manda, ninapiqi bota, cumelenoterama, hanta istitima ininoma beta, intahero, anomanisiqe mostanimano nantelaha, heqenoqere, chinahiabobota habele.***

The Apalachees have another god called Anoquayaqe and the Timucua make their [own] lord, and every country and every town creates another god and believes in him. . . . Now the one God Utina will know about you if a person wants to commit a wicked sin, refusing a good commandment, envying others [wanting good and happy things to finish coming [to others]], and acting wickedly.

k. ***Caqi hitima, ano ninachalasobota, beta, hanimano, hachaqueniqe ninachalasobote?***

Chinahiabobo haue quenihabela. Naquenihabemano, hachibueno care tera, ininoma, ayehibuanoterarabama, acatalaterarabama, hanta, himenima, minecabeta, Christianolemoqe, taeyamohaue hachibueno, care, terabama, elono teraco inereqe, inema elotamoqe nanemi machinotera, ysaco maninotera toomama nohoi, toomama, hachibueno caretera qebèta naqua homa michu, enemohauemanda enemohanimano, nacupananochiqequa, oraoramota, ano seyacota eyamohaue, cha! cha! qebeta hibua michuqua, tera, atimoma, nimelachela, mota hibuatela.

If this devil is tempting us, why does he tempt us? You will know. Refusing good things, sins, the excellent chair, the excellent bed, when we come to the Lord, those who are Christians will live away from here and will sing all the good songs, every excellent thing, the eternal rest, and all good desires, all. . . . [W]e will want to see them all end, and although we see them, we will delight in them and talk happily and live in ecstasy, and say "Oh, oh" for that good [past?] life, . . . I am free of [my past life].

l. ***Acu equelacote pilanicote nafuina, cume yuricota nabirichita, hachinaramita ninapiqibota, hacha masiboqiti, honihequa hebuano, vquasta cumeletana, vruta, mosotequa, honihe intanaqua, mota, tacananemima, nafuina, heca hanta, mine, ecate, hachinaramimoheti, manda chinachalasobohalecu, mantequa, Dios vtina, aro ta, elama Dios vtinala nimohaue.***

Every day and night, our minds and hearts are angry and [wrathful?], we are always envious. What if they say, "I will take things as I want, and along with this, I will be this way." We will say that we refuse the eternal flames, they always want to tempt you, [saying that] that the sun is Dios Utina, that there are many gods Utina.

m. ***Acuma, Diosilamoqe, yyolaco, Dios vtinala moqe. Maha, ayeco, vtinalamoqe mosotanimano, ona, mosota, hi quita, naiquitaqere, yano.***

Ca, inemimano, anoyoquareqe cumelesota, elaco anocomitota, vtinachieta, aparòta, naquosota tamalota, nabosotachiqe, moqe. Acuco, vtinale, aparota, naqua, mostachiqe, chapico, cuiuco, abayco acunaqua mosta [f. 15v.] hachiqe, moqe hachipileco, utinalamoqe.
The moon is God, snakes are God Utina. Or when they say trees are Utina, indeed, it is ended and finished. Furthermore every other person says that the sun is their lord, they prepare and worship and make and entreat and honor Utina. . . . [T]he moon is Utina, and therefore they worship it. [T]hey say, the *chapi*, the fish, the *abay*, are all [gods] they believe; they say [there should be?] ceremonies, and they say that an animal is Utina.
n. ***Na emaco, mostanimano, Dios vtinama, nahiabomohabele, nachalasabota chimasiboqiti, Dios vtina nuta honihe, cumelatanaqua vquatèqua, hecate honihe, inta naqua, hachinaramita, nàqua chimobohabelecu, manda, nisisobotale.***
If one says to you (pl.), tempting you, "they will know that the wooden thing is like God Utina, and because I don't know God Utina, I acted wickedly and learned this." [T]hen [you will say], "We and I used to be this way, and therefore we continue to want to speak to you. . . ."

Objects of Worship

To understand the text, it is also important to note that Utina is the native Timucua word for "god," and can be applied to both the Christian god and to native gods. Diosi and Diosi Utina refer exclusively to the Christian god. Thus in (1m), "Acuco, vtinale" means "The moon is Utina" or "The moon is God."

The items listed in (1m) and (1n) are the following. Translations for the first five are relatively easy, but the last two words are puzzling.

- *ela* "sun"
- *acu* "moon"
- *iyola* "snake"
- *aye* "tree"
- *na ema* "wooden things"
- *abay* ?
- *chapi* ?

In the following sections, I explore the correct translations of *abay* and *chapi* in more detail, and attempt to connect the linguistic explication of this text to current archaeological findings in the Timucua region.

What Are Abay?

Fortunately, Pareja discusses *abay* in another context, which helps us better understand the meaning of the word. In the discussion of God's creations on the fifth day, we find the following Spanish passage:

(2) *En el quinto dia, que es Iueues, como para adornar la tierra criò Dios en ella el Mar, Rios, y lagunas, y en estas aguas criò grande numero de Peces, de los quales hizo Cacique ò señor al hombre, y le diò sabiduria, para pescallos.*
On the fifth day, which is Thursday, to adorn the earth, God created on it the sea, rivers, and lakes, and in these waters, he created a great number of fish, and he made man the cacique or master of them, and he gave the wisdom to fish them.

The Timucua translation of this portion follows:

(3) a. *Equela namaruama, Iueues equelamante, cume areconolehabema, Dios vtinama, areconimano, moca carecote, ybimacarecote nubalacarecote, aquecarecote, caqi vtima, isamolota quanunta nahulubontasiro manda, areconelehachaquene?*
On the fifth, the day called Thursday, one must understand that God Utina made the seas, the rivers, the lakes, and the air to wash and adorn the earth and so that one could farm it. Why did he make them?
b. ***heca, ninapichibota sontela caqi, ibine oyoma, cuyu, inereqeine homama, arecota, vchuco, siacatoco, ytorico chayoco, aquatiro l cunachuaco, chayoco abayco, caracasico, tanitoco, echacaco tococo.***
He provides them for us and made each fish in the water, the whale, the *siacato*, the alligator, the *chayo*, the *aquatiro* or *cunachua*, the *chayo*, the *abay*, the *corvina*, the *tanito*, the mullet, and the *toco*.
c. ***Pueloco guacapeco henosoco tumeco, chapoco, sucu sico cuyuqichico, inereqe inema, melo toomamate henta hauema hiqui hiquimosota, mine bendicionima, na ecasibota, coesa, qiemi nahisiro, manta abosintamaca, masibonige.***
The *puelo*, the *guacape*, the *henoso*, the *tume*, the *chapo*, the *sucusi*, all the little fish and all the shellfish to be eaten, he caused completely. They are brought as his blessing, the things which he wanted his children to have, he said and they existed.

How can we understand the list of species listed here? Fortunately, Pareja's *Arte* gives Spanish translations for several words on the Timucua list.[7] They are *uchu ballena*/whale, *echaca liza*/mullet, *caracasi corvina*/corvina, and *ytori caimán*/alligator. Their presence in the list helps anchor our understanding of what is happening at this point in the text.

Thus we can see that this is a list of animals which live in the sea, each suffixed with -co, a marker of coordination. But how can we interpret the names of the Timucua species that do not have Spanish translations?

I would like to suggest that there is a possible logic to this text, which begins with whales and ends with shellfish. The initial species on the list are whale, siacato, and alligator—animals that are partly above the water and

7. Pareja, *Arte y Pronunciacion*.

partly below. The final species (shellfish) are those that are at the very bottom in the water. Thus the author of this text seems to have organized the species listed by reference to their verticality, where the order is

Whale > *siacato* > alligator > *chayo* > *abay* > *chayo* > fish > little fish > shellfish

Thus although we cannot know exactly what *siacato*, *chayo*, and *abay* mean, it is likely that they share some properties with whales and alligators, large species that are partially above and partially below the water. Thus likely candidates, given the ecology of this part of Florida, are manatee, dolphin, and shark.

Similar considerations apply to *abay*. The text of (1m) says that people worship both *cuyu* "fish" and *abay*, which suggests that *abay* is not a kind of fish. Manatees and dolphins both have some human-like features that might make them likely objects of devotion, and thus they are the likeliest candidates for *abay*. There are also archaeological considerations that favor an identification of *abay* with "manatee."

Archaeological sites in Florida with carefully researched faunal remains generally contain large numbers of bones associated with fish, deer, and other animals that were likely part of the local diet. However, several sites in locations within or near Timucua territory show a surprising absence or near-absence of manatee bone. For example, no manatee bones are currently attested at the Crystal River site (8CI1) in Crystal River, Florida, despite the fact it is adjacent to an area that is a currently winter haven for manatees. Similarly the faunal remains from Mission Catalina de Guale, on St. Catherine's Island, Georgia, also show no manatee bones.[8]

I suggest a possible connection between the Timucua texts that speak of reverence for a sea creature called the *abay* and this archaeological result. While we cannot be certain, taking *abay* to be the Timucua word for "manatee" nicely connects these two observations.

---

8. The Crystal River site is discussed in Thomas J. Pluckhahn and Victor D. Thompson "Woodland-Period Mound Building as Historical Tradition: Dating the Mounds and Monuments at Crystal River (8CI1)," *Journal of Archaeological Science: Reports* 15 (2017): 73–94. The Santa Cataline de Guale in Clark Spencer Larsen, Inui Choi, Anne E. Fresia, et al., *The Archaeology of Mission Santa Catalina de Guale, 2, Biocultural Interpretations of a Population in Transition*, Anthropological Papers of the AMNH, no. 68 (Washington, DC: American Museum of Natural History, 1990). I thank Susan de France and Trevor Duke for discussion of these results.

What Are Chapi?

In several passages from the Timucua corpus, *chapi* is translated as "idol," as in the following example[9]:

> (4) ***Honiheno qere naniquosonyhaue nimatileheleqete antamano vtinaeyo etenta ynostanchu heqeno Christiano leta vti nanocomi acona etentatiyacu chapico etentantiqua Diosi vtina nocomima etentanico naniquosonihaue nimatetile heleqete.***
> *Quanto mayores gracias os deuo yo dar, porque soy Christiano, y no pagano; y porque adoro a vos que soys verdadero Dios, y no piedras, ni demonios.*
> As for me, I cannot fail to thank you, for previously I served other gods. But now I am a Christian and I adore the true God; the adoration of idols is prohibited because we worship the true God Utina.

Archaeologists have excavated a number of wood sculptures from east-central Florida sites that may be relevant to our understanding.[10] The most well-known of these is the Hontoon island "owl" sculpture. There are also figures that appear to be an otter, and a pelican. A related wood sculpture of a seated figure with hands raised to the chest has been found at Tomoka State Park.

Is *chapi* the Timucua word for this kind of sculpture? There are a few other material objects associated with the Timucua that seem likely candidates for being called "idols" by the Spanish, and so I will take this as indication of a probable connection.

In most of the texts, *chapi* seems to equate to an object of worship or adoration, roughly equivalent to "idol" or "icon" in Spanish. However, we see a difference (and enlightening) use of the word on folio 93 of the *Catecismo*:

> (5) ***Quenìqe nia, ebo habeleta, viro hono pochama, nìa vnamima chorosotaqe, nia hono pochamìma te pìtatequa vìro honopochamichu, yuchaqua, naha bososinta naya mesintamoqe naquana yache abo ma, soromìtequa vle, chapì minosotela.***
> So when a woman is going to give birth, [he/it] causes the man's seed to flow into the woman's body, and the woman's seed descends and both are received and mixed together. Immediately this penetrates the yache abo and sends the child's chapi.

In this passage, *chapi* seems to mean something like "(animating) spirit, soul." In the theology of Aristotle, the soul of a male fetus entered forty days after conception, and the soul of a female fetus entered ninety days after con-

9. Pareja, *Catechismo y breve exposición*, 1612a, f. 45v.

10. See Joanna Ostapkowicz, et al., "East-Central Florida pre-Columbian Wood sculpture: Radiocarbon Dating, Wood Identification and Strontium Isotope Studies," *Journal of Archaeological Science: Reports* 13 (2017).

ception.[11] This was a widespread Catholic understanding at the time of the Timucua publications. Yet these disparate senses of *chapi* present a linguistic problem. What does *chapi* truly mean if in one sense it appears to mean "soul/spirit" and in another sense it appears to mean "idol/icon"? How may we reconcile these two different senses of *chapi*?

Perhaps the answer to this puzzle lies in the idea of items like wood sculptures that are infused with an animating spirit. The idea of a soul/spirit entering into statues or other inanimate objects is well attested during the classical period.[12] And if we look further afield, we also find that in many Polynesian cultures, wooden sculptures, such as the Hawaiian *ki'i* were taken to be infused with *mana*, roughly translated as "power, spirit."[13]

These conclusions are (intentionally) speculative, but provide a way of connecting the linguistic and archaeological evidence to better understand the role of statues in Timucua religious practice.

Conclusion

While we are very far from a full understanding of Timucua religious practice prior to Christianity, I have argued in this chapter that a close reading of the Timucua text in Pareja's *Catecismo* gives us important insight. We know of many early Christian "heretical" practices only through their condemnations in the works of authors such as Irenaeus. In a similar way, the authors of this Christian Timucua text have singled out and condemned selected traditional religious practices. We are fortunate that these condemnations have preserved knowledge of traditional practices for our current understanding.

---

11. See discussion in Norman M. Ford and Norman D. Ford, *When Did I Begin? Conception of the Human Individual in History, Philosophy and Science* (Cambridge University Press, 1991).

12. See Nigel Spivey, "Bionic statues," *The Greek World*, 464–74 (Routledge, 2002); and Jason Q. Von Ehrenkrook, "Sculpting Idolatry in Flavian Rome: (An) Iconic Rhetoric in the Writings of Flavius Josephus" (PhD diss., University of Michigan, 2009).

13. J. Halley Cox and William H. Davenport, *Hawaiian Sculpture* (Honolulu: The University of Hawaii Press, 1974).

Chapter 5

Manufacturing Sin: Francisco Carranco, O.F.M., and the Inquisition in the Diocese of Cuba, 1604–1611

LEONARDO FALCÓN

Francisco Carranco, O.F.M., served for at least seven years as the first officially designated commissary of the Inquisition in Havana. His assignment in 1605 marked the formal establishment of the Holy Office on the island. Havana was part of the Santiago de Cuba diocese, which encompassed the islands of Cuba and Jamaica as well as the Provincia of La Florida.[1] He lived in Havana until at least 1611 where he also served as guardian for the Franciscan convent of La Purísima Concepción. Between 1595 and 1604, he held similar positions in Veracruz where he was particularly active in censorship activities prescribed by the Inquisition.[2] Carranco lived to serve the Spanish Empire, Franciscans, Catholic Church, and the Inquisition during a period of significant political change.

During the short time that Carranco worked in Cuba, he authored over two hundred pieces of correspondence sent to the Inquisition tribunal in

---

1. According to several archival documents, Carranco was only assigned as commissary of the Inquisition for Havana and not for the entire diocese. See Archivo General de la Nación (henceforth AGN), Inq., vol. 1578, exp. 137, f. 1, and AGN, Inq., vol. 1566, signatura (henceforth sig.) 13386, exp. 10, f. 20. His attempts to extend his powers over the diocese, particularly in St. Augustine in Florida, were a source of contention with the local authorities. I expand on his struggles with the local authorities as well as the irregular nature of some of his proceedings in my dissertation. Leonardo Falcón, "Manufacturing Sin on the Frontier of Heresy: Bishops, Franciscans, and the Inquisition in Cuba During the Long Sixteenth Century, 1511–1611)," Ph.D dissertation, Florida International University, Miami, 2019.

2. The records regarding his tenure as commissary of the Inquisition, both in Veracruz and Cuba are contradictory. José Manuel López Mora, *Inquisición de Veracruz: Catálogo de documentos Novohispanos en el AGN—Estudio preliminar y notas* (Veracruz: Colección Rescate, Universidad Veracruzana, 2009), 139, 509. This catalogue lists Carranco as commissary of the Inquisition in Veracruz only during 1604, yet he is mentioned as commissary in several other documents as early as 1599 and his nomination as commissary of the Inquisition for Veracruz dates to 1595: AGN, Inq., vol. 200, exp. 4, f. 6.

Mexico, which had jurisdiction over the Santiago de Cuba bishopric and its satellite provinces until 1610. The documents included *procesos* (proceedings or trials), *denuncias* (complaints), and other miscellaneous letters describing possible proceedings, complaining about the lack of resources and support he faced, or detailing his confrontations with local authorities. The sheer number of Carranco's letters represent a significant increase over the twelve Inquisition-related documents sent from Cuba to Mexico during the previous twenty years. The upsurge in communication with the Tribunal in Mexico shows Carranco's eagerness to enforce the laws governing the Catholic Church as stipulated by the canons issued during the Council of Trent (1545–1563). Moreover, his religious zeal was in consonance with those of his counterparts on both sides of the Atlantic. His actions indicate that he was willing and able to comply with the responsibilities of an Inquisition agent as prescribed in the Inquisitor's manual and in the instructions issued by the Inquisitor general in Spain.

Many of Carranco's proceedings, however, were out of the ordinary. His *ad libitum*[3] interpretation of what constituted a religious crime exceeded the parameters specified by the Supreme Tribunal of the Inquisition to the point of *manufacturing sin*.[4] Some of his accusations fell outside the boundaries established by the Council of Trent and others went beyond the manual followed by Inquisition officials. In several instances, his practices were extreme and overtly defiant of religious and secular authorities. He overextended his powers as commissary overstepping the boundaries of his position. Although he accused a plethora of individuals from every social group, he paid special attention to influential people and to those of the upper classes. Underpinning Carranco's actions was a constant battle with local diocesan religious authorities over the legal reach and execution of his office within the ecclesiastic jurisdiction and the rank to which he had been assigned.

In this work I examine some of Carranco's documents that raised the hackles of peers and superiors to understand the ideologies and goals that motivated him to produce such a prolific caseload. I also study the friar's battle with the local bishop to highlight quarrels over establishing and delimiting jurisdiction and authority in the territory where both served. When considered within the larger context of administrative reorganization taking place throughout the circum-Caribbean during the early years of the seventeenth century, Carranco's actions demonstrate a plan that had little to do with moral cleansing. They were neither coincidental nor the ordinary result of his admin-

3. Latin expression, literally meaning "according to [one's] pleasure/preference" or extemporaneous.

4. The title of this work implies that Carranco intentionally exaggerated his practices and inflated his accusations, particularly those aimed at influential individuals to gain name recognition with the Inquisition network.

istrative functions. Carranco's actions were part of his carefully orchestrated plan to justify the creation of an Inquisition tribunal in Havana, with jurisdiction over Jamaica and La Florida. Once created, Carranco himself hoped to preside as the Inquisitor. As such he could oversee and enforce the Catholic purity of Spanish subjects and prevent infiltration of disruptive heretical individuals and ideas.

Carranco's years in Cuba coincided with a reorganization period of the Church throughout the Spanish Empire, especially in the circum-Caribbean, following the deaths of Phillip II of Spain in 1598 and Elizabeth I of England in 1603. The reorganization included establishment of new dioceses, allowing new religious provinces and (most meaningful for this research and for Carranco's intentions and actions), the creation of a new Inquisition tribunal in one of the region's port cities.

Overt communication among the local civil and religious leadership and the Council of the Indies about creating a third tribunal in the Americas began in 1576.[5] In 1577 the viceroy of Peru, Francisco de Toledo, complained to the Council about how exhausted his subjects were because of traveling such long distances upon request, either as witnesses or accused, by the tribunal in Lima.[6] He also described the dangers his people faced when traveling and unnecessary expenses for trips that, he added, were usually in vain. The viceroy proposed establishment of two new tribunals in the new kingdom, one in Quito and the other in La Plata, led by the bishop of each diocese and two local judges. This would limit the number of new Inquisition employees as well as salaries. Toledo recommended that the Council instruct the Inquisition personnel to send to tribunals only individuals whose crimes were considered grave, adding that all minor cases should be handled at the local level.[7] The viceroy's complaints and recommendations indicated the need to increase the Inquisition's presence in the Americas to control religious unorthodoxy, as well as to reorganize this institution to more efficiently handle the extensive territories and population growth in the region.

Similar concerns were expressed by religious authorities throughout the colonies. They increasingly named the presence of non-Catholics as a reason to establish new tribunals. They also complained about their inability to efficiently visit population centers in their dioceses because of vast distances, citing this as the main cause for the rapid emergence of religious dissidence

---

5. José Toribio Medina, *Historia del Tribunal del Santo Oficio de la Inquisición de Cartagena de las Indias*, 2nd ed. (Bogotá: ABC Editores, 1952), 42.

6. "[C]uán vejados estaban sus vasallos del Perú, porque siendo tan vasto el distrito del Tribunal se les llamaba á Lima, ya como testigos ó como reos." From José Toribio Medina, *Historia del Tribunal del Santo Oficio de la Inquisición de Cartagena de las Indias* (Santiago de Chile: Imprenta Elzeviriana, 1899), 36.

7. Ibid.

and unorthodoxy in the Americas. By 1579 the authorities on the island of Hispaniola were requesting a new tribunal for Santo Domingo and reiterated their petition in 1585.[8] They were supported by members of the Inquisition tribunal in Mexico City, which in 1594 requested the creation of an independent tribunal in that Caribbean port city.[9] In all three instances the reasons given to establish a new tribunal were the same: the port cities of the Caribbean were constantly visited by "pirates and corsairs, English and French, all Protestants, which demanded from the King and his Council defense of the holy Catholic faith."[10] In May 1594 the religious authorities wrote directly to King Phillip II, reminding him that the Council of the Indies had already recommended establishment of a new Tribunal in Hispaniola since March of that year.[11]

The Council and the colonial authorities complained to the King that pirates' and corsairs' constant and increasing raids of the port cities were devastating, destabilizing the social and moral order of the colonies. They added that the constant kidnapping of prominent individuals and requests for astronomical ramson to free them had become so common that it was impossible for the authorities to rescue them, contributing to their failure to keep order.[12] They claimed that the presence of an Inquisition tribunal in the Caribbean would serve not only as a deterrent to pirates and corsairs but also to raise the Catholic morality of the local population and to keep the number of foreigners—Protestants—to a minimum.[13]

At the turn of the seventeenth century, the clergy's frustration with ongoing delays in decision making to establish new tribunals in the Americas was evident in the correspondence sent to Madrid. More bishops representing several dioceses in the New World became active in the discussions. Each voiced his concerns about the social and religious disarray as well as lack of religious personnel in his respective diocese.[14] Two Inquisition tribunals, in

8. AGI, Santo Domingo, 868, leg. 3, f.122r.–122v.

9. Medina, *Historia*, 1899 ed., 36.

10. AGI, Santo Domingo, 868, leg. 3, f. 122r.–122v.

11. Ibid., 43.

12. "*Rescates*" means ransom; yet, in the case of the Caribbean it was also used to describe the illegal trade that took place between locals and foreign pirates and corsairs. For a detailed examination of this phenomenon, see Irene A. Wright, "Rescates: With special reference to Cuba, 1599–1610," *Hispanic American Historical Review* 3, no. 3 (1920): 333–361.

13. Medina, *Historia*, 1899 ed., 43.

14. In 1599, the archbishop of Santa Fé de Bogotá, Bartolomé Lobo Guerrero, who had been Inquisitor in Mexico City (1593–1598), wrote to the Council of the Indies requesting that a tribunal be established in Bogotá. Lobo Guerrero reminded the Council that the discussion to establish the tribunal in his diocese had started years previously with no resolution, but that such tribunal had become extremely necessary with the passage of time as the population continued to grow and heresy and religious ignorance were ram-

Mexico and Lima, were insufficient to oversee the large population and extensive territories recently conquered by the Spaniards in the Americas. As guardian of the Franciscan convents and commissary of the Inquisition first in Veracruz and later in Havana, Carranco was at the intersection of communication to and from the metropolis. He most likely was aware of such conversations and therefore worked diligently during his time in Havana to favor that Cuban city as recipient of the new tribunal.

Not coincidentally, these measures to amplify and to strengthen the Catholic presence and influence in the region were a direct result of the non-Spanish presence in the region, epitomized by English Protestants establishing the Jamestown colony in 1607. The foreign settlement was dangerously close to St. Augustine in Florida and threatened Spain's hegemony.[15] Meanwhile, Cuba and its dependencies underwent a political reorganization that divided the island into two administrative regions.[16] The division increased Havana's defensive capabilities as it narrowed its administrative focus and concentrated its limited resources on the city instead of the entire island. Cuba, as the administrative epicenter of the circum-Caribbean, was crucial to the Spanish Empire and correspondingly morphed into a bastion of protection on all fronts. Havana housed in its bay the crown's treasure ships until their departure towards Spain, as such it had to be utterly fortified.[17]

---

pant throughout the realm. He gave extensive reasons, similar to those expressed by Toledo from Lima, and even noted that establishing a tribunal in Bogotá with jurisdiction over Cartagena, Santa Marta, Popayán, Venezuela, and Quito would relieve some of the burden from the Lima tribunal. Lobo Guerrero recommended that the new tribunal salary structure be similar to that of the tribunals in Lima and Mexico and if necessary the money could come from additional taxes levied on the *"indios vacos"* (indigenous who were not part of an *encomienda* and who paid taxes directly to the Crown). Medina, *Historia*, 1899 ed., 41.

15. While Jamestown is considered the first permanent English settlement in the region, it was not the first attempt. See Karen O. Kupperman, *Roanoke: The Abandoned Colony*, 2nd ed. (Lanham, MD: Rowman and Littlefield Publishers, 2007). French Huguenots had also attempted to settle in the region. See John T. McGrath, *The French in Early Florida: In the Eye of the Hurricane* (Gainesville: University Press of Florida, 2000). In 1603, five hundred English and French men who had disembarked in Jamaica with ambitions of settling in the New World, were taken aboard Spanish ships. The following year the governor of Cuba, Pedro de Valdés, received news of an unidentified enemy building a town (*poblado*) in Florida's San Carlos Bay. Both territories were under the same diocesan jurisdiction, namely the Cuban diocese. See Irene A. Wright, *Historia documentada de San Cristóbal de la Habana en la primera mitad del siglo XVII* (Havana: Imprenta El Siglo XX, 1930), 41.

16. Hortensia Pichardo, *Documentos para la historia de Cuba*, vol. I (Havana: Instituto Cubano del Libro, Editorial de Ciencias Sociales, 1973), 141.

17. Several highly specialized and outstanding academic works analyze the Caribbean, especially Cuba, and its complex and vital role within the Spanish Empire's plans during the sixteenth and seventeenth centuries. The pivotal work of Paul Hoffman thoroughly documented how Cuba grew rapidly both in population and importance as a defensive post

The Spanish monarch Phillip III and the Council of the Indies agreed with the local authorities' recommendations. They perceived the Caribbean not only as the Empire's military ultimate line of defense but also as the rampart to safeguard the ideological and religious integrity of the Spanish American realms. The Diocese of Santiago de Cuba and its satellite territory of St. Augustine in La Florida formed the easternmost Spanish frontier of the New World. Hence, they were particularly important for the overall imperial religious initiatives to protect Spanish possessions. The defensive role of the Church in the Caribbean went, therefore, hand in hand with that of the military.

Increasing religious personnel numbers and establishing an Inquisition tribunal in the Caribbean were as necessary as fort construction and expanding Spanish military presence. Religious and civilian authorities in Cuba requested the establishment of the Inquisition on the island as necessary to fight "those heretic enemies against whom there is no civil or religious recourse."[18] Carranco's assignment as commissary of the Inquisition for the Cuban diocese was part of that growth in religious personnel for defense of the region.[19]

In the preface to the latest edition of *The Spanish Inquisition: A Historical Revision,* Henry Kamen refers to the extensive historiography within and outside of academia about this religious institution. He mentions popular histories, novels, and essays and highlights the importance of ongoing debates about various approaches to studying the Inquisition as well as the diverse interpretations of its functions.[20] In the introduction to her seminal work on the Inquisition in New Spain, Asunción Lavrin indicates that "the Spanish Inquisition re-created itself in the Americas in only three locations, but its influence in shaping the religious culture of Spanish America belied the small number of offices in such a vast territory."[21] Indeed, the Spanish Inquisition and its role in the Americas have been amply covered; however, there is no academic work about the Inquisition in Cuba.

---

within the region. Paul E. Hoffman, *The Spanish Crown and the Defense of the Caribbean, 1535–1585: Precedent, Patrimonialism, and Royal Parsimony* (Baton Rouge: Louisiana State University Press, 1980).

18. "Contra estos herejes enemigos no aprovechaba rigor de justicia seglar ni eclesiástica." Fragment of a letter sent by governor of Cuba, Pedro de Valdés, cited by Irene A. Wright. She also mentions similar requests from the bishop of Cuba, Juan de las Cabezas Altamirano, but does not provide further sources. Wright, *Historia Documentada*, 1930, ft. 4.

19. Carranco is mentioned in minor remarks and annotations in the historiography of the topic, yet my research indicates that his role during these crucial historical moments was significant and thus overlooked and underappreciated.

20. Henry Kamen, *The Spanish Inquisition: A Historical Revision*, 4th ed. (New Haven, CT: Yale University Press, 2014).

21. Asunción Lavrin, Introduction to John F. Chuchiack IV, *The Inquisition in New Spain, 1536–1820: A Documented History* (Baltimore: John Hopkins University Press, 2012), xiii.

Those who have addressed the Inquisition on the island have done so in passing, mentioning disagreements between tribunal officials with the local authorities while others have limited their work to compiling a list of records housed at various archives. At most, analysis of the Inquisition in Cuba has been relegated to folktales and footnotes, with cursory analysis and dismissal of its sociopolitical and religious role. Examples of the latter are two publications that directly refer to the Inquisition in Cuba. One is anthropologist Fernando Ortiz's *Historia de una Pelea Cubana contra los Demonios*, which is characterized as a semi-historic and folkloric work on the idea of demonology with colorful and extravagant episodes about a fight in the villa of Remedios.[22] Ortiz, who relies mostly on the works of Toribio Medina on the tribunals in Mexico and Cartagena, dedicates a few pages to the Inquisition, perpetuating numerous errors along with the myth of an uneventful and relatively modest institution.[23] The other work is an article turned into a booklet and published in 2001 by Cuban journalist Tania Chappi. The brief work summarizes a few inquisitorial events and individuals, echoing a legendary tale previously mentioned by Ortiz about a group of *amujerados*,[24] allegedly burned by the Inquisition in Havana.[25] Many others who wrote about early colonial Cuba or the Inquisition in the New World have entirely ignored this institution's role in the island's historical processes or simply repeated the abovementioned references.[26]

This lack of historiography is peculiar because the first American Inquisition activities began in the Cuba as early as 1516.[27] From the onset of the Spanish colonization of the New World, numerous individuals in Cuba, natives as well as Europeans, were accused of religious crimes and prosecuted on site as detailed in the writings of Bartolomé de Las Casas. Some of the accused were tried, tortured, and punished, as documented in the fragmented archival records on the subject.[28] Indeed, those cases could be designated as

---

22. Fernando Ortiz, *Historia de una Pelea Cubana Contra los Demonios* (Madrid: Ediciones ERRE, S.I., 1973). Cited by Gerardo Enrique Chávez Espíngola, "Imaginario popular. Mitología Cubana: Posesión satánica—historia y fantasiario popular," *Cubarte—El Portal de la Cultura Cubana*, August 2011, available at www.cubarte.cult.cu/periodico.

23. Ortiz, *Historia*, 373.

24. The closest translation is "effeminate men."

25. Tania Chappi, *Demonios en La Habana: Episodios de la Inquisición en Cuba* (Havana: Oficina del Historiador de la Ciudad de La Habana, Ediciones Boloña, 2001), 89. The case is mentioned by Ortiz, *Historia*, 374, and perpetuated in Cuban lore; however, Ortiz cites no sources.

26. See previously cited works of José Toribio Medina. See also Leví Marrero, *Cuba: Economía y Sociedad*, vol. V (Madrid: Editorial Playor, S.A., 1976).

27. Martin Nesvig, *Ideology and Inquisition: The World of the Censors in Early Mexico* (New Haven, CT: Yale University Press, 2009), 104.

28. Bartolomé de Las Casas, "Memorial de remedios para las Indias, 1516," in Juan Pérez de Tudela Bueso, *Obras Escogidas*, vol. 5, Biblioteca de Autores Españoles, Colección Rivadeneyba (Madrid: Real Academia Española, 1958), 15.

"Inquisitorial" because of the similarity between the judicial procedures followed by the religious personnel in Cuba and those conducted by the tribunals of the Holy Office elsewhere. Furthermore, the Inquisitorial actions of friars, bishops, and their delegates in the Cuban bishopric were prescribed and legitimized by both the Spanish Crown and the Vatican.[29] Their Inquisitorial powers were intrinsic but secondary to the office, as they largely served other functions within the Spanish Empire's religious administrative apparatus in the colonies. Yet, it was Carranco's assignment as commissary that marked the official presence of the Inquisition in Cuba.

Created in the 1550s, the commissary position was part of the Spanish Crown's efforts to restrain the expansion of Protestantism. One strategy was to expand and strengthen the presence of the Inquisition beyond the towns and cities that hosted a tribunal. Commissaries were key agents in the ecclesiastic judicial system and served as the Inquisition's eyes on the outskirts and hinterlands of tribunals' jurisdictions. They were often the people's only interaction with the Inquisition and thus were constantly mistaken as Inquisitors, which benefitted the Holy Office's deterrent role. Carranco was appointed commissary in Havana at a time of demographic growth in the Caribbean, which intensified the need to exert control over new arrivals and their ideas. Consequently, there was an explosion of commissariats in the Mexican tribunal and its dependencies to aid in maintaining the desired control.[30]

The large number of commissaries posted throughout the New World was partially responsible for their clashes with local authorities. Clashes were especially acute when commissaries were assigned to cities where the "ordinary Inquisitor" (the local bishop) kept his residence and many times his own ecclesiastic tribunal. Because most of the new commissaries were appointed without the ordinary's approval, this practice "fractured" the diocesan structure and added new levels of bureaucracy to an already complicated and obscure judicial system. In the absence of a bishop or under his orders, some commissaries

---

29. From the time of the Europeans' establishment in the Americas until 1569–1570, when the tribunals in Lima and Mexico were created, members of religious orders, bishops, and their delegates operated as inquisitors. Their role was indirectly legitimized first by their religious commission to evangelize the natives and maintain religious orthodoxy among the Spaniards, and second by the papal bull *Exponi Nobis Fecisiti* issued in 1522, also known as *Omnimoda*. This initial inquisition has been classified as apostolic or primitive by Richard Greenleaf and José Toribio Medina. See Richard E. Greenleaf, *The Mexican Inquisition of the Sixteenth Century* (Albuquerque: University of New Mexico Press, 1969), 7–11; José Toribio Medina, *La primitiva inquisición americana (1493–1569): estudio histórico* (Santiago: Imprenta Elzeviriana, 1914).

30. Pedro Miranda Ojeda, "Las comisarías del Santo Oficio de la Nueva España, siglos xvi–xvii," *Contribuciones desde Coatepec* (2010), available at revistacoatepec.uaemex.mx/article/download/202/197. Dr. Miranda Ojeda has published numerous articles analyzing the role of the commissaries in New Spain.

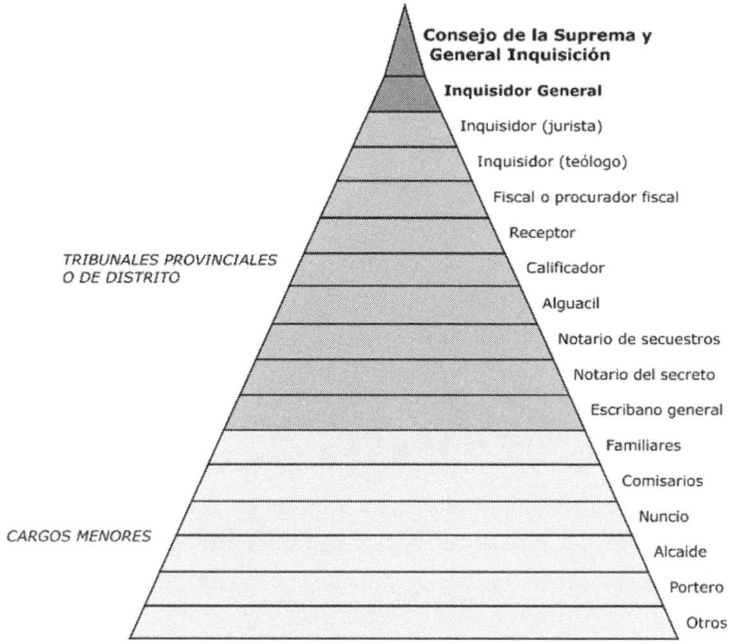

FIGURE 1. Ranking system within the Inquisition apparatus. The commissary post, held by a member of the clergy, ranked below that of a *familiar*, which was held by a layperson. This is an indication of both how low Carranco was in the jurisdictional hierarchy and how limited his powers were.[31]

acted as ordinary Inquisitors within their jurisdiction and a few even presided over a small tribunal with the necessary personnel to handle minor cases.[32]

The office of commissary was reserved for a clergyman, either regular (a member of a religious order) or secular (diocesan priest). Since it was an unpaid service to the main tribunal, commissary posts were granted to local, well-established priests, or as in the case of Carranco, to the local superior of a religious order. While it was the lowest-ranking office for the clergy within the Inquisition structure (see Figure 1), the commissary post was also regarded by many as a stepping stone to a higher, paid office such as that of a regional Inquisitor. In exceptional cases based on family ties and individual prominence, some commissaries were promoted to the Inquisition's supreme

31. "La Inquisición Española: Origen," posted by Livia Drusila in Historia Moderna, *El Sondeo H: Blog de Historia y Archeología*, November 2014, available at https://elsondeoh.wordpress.com/2014/11/14/la-inquisicion-espanola-origen-y-desarrollo/.

32. Ibid. See also Chuchiack, *Inquisition*, 20. This, however, was not Carranco's case in Havana, since—discussed shortly—he constantly complained about not having sufficient personnel to function, and the bishop for the Diocese of Cuba lived in Havana.

tribunal in Spain. In the absence of an influential family member within the Inquisition apparatus, the more cases a commissary sent to the tribunal, the more his name was heard by his superiors, and therefore the greater the probability of his ascension through the ranks of the ecclesiastic judicial system.[33]

Prior to his relocation to Cuba, Carranco had already been involved in an Inquisition legal case from the island. In 1604 the commissary informed his superiors in Mexico City and Seville about the transfer of a Flemish prisoner named Pedro Pedro from Havana to Spain.[34] After being tried for Lutheranism in Mexico in 1598, Pedro[35] was sent in 1603 to Havana for incarceration but escaped upon arrival. The document forwarded by Carranco included his comments on the case and transcripts for interrogations of seven witnesses who confirmed Pedro's escape. The men interviewed by the local authorities in Havana described the consequent year-long, citywide manhunt ordered by the governor of Cuba, Pedro de Valdés, who offered a reward of one hundred *reales* to the heretic's capture. The sum was to be paid by the captain of the *Nao*, who had transferred the prisoner to Havana and from whose custody he had escaped. All witnesses mentioned collaboration by the authorities in recapturing the fugitive and his subsequent transport to a highly secure local prison. Deportation from the island to Seville had been initiated by the diocesan procurator, Luis de Salas, who served as commissary of the Inquisition in Havana, delegated by the local bishop, Juan de las Cabezas Altamirano.[36]

The Inquisition's focus on persecuting, prosecuting, and eliminating Protestants was common during the post-Tridentine militancy of the Catholic Church throughout the Spanish Empire. Its intent was to uphold, guarantee, and safeguard the religious orthodoxy of all Crown subjects. Heretics had to be removed from the Church "so that they do not infect the faithful with their contagion because putrescent meat must be cast out. The mangy sheep must be removed from the flock and destroyed."[37] The infiltration of non-Catholic ideologies was perceived as dangerous to the Spanish Crown and prevention became for some more than an official obligation, but rather an obsession.

In the Caribbean, the periphery of Spanish Catholicism, eradicating Protestants served the additional preemptive function of impeding their access to mainland colonies. Capturing and deporting one heretic from Havana was

---

33. For an in-depth study about the commissariats, see the work of Sara T. Nalle, "Inquisitors, Priests, and the People during the Catholic Reformation in Spain," *The Sixteenth Century Journal* 18, no. 4 (1987): 557. See also Kimberly Lynn, *Between Court and Confessional: The Politics of Spanish Inquisitors* (New York: Cambridge University Press, 2013).

34. AGN, Inq., vol. 368, exp. 75, f. 282A–289.

35. AGN, Inq., vol. 165, exp. 2, f. 114.

36. AGN, Inq., vol. 368, exp. 75, f. 282A–289.

37. *Decretum*, causa 24, cited in Nesvig, *Ideology and Inquisition*, 1.

an act of safeguarding Spanish religious orthodoxy as well as a warning to Protestants to stay away from the colonies. The government of the island, therefore, did not spare its limited resources to find and deport Pedro Pedro, and the authorities' level of collaboration with Inquisition officials throughout the Caribbean was quite efficient. Soon after Carranco's arrival in Havana, the nature of this interaction and collaboration changed as the authorities involved in the affair involving the Flemish man became entangled in Carranco's inquisitorial crusade in which most were accused.

In December 1605, after being appointed by the Inquisition as commissary for Havana and prior to traveling to the island, Carranco gave his replacement, Friar Balthazar Morales, detailed instructions about the responsibilities of his position and role. As commissary in the port of San Juan de Ulúa in Veracruz, Morales was to lead with decorum, communicate with determination, and act with a firm hand. As the functionary in charge of censorship of incoming literature, he should demand that secular authorities to be first to board the newly anchored ships to conduct a thorough inspection of the cargo. Carranco instructed Morales to search the vessels, interview the sailors, and confiscate any suspicious literature. Upon locating any book printed in Holland or Zeeland, Morales was ordered to burn it at once.[38]

Carranco was delegating to others instructions he had received from the Inquisition authorities in Spain, to toss any unorthodox book into the fire "because they can endure for centuries and infect those who come after their publication. And while the voices of heretics can only fill a city, books can pass from region to region, from kingdom to kingdom."[39] The letter to Morales showcased Carranco's experience as an officer of the Inquisition as well as his comprehensive knowledge of personnel behavior and responsibilities in a port city. The directives were also an indication of his authoritarian tendencies and leadership capacity, as well as his intolerance of unorthodox religious practices and for those who disrespected his office as commissary.[40]

His appointment pleased Juan de las Cabezas Altamirano, bishop of the Santiago de Cuba diocese. The prelate wrote to the authorities in Mexico thanking them for accepting his previous requests to have "in the City of San Cristobal de la Habana a Commissary and other ministers the Holy Office

38. AGN, Inq., vol. 1566, exp. 8, f. 2.

39. Diego de Simancas, *De catholicis institutionibus*, cited in Nesvig, *Ideology and Inquisition*, 1.

40. During Carranco's time as commissary in Veracruz, he participated in numerous searches at the port, confiscating and destroying numerous books; however, on certain occasions he allowed for less rigorous searches. See Nesvig, *Ideology and Inquisition*, 239–40. See also a record in which Carranco permitted the passage of numerous recently printed books of unknown reputation, including *Don Quijote de la Mancha*. AGN, Inq., vol. 275, exp. 13, f. 309, f y v.

has in other port cities."[41] He felt relieved that additional religious personnel would serve the spiritual needs of his flock and would aid in correcting the city's moral disarray. Altamirano, who was in Florida conducting a canonical visit when Carranco arrived in Havana, continued by praising the Franciscan friar's expertise and knowledge of canon law and Inquisition rubrics as demonstrated by the many years he served as commissary in Veracruz. He also acknowledged Carranco's well-known Christian virtues and expressed his confidence that the new commissary would be of great help and benefit to his people.[42]

Altamirano's relief and excitement had as much to do with the assistance he expected to receive from Carranco as a friar as with his role as Inquisition commissary for the port city. His duties as a friar implied serving the spiritual needs of the population and contributing to the Christianization of the locals. As an Inquisition officer, Carranco was to deter, if not control and avoid, problems caused by heretic pirates and the infamous *rescates* affecting most of the population, including clergy. The bishop himself was held for ransom by pirates only two years before his trip to La Florida.[43]

Altamirano arrived in Cuba in 1603 from Hispaniola where he had served as provincial of the Dominican friars and as professor of theology and canon law. During the first years of his tenure as bishop of Cuba, Altamirano attempted to curtail the problems caused by *rescates* and the circulation of Protestants throughout his diocese by increasing the presence of religious personnel in Cuba, Jamaica, and Florida. As part of such efforts, he also conducted canonic visits throughout diocesan territories as mandated by the Council of Trent and enlisted the collaboration of the local civil authorities.[44] The presence of an Inquisition officer in Havana was certainly a powerful weapon in Altamirano's defensive plans and postings.

---

41. Original text: "Para que en la villa de San Cristoval de la havana huviesse comisario y los demas ministros quel santo officio acostumbratener en los pueblos que son puertos de mar." AGN, Inq., vol. 1578, exp. 137, f. 1.

42. Ibid.

43. In 1604, Bishop Juan de las Cabezas Altamirano was taken prisoner by a French pirate who demanded an exorbitant amount of money as ransom (*rescate*). The bishop was rescued by a slave with the help of locals. The event is well known in Cuban history and literature as it was the basis for what is considered the first poem written on the island, called "Espejo de Paciencia." There are numerous works dedicated to these events. See, for instance, Graciella Cruz-Taura, *Espejo de Paciencia y Silvestre de Balboa en la Historia de Cuba*, Estudio Edición Critica de Espejo de Paciencia y edición documental (Madrid: Iberoamericana; Frankfurt am Main: Vervuert, 2009).

44. While Altamirano is mentioned in numerous works, the most complete biographical information comes from Victor Francis O'Daniel, O.P., "The Right Rev. Juan de Las Cabezas de Altamirano: The First Bishop to Visit the Present Territory of the United States (1562–1615)," *The Catholic Historical Review* 2, no. 4 (January 1917): 400–414.

Pedro de Valdés, governor of Cuba, also actively participated in Altamirano's anti-Protestant network; on several occasions De Valdés wrote to the Spanish king and Council of the Indies demanding support to eradicate foreigners. The governor was involved in the construction and improvement of numerous defensive structures in Havana and surrounding areas.[45] He was concerned with transient merchants and traders, described as heretics and thus enemies of the Crown who "inspired horrors among the Catholic colonists of Cuba. . . . [These] Protestants, Calvinists, and Lutherans, . . . distributed heretical books translated into Spanish, thereby jeopardizing the souls, especially of the rustics, [and] particularly the Indians and the blacks, barbarous peoples, among whom they . . . proselytized." The governor described the relationship between the heretics and "his most Catholic majesty's subjects in Cuba" as more than business relations. They were known for "eating and drinking and sleeping together." Furthermore, in the absence of physicians, the locals took their sick to the pirates to be treated and, he continued, both civil and religious authorities were heavily involved with the pirates; in fact, "more than one *cura* was implicated, and they were slower than their flocks to reform."[46]

As the official representative of the Inquisition in Havana, Carranco joined forces against such disorder. He arrived in the city sometime between January and March of 1606, and was expeditious in his office from his arrival. During the first week of April, he sent a first set of letters to the Inquisition authorities in Mexico summarizing a series of complaints previously filed under the jurisdiction of local bishops. He highlighted that many of those cases had not been concluded and requested permission to reopen some of them. He also expressed the "extreme need" for more Inquisition personnel in Havana and requested that the Mexican tribunal appoint four additional *familiares* (informants), asking that one of them should live among the soldiers (*gente de guerra*) as they needed order. Carranco also asked for one constable (*alguacil*), and two additional notaries to support his work. He recommended for the posts several candidates who already lived in Havana and others from Veracruz who had experience working with the Inquisition. He described the city as crowded and busy, with problems of all kinds, but most importantly, he reiterated, Havana was a port city requiring more Inquisition officers to safeguard the Catholic faith "from the large transient population that constantly roams the streets of the city."[47]

---

45. Ismael Sarmiento Ramírez and Aroa Huerta Quintana, "Una Mirada a la Isla de Cuba en Tiempos del Gobernador Pedro de Valdés, a Través de Sus Cartas al Rey (1602–1608)," *Caravelle* 106 (2016): 99–120.

46. Valdés to King, cited in Wright, *Rescates*, 338–339.

47. AGN, Inq., vol. 1573, sig. 13396, exp. 14, f. 3. The files contain annotations about when the letters were received by the tribunal in Mexico, and some include a note

Carranco's request for additional personnel immediately after his arrival suggests either an early realization for the need of an Inquisition tribunal in Havana or that it was part of a premeditated long-term strategy. Tribunals were established by royal decrees after lengthy discussions within the Council of the Indies where pro and con arguments were debated. Carranco arrived in Havana during the aforementioned active and lengthy discussions in Spain and the colonies about establishing a tribunal in the Caribbean. As of early 1606, a decision on this matter had not yet been announced. Hoping that Havana would be considered for tribunal location because of its strategic position and the aggravating presence of Protestants, Carranco immediately launched a busy career as commissary in the port city.

The years in Veracruz as part of the network of Inquisition officials had made Carranco aware of the prerequisites necessary for the establishment and functioning of a tribunal. The authorities required enough evidence that a tribunal was needed and expected it to be financially self-sufficient.[48] They demanded experienced personnel, knowledgeable of both canon and civil law and procedures, to serve as tribunal employees. The men selected would prosecute heretics, blasphemers, bigamists, and those guilty of other immoral acts as defined by Catholic canons and, therefore, must know definitions and required punishments. They had to abide by strict procedures and rubrics similar to those followed by the civil and criminal judges, which entailed a high level of education.[49] To function properly, the tribunal depended on a net of reliable informants, the *familiares*, who would identify and denounce unorthodox behaviors and acts. They were an extension of the Inquisition personnel and an additional deterrent presence, particularly in remote places.[50]

To justify his petition, Carranco had to document a caseload sufficiently large enough to prevent his effectiveness as an agent of the Inquisition and serious enough to merit additional skilled personnel. A significant number of accusations, particularly if they had the potential for scandal, was a good beginning. In the course of four days, 20–24 April 1606, Carranco wrote nine accusations, seven of them accusing people of heresy, witchcraft, and suspected Judaism. The accused were people living in Havana and the charges matched the type of crimes that could be filed based on Church canons and the current Inquisition manual.[51]

---

stating that a response was sent. Only a few files in the archive contain the mentioned response—either they no longer exist or are in a different file or archive that has not been accessed.

48. Chuchiack, *Inquisition*, 26–28.

49. Ibid., 30.

50. Ibid., 26.

51. AGN, Inq. vol. 1566, sig. 13386, exp. 10, f. 20 (CAJAS). In the letters Carranco mentions having a separate set of testimonies about his accusations but these have not been found.

Two of the cases filed in April 1606 differed from the rest in that the accused lived in St. Augustine in La Florida. This became Carranco's first territorial infraction because the two resided outside his immediate territorial jurisdiction; Carranco was designated as commissary for Havana only and not settlements in La Florida. In addition, one of the men accused by Carranco was the governor of Florida, Pedro de Ybarra. This constituted Carranco's first attempt to implicate a high-ranking functionary of the Spanish Empire, which increased the profile of the potential case. Along with Ybarra, Carranco accused a Frenchman whose name was not revealed in the document.[52]

Carranco denounced the governor for failure to arrest the Frenchman for making blasphemous statements in public that scandalized the Indians. He had been heard in the streets stating that only God should be venerated, and not the cross or any other religious images. Carranco asserted that Ybarra's refusal to detain the Frenchman was the result of certain beliefs evidenced in certain statements made by the governor. According to the commissary, Ybarra's statements contradicted the laws of the Church and rejected the king's decrees.

The friar made other serious accusations against Ybarra, including the practice of sorcery and issuing heretical statements about the Virgin Mary. Carranco based his accusations on a letter he received from Father Francisco de Pareja, guardian of the Franciscans in St. Augustine. According to Pareja, both Ybarra and his heretic friend (the Frenchman) were also known for reading books of dubious religious orthodoxy.[53] Aside from the gravity of the accusations appearing in the document, the letter shows that at the time of his arrival in Cuba, Carranco had already participated in and benefitted from an Inquisition system of informants embedded in the Franciscan evangelization network. In addition, because he was trusted by certain leaders of his order, such serious accusations against important individuals became credible. This kind of support was crucial to entrench his influence and expand his reach as a potential Inquisitor.

The letter echoed what had been previously maintained by the colonial authorities regarding the close relationship among locals and foreigners that permeated all sectors of society. It also depicts the absence of a Catholic moral code among the population at large and their disregard for secular and religious authorities. Even graver, however, was Carranco's reference to the lax attitude of the leadership in matters of faith and their unwillingness to enforce Crown law. He reiterated the inadequate numbers of Inquisition personnel, the vast territorial expanse of the diocese, the distance between Havana and St. Augustine and between both towns and Mexico City as obstacles to enforcing Inquisition authority. He recognized that the cases in St. Augustine were even more difficult, since his jurisdiction was limited to Havana, as stated

52. Ibid.
53. Ibid.

in his credentials. The remedy, he claimed, was to extend his powers to bring St. Augustine into his jurisdiction.[54]

The letter is the first instance in which Carranco, at least in writing, challenged the authority of Juan de las Cabezas Altamirano, bishop of the Cuban diocese, as *inquisidor ordinario*. Furthermore, he accused Altamirano of not enforcing the rules of the Inquisition and failing to prosecute or at least reprimand Ybarra because the two had a very close relationship. He added that since his arrival in Havana the bishop included in every document all of his titles, including that of ordinary Inquisitor, which prior to Carranco's arrival, did not appear. Carranco claimed that the bishop, who was still in Florida, was interfering in Inquisition matters in St. Augustine by visiting certain ships anchored there and ordering the destruction or safeguarding of selected heretical books. Carranco also complained about the lack of support he was receiving from local authorities, who in several instances had demanded to see his credentials and prevented him from doing his work.[55]

The commissary used his momentum to disclose secret communications he had sent to the supreme tribunal in Sevilla, in which he questioned the jurisdiction of the Mexico City tribunal over Florida. In his opinion, Florida would be better served under his jurisdiction from a tribunal in Havana rather than the Mexican one and even less from the one in Seville. He referred to an earlier letter sent to the Mexican tribunal asking for credentials specifically stating his Inquisitorial powers over Havana and St. Augustine. Toward the end of the letter he softened his demands, stating that regardless of his suggestions, he would accept whatever the authorities decided.[56] Carranco's alleged communication with the supreme tribunal is an additional indication of his ulterior intentions of establishing a new Inquisition tribunal under his direction.

The accusations levied against Governor Ybarra and Bishop Altamirano were just the beginning of a parade of manufactured sins and/or exaggerated charges filed by Carranco against high-profile individuals. Typical of Inquisition agents, Carranco targeted people of sociopolitical and economic importance as subjects of his investigations.[57] A guilty verdict of an important person would guarantee a considerable financial reward if property was thereafter sequestered. In addition, denunciations filed against influential or socially vis-

54. Ibid.

55. Ibid.

56. Ibid.

57. While Inquisition tribunals and their dependencies did receive subsidies from imperial coffers, they were expected to be financially self-sufficient. The main source of revenue was confiscated properties and wealth of high-profile individuals. See Chuchiack, *Inquisition*, 26–29. The Inquisition was also a career for some of its officials who amassed significant wealth from properties confiscated. For an in-depth study of careerism within the Inquisition apparatus, see Lynn, *Between Court and Confessional*.

ible people had better chances of being heard by the tribunals because of their prominence or potential for scandal. The allegations against Ybarra and Altamirano initiated Carranco's pattern of overstepping his boundaries, and while this could have negative consequences, it was a risk worth taking, since it guaranteed that his name would be recognized at the Mexican tribunal. He seized every opportunity to push the boundaries of his office, and his post in Havana granted him a number of such opportunities.

Carranco's combined role as guardian of the Franciscan friars and commissary of the Holy Office in Havana turned him into a regional administrative agent. While the Inquisition office did not grant him jurisdiction over Florida, his membership and rank within the Franciscan Order did, and his superiors used this confluence of powers. Not long after accusing Ybarra, Carranco was sent—sometime in April or May 1606—to St. Augustine by the regional Franciscan superior to mediate in a conflict over jurisdictions between the members of his order and the governor of Florida.[58] He was welcomed at the port by the other man he had accused, Bishop Altamirano, who was still in Florida conducting his canonical visit.[59] The three men were able to successfully resolve the issues at hand. Carranco made use of his powers by removing some friars from St. Augustine, forbidding others from interacting with the governor, and threatening those who failed to abide by his orders with excommunication. His tenacious nature as a mediator added to his rising profile and contributed to the governor's trust in the friar during future conflicts.[60] Carranco and Altamirano returned to Havana on the same ship, arriving in early October 1606.[61]

Within days of his return, Carranco sent to the Mexican tribunal a new batch of accusations. The crimes alleged by the commissary were common ones such as bigamy, witchcraft, blasphemy, and solicitation. One accusation, however, went beyond the typical.[62] On 17 October, Carranco wrote to the tribunal mentioning the detention of a woman named Magdalena de Cardenas. He had detained her at the request of General de Carrera de las Indias Alonso de Chavez Galindo, captain of the ship she boarded in Veracruz. Car-

---

58. Maynard J. Geiger, O.F.M., *The Franciscan Conquest of Florida (1573–1618)* (authorized facsimile, Ann Arbor, MI: University Microfilm, 1969 [PhD diss., The Catholic University of America, 1937]), 206.

59. Ibid., 213.

60. Ibid., 216–222.

61. Altamirano wrote to the king on 8 October 1606, informing him of his return with Carranco. AGI, Santo Domingo, 150. Copy in possession of the author obtained from the John Batterson Stetson Collection, University of Florida, cited as AI, 54-3-1.

62. The uniqueness of this case merits coverage as it is central to understanding Carranco's *ad lib* interpretation and application of the laws, which reflects on his aspirations for a higher post within the Inquisition.

ranco stated in the letter that Chavez knew that Magdalena was married in Tabasco, but also knew her as a professed nun from the Convento de La Pasión, in Seville.[63] During the next two years Carranco directed a trans-Atlantic investigation (Veracruz, Havana, and Seville) to uncover the truth about Magdalena's status. As a result, Magdalena was forced to spend the same amount of time and a considerable sum of money fighting those charges while being detained in Havana.

Magdalena's case was unusual and full of procedural irregularities from its beginning. Indeed, she had arrived in Havana from Veracruz, but in March, seven months before Carranco wrote the letter.[64] She had been imprisoned in Havana, without the commissary informing the tribunal in Mexico of the denunciation against her. Magdalena had been detained by Carranco as requested by General Chavez Galindo, but neither the commissary nor the general had the authority to order her detention. According to the instructions for Inquisitors, only theological qualifiers (*calificadores*) could decide if an arrest was warranted.[65] Not only was Magdalena detained without proper procedure, but after her detention, Carranco left for Florida, where he remained for several months. He had left Magdalena in a legal limbo, detained at a private home of a trusted *vecino*. This was not only inappropriate, but also unnecessary and ultimately, illegal.[66]

Adding to the irregularities of the case was the nature of the actual charges. The alleged crime committed by Magdalena was to be married while also a professed nun.[67] This was not a crime specifically listed in canon law nor was it included or defined in the Inquisitor's manual. Of course, neither status (nun or married) constituted a crime; however, living as both was considered a minor violation because they were considered mutually exclusive. A professed female religious could not marry unless her religious status was annulled by a canonic dispensation from the local bishop and the superior of

63. AGN, sig. 12113, vol. 283, part 2, f. 551. The document is filed incorrectly under 1608.

64. This is inferred from a letter mentioning Chavez's arrival aboard the *Nao* in Havana in March, available at http://biblio.juridicas.unam.mx/libros/1/163/12.pdf. In the letter accusing Magdalena in which Carranco mentions that it happened before he left for Florida and for that reason he had left another Franciscan friar in charge of investigating the matter. AGN, sig. 12113, vol. 283, part 2, f. 551.

65. Valdés, Instrucciones, Article 1, reproduced in Chuchiack, *Inquisition*, 59, and Nesvig, *Ideology and Inquisition*, 71. For an extensive discussion on the legal evolution of *calificadores* and their roles within the Inquisition apparatus, see Nesvig, *Ideology and Inquisition*, 70–74, and Chuchiack, *Inquisition*, 20.

66. Carranco's violation of procedural practices pertaining to an arrest will be repeated later; because the people arrested were clerics, it had graver consequences. The case will be discussed after Magdalena's for the sake of chronology.

67. The document reads "*casose siendo monja profesa.*"

her order. Conversely, a married woman could not become a nun unless she was widowed.

A denunciation or case such as Magdalena's could not be found in the canons or case law consulted. One case, dated 1553, tells of Isabel de Chavez, a runaway Benedictine nun who was captured attempting to escape to the New World. Isabel was thereafter held in a convent in Seville and then transferred to the monastery from which she had fled.[68] Another case pertains to a nun taken by the authorities from a convent in 1500, to question her about an alleged marriage. The nun was given the options of leaving the convent to return to her alleged husband or staying at the convent to remain a nun.[69] The women in these cases were not arrested or charged with a crime before the Inquisition. One woman was returned to her convent and the other given the option to choose, which were the usual procedures and outcome for these types of cases.[70] While other instances may have existed, they were probably hidden from public knowledge to safeguard the reputation of the individual and/or the convent. Magdalena's case as a runaway married nun gained notoriety as part of Carranco's plan to gain power and influence.

The only way to legally explain Magdalena's detention, charges, and subsequent ordeal is Carranco's spontaneous interpretation of canon law as he attempted to create a highly visible case or to establish a legal precedent. Section IX of the canons issued by the Council of Trent addressed the issue of clergy members, secular (diocesan) or regular (members of religious orders), who marry without receiving dispensation. The canon considered them to be violating the sacrament of marriage and therefore, as "anathema."[71] Nuns,

---

68. AGI, Indiferente, 424, leg. 22, f. 511r., 1553-9-6, "Real cédula a Juan Martínez Silíceo, arzobispo de Toledo, primado, y del Consejo del Emperador, pidiéndole haga trasladar a Isabel de Chaves, monja profesa de la Orden de San Bernardo, del monasterio de San Clemente de Sevilla al monasterio de Nuestra Señora de la Piedad de Vallecas, donde vivía antes de su frustrada huída a Indias." Royal decree to Primate Juan Martínez Silíceo, archbishop of Toledo, and to the Emperor's Council, asking them to transfer Isabel de Chaves, professed nun of the Order of Saint Bernard, from the San Clemente Monastery in Seville to the Nuestra Señora de la Piedad Monastery in Vallecas, where she lived before her failed attempt to run away to the Indies.

69. Archivo de Simancas, RGS, leg. 150,003,268, 1500-3-24. "Cumplimiento de la carta inserta, fechada en Sevilla, a 11 de febrero de 1500, por la que se mandaba sacar del monasterio de Santa Clara de Zafra a María de Carbajal para alegar si estaba casada con Francisco Villalobos o si quería seguir de monja." In accordance with the attached letter, dated 11 February 1500, in Seville, which ordered the removal of Maria de Carbajal from the Santa Clara Monastery in Zafra, to testify whether she was married to Francisco Villalobos or whether she wished to remain a nun.

70. For a discussion on this, see Linda Elizabeth Mitchell, *Women in Medieval Western European Culture* (New York: Garland Publishing, 1999).

71. Council of Trent, Canon IX, Session 24, 196. "If any one saith that clerics constituted in sacred orders, or regulars who have solemnly professed chastity, are able to

however, are not clergy, and the term "regulars" in canon law was applied only to friars and monks.[72]

Even so, Carranco, by interpretation or by analogy, extended this classification to a female religious person. Since Canon X as issued by the Council of Trent assigned cases regarding marriage irregularities to ecclesiastic tribunals, Carranco decided to formally charge Magdalena with a crime he fabricated.[73] Still, an Inquisition tribunal was different from an ecclesiastic one. This is not to say that nuns were exempt from canon laws. On the contrary, all lay and religious people alike were subjected to Church law. In the literature consulted, however, there is no precedent on which to ground Magdalena's prosecution. This, and Magdalena's economic status, brought additional significance and public attention to Magdalena's case—also as planned by Carranco.

Carranco did follow procedure by ordering an investigation regarding the case, which as expected produced contradictory testimonies. Several people interviewed in Havana, including those who "housed" Magdalena, testified that she had been a nun in Seville. Some described, in detail, the circumstances under which they met, and others rendered an account of her religious profession ceremony and subsequent celebrations. People interviewed in Veracruz declared that she was married in Tabasco to a man from Nueva Granada named Antonio de Guevara. The third group of witnesses included members of her family and the nuns of La Pasion. They were interviewed in Seville and all affirmed, with striking similarity in their statements, that she had never been a nun.[74]

---

contract marriage, and that being contracted it is valid, notwithstanding the ecclesiastical law, or vow; and that the contrary is nothing else than to condemn marriage; and, that all who do not feel that they have the gift of chastity, even though they have made a vow thereof, may contract marriage; let him be anathema."

72. There is an extensive discussion about this in the Catholic encyclopedia *New Advent* that highlights all the laws excluding nuns from the concept of regulars. The apostolical constitutions about the cloister of regulars, and notably the exclusion of women, are all after the Council of Trent. Regarding the inclusion of women, the sources are "Regularium," 24 October 1566, and "Decet," 16 July 1570, both from Pope Pius V; "Ubi Gratiae," 13 June 1575, by Gregory XIII; "Nullus," section 18, 25 June 1599, by Clement VIII. Regarding the egress of religious, see the following constitutions: "Ad Romanum spectat," sections 20 and 21, 21 October 1588, by Sixtus V; "Decretum illud," 10 March 1601, by Clement VIII (on the question of journeys to Rome); and the decree "Nullus omnino," 25 June 1599, by Clement VIII (for Italy).

73. "If any one saith that matrimonial causes do not belong to ecclesiastical judges, let him be anathema." Canon X, session 24, 197.

74. This information about Magdalena has been summarized from numerous letters and testimonies concerning her case. AGN, Inq., vol. 283, 2nd part, sig. 12113, f. 51, 119 (out of order), 551–53. The documents were filed incorrectly under 1608 and several of them were within other documents.

Magdalena probably knew the Inquisition procedures well or was being counseled appropriately. She hired an attorney, Adriano de Eraso, instead of relying on the one who would be assigned by the Inquisition tribunal for her defense. Eraso, who worked as an assistant attorney at the ecclesiastic tribunal in Seville, presented her case before the grand Inquisitor, Cardinal Fernando Niño de Guevara, in that city, and within a few months produced a verdict from the cardinal attesting to Magdalena's innocence. Magdalena's attorney sent the verdict to Havana immediately. For unknown reasons, however, the Mexican tribunal did not order Magdalena's release, and instructed Carranco to keep her in a safe place in Havana, which he did. After two years of struggle and four thousand ducats spent on legal and sundry other expenses, and with the intervention of the governor of Havana, Magdalena was escorted to a ship and returned to Veracruz.[75]

Although this research departs from the premise that Magdalena may have been a runaway nun who married in Tabasco, finding evidence of her status would require additional research and access to documents. Yet, the truth about Magdalena's civil status is of less relevance than the fact that Magdalena's case represents extraordinary practices and extreme procedures. As such Magdalena was used by Carranco in an attempt to advance his career and his goal of establishing a new tribunal in Havana.

In order to gain more attention, Carranco constantly complained in his letters about the lack of responses his cases received from the Inquisitors attached to the Mexican tribunal. He finally got the attention he wanted when he decided to denounce Luis de Salas, the procurator[76] of Havana. In addition to his prominent position, the man was Bishop Altamirano's very close and trusted friend.[77] The case was among a few of Carranco's accusations that culminated in a full-blown trial at the Inquisition tribunal in Mexico City. It was

---

75. Ibid. Details of Magdalena's case are the focus of a chapter in my dissertation.

76. A procurator (*provisor* in Spanish) is a bishop's deputy for a region with no bishop or too large for a single bishop to control by himself. Cuba was one such diocese whose jurisdiction encompassed to the island of Jamaica and La Florida province. The see of the diocese was in Santiago de Cuba, even though Altamirano spent most of his time in Havana. The Havana see was established in 1787, and the city's first bishop was installed two years later.

77. This case supports my arguments and is further analyzed in my dissertation. It has been mentioned by other authors such as Graciela Cruz-Taura, *Espejo de Paciencia y Silvestre de Balboa en la Historia de Cuba: Estudio Edición Critica de Espejo de Paciencia y edicion documental* (Madrid: Iberoamericana; Frankfurt: Vervuert, 2009). It is cursorily listed by Eugenio Alonso in *Mohinas de la Inquisición*, available at http://www.kislakfoundation.org/prize/200201.html. Both Cruz-Taura and Alonso approach the case from a different perspective and Carranco is not a focus of their investigations. Cruz-Taura focuses on Altamirano at the center of Espejo de Paciencia, a poem about his capture and rescue, while Alonso centers on the persecution of Judaizantes ("Judaizers"), briefly passing over Altamirano and Carranco's time period.

so notorious that it even reached the Inquisition Supreme Tribunal in Seville. The case supported Carranco's assertions to the courts and local authorities in Havana that he was the de facto highest-level Inquisition authority in the city. This claim was vehemently rejected by Bishop Altamirano whose jurisdictional rights were challenged by Carranco.

On 13 March 1608 the case opened at the Inquisition tribunal in Mexico City. Carranco filed charges against the procurator of Havana and three high-ranking priests for not accepting his appointment as commissary. The chief complaint was that these priests, ordered by Bishop Altamirano, were waging a campaign to diminish his authority and power over the population. He added that they were responsible for his inability to file more cases. Carranco accused the men of convincing witnesses not to testify against some of the people he had accused and of scandalizing the local population by undermining the Inquisition tribunal's decisions. He provided details of how the procurator, an informant, and an attorney had legally challenged his position by filing formal complaints against him and how he had no other recourse than to excommunicate them.[78]

Carranco made reference to other communications with the Mexican tribunal that predated the official legal case. He allegedly informed the authorities in Mexico about the problems he had with the priests and requested instructions on how to proceed.[79] It is obvious the tribunal never received such letters and even worse, they had never ordered the priests' arrest. The Inquisition officials were puzzled by Carranco's actions and demanded an explanation about his procedures. He accepted his responsibility in ordering the arrest but justified his actions using a previous communication from the tribunal.[80] As the commissary of the Inquisition, he believed he was responsible for detaining these men and sending them to the tribunal.

Regardless of his interpretation of his commission, Carranco knew he was acting beyond his legal prerogatives. He ordered the arrests while Bishop Altamirano was absent from Cuba conducting a canonical visit in Jamaica. He knew that the bishop would have prevented the arrests had he been on site. He was also aware that the civil authorities would not cooperate with him in detaining such high-ranking ecclesiastic officials, and thus, as he told the tribunal, the arrests were conducted in secret and at night. The priests had been transferred in a small boat, also at night, without consent of the

78. AGI, inq., vol. 282, sig. 12112, exp. 4, 5, 6, f. 1–147.

79. These letters have not yet been located in the archives, but Carranco's summary sheds light on the evolution of the case.

80. Ibid., f. 211–213. "[Q]ue V. Sa me manda que si pasaren adelante en el impedir exercicio de my oficio . . . y en tan grave delito como es notifficarme que cesse en el exercicio de todo mi oficio mande prenderlos e ymbiarlos presos y a muy buen recado. . . ." Because your honor has ordered that anyone preventing my role, particularly in a case as serious as ordering me to halt, I will arrest them and send them (to the tribunal).

guards, who, because of this oversight, were arrested in turn by the governor of Havana.[81]

During the process, the Inquisitor in Mexico requested information from all the people involved in the case, including Bishop Altamirano. While he was central to the case, he was never formally accused of anything by Carranco or the tribunal. That would have been a violation of canon law as well as a transgression of the Inquisition's judicial powers. As a member of the Royal Council, the bishop responded directly to the monarch, whom he had already informed of the jurisdictional debates and illegal arrests. In addition, Altamirano as the ordinary Inquisitor for the entire diocese, he responded directly to the Supreme Tribunal in Seville. In the bishop's written testimony, he reminded the Mexican tribunal about all these hierarchical protocols and of the dangers in violating them. Next, he turned to blaming Carranco's overstepping of boundaries and illegal actions as the root of the problem.[82]

In the letter, Altamirano told the Mexican Inquisitor that from the day of his arrival in Havana, Carranco acted as if he were the Inquisitor of Cuba, in complete disregard for his legal authority as bishop of the diocese. He accused Carranco of usurping all of his responsibilities and rights as Inquisitor, and that upon his arrival he had informed Luis de Salas that he would take the title of Inquisitor from the bishop.[83] Furthermore, Carranco had even tried to take over the bishop's jurisdiction in Florida and Jamaica. The bishop reminded the tribunal that his office was superior to theirs, citing both canon law and tradition as the sources of his legal superiority. He added that the authority of the Inquisition Tribunal rested on the delegation of and by the bishops. Altamirano stated that the Inquisitors should remember that the bishops' authority above all persons and institutions came "from our consecration, oath, and particular profession, which we bishops know as pontifices of the Church of God and successors of the Apostles as it was determined by the Holy Council of Trent."[84] No one in that tribunal or in his diocese, the bishop reiterated, was superior to his office.

Altamirano challenged Carranco and the tribunal to produce a document to justify Carranco's authority that would carry greater legal weight than the

81. Ibid. "[S]e le despacho una canoa de noche, que por averla dexado salir por el puerto los soldados questavan de posta los tiene oy pressos el governador." They were sent in a canoe at night and because the guards stationed at the port let the boat pass, they have been arrested by the governor.

82. Ibid., 212.

83. Ibid. "[A]via notificado al Procurator de la Havana el beneficiado Luys de Salas que nos quitase el titulo de Inquisidor." Upon his arrival he notified the procurator of Havana, the incumbent Luys de Salas, to take away our title of Inquisitor.

84. Ibid., 217. "[E]s consedida en razon de nuestra consagracion y juramento y profession particular la cual sabemos de la fe los obispos como pontifises en la iglesia de Dios y susesores de los apostoles como esta determinado en el sancto consilio de Trento."

royal decree in which the king of Spain had named him "Inquisidor Ordinario" for the island of Cuba, Florida, and Jamaica. He went on to enumerate with dates and names of witnesses, all instances in which Carranco had attempted to, or had managed to, interfere with his duties and rights as Inquisitor. He had constantly reminded the Mexican tribunal of its failure to produce any document, other than a letter introducing Carranco's credentials and posting as commissary, that would supersede his authority as Ordinario.[85] Altamirano's statements displayed his knowledge of canon law and litigation practices as well as serving as an illustration of the hierarchical and judicial protocols governing ecclesiastic jurisdictions.

The bishop's role as the highest authority over a diocese was indisputable and Carranco knew it. He, however, challenged Altamirano's title, role, and power before the Inquisition tribunal as a way of reinforcing his own role as an agent of the Inquisition. He managed to gain the support of the tribunal in Mexico and added a large number of supporters among the Inquisition personnel. Yet in Cuba both civil and religious authorities, including the governor and his entire advisory council, sided with the bishop, and expressed their discontent with the commissary in numerous letters to the Mexican Inquisition tribunal.[86]

The case against the procurator and other priests was dismissed because the Mexican tribunal ruled they were acting under direction of their superior. They returned to Havana and resumed their administrative and ministerial duties. The validity of Carranco's assignment as Commissary in Havana and his actions as such, as far as the records show, were upheld because he remained in Havana at least until 1611 as commissary of the Holy Office.[87]

The bishop, however, was not satisfied with the verdict. He continued writing letters to the Crown requesting an intervention. In July 1608, Altamirano wrote a letter to the Mexican tribunal filing charges against Carranco, requesting his incarceration for the illegal arrests of the procurator and the other priests, among many other excesses.[88] The bishop was right about the illegal nature of Carranco's action. The same had occurred with Magdalena's arrest. However, only the *calificadores*, who were experts in civil and canon

85. Ibid., 216–219.

86. AGN, Inq., vol. 282, sig. 12113, exp. 5, f. 226–227.

87. Cruz-Taura, *Espejo*, 26.

88. AGN, Inq., vol. 283, part 1, sig. 121113, exp. 6, f. 23–26. While copies of letters from the bishop as well as Carranco's response are in my possession, additional research at the AGN is necessary to complete this case. It is obvious Carranco was not arrested because he continued as commissary in Cuba (at least) until 1611. The case may not have proceeded because the bishop was assigned to the diocese of Guatemala a few months after he filed the complaint against Carranco. AGN, Inq., vol. 292, sig. 12122, exp. 7, f. 23–29.

law, could approve an arrest after reviewing the allegations against Carranco. He was not arrested.[89]

There is no evidence in the records of the Inquisition's supreme tribunal in Seville, the king, or the Mexican tribunal about why they did not respond to Altamirano's letters. Perhaps these bodies attempted to appease both parties by refusing to formally side with no one. A more likely explanation is that in 1608, the year during which the quarrel between the commissary and the bishop was "solved," the Council of the Indies and the Crown decided to establish a new Inquisition tribunal in Santo Domingo, Hispaniola. That decision could have been influenced by the dispute between Altamirano and Carranco or was adopted in order to end their disagreements. Even though a royal decree was issued, the tribunal in Santo Domingo never materialized.[90]

In 1609, Altamirano was made bishop of Guatemala and a year later left Cuba for his new post. In the same year, 1610, a new tribunal was finally established in the Caribbean, but not in Santo Domingo as earlier decreed by the Crown or in Havana as desired by Carranco. Instead, the tribunal was established in Cartagena de Indias in the New Granada.[91] Henceforth, Carranco stopped manufacturing sin. There were only two more letters written by Carranco from Havana after 1610. The first was sent to the supreme tribunal in Seville complaining about the inconvenience of Havana being placed under the jurisdiction of Cartagena.[92]

The other letter was Carranco's response to the authorities in Mexico after being recalled to Veracruz to serve as commissary in that port city once again. On 5 May 1611, Carranco wrote what seems to be his last letter from Cuba. He thanked the tribunal for reassigning him to Veracruz and expressed his gratitude to the Inquisitor for being the "only man in the kingdom who appreciated and remembered him." He prayed that God would grant him strength and health to continue serving as a friar and commissary. Carranco then informed the authorities in Mexico City that he had not been able to return to Veracruz because his replacement had not arrived. He also told them that he had not yet boarded ship because he was so poor that he could not "even purchase an umbrella to protect . . . [himself] against inclement weather" during the trip. He cursorily communicated the arrival of an order issued by Altamirano for his arrest, but that the new bishop who was already

89. The order to arrest Carranco was never carried out because Altamirano had already left Cuba when the order arrived (if it arrived) and the new bishop did not act on it. This is inferred from Carranco's last known letter. AGN, Inq., vol. 292, sig. 12122, exp. 5, f. 19–20.

90. Medina, *Historia* (1899), 34.

91. Ibid. As of this writing, no historian has suggested an explanation of the decision. See AGN, Inq., vol. 1568C, sig. 13390/5, exp. 366, f. 2.

92. AGN, Inq., vol. 292, sig. 12122, exp. 31, f. 141–142.

in Havana, did not enforce it. Carranco ended the letter stating his intentions to leave Havana for Veracruz in the next ship.[93]

Through the first decade of the seventeenth century Carranco's role and influence as commissary of the Inquisition, whether accepted or not by the authorities, expanded rapidly from Veracruz into the greater Caribbean region. Besides producing a profuse caseload in Havana, Carranco also mediated in a Florida jurisdictional conflict. It is unknown but probable that in its dual role as commissary of the Inquisition and guardian of the Franciscan convent in Havana, he also participated in the establishment of Franciscan missions in Florida. He was recognized by his superiors as diligent and reliable, and was perceived as an efficient agent of the Inquisition in the Caribbean. Carranco was also trusted within the Franciscan network in the region and navigated through it effortlessly.

He additionally recognized and used the political prominence of Havana at the time he served there. The city had just been made captaincy general in 1607, and its proximity to the recently established Protestant settlement of Jamestown in the same year, made it the ideal place for the new tribunal he so much sought to establish. He knew the time was right to shine as commissary and to seek ascension through the ranks of the Inquisition because he was aware of the discussions about creating new tribunals in the New World.

As a member of the Spanish imperial administration Carranco learned to navigate the hazy waters of jurisdictional boundaries. He was astute enough to manipulate and negotiate legal precepts and processes to the benefit of his office. His life was grounded in serving the Church, the order, and the empire, and his goals propelled and justified his actions. Most of time, he relied on canon law and acted in accordance with the Inquisitor's instructions and manual. As such they were within his prerogatives and legal authority as commissary. At other times Carranco's actions were exaggerations of his functions and premeditated overreaching his legal jurisdiction and responsibilities. In both instances his actions were consciously undertaken toward pursuit of his long-term goals.

By targeting well-known people and implicating them in manufactured sin and quarreling over jurisdictions, he attempted to establish himself as a powerful figure in the region. His mission was to safeguard the Catholicity of the king's subjects and to prevent heretics from infiltrating the colonies. For that, he attempted to pass over the local authorities, making even more obvious his aspirations to a higher office within the Inquisition apparatus. His emphasis on the importance of a permanent Inquisitor post in Havana was demonstrated in the first and last letters he wrote from Cuba. In the first one he requested

93. AGN, Inq., vol. 292, sig. 12122, exp. 5, f. 19–20.

Inquisition personnel to aid his endeavors. In the last one, he complained about the establishment of the new Inquisition tribunal in Cartagena.[94]

Although his efforts to install a new tribunal in Cuba were unsuccessful, the study of his actions and of the trail of cases he left behind serve as a departure point in documenting the history of the Inquisition in Cuba. They are also key to reevaluating the role of the Inquisition and its agents in the greater Caribbean. Carranco's life and caseload documents serve in reconstructing the lives of peoples residing in or passing through Havana in the early seventeenth century. Furthermore, this study begs for a reassessment of Inquisition networks to produce a more accurate historical interpretation of life in the hinterlands of the Spanish Empire. Finally, this work serves as a departure point for studying the Inquisition and the Franciscan Order as trans-Atlantic agents of the empire in the circum-Caribbean context.

94. AGN, Inq., vol. 292, sig. 12122, exp. 31, f. 141–142.

Chapter 6

Asymmetries of Power: Timucua–Apalachee Relations in the Early Eighteenth Century

Alejandra Dubcovsky

What was the relationship between Timucuas and Apalachees? Were they enemies or allies? How did these two powerful, numerous, yet distinct Native polities interact with one another? Timucuas and Apalachee had a long and complicated history that predated European incursions into their homelands (what is now northern Florida, southern Georgia, and eastern Alabama). Before Pedro Menéndez de Avilés established San Agustín in 1565, Hernando de Soto traversed through Apalachee in the 1540s, or even before Christopher Columbus sailed in 1492, Timucua and Apalachee worlds intersected without overlapping. Longtime neighbors, sometimes allies, and other times rivals, Timucua and Apalachee had lived alongside one another for centuries. Of course during those times, Timucuas and Apalachees were not "Timucuas" and "Apalachees"; it was the Spaniards who imposed those appellations.[1]

"Timucua" and "Apalachee" became shorthand, simplifying what were constellations of people with affiliations more closely tied to their local towns, kin networks, and dialects than to a single, unified nation. On the ground,

1. For Timucua relations with their neighbors, see Jonathan DeCoster, "Entangled Borderlands: Europeans and Timucuans in Sixteenth-Century Florida," *Florida Historical Quarterly* 91, no. 3 (2013): 375–400; Jerald T. Milanich, *The Timucua* (Cambridge: Blackwell Publishers, 1996), 187–188, 198–212; Diana Reigelsperger, "Interethnic Relations and Settlement on the Spanish Florida Frontier, 1668–1763" (PhD diss., University of Florida, 2013); John Worth, "Spanish Missions and the Persistence of Chiefly Power," in *The Transformation of the Southeastern Indians, 1540–1760*, ed. Robbie Ethridge and Charles Hudson, 39–65 (Jackson: University Press of Mississippi, 2002). For Apalachee relations with their neighbors, see Joseph Hall, "Anxious Alliances: Apalachicola Efforts to Survive the Slave Trade, 1638–1705," in *Indian Slavery in Colonial America*, ed. Alan Gallay, 147–184 (Lincoln: University of Nebraska Press, 2015); James W. Covington, "Apalachee Indians, 1704–1763," *Florida Historical Quarterly* 50, no. 4 (April 1972): 366–384; John H. Hann, *The Apalachee Indians and Mission San Luis* (Gainesville: University Press of Florida, 1998), 106; John H. Hann, *The Land between the Rivers.* (Gainesville: University of Florida Press, 1988), 106; Steven C. Hahn, *Invention of the Creek Nation*, 1670–1763 (Lincoln: University of Nebraska Press, 2004), 40–47.

the harmony afforded by sharing a common name or, at the very least, a name commonly recognized by competing European powers, was limited. Throughout the eighteenth century—even after three hundred years of interaction with Spanish, English, and French colonial forces—Timucuas and Apalachees used their local towns and communities to self-identify, discern friend from foe, and establish ties. Though the destabilizing effects of European colonization in the Southeast cannot be overstated, neither can the enduring power of indigenous self-governance, politics, and agency.

Timucua and Apalachee histories were closely intertwined. Yet we know little about their relations with one another. Indigenous groups, especially during the long colonial period, are most often studied through their interactions and exchanges with European powers. The focus on Euro–Native relations, as opposed to inter- or intra-Indian relations can be easily explained. Documentary sources are often the first-named culprit. After all, Euro–Native exchanges produced not only a great number, but also a great variety of written sources that are still preserved in colonial archives. While Spanish, French, and English officials all wrote about their interactions with Timucuas and Apalachee, there are a very limited number of documents detailing what Timucua and Apalachee officials thought of these exchanges and, even less, what they thought of their Native neighbor's responses to these same dealings.

Sources alone do not bear all the blame, however. More at fault is the underlying assumption produced in these written documents and then replicated by later historians that the Native groups and interactions that mattered were those that took place with Europeans.[2] This essay seeks to redress this historical myopia by centering Timucua and Apalachee relations with one another. It argues that Apalachee and Timucua relations were multidirectional. Even as most Timucua and Apalachee towns allied themselves with the Spaniards, Timucuas and Apalachees continued engaging in diplomacy, war, and trade with each other (as well as their other Native neighbors, including, but not limited to the Guales, Chacatos, and Apalachicolas).[3]

---

2. For the importance of understanding Indian history in its own proper context, see Alyssa Mt. Pleasant, Caroline Wigginton, and Kelly Wisecup, "Materials and Methods in Native American and Indigenous Studies: Completing the Turn," *The William and Mary Quarterly* 75, no. 2 (April 2018): 207–236; Juliana Barr, "Geographies of Power: Mapping Indian Borders in the 'Borderlands' of the Early Southwest," *William and Mary Quarterly* 68, no. 1 (2011): 5–46; Barr, "There's No Such Thing as 'Prehistory': What the Longue Durée of Caddo and Pueblo History Tells Us about Colonial America," *The William and Mary Quarterly* 74, no. 2 (2017): 203–240.

3. For economic initiatives and political developments in Apalachee, see Hann, *The Apalachee Indians*, 17; Amy Bushnell, "The Menéndez Marquéz Cattle Barony at La Chua and the Determinants of Economic Expansion in Seventeenth-Century Florida," *Florida Historical Quarterly* 56, no. 4 (April 1978): 407–431; John F. Scarry, "The Apalachee Chiefdom: A Mississippian Society on the Fringe of the Mississippi World," in *The Forgot-*

In this essay, I focus on a single incident, the trial of a Timucua man in 1695, to show how Timucua–Apalachee relations unfolded and shifted. The relations between these neighboring nations, which had always been tenuous, became increasingly fraught in the last decades of the seventeenth century. Highlighting the divisions and tense connections among and within Timucuas and Apalachees reveals the often-unseen, yet profound influence of intra-Indian relations in the colonial world. It was these interactions with one another, rather than their connections with Spanish officials and friars, that shaped the contours of everyday life for Timucuas and Apalachees.

Timucuas and Apalachee

Who were the Timucuas and the Apalachees? These Southeastern Native groups had distinct language, governmental, and economic traditions. Timucuas had about thirty-five separate chiefdoms. Archaeological evidence suggests that there were possibly 200,000 Timucuas living in the region before the advent of Spanish colonization, but by the late sixteenth century the population had declined drastically and was closer to 27,000.[4] Timucuas farmed, but most of their diet came from fishing, hunting, and foraging for palm berries, nuts, and acorns. Their societies, like those of most Southeastern Indians, were matrilineal and remained so even after Spanish colonization. It took until the 1590s for the Timucuas to welcome Spanish friars into their towns. Timucua chiefs had practical, political, and religious motivations for inviting the Franciscans. Timucua elites sought the goods, access, and military alliance

---

ten Centuries: Indians and Europeans in the American South, 1521–1704, ed. Charles M. Hudson and Carmen Chaves Tesser, 156–178 (Athens: University of Georgia Press, 1994); Patrick Lee Johnson, "Apalachee Identity on the Gulf Coast Frontier," *Native South* 6, no. 10 (2013): 110–141. In 1647, Apalachees had revolted and expelled Spanish officials and missionaries from the area. See John H. Hann, "Late Seventeenth-Century Forebears of the Lower Creeks and Seminoles," *Southeastern Archaeology* 15, no. 1 (Summer 1996): 66–80; Paul E. Hoffman, *Florida's Frontiers* (Bloomington: Indiana University Press, 2002), 101–102, 124–126; Jennifer Baszile, "Apalachee Testimony in Florida: A View of Slavery from the Spanish Archives," in *Indian Slavery in Colonial America*, ed. Alan Gallay, 147–184 (Lincoln: University of Nebraska Press, 2015), 185–206; George E. Lankford, "Chacato, Pensacola, Tahomé, Naniaba, and Mobila," in *Handbook of North American Indians*, vol. 14, *Southeast*, ed. Raymond D. Fogelson and William Sturtevant (Washington, DC: Smithsonian Institution, 2004), 664–668; Ives Goddard, et al., "Small Tribes of the Western Southeast," in *Handbook of North American Indians*, vol. 14, 174–190.

4. John E. Worth, *The Timucuan Chiefdoms of Spanish Florida*, vol. 2, *Resistance and Destruction* (Gainesville: University Press of Florida, 1998), 9–10; John H. Hann, "1630 Memorial of Fray Francisco Alonso de Jesus on Spanish Florida's Missions and Natives," *The Americas* 50, no. 1 (1993): 85–105.

that accompanied Spanish missions.[5] Within a century, nearly all the Timucua chiefdoms had received Franciscan friars and/or built missions. By doing so, Timucua leaders had done more than form a partnership with San Agustín; they had also managed to retain political power in a changing world.[6]

Spanish presence slowly reorganized the Timucua. Throughout the seventeenth century Timucuas harvested more corn than ever before. They also saw their gender roles become unbalanced, as Timucua men increasingly supplied labor outside their communities. Spanish pathogens further destabilized Timucua communities, reducing what was once a sizeable population to mere thousands.[7] Timucuas proved resilient and flexible. They renegotiated their alliances and developed inventive ways to not merely survive, but to remain an autonomous and self-governing nation. A clear expression of their power came in the 1656 Timucua rebellion. They mounted a calculated attack on Spanish officials to protest unfair labor demands and incursions on their lands and resources by cattle ranches and other Spanish enterprises. They also pointed to the growing slave raids in their lands and the lack of protection afforded by the Spaniards.[8] The short-lived rebellion reminded Spanish officials that, despite their missions and efforts in the region, they had limited control over Timucua.

Apalachees proved instrumental in helping the Spanish military officials suppress violence in Timucua. The failed 1656 Timucua rebellion forced a change in Timucua leadership, which saw many of its chiefs removed and replaced by minor figures who had remained loyal to the Spaniards. Timucua towns and missions, previously located on Timucua-selected and ancestral lands, were relocated closer to El Camino Real, the main Spanish road. A purposeful attack on Timucua autonomy, these geographical and politically imposed changes did not manage to fully compromise Timucua sovereignty or sense of identity.[9] At the close of the seventeenth century, Timucuas remained a central Spanish ally and force in Florida.[10]

---

5. John E. Worth, *The Timucuan Chiefdoms of Spanish Florida*, vol.: *Assimilation* (Gainesville: University of Florida, 1998), 35–54; Alejandra Dubcovsky, *Informed Power: Communication in the Early South* (Cambridge, MA: Harvard University Press, 2016), 68–72.

6. "Visitation of Timucua," 13 February 1657, in Testimonio de Visita of Governor Diego Rebolledo. Escribanía de Camara, leg. 15, no. 188, bnd. 1467, reel 12, Stetson Collection, P.K. Yonge Library of Florida History, University of Florida, Gainesville (PKY hereafter for archive location).

7. Paul Kelton, *Epidemics and Enslavement: Biological Catastrophe in the Native Southeast, 1492–1715* (Lincoln: University of Nebraska Press, 2007), 82–87.

8. Worth, *Timucuan Chiefdoms*, vol. 2, 35–76; Justin B. Blanton, "The Role of Cattle Ranching in the 1656 Timucuan Rebellion: A Struggle for Land, Labor, and Chiefly Power," *The Florida Historical Quarterly* 92, no. 4 (2014): 667–684.

9. Jerald T. Milanich, *Laboring in the Fields of the Lord: Spanish Missions and Southeastern Indians* (Washington, DC: Smithsonian Institution Press, 1999), 161–164.

10. For a survey and population census of these towns, see efforts by Joseph Primo de Rivera in April 18, 1717, reel 36, Stetson Collection, PKY, and John H. Hann, "St.

The history of the Apalachees follows many similar patterns. Apalachees were also farmers, and grew a variety of crops, including corn, beans, and squash. They were also matrilineal.[11] They did not speak Timucua; instead their language derived from the Muskogean family.[12] Their towns, much like the Timucuas, had two to three hundred houses—with big towns surrounded by smaller satellites communities. Although Apalachees interacted with the Spaniards since the *entradas* of the mid-sixteenth century, it took until the first decade of the seventeenth century for Spanish officials and missionaries to make headway in Apalachee. After much trial and error Spanish officials established San Luis, the main Spanish garrison in Apalachee that would grow steadily and boast a population close to 1,400 on the eve of the eighteenth century. By that time, Apalachee had close to eleven mission towns serving between 8,000 and 9,000 neophytes.[13]

The process of missionization was a bit more fraught, slow, and contentious in Apalachee than in Timucua. In 1647, a group of Apalachees in the town of Bacuqua killed the newly appointed lieutenant governor, Claudio de Florencia, along with his family and several Franciscans. The causes of the 1647 Apalachee Revolt were rooted in tense Apalachee–Spanish relations as well as shifting politics within Apalachee itself. Timucuas rallied behind their Spanish allies and helped suppress the uprising. As would come to pass in the Timucua rebellion nine years later, these neighboring Native groups allied with the Spaniards. In 1647, Apalachees would feel the brunt of a Spanish–Timucua offensive; in 1656, they would repay the favor and help the Spaniards regain control of Timucua.[14]

Augustine's Fallout from the Yamasee War," *The Florida Historical Quarterly* 68, no. 2 (1989): 180–201.

11. "General Inspection that Capitán Joaquín de Florencia Made," Archivo General de Indias (AGI) Escribanía de Cámara (EC) 157A, f. 63–64.

12. Thomas Buckingham Smith, [Documents in the Spanish and Two of the Early Tongues of Florida (Apalachian and Timuquan)] (Washington, DC: 1860). John Carter Brown Library, Providence, Rhode Island.

13. Patrick Lee Johnson, "Apalachee Identity on the Gulf Coast Frontier," *Native South* 6, no. 10 (2013): 110–141; Hann, *Apalachee: Land Between Rivers,* 160–180; Scarry, "The Apalachee Chiefdom"; Bonnie G. McEwan, "The Apalachee Indians of Northwest Florida," in *Indians of the Greater Southeast: Historical Archaeology and Ethnohistory*, ed. McEwan, 57–84 (Gainesville: University Press of Florida, 2001).

14. Testimony of Manuel Calderón, May 7, 1660, in Caja de San Agustín de Florida, Residencia a Diego Rebollo, AGI Contaduría, 963; Worth, *The Timucuan Chiefdoms of Spanish Florida*, vol. 2, 66–87; Aubrey Lauersdorf, "'To gain control over their Indians with the aid and support of Your majesty': The Role of Internal Factionalism and Inter-Province Relations in the Establishment and Destruction of Apalachee's Missions, 1607–1647" (paper presented at Ethnohistories of Native Space, American Society of Ethnohistory, Nashville, TN, November 9–12, 2016).

In the 1660s, Timucua and Apalachee communities faced new challenges. Slaving raids sponsored and supplied from English colonists first from Virginia and then from South Carolina did much to destabilize the region. The earliest of these attacks carried out by Westos, Savannahs, Yamasees, and Apalachicolas targeted the Guale, who lived along the present-day Georgia coastline. Slowly and steadily, as Guale Indians retreated south, slave raiders shifted their attention to what the Spaniards called *la tierra adentro* (literally the land within). Apalachee and Timucua communities began feeling the brunt of these attacks by the 1680s.[15]

Northern Timucua towns were particularly exposed, and soon Timucua chiefs began complaining that as their people suffered increasing attacks and devastation, Spanish officials did little to support them. With a shrinking number of people under their command, Timucua caciques were afraid of losing more than their families and friends; they also feared losing their power, relevancy, and livelihood. Instead of offering aid to the Timucuas, Florida governors like Diego de Rebodello used the *gasto de Indios* to win favors from the Ais, who resided in strategically important locations, and the Apalachees, who grew far more corn.[16] Timucua chiefs complained that the Spaniards favored these other Indians over the Timucua, who were not only longstanding Spanish allies, but also far more committed to Florida's missionization project. Lucas Menéndez, chief of the town of San Martín in Timucua, complained that while he had no Spanish goods "if he were cacique of Ays, or another pagan [community], that the Governor would give it to him."[17]

By the 1690s, Timucua caciques were acutely aware of their vulnerability, especially vis-à-vis Apalachee strength. Timucua towns suffered slaving raids, faced increasing Spanish demands, and received fewer goods and support; Apalachee, on the other hand, seemed to be growing. Apalachee towns were further removed from the paths that slave-raiding parties took and had thus managed to remain mostly intact. In 1695, Apalachees had welcomed Chacato Indians to establish towns within their lands, not only increasing the population of Apalachee, but also demanding tribute from the Chacatos.

---

15. Alan Gallay, *The Indian Slave Trade: The Rise of the English Empire in the American South, 1670–1717* (New Haven, CT: Yale University Press, 2002), 145–180; Christina Snyder, *Slavery in Indian Country: The Changing Face of Captivity in Early America* (Cambridge, MA: Harvard University Press, 2010), 70–78.

16. Letter by Diego Obispo de Santiago de Cuba, 3 February 1698, Havana, Indiferente Virreinal, Caja 0673, exp. 001, Archivo General de la Nación (AGN), Mexico City; Alejandra Dubcovsky and George Aaron Broadwell, "Writing Timucua: Recovering and Interrogating Indigenous Authorship," *Early American Studies: An Interdisciplinary Journal* 15, no. 3 (2017): 409–441.

17. "Captain Martín Alcayde de Cordoba," 2 May 1660, in Visita, reel 12, Stetson Collection, PKY.

The Apalachees "agreed and consented at once that they would give the said land to them and that in respect to what pertained to them on their part, they [Chacatos] make a free gift to them and cultivate them, provided that they are to understand that . . . [they] are to belong to the cacique of this village."[18]

Timucua people took notice. Once comparably influential Timucua towns were now lagging behind Apalachee.[19] A minor, yet violent incident on the border towns between Timucua and Apalachee exposed the shifting asymmetries of power in the region. The trial of a Timucua man reveals the proximity and interconnectedness of Timucua and Apalachee lives, while also emphasizing the growing difference in status and power of these two neighboring groups.[20]

Santiago the Hero, Santiago the Murderer

One Sunday afternoon during the early months of winter in 1695, Santiago, a fifty-eight-year-old Native man from the Timucua town San Pedro de Potohiriva, went to hunt. There was nothing surprising about his decision to go searching for prey or the paths he took toward the Timucua-appointed hunting grounds. The surprise came later that night. Santiago returned to San Pedro much later than he was expected, and instead of a deer, rabbit, or bird, he had with him a scalp. Yelling loudly and rousing the town from sleep, he showed everyone his trophy and made his way to the council house. Santiago spent the rest of the night in the council house telling and retelling his heroic deed. He claimed that on his way to the hunting grounds he had stumbled on an Apalachicola raiding party. Rather than cower in fear, Santiago faced the four, well-armed men intent on capturing and enslaving Timucuas. With the element of surprise on his side, Santiago managed to overcome the Apalachicola enemy, wound one of the raiders, and scalp another who had fallen behind. Santiago had then triumphantly marched into his town carrying and displaying the enemy scalp.[21]

---

18. "Visitation of San Luis de Tamaili," 9 December 1674, in Hann, *Visitations,* 178.

19. Hann, *Apalachee: Land Between Rivers,* 264–283.

20. This trial is one of many documents filed under "Visitation of Florida," a survey of Spanish missions and dealings in the colony conducted from 1694 into early months of 1695. AGI, EC 157A, Cuaderno I. See also John H. Hann, "Apalachee Counterfeiters in St. Augustine," *The Florida Historical Quarterly* 67, no. 1 (1988): 52–68.

21. "Declaración de Santiago," March 2, 1695, Autos Hechos de Oficio de la Justicia, por el Ayudante Andrés García, Teniente de la Provincia de Timucua, contra Santiago, natural del Pueblo de San Pedro, año 1695, AGI, EC 157, folio 176. The bulk of the trial has been translated in John Hann, *Visitations and Revolts in Florida, 1657–1695,* Florida Archaeology series, no. 7 (Tallahassee: Florida Bureau of Archaeological Research, 1993). I use his translations in this work. Thus, the *declaración* appears in Hann, *Visitations,* 281.

During the last couple of years, Apalachicola Indians had intensified their attacks on the Timucua. They had captured and enslaved Timucuas, in particular women and children who lived beyond the Camino Real.[22] As the town of San Pedro celebrated Santiago's bloody success, uneasy conversation spread throughout the small village. Apalachicolas had never dared to send slaving parties so near the mission town before. Santiago had been lucky, but the risk was far from over. Men rushed to their monitoring posts and kept a watchful eye, unsure if a larger enemy force was soon to arrive. As dawn broke and the enemy failed to appear, the town celebrated its safety and thanked Santiago for his bravery and quick thinking. The enemy, at least momentarily, seemed defeated.

Santiago did not remain a hero for long. News of his actions spread beyond this western Timucua town. San Pedro was part of the Ustacan-speaking towns at the western-most edge of Timucua. This location meant that the town was far closer to the Apalachee territory and the main Apalachee town of Ivitachuco than to Santa Fé, where Spanish forces and officials charged with supervising Timucua usually resided. To that effect, news of Santiago's exploits reached Don Patricio, the chief of Ivitachuco, well before André García, the lieutenant in charge of the Timucua region, had any sense of what had happened that Sunday night after mass. By the time Lieutenant García heard of Santiago, the Timucua man from San Pedro and his Apalachicola scalp were already infamous. While many in San Pedro praised Santiago's bravery, other Timucua and Apalachee people questioned his claims. Apalachee headmen like Don Patricio and Timucua leaders from San Matheo, another of these Ustacan Timucua towns that bordered Apalachee, accused Santiago of murder. They claimed he had killed an innocent Chacato woman.

Lieutenant García had no idea which story was true. If Santiago had killed an Apalachicola Indian, then he needed to increase protection in these Timucua–Apalachee border towns and keep Apalachicola slave raiders away. If Santiago had killed a harmless woman and the principal Apalachee leaders were correct, then the Spanish official needed to punish the Timucua man. Unsure what to do, Lieutenant García traveled to the border of Timucua and Apalachee. Although supposedly in charge of the entire Timucua province, he had, at best, limited control over this vast territory. He lived and operated much closer to San Agustín than to Apalachee, and as he headed west, he moved into a geopolitical world he hardly understood. It was not just the Timucua dialect that changed; it was that the people in these border towns had different concerns.[23]

The lengthy trial procedure offered no clear verdict—though later testimony seems to place Santiago in San Agustín serving a sentence of hard labor,

22. Milanich, *The Timucua*, 208.
23. Hann, *Visitations*, 278.

which suggests that he was convicted of murder. The 1695 trial of Santiago, supposedly concerned with evaluating the innocence or guilt of this San Pedro man, quickly became a battle of power between Timucua and Apalachee. Lieutenant García hired multiple interpreters, granted Santiago legal representations, and interrogated many witnesses. He claimed he took all these precautions "in order to make the investigation and inquiry that was most appropriate."[24] But long before the lieutenant began his investigation, the Apalachee chiefs of Ivitachuco and the Timucua leadership of San Matheo had already launched their own inquiries. Lieutenant García was merely trying not to fall behind or get too entangled in a complex web spun from intra-Timucua rivalries and Apalachee–Timucua relations. He failed at both tasks.

Apalachees in Timucuas

The two star witnesses against Santiago were Apalachee. Chucuta Antonio, the only witness who personally interacted with the Chacato woman Santiago had allegedly murdered, was an Apalachee Indian from the town of Ivitachuco. Lázaro, the trial's first witness, was also from Ivitachuco. Although his current residence was unclear, his testimony suggests that he had lived and traveled throughout Timucua.[25] Although the trial focused on whether Santiago had killed an Apalachicola slave raider or a Chacato woman, the movements of these Apalachee men hint at more than the porous nature of border towns; they also reflected the complicated relations between Timucuas and Apalachees in the 1690s.

Timucua and Apalachee were both Spanish allies and had both welcomed Franciscan missions, but that is where the similarities ended. The rising power of the grain-producing towns of Apalachee clashed with the struggling and increasingly raided towns of Timucua. The 1695 trial showed the uncomfortable proximity of Timucua and Apalachee, and the asymmetrical relations between these Native neighbors.

Chucuta Antonio lived right on the outskirts of San Pedro, but so close he "heard the barking of dogs in the place."[26] Why did he not live within the town? Perhaps the chief of San Pedro had not permitted the Apalachee man to reside within his town. Or perhaps Chucuta Antonio had specifically chosen his place of residence. After all, his house was located next to a small crossroads—at the meeting point of the trail that connected San Pedro to the Camino Real. In other words, Chucuta Antonio could monitor those who

---

24. Opening Remarks, Santiago's Trial, AGI, EC 157, folio 173, Translation in Hann, *Visitations*, 276.

25. Ibid.

26. Testimony of Chucuta Antonio, Febuary 29, 1695, in San Matheo, AGI, EC 157, folio 175; Translation in Hann, *Visitations*, 278.

went in and out of San Pedro as well as those who passed by. Why did the leading men of San Pedro allow this Apalachee man access to their town, but live just beyond their control? This unfavorable arrangement for the San Pedro Timucua hints at their declining control over their trails and towns.[27]

Chucuta Antonio might have lived by himself, but he was under the protection of the chief of Ivitachuco. Whether welcome or not in San Pedro, Chucuta Antonio had powerful Apalachee connections that seemed to grant him access into Timucua spaces. Lázaro, the other Apalachee witness from Ivitachuco, displayed a similar kind of attitude toward Timucua. Lázaro, like Chucuta Antonio, was a foreigner in Timucua lands; yet he too acted with the privileges of an insider. During Santiago's trial, Chucuta Antonio, though living near San Pedro, purposefully chose to give his declaration in San Matheo, a town far less sympathetic to Santiago and under increasing Apalachee pressure. Lázaro gave his testimony in Machaba, showing the extent of Apalachee travel through Timucua paths.[28]

By the 1690s, Apalachee presence in Timucua was quite common. Chucuta Antonio, for example, had lived outside San Pedro for several years before Santiago faced murder charges. Lázaro, on the other hand, had purposefully traveled to Timucua to comply with the "order of Patricio, principal cacique of Ivitachuco of the province of Apalachee." Don Patricio of Ivitachuco had requested that Lázaro travel east and investigate the claims of Santiago.[29] As one of the most important caciques of Apalachee, Don Patricio wanted to know what had happened that Sunday afternoon when Santiago had gone hunting. Had Santiago killed a Chacato woman belonging to the communities who had recently relocated to Apalachee? Had Apalachicola raiders truly ventured that far into Timucua?

Don Patricio's interest in the case could have been rooted in concerns with public safety. If slave raiders had indeed come to San Pedro, it would only be a matter of months before they targeted Apalachee towns; the cacique of Ivitachuco needed to be prepared. But his meddling in Timucua affairs also could have been about Apalachee authority. Santiago's lawyer, Antonio Ponce de León, suggested that Don Patricio's interest in the case had little to do with a murdered woman or slave raiding; instead, the cacique of Ivitachuco

---

27. For the importance of Native paths, see Joshua A. Piker, "'White & Clean' and Contested: Creek Towns and Trading Paths in the Aftermath of the Seven Years' War," *Ethnohistory* 50, no. 2 (Spring 2003): 315–347; Angela Pulley Hudson, *Creek Paths and Federal Roads: Indians, Settlers, and Slaves and the Making of the American South* (Chapel Hill: University of North Carolina Press, 2010), 4–18; Dubcovsky, *Informed Power*, 99–127.

28. Opening Remarks, Santiago's Trial, AGI, EC 157, folio 173; Translation in Hann, *Visitations*, 276.

29. Testimony of Chucuta Antonio, Febuary 29, 1695, in San Matheo, AGI, EC 157, folio 175; Translation in Hann, *Visitations*, 278.

wanted to monitor who traveled, hunted, and moved throughout the region. Ponce de León argued that it was no surprise that the main "witnesses are both natives of the village of Ivitachuco and vassals of the said cacique." Santiago's only crime, argued his lawyer, had been moving around Timucua and protecting his town; Don Patricio was the one who was overreaching, attempting to exert influence beyond Apalachee.[30]

The Timucuas did not all rally behind Santiago, however. Diego, a leading Timucua man from the town of San Matheo revealed that "he was sent by the caciques and leading men of the said place of San Matheo with three other Indians; and that he walked with other Indians from the said place of San Pedro, looking for a trace of the murder."[31] It was clear from his statement that San Matheo leadership thought Santiago was guilty—they were looking for a "trace of the murder," not for a trace of the enemy. They went looking through the trails around San Pedro seeking answers.

Frustrated by the lack of findings, Diego and the rest of the San Matheo men turned west, back towards their hometown. They had not traveled long when a group of San Pedro men approached them. The San Pedro Timucuas entreated the San Matheo Timucuas to lie. The San Pedro delegation told Diego: "he should return and that he should tell them in his place of San Matheo that he had seen the traces" of the body.[32] Diego refused, evincing a larger inter-Timucua struggle, especially in these border towns with Apalachee. The San Pedro Natives wanted more than to secure the innocence of Santiago; they wanted to keep the cacique of Ivitachuco away from their town. San Pedro leaders did not want Apalachee men investigating, interfering, and dictating their local politics. Diego as well as the other men from San Matheo took the opposite strategy. Instead of trying to remain separate from Ivitachuco, they had echoed Don Patricio's initiative and attempted to support his efforts. As San Pedro tried to move away from Apalachee influence, San Matheo embraced Ivitachuco.[33]

Santiago's trial showed the growing divisions among western Timucua towns. It also revealed the diverse and innovative ways in which Timucuas

---

30. John Hann and Amy Bushnell, the two scholars who have examined the case, strongly disagree on the veracity of this claim. Bushnell blames Don Patricio for falsely incriminating Santiago and Hann argues that Santiago merely had a good lawyer. Although there is evidence that supports both claims, what is truly more evident are the complex relations among Chacatos, Apalachees, and Timucuas. Amy Bushnell, "Patricio De Hinachuba: Defender of the Word of God, the Crown of the King, and the Little Children of Ivitachuco," *American Indian Culture and Research Journal* 3, no. 3 (1979): 1–21; Hann, *Visitations*.

31. Diego's testimony in San Matheo, 20 February 1695, Santiago's Trial, AGI, EC 157, folio 174; translation in Hann, *Visitations*, 278.

32. Ibid.

33. Ibid.

attempted to deal with the increasing and violent threats on their authority. Some western Timucua towns used the murder case to seek and display their loyalty to the more powerful Apalachee towns. Rather than support San Pedro, towns like San Matheo joined Ivitachuco in accusing Santiago of murder. Other Timucua towns resented the growing Apalachee presence and influence in the area and thus refused to support the persecution of a Timucua man—they mostly remained quiet, unwilling to support a rival, but not quite willing to march against them.

The 1695 trial of Santiago of San Pedro reveals the physical, political, and economic proximity of Timucua and Apalachee, providing insight into the asymmetrical ways these indigenously centered relationships unfolded. For centuries Apalachee and Timucua lives, experiences, and struggles had been closely connected. But by the end of the seventeenth century, Apalachees had a noticeable presence in and exerted significant influence over western Timucua. While these intra- and inter-Indian exchanges are often treated as secondary to European–Native relations, Santiago's trial helps bring them back to the forefront. It also shows that for the vast majority of people living in the area, it was these intra- and inter-Indian exchanges that enabled them to make sense of their changing world.

Chapter 7

Guns for Godliness: The Yamasees in St. Augustine

DENISE I. BOSSY

A junta in the city of St. Augustine on October 6, 1723 comprised of Spanish officials—including the governor, the vicar of the parochial church, and the head of the convent and chapter house of St. Francis—clearly identified the key to Indian conversion.[1] Eight years earlier, a large contingent of Yamasee Indians had opened negotiations with the Spanish. Both parties hoped that the Yamasees might relocate to La Florida from South Carolina. Initially settling to the north of the city, by 1717 the Yamasees had subsequently established three towns: two to the south of St. Augustine in an area known as Las Rosas de Ayamón (roughly sixteen miles south of the city) and a third closer to the presidio.[2] In a census taken by the Spanish that year, they identified 16 percent of those Yamasees to be either new or old Christians but the majority were still identified as practicing Yamasee religion. In other words they were "heathen," as the Spanish interpreted it.[3]

In the intervening years, the Spanish marshaled numerous resources to promote the Yamasees' further conversion. So it was no small matter when, in 1723, the Spanish zeroed in on the singularly most important thing that they could do to ensure the Yamasees' subjection to the Spanish Crown and con-

1. Governor Antonio de Benavides with Pedro Lorenzo de Azevedo (vicar of the parochial church) and Reverend Domingo Garcia (head of the convent and chapter house of St. Francis).

2. Amanda Hall, "The Persistence of Yamasee Power and Identity at the Town of San Antonio de Pocotalaca, 1716–1752," in *The Yamasee Indians: From Florida to South Carolina*, ed. Denise I. Bossy (Lincoln: University of Nebraska Press, 2018), 223–224. For other significant studies of the Yamasees in St. Augustine, see also Andrea P. White, "Refuge among the Spanish: Yamasee Community Coalescence in St. Augustine after 1715," and Susan Richbourg Parker, "Chief Francisco Jospogue: Reconstructing the Paths of a Guale-Yamasee Indian Lineage through Spanish Records," in *The Yamasee Indians*, 251–308.

3. The total Yamasee population at the time was approximately 419 including 10 women identified as Yamasee and/or Apalachee. Of these, 68 were identified as Christians in the census. Primo de Rivera Census, in John H. Hann, "Fallout from the Yamasee War," *The Florida Historical Quarterly* 68 (October 1989): 184–186. See also Census of the Inhabitants of the Indian Villages Near St. Augustine in April 1717, HC box MS 2003, bnd. 1: 25, John Hann Collection, PK Yonge Library, University of Florida, Gainesville (hereafter JHC).

version to Catholicism. And the answer may prove surprising. The key, the assembled political and religious leaders of St. Augustine declared, was guns. To be precise: 600 guns, 6 to 12 barrels of gunpowder, and 6,000 flintlocks.[4] Moreover, they couldn't be just any guns. They needed to be the light hunting muskets that the Yamasees preferred and which they had long acquired through trade with the British of Carolina. The alternative to not acquiring these guns for the Yamasees was just too terrible to contemplate. Without them, the Spanish junta explained, it would be "impossible" to "keep the Indians in our friendship." It would be a "great sorrow," they elaborated, "that because of this lack, so easy to remedy" that "the chance is lost of the propagation of the Holy gospel and the zeal with which His Lordship is seeking its greater extension."[5]

This surprising exchange and the great lengths to which the religious and political authorities of St. Augustine were willing to go in order to keep the Yamasees in the struggling city, open up a number of questions about what "conversion" meant to the Yamasees, to the Spanish, and to other Indians then living in St. Augustine. In 1717, the Yamasees were one of the most powerful Indigenous polities in the Native South and had a wealth of experience with both Spanish Franciscan and British Anglican missionaries and religious institutions. The Yamasee nation included citizens who had engaged with Franciscans since the late sixteenth century, most notably the Guales who governed and populated at least five of the Yamasees' ten or more towns in South Carolina.[6] The emigration of hundreds of Yamasees to St. Augustine between 1715 and 1717 fundamentally challenged and reshaped religious encounters in that city. While the Spanish attempted to publicly barter guns for godliness, the Yamasees negotiated, rejected, and cajoled the Spanish into aligning with their own geopolitical goals and religious expectations. Carefully witnessing and learning from this were several hundred Indians who overtly defined themselves as "old Christians" as well as "heathens" from South Florida who had only recently opened diplomatic conversations with the Spanish.

Historians of the Franciscans missions in La Florida have yet to fully and rigorously investigate what conversion meant from the perspectives of the Guales, Timucuas, Apalachees, Yamasees, Apalachicolas, Calusas, Ais, and other Native communities who engaged with, rejected, and reformulated Catholicism to suit their own cultural frameworks and needs. To be sure, since the 1970s there has been a decided effort "to question the criteria for Franciscan

4. Of these 450 were intended for the Yamasees in St. Augustine and the remaining 150 for the Yamasees in West Florida.

5. Junta, St. Augustine, October 6, 1723, Arms from Movilla for the Yamasee, 1723, JHC, 9.

6. In 1715, the Guale-Yamasee towns located in southern Carolina were: Pocotaligo, Huspah, Pocosabo, Sadketche, and Euhaw. In addition, there may have been a sixth Guale-Yamasee town called Tulafina.

successes." Yet despite the significant work by a number of archaeologists and historians to recover Indian perspectives and move away from narratives celebrating Catholic successes in conversion, some scholars continue to hold onto older tenets of what one historian calls "Christophilic triumphalism."[7] They presume that conversion meant to Native peoples what the Franciscans understood it to mean: the replacement of the central tenets of Indigenous systems of faith with those promoted by Franciscan Catholics operating in La Florida. While these scholars might recognize the syncretic elements of this process of cross-cultural religious encounters, they implicitly or explicitly suggest that when Indians "converted" to Catholicism—most commonly measured by the Franciscans in terms of baptism—that they understood the fundamental aspects of Catholicism in a way that reflected the teachings of the Franciscan missionaries who sought to colonize their very souls. Moreover, they often presume that Catholicism displaced Indigenous systems of faith in the process.

To more rigorously examine how Indians of La Florida understood and engaged with Catholicism and how those understandings and engagements differed over time and space and even in the same time and same space, requires that we focus squarely on Indigenous people. Only by centering Indians in our analysis can we see that Franciscans were generally on the margins of complex Indian worlds and that the true "converts"—in the Catholic sense—represented a very small number of the tens of thousands of Indians who engaged with, pushed back against, selectively and intentionally adopted elements and rejected other aspects of Catholicism even as they might, for instance, engage in the ceremony of baptism. Fortunately, historians in other fields have already made meaningful progress in reconstructing how American Indians "translated" Christian theology and practice into their own Indigenous religious systems, to use the construct of one scholar. These studies offer useful methods for scholars of La Florida.[8]

---

7. David J. Weber, "Blood of Martyrs, Blood of Indians: Toward a More Balanced View of Spanish Missions in Seventeenth-Century North America," in *Columbian Consequences*, vol. 2: *Archaeological and Historical Perspectives on the Spanish Borderlands East*, ed. David Hurst Thomas (Washington, DC: Smithsonian Institution Press, 1990), 430–433. Especially important studies that seek to more rigorously interpret the Florida missions from Native points of view include John E. Worth, "Spanish Missions and the Persistence of Chiefly Power," in *The Transformation of the Southeastern Indians, 1540–1760*, ed. Robbie Ethridge and Charles Hudson (Jackson: University Press of Mississippi, 2002), 39–64; Jerald T. Milanich, *Laboring in the Fields of the Lord: Spanish Missions and Southeastern Indians* (Washington, DC: Smithsonian Institution, 1999); Amy Turner Bushnell, "These people are not conquered like those of New Spain": Florida's Reciprocal Colonial Compact," *The Florida Historical Quarterly* 92 (Winter 2014): 524–553.

8. See especially David Silverman, *Faith and Boundaries: Colonists, Christianity and Community among the Wampanoag Indians of Martha's Vineyard, 1600–1871* (New York: Cambridge University Press, 2007); Daniel K. Richter, *Facing East from Indian Country: A Native History of Early America* (Cambridge: Harvard University Press, 2001), 69–109.

In much of my own work on these questions, I find that Indians more often than Franciscan or Anglican missionaries were the ones to set the terms of their religious relationship in the Native South.[9] Few Southeastern Indians can be said to have ever understood themselves to be practicing Catholics in the way that the Franciscans and other Spaniards would have expected. One has only to move beyond the rhetoric of those Spanish letters and reports whose express purpose was to justify further investment in Catholic enterprises in order to see Indian points of view come through these very same accounts. Franciscans traveled into Indian communities with decidedly imperial aims. Rarely did they fully understand what was happening in the Indigenous worlds in which they now lived. Few Franciscans achieved mastery of Indigenous languages in La Florida, to say nothing of Indigenous religions, and most lived alone in Indian towns and polities, where they were often kept on the margins of community life.[10] In the late 1730s, the Spanish were still calling for Franciscans to achieve basic mastery of Indigenous languages and to develop dictionaries to facilitate this process. Several friars explained that Indians actively tried to impede the acquisition of language skills, hiding the notebooks in which Spanish priests "write their language."[11] Even in and around St. Augustine where, after 1706, the Franciscans sought to keep the collapsed mission system alive in the wake of the destruction of Guale, Timucua, and Apalachee, that small number of Indians who had integrated Catholicism into their Indigenous cultural frameworks, continued to barter religion for goods and rights, understanding conversion to be part of an alliance with the Spanish predicated on tangible as well as spiritual returns.

Consider the junta's desperation to acquire guns for the Yamasees in the 1720s. The major impetus for this project came from the lobbying efforts of the Yamasees themselves. What began as ardent conversations in 1722 led to a formal

---

9. Denise I. Bossy, "Spiritual Diplomacy: Reinterpreting the Yamasee Prince's Eighteenth-Century Voyage to England," in *The Yamasee Indians: From Florida to South Carolina*, ed. Bossy (Lincoln: University of Nebraska Press, 2018), 131–162.

10. This is most recently revealed by the important work of Broadwell on the *Confessionario* long believed to have been written by Fray Francisco Pareja. Using the *Confessionario* to reconstruct the Timucua language, Broadwell has discovered that native Timucua speakers, not Pareja, were responsible for the translations. Moreover, these Indigenous scholars transformed Spanish queries and constructs, translating them not simply into the Timucua language but also culture and worldview and indigenizing what Catholicism meant in the process. See Broadwell, this volume, and also Alejandra Dubcovsky and George Aaron Broadwell, "Writing Timucua: Recovering and Interrogating Indigenous Authorship," *Early American Studies* 15 (Summer 2017): 409–441.

11. Manuel de Montiano to the King, July 16, 1738, Florida's Friars and Missions in the 1730s, JHC, 8–9; Fray Juan Calleja, Fray Pedro Morales, Fray Antonio Navarro, Fray Francisco Gomez, Fray Ignacio Venegas, Fray Pablo Rodriguez, and Fray Pedro de Leon y Cordero to the King, March 6, 1735, Florida's Friars and Missions in the 1730s, JHC, 28–29.

petition in 1723 when four Yamasee caciques—Don Francisco Bentura, Don Dionicio Aquilacje, Don Phelipe de la Tama, and Don Antonio de Pocotalaca—wrote to the Spanish, carefully but briefly couching their request for guns in terms that would resonate with their audience. The Yamasees reminded the Spanish officials that they had come to the presidio in 1715 "of our own will for the sole purpose of following the evangelical Law and to submit our obedience to so Catholic a monarch and sovereign king and lord of the Spains." And since that fateful decision, they had been under nearly constant attacks both in St. Augustine and also in San Marcos de Apalache in West Florida. In this same sentence, the Yamasees virtually cast themselves as martyrs for Catholicism. Under the kingdoms of God and the Spanish Crown, they pronounced "we are always persevering up to the point of sacrificing our lives."[12] Yet, it is worth noting that their letter includes only one sentence referencing Catholicism. The rest is expressed in overtly political terms, as we shall soon see. And this stands in contrast to the memorial by an "old Christian," which I analyze below.

Helping the Yamasees to craft their request was the interpreter Antonio Pérez. Indeed, Pérez wrote the letter, since none of the Yamasee caciques could write in Spanish or perhaps at all. Pérez well understood how to navigate Spanish expectations in order to forward Indigenous agendas. He had been the cacique of the Guale community of Santa Catharina, was Guale on his mother's side, possibly Spanish on his father's side, and had long served as the presidio's interpreter to Guale, Yamasee, and Creek Muskogee speakers.[13] Pérez might even have personally known or had kin connections with the Yamasees who had recently relocated to St. Augustine. Many of the Yamasees now in the city were Guales who had returned to La Florida, after having relocated from Guale-Mocama to Yamasee between 1685 and 1702. Among them were the Pocotalacas, whose cacique was one of the four representing the larger Yamasee population in the petition.

But while the Yamasee caciques cast themselves as Catholics in order to acquire the guns, they also revealed the driving reason that they wanted, indeed needed, the guns. They were still involved in the aftershocks of the

12. Don Francisco Bentura, Don Dionicio Aquilacje, Don Phelipe de la Tama, and Don Antonio de Pocotalaca to Governor Antonio de Benavides, May 20, 1724, Arms from Movilla for the Yamasees, JHC, 18–19.

13. Governor Juan de Ayala y Escobar to the King, April 18, 1717, Account of the 1717 Visit of 157 Creek to St. Augustine, JHC, 41. Antonio Pérez Campaña was identified as the cacique of Santa Catharina de Guale in the 1711 census and also the interpreter for the 1715 Yamasee and Creek diplomatic party that opened discussions about Yamasees relocating to St. Augustine. Census of Santa Catharina de Guale, Fray Joseph Pimentel de Ruedas, January 10, 1711, Native Village Census of 1711, JHC, 7–8; Testimony of Yfallaquisca, the War Captain of Satiquicha in Apalachicola, through the interpreter Antonio Pérez Campaña, Christian Guale Indian, resident among the Yguaja, May 28, 1715, AGI SD 843/30, John E. Worth Collection.

Yamasee War. In April 1715, the Yamasees with their Lower Creek allies and kin had initiated a war against the British to stop the enslavement of their family members and to check the illegal usurpation of their lands by colonial settlers, the theft of their property, their economic exploitation, and the abuse of their leaders and women by white traders. They were by no means alone. Within days, they were joined by Indians who lived along the Savannah River. Within weeks, more Lower Creeks, Catawbas, Waterees, Cherokees, and then Upper Creeks, Choctaws, and even a number of Chickasaws collectively killed the majority of British traders then in their towns. A smaller number of Indians engaged in direct assaults on the colony, a series of events that virtually destroyed Carolina.

The Yamasees had intended to use violence to renegotiate but not sever their relationship with the British. However, by May 1715, the Yamasees were forced to flee the homelands that they had occupied for the last twenty years along the Broad River. Roughly a third of the Yamasees decided to relocate to St. Augustine, and the rest went either to the Chattahoochee River with their Creek kin or to old Apalachee in West Florida.[14] For decades to come, the Yamasees—especially those near St. Augustine—remained at war with the British and, to a certain extent, with select Creek, Yuchi, and Chickasaw Indian bands. There were frequent attacks on the Yamasees in St. Augustine. And the Yamasees (and Spanish) also frequently struck the southern settlements of Carolina. This was the context in which the Yamasees repeatedly called for the Spanish to supply them with muskets, powder, and shot.

Lacking the arms and ammunition to successfully defend their communities, the Yamasees had, they explained, lost their "valor and reputation," which had once "extended through all these provinces." If they did not take revenge, they had little hope of defending themselves against the British and their "partisan" Indians who openly intended to effect the "extinction of us over time." To reestablish their martial reputation, the Yamasees needed two things from the Spanish: the license to take revenge (despite a suspension of armed conflict between Spain and Great Britain) and guns. Once a well-armed people, the Yamasees had brought numerous muskets with them to St. Augustine but now had few left and even those were "incapable for making either an attack or a defense." They were good only for ceremonies, the Yamasees explained.[15] The cost of alliance with the Spanish was proving steep. If cut off

14. William L. Ramsey, *The Yamasee War: A Study of Culture, Economy, Conflict in the Colonial South* (Lincoln: University of Nebraska Press, 2008); Steven C. Hahn, "The Long Yamasee War: Reflections on Yamasee Conflict in the Eighteenth Century, in *The Yamasee Indians: From Florida to South Carolina*, ed. Denise I. Bossy (Lincoln: University of Nebraska Press, 2018), 191–220.

15. Don Francisco Bentura, Don Dionicio Aquilacje, Don Phelipe de la Tama, and Don Antonio de Pocotalaca to Governor Antonio de Benavides, May 20, 1724, Arms from

from a ready supply of guns and ammunition, the Yamasees would have to leave or face their very annihilation.

The junta's desperation to acquire guns for the Yamasees was a direct response to Yamasee demands for those guns. However, for at least seventy years, Franciscans and the Spanish more generally had actively tried to acquire guns and ammunition for Indians whom they sought to convert. Although scholars have long characterized the Spanish as loathe to arm Indians in La Florida, in fact by the second half of the seventeenth century the Spanish increasingly and actively sought to do just that. They were pushed to this policy not just by English colonizers, who certainly played a crucial role, but also by Indian communities in and beyond La Florida.

By the mid-seventeenth century, assaults on the missions north and west of St. Augustine by gun-wielding Westo Indians allied with the English of Virginia had prompted Indians to arm themselves (when possible) and the Spanish to provide some arquebuses, shotguns, and training in firearms to Indian leaders and warriors.[16] By the 1670s and 1680s, the expansion of the English of Carolina into territory claimed by the Spanish and the intensification of slave and pirate raids on the missions prompted the Spanish to intensify their Indian arms program. Yamasees, Creeks, and others launched a series of episodic slave raids against the missions. Not only did they seek captives to sell in the English slave markets but they also sought to persuade those Guales, Timucuas, and Apalachees who remained in La Florida to join their polities.

By the 1680s each Indian mission town in La Florida had shotgunners and arquebusiers at the ready.[17] As historian Amy Turner Bushnell has recently argued, not only had "the Spanish . . . given up the idea of keeping guns out of the hands of Indian commoners" by this point but they "would have armed all of their allies, had they been able."[18] Perpetually suffering from an inadequate number of Spanish soldiers to staff the presidios in St. Augustine and

---

Movilla for the Yamasees, JHC, 18–19. Guns only lasted eight to ten years, even with regular repair, as one Apalachee cacique explained. Memorial of Francisco Luis, Native, to Antonio de Arredondo, September 20, 1736, Florida's Friars and Missions in the 1730s, JHC, 42–47.

16. For an overview of the Westos see Eric Bowne, *The Westo Indians: Slave Traders of the Early Colonial South* (Tuscaloosa: University of Alabama Press, 2005).

17. The rest of the Indian men were expected to have fifty arrows ready in their quiver in case of invasion. General Auto of the Visitation of Guale, December 21, 1685 and Auto and Orders for Guale and Mocama, December 29, 1685, in *The Struggle for the Georgia Coast: An 18th-Century Spanish Retrospective on Guale and Mocama*, trans. John E. Worth (Athens: American Museum of Natural History; distributed by the University of Georgia, 1995), 112, 119.

18. Amy Turner Bushnell, "Living at Liberty: The Ungovernable Yamasees of Spanish Florida," in *The Yamasee Indians: From Florida to South Carolina*, ed. Denise I. Bossy (Lincoln: University of Nebraska Press, 2018), 34.

Apalachee along with the small garrisons in each mission province, the Spanish relied on Indian men to serve in standing militias.[19] That they could do so in only limited numbers in the second half of the seventeenth century was more a product of their own supply problems rather than of a strong ideological stance against arming Indians in and near mission towns.[20]

Desperate for guns to put into the hands of his flock on Amelia Island, for example, one Franciscan friar made a remarkable journey to South Carolina where he opened an illegal and furtive trade in guns with the English, who were then ardent enemies of the Spanish. In the winter of 1687, Fray Símon de Salas was sent by Governor Diego de Quiroga y Losada on a mission to woo the Yamasees back to La Florida. In the early 1660s, the Yamasees had begun to move into Guale-Mocama, Apalachee, and Apalachicola, fleeing slave raids that devastated their ancestral homelands in interior Georgia. Most Yamasees moved to the coast, where they created lasting bonds with many of the Guales. When the Yamasee core severed their ties with the Spanish in the early 1680s and moved north, hundreds of Guales joined them and became Yamasee citizens. Together, they made new homes nearby and a new alliance with the English of Carolina.

A major impetus for the Yamasee and Guale exodus was their shared desire to live as they desired, especially when it came to religion. Spanish documents suggest that the Yamasees were familiar with the Fundamental Constitutions of South Carolina and that this was part of their attraction to the colony. Crafted by the philosopher John Locke, the Fundamental Constitutions not only protected but promoted freedom of religion. (Locke and his patron, one of the Lords Proprietors who owned Carolina, were Dissenters.) With incredible prescience, Locke thought also to recognize the legitimacy of American Indian religions in the Fundamental Constitutions. Could he have guessed that the Yamasees would learn about this? It seems unlikely, and yet the Spanish

---

19. General Auto of the Visitation of Guale, December 21, 1685, in *The Struggle for the Georgia Coast*, 109. In 1680, for instance, when Cabrera assumed the governorship, he reported that there were only 140 men in fighting shape able to serve in the following posts: 30 to Apalachee for the fort and post with a squad leader, 6 in Timucua province, 6 at the Matanzas lookout, 6 in the bar of St. Augustine, 4 on the St. Johns River (Salamoto), and 12 in Guale. That would have left 75 men at the Castillo. Juan Marquez Cabrera to the King, December 8, 1680, Cabrera Documents, JHC, 8–9.

20. In 1685, for example, Cacique Lorenzo Santiago (Mocama) explained that the arquebusiers and shotgunners "do not have powder or balls, nor do they find themselves in a position to buy them, although they would like to." Visitation in Santa Cruz de San Buenaventura, 1685, in *The Struggle for the Georgia Coast: An 18th-Century Spanish Retrospective on Guale and Mocama*, trans. John E. Worth (Athens: American Museum of Natural History; distributed by the University of Georgia, 1995), 111. In 1687, there were more than three hundred firearms in Apalachee belonging to Indians and Spaniards, but little powder or balls. Statement of Captain Jacinto Roque, May 30, 1687, Matheos Phases I–II, JHC, 43.

noted that the Yamasees had not only repeatedly rejected efforts by the Franciscans in Guale-Mocama to convert them but had left La Florida because they wanted to live as they pleased with "liberty of conscience."[21]

The exodus of Guales continued during the 1690s and into the early eighteenth century, and the number of Yamasee towns increased in southern Carolina apace. Fray Salas had gone to Charleston in 1687 not just to woo the Yamasees back but also to prevent the last remaining Guales from following their lead. To do so, he understood, he needed guns. Salas had served as the *doctrinero* to both Guales and Yamasees on Sapelo Island and those who now remained on Amelia Island. While in Charles Town, he made plans to open a surreptitious trade with the English governor of the colony, exchanging Spanish horses from Apalachee for English firearms.[22] That July a Scottish delegate from South Carolina arrived on *The Sabina* with a boatload of arms, powder, and shot, ready to do business with Salas. Among the arms were two muskets that Salinas had specially ordered for himself. The rest was clearly intended for the Guales who lived on Amelia Island in three refugee towns.[23] But not only did this singular effort to acquire English guns for Guale converts fail (it was, after all, illegal trade), but the Spanish also failed to stem the tide of Guale emigration to Yamasee. By 1701, there were only two hundred Guales left in

---

21. In Article 97, a church was defined as any seven or more people who agreed in any religion. The impetus for this article was that "natives of that place" would be "utter strangers to Christianity" and "unavoidably of different opinions concerning matters of religions, *the liberty whereof* they will expect to have allowed them" (emphasis added). By not compelling Indians to convert and by peacefully tolerating differences of religious opinion, the hope was that Indians (as well as Jews and from Christian dissenters) might be won over. The Fundamental Constitutions of Carolina, March 1, 1669, https://avalon.law.yale.edu/17th_century/nc05.asp (accessed January 3, 2019). Governor Torres y Ayala to the King, February 7, 1697, Hann, Matheos Part VI, 103. See also Tomás Menéndez Márquez and Francisco de la Rocha to the King, October 4, 1686, Hann, Matheos Phase III, 95. Scholars have recently made a similar argument about Yamasee self-determination but have not connected this to their familiarity (and also that of the Spanish) with Locke's Fundamental Constitutions. Bushnell, "Living at Liberty"; Keith Ashley, "Yamasee Migrations into the Mocama and Timucua Mission Provinces of Florida, 1667–1683: An Archaeological Perspective," in *The Yamasee Indians: From Florida to South Carolina*, ed. Denise I. Bossy (Lincoln: University of Nebraska Press, 2018), 64–65.

22. J.G. Dunlop, ed., "William Dunlop's Mission to St. Augustine in 1688," *The South Carolina Historical and Genealogical Magazine* 34 (January 1933): 10–12. Salas had already engaged in trading while in Charleston and had ordered two firearms, which Dunlop brought with him to La Florida along with bills of sale for Salas's debts. Salas had a long career in La Florida: he arrived in 1678 and beginning in 1705 served as the provincial commissary. Maynard Geiger, *Biographical Dictionary of the Franciscans in Spanish Florida and Cuba, Franciscan Studies*, vol. XXI (Patterson, NJ: St. Anthony Guild Press, 1940), 101–102.

23. Salas's trade was illegal, a point he made clear in his response. He beseeched the Scottish envoy not to reveal that he had traded with the English in Carolina, promising to reward him with gold and silver if he kept the secret.

the province. The rest, as the governor explained, "have been going little by little to the Yamasees and to places bordering on St. George (Charleston)."[24]

The attempt to acquire guns for the Yamasee Indians in the 1720s thus fit into a longer practice of the Spanish arming Indians who lived in at-risk mission towns. Moreover, it reveals the agency of the Yamasees and others in demanding that the Spanish acquire these guns for them. Because the Spanish emphasized Catholicism as crucial to alliance, the Yamasees applied this language when they forcefully requested guns and other tangible goods. Meanwhile, they sought religious self-determination. This had not changed when they returned to La Florida in the wake of the Yamasee War. And it is to that which we now turn.

By 1711, the Spanish counted only seven mission communities in La Florida with a total population of 401 inhabitants: Timucuas, Apalachees, Guales, and Ais. (It is worth noting that there were only 61 Guales left in St. Augustine by this point.) With the exception of the 137 Ais, the rest were the "old Christians"—264 Indians who had engaged with Catholicism for generations and had decided to stay in La Florida even as the majority of their community members were either forcibly removed or killed by slavers or chose to leave for Carolina, Louisiana, or Creek and other Indian communities. The Ais had only recently begun to consider an alliance with the Spanish, compelled to do so by slave raids largely led by the Yamasees in South Florida. Although 12 Ais were counted as "converted," in 1711 the vast majority (88 percent) were still "heathen." Both the old Christians and new "heathens" were huddled around St. Augustine "within a pistol shot" of the Castillo de San Marcos, where they hoped to remain safe.[25]

These were the survivors of unprecedented levels of violence and loss. What had once been an expansive Franciscan mission system that stretched north along the coast into present-day southern Georgia and west across northern Florida into present-day Tallahassee had all but collapsed. Episodic revolts and small-scale epidemics coupled with flight from the missions had been further exacerbated by direct assaults encouraged or led by the English out of Virginia and South Carolina. Over the course of 66 years, more or less, the Indians who

---

24. Governor Don Joseph Zúñiga y Cerda to H.M., June 22, 1701; 1701 Visitation of Guale and Mocama, JHC.

25. Governor Francisco Córcoles y Martínez to the King, April 9, 1711; Report on San Luis de Talimali alias Abosaya by Fray Phelipe Ossorios Maldonado, January 8, 1711, Report on Santa Catharina de Guale by Fray Joseph Pimentel de Ruedas, January 10, 1711; Report on Santo Thomas de Santa Fe alias Esperanza by Fray Alonso Santurro, January 13, 1711; Report on San Juan del Puerto by Fray Salvador Bueno, January 13, 1711; Report on Nombre de Dios by Fray Manuel de Urisa, n.d.; Report on Tolomato by Fray Pedro de Lastra, n.d.; Report on the Indians of la Costa (Ais) by Fray Joseph Lopez, n.d., Native Village Census of 1711, all in JHC, 2–14.

lived in the communities of the three major mission provinces—Timucua, Guale, and Apalachee—suffered a progressively intensified campaign of slave raids. Many of these raids were spearheaded by the Yamasees and Creeks, who sought both to procure captives for the English slave markets and to recruit Indians to abandon Florida and join their confederacies.

The most destructive were the two campaigns where the Carolinians took the lead. Joined by hundreds of Yamasee Indians, Governor James Moore and his companies effectively dismantled the remaining Guale-Mocama missions in 1702 during their assault on St. Augustine. Despite burning much of the town, Moore failed to take the Castillo and so turned to La Florida's stronghold: the northern mission chain of Apalachee, in 1703–1704. This was followed by more raids by the Creeks and Yamasees that not only finished off the remaining Apalachee towns but also the Timucua and then pushed south into the Florida peninsula where Ais, Calusas, and others had long resisted Spanish colonization including missionization.

The Spanish were thus overjoyed when the Yamasees and some of their Creek kin and allies opened negotiations in May 1715 to relocate to La Florida. The most immediate effect of the Yamasees' relocation was a ballooning of the mission population. In 1717, the Spanish counted 946 Indians living near St. Augustine in ten towns. The influx of Yamasees and their affiliates along with largely unconverted Indians seeking refuge from other parts of Florida (primarily Mayacas) had more than doubled the size of the Indian population. And the Yamasees now comprised a bit less than half of that population (44 percent).[26]

The Yamasees fundamentally changed what religious encounters meant in the missions near and of St. Augustine and not only for themselves but also for other Indians. A total of 247 "old Christians"—Timucuas, Apalachees, and Guales—had formed the majority of the Indian population around St. Augustine in 1711, where they lived in six towns comprised entirely of Indians identified as long-standing Catholics. When the non-Catholic Ais began to arrive around 1711, they lived in their own distinct community. Moreover, few (if any) Ais stayed in St. Augustine and none appear on the next census.

The immigration of over 400 Yamasees by 1717 transformed all of this. The Yamasees reconstituted three of their own towns—Tamaja, Pocosaba, and Pocotalaca—and some Yamasees also joined other towns. For example, in the Mocama town of Palica, 42 Yamasees (including Ichisis) moved in alongside the 90 Christian Timucuas (Mocamas and Salamototos). And Santa Catharina de Guale's population grew from 61 in 1711 to 125 people in 1717. At least some of this population growth must have been a result of

26. Primo de Rivera Census, in John H. Hann, "Fallout from the Yamasee War," *The Florida Historical Quarterly* 68 (October 1989): 184–186.

Guale-Yamasees rejoining their Guale kin. Only four missions now remained solely in the hands of the "old Christian" Indians.[27]

The Spanish set to work, attempting to convert all of the Yamasees to Catholicism by focusing first of all on persuading Yamasees and other "heathens" to accept baptism. Writing to the king in 1723, Governor Benavides proudly pronounced that since taking the governorship in 1718 he had not only dedicated himself to the conversion of the Indians but that his work and the collective work of the Franciscans had paid off. In the space of those five years, he claimed, 658 Indians had been baptized (193 children and 465 adults). Of these, almost a third were Yamasees (29.5 percent; 55 Yamasee children and 139 Yamasee adults).[28] Conflating baptism with conversion, Benavides, proclaimed that he expected the "conversions" to increase and he documented as much in his formal visitation report just two years later.

By 1726, according to Benavides, nearly all of the Yamasees living near St. Augustine had "converted," save four "heathen." But the Yamasee population of St. Augustine had sharply declined from roughly 419 in 1717 to just 167 in 1726; a decline of over 60 percent. This was a direct result of years of attacks by select bands of Creeks and Yuchis, the very series of attacks that had prompted the Yamasees to demand guns in 1723. With incredible prescience, the Yamasees realized that their communities in St. Augustine and in West Florida faced certain destruction.[29]

Although Governor Benavides claimed that Yamasees who accepted baptism became Catholics, a memorial written by an Apalachee on behalf of the "old Christians" and a series of letters by Franciscans who had come from Spain to La Florida in the 1730s, collectively challenged this notion. Instead, they demonstrate the Yamasees had also successfully reformulated religious encounters across the missions by this period. Taken together, we can begin to reconstruct a better sense of how different Indian and Spanish factions understood Catholicism and the role of religion in Spanish–Indian relations by situating their experiences in a broader historical context.[30]

---

27. The tenth town was Jororo, inhabited by Mayacas of whom 33 percent (11 of 33) were identified as Christian in 1717.

28. Governor Antonio Benavides to the King, March 8, 1723, in *Missions to the Calusas*, ed. and trans. Hann, 359–362. No total population figure was offered in this report, only the numbers of Indians baptized.

29. Governor Benavides, Report of Visitation of Settlements near St. Augustine and San Marcos de Apalachee, December 1–11, 1726, in *Missions to the Calusas*, 363–367. This is in contrast to the new mission towns in Apalachee, where many of the Yamasees were still identified by Benavides as heathen.

30. Part of this was the result of an ongoing struggle between American- and Spanish-born friars—*criollos* and *peninsulares*, respectively—for control over the dwindling missions near St. Augustine. This political and cultural battle has been discussed by other scholars of Florida and had long been and would continue to be a common problem in Spanish

The 1736 memorial of Francisco Luis offers a glimpse into how Indians who had lived in missions before the collapse of the mission system and subsequently relocated to St. Augustine understood their engagement with Catholicism. Luis self-identified as one of the "old Christians," that is the small number of Apalachees, Timucuas, and Guales who had never left La Florida and who had decided to live in or near St. Augustine after 1706. They were the descendants of Indians who had engaged with the Spanish and Catholicism for generations by this point, most for well over a hundred years.[31] Representing the "native Indians and leading men[,] . . . old Christians[,]" he now lodged a lengthy series of complaints.

In sharp contrast to the Yamasees caciques' 1723 letter, Luis's memorial is suffused with both Catholic language and also direct discussion of Catholic practices, as he understood them. Significantly, Luis focused on what he perceived to be profound changes in how the Spanish (especially the governor) treated the "old Christians," changes that had occurred as a direct result of the new world order in the post–Yamasee War period. Luis was particularly critical of Governor Francisco Moral Sanchez's policy of inviting "heathen" Indians to St. Augustine to engage in diplomatic exchanges, including gift giving.

Although all of La Florida's governors had similarly engaged in this type of diplomacy since St. Augustine's founding, the Apalachees' once extraordinarily powerful and populous polities had been dismantled in a series of traumatic slave raids by the Creeks and Yamasees, as had the Guales and Timucuas. To then witness the Spanish welcome Yamasee refugees and Creek diplomats to St. Augustine must have felt like a betrayal by the Spanish. As Luis made clear, he resented the "heathen Indians" and believed that they upended the world that the Indians and Spaniards of St. Augustine had created through over a century of mutual accommodations. At the same time, his memorial focuses squarely on Indian labor abuse and the failures of the governor to justly distribute Spanish goods owed to the Indians (through the *gasto de indios* and *situado*).

In the memorial, Catholicism functions as a barometer of morality—a way to distinguish "old Christian" from "heathen"—but most importantly as a marker of identity. For even as they remained Apalachee, Timucua, and Guale, these "old Christians" were also members of the Spanish political body. And that, as Luis's memorial sought to remind his audience, entitled the "old

---

communities across the Americas as Spanish lay and religious officials with different cultural experiences fought for power. But in St. Augustine, this struggle also reflected the reality that Yamasees more often than not set the terms of their spiritual and political alliances with the Spanish. By the 1730s, Spanish *criollos* had largely accepted this reality but the arrival of *peninsular* friars in 1735 from Spain shed new light on this reality.

31. Memorial of Francisco Luis, Native, to Antonio de Arredondo, September 20, 1736, Florida's Friars and Missions in the 1730s, JHC, 42–47.

Christian" Indians to fair pay for their labor, protection from labor abuse, goods from the Crown, and a Spanish official to serve as their advocate. For the "old Christian" Indians, Catholicism was thus part of a transactional relationship with the Spanish. At the heart of this relationship was the Spaniards' profound dependency on Indian labor.

Since the seventeenth century, Indians in La Florida whose polities accepted missionaries had labored under the *repartimiento* system wherein they worked on behalf of the Spanish in exchange for goods and, at times, cash payments. Caciques, recognized as lords (or dons) and entitled to labor exemptions as well as endowed with the authority of selecting the laborers, had long benefited from this system, receiving goods and money in exchange for the labor of their people. This system not only reinforced but expanded the power of those caciques, who exerted a new level of control over labor (and land) and the redistribution of Spanish gifts.[32]

But, as Luis explained, the frequent presence of "heathen Indians" who came to St. Augustine made it plain that the Spanish did not treat all Indians in the same way. The old Christian Indians made charcoal for the forge, palms for Spanish houses, cut firewood and logs for construction projects, served as messengers at all times of the day and even the night for the governor (sometimes traveling 200 leagues at a moment's notice), and spent long periods of time away from their wives and children when hunting for the Spanish. Moreover, the Spanish abused the old Christian Indians. They were severely underpaid or not paid at all. Worse still, they were often beaten, shackled, and even incarcerated—caciques as well as commoners.

Additionally, Luis noted, the *gasto de indios*—the yearly expenditure sent by the king to be distributed to Indians in La Florida—was not being fairly distributed to the Christian Indians of St. Augustine. While the governor gave the old Christians a small, miserly distribution of goods, he lavished the "heathen" Indians—particularly Creek diplomats who visited St. Augustine—with an abundance of liquor and goods including muskets, powder, and shot. Moreover, these very same heathen Indians openly proclaimed that they had no intention of converting or even politically allying with the Spanish because they could clearly see that the Spanish treated their "old Christians . . . worse than if we were slaves." In "their own provinces" they were "free from all this." Why convert, why "come among the Spaniards to be slaves?"

---

32. Amy Turner Bushnell, "Ruling 'the Republic of Indians' in Seventeenth-Century Florida," in *Powhatan's Mantle: Indians in the Colonial Southeast*, ed. Gregory A. Waselkov, Peter H. Wood, and Tom Hatley, 2nd ed. (Lincoln: University of Nebraska Press, 2006), 195–209; Bushnell, *Situado and Sabana: Spain's Support System for the Presidio and Mission Provinces of Florida*, American Museum of Natural History, Anthropological Papers, no. 74 (Athens, GA: Distributed by the University of Georgia Press, 1994).

The types of labor abuse that Luis described were not new. Apalachees, Guales, and Timucuas had lodged the same kinds of complaints since the seventeenth century. They frequently charged Franciscans as well as Spanish officials, soldiers, and ranchers, with labor and other forms of abuse. Luis was not describing a profound change in what was a fundamentally exploitative system. Rather, what was new was the context in which Luis and other old Christians suffered this abuse. The "heathen" Indians were not subjected to the same labor exploitation because they were members of independent, self-governing Indian polities. Yet the Spanish overtly diverted goods to the "heathens" that rightly belonged to Luis and his compatriots. What's more, the "heathens" loudly and publicly criticized not only how the Spanish treated the old Christian Indians but implicitly questioned the willingness of Luis and others to put up with such treatment. Seeking to remind the Spanish of the great costs of their allegiance to the Crown, Luis noted: "were it not for our looking to our lord and to our King and as we are old Christians, we would have long ago gone to our provinces in accord as we are scourged."[33] But those provinces no longer existed. Adding insult, Luis surely knew that small communities of Yamasees and Creeks were now the ones living in old Apalachee.[34]

Luis did not remark on the Yamasees in St. Augustine; instead he created a straightforward insider–outsider dichotomy, defining "old Christian" Indians as those who lived in the town and "heathen" Indians as those non-Catholic Indians who episodically came to St. Augustine for diplomacy. Writing during the same period, however, the Franciscan missionaries who worked among the 350 Indians hanging on in mission towns in or near the presidio more explicitly discussed the decline of that population and of their Catholic practices and ideals. Most relevant to this study, they further identified the Yamasees and other "heathens" as the most problematic of their charges.[35]

In a particularly scathing letter to the king in 1736, the auxiliary bishop to La Florida wrote that the missions of St. Augustine ought not to even be

---

33. Memorial of Francisco Luis, Native, to Antonio de Arredondo, September 20, 1736, Florida's Friars and Missions in the 1730s, JHC, 42–47.

34. John E. Worth, "The Yamasee in West Florida," in *The Yamasee Indians*, 309–28.

35. A number of accounts also discussed the frequent reassignment of friars from one *doctrina* to another, which created severe problems both in terms of friars acquiring the necessary language skills to communicate and also inhibited the development of meaningful relationships between friars and the communities in which they worked. Certification of Francisco Menéndez Márquez, February 25, 1735; Fray Juan Calleja, Fray Pedro Morales, Fray Antonio Navarro, Fray Francisco Gomez, Fray Ignacio Venegas, Fray Pablo Rodriguez, and Fray Pedro de Leon y Cordero to the King, March 6, 1735; Manuel de Montiano to the King, July 16, 1738, Florida's Friars and Missions in the 1730s, JHC, 26–34 and 7–9. Even at this very late stage in Spanish missionization efforts in La Florida, Montiano called for the composition of language materials (dictionaries) because so few missionaries were able to effectively communicate with their Indian charges.

called missions. None of the conversions by "heathens" that the missionaries claimed and counted were sincere. Rather, these heathens had converted because they were given goods. "Find me stupid," the bishop exclaimed, but they were not instructed in the faith and did not even understand what was happening during the ritual itself. "For they gave them the water fifteen days after their arrival and they soon returned to their heathenism." Bishop San Buenaventura and many of the newly arrived Spanish friars laid the lion's share of the blame at the feet of the *criollo* Franciscans, whom they claimed had given in to the demands of the many heathen Indians in the missions and "let them live as they wish." This practice, the bishop claimed, was one "which the ancient Indians regret."[36]

Writing about their efforts in these missions, Franciscans consistently described the challenges of ministering to unconverted Indians. At Nombre de Dios de Macaris, Fray Veteta struggled to balance the different expectations and experiences of the town's population. Macaris was a small community of 46 Timucuas, Apalachees, and Yamasees. Although Veteta complained about all of his charges, the Timucuas and Apalachees were "of the less evil ones and ones who speak of themselves and consider themselves as old Christians." The implication was, quite clearly, that the Yamasees were the most "evil" and most difficult to minister to.[37]

The *doctrinero* of the Yamasee town of Pocotalaca inventoried an impressive list of problems in the 47-person community under Cacique Antonio Jospo. Like his fellow friars, Fray Mora complained that the town's close proximity to the presidio meant that the Yamasees had frequent contact with Spaniards and easy access to alcohol: "Indian men and women find themselves given over thus to drink as well as to other greater things that are against God." This, Mora believed, had catalyzed numerous other problems. At Pocotalaca, the Yamasees neglected their duties to keep the church clean and orderly and similarly did not care for their homes or plant crops. Yamasee men beat and even killed their own wives, he contended. Perhaps most upsetting to Mora was that he had absolutely no authority over his supposed charges and here he spoke not only of his only mission but more broadly of what his fellow friars experienced in the other eight missions. The Indians came and went as they wished, paying their friars little mind. They did not ask permission of their friars or caciques to travel beyond the limits of their small towns, they did not attend mass on the feast days, and they did not even marry in the church. Most dangerous of all, they had "laid hold of the idea of our

36. Bishop Fray Francisco de San Buenaventura to the King, April 29, 1736, Florida's Friars and Missions in the 1730s, JHC, 35–36.

37. Report of Fray Manuel Veteta, July 8, 1738, Florida's Friars and Missions in the 1730s, JHC, 21–24.

having usurped spiritual jurisdiction over them" and they rejected the authority of friars (and even caciques) in both the "temporal and spiritual spheres."[38]

This was not only a problem with the Yamasees, but with the smaller population of "heathens" from south Florida who had episodically experimented with living near the presidio in search of protection from slave and other raids by first the Yamasees and then the Creeks. As the friar of Casapullos explained, one of the major challenges was that the heathens—in this case Jororo, Pojoy, and Amacapiras, as well as Casapullo—came and went from the mission, withdrawing to the "woods" and even leaving altogether. And some of the purportedly "baptized Indians" joined them. Facing such a diverse group of Indians who deployed mobility to resist his efforts to inculcate them in Catholic practices, the fray felt compelled to honestly admit that the entire population of the town, including those baptized were not truly Catholic: "I am speaking thus on my conscience that these like the rest are Christians only in name."[39]

Two major factors contributed to the problems identified by the friars. First, many Yamasees and, indeed, many supposedly "converted" Indians had long contested Franciscan efforts to transform their cultural practices and beliefs in alignment with Spanish Catholic expectations. Mora's complaint that the Yamasees of Pocotalaca were "living as they wish" and according to "their own free will" echoes similar complaints of the Yamasees in the late seventeenth century, as we have already seen. And both before and after the 1706 relocation of the "old Christians" to St. Augustine, friars had long complained of similar problems in all of the major mission provinces and also in those places where their efforts were almost universally rejected, like Calusa and Apalachicola (the Lower Creeks' ancestors' homeland).

What concerned the Franciscans now was that they believed that even those "old Christians" were straying. In San Juan del Puerto, the friar reported that the Timucuas were "failing me on the whole matter of obedience in spiritual matters as well as in temporal ones."[40] At Tolomato, the three resident friars noted that all of the *doctrinas* were in a "wretched state." Even many of the 24 *vecinos*—Indians who had moved out of mission communities and into St. Augustine proper—refused to recognize the convent as their *doctrina*, claiming that the parish priest had no authority over them. In his words, "they live at their liberty."[41] Although the Franciscans (and Benavides) largely

38. Report of Fray Antonio Fernandez de Mora, July 10, 1738, Florida's Friars and Missions in the 1730s, JHC, 15–17.

39. Report of Fray Luis Quixano, July 8, 1738, Florida's Friars and Missions in the 1730s, JHC, 14–15.

40. Report of Fray Joseph de Hita, July 6, 1738, Florida's Friars and Missions in the 1730s, JHC, 17.

41. Here the priest was referring both to the *vecinos* and also to the "serving Indians" who similarly did not "recognize the convent as their *doctrina*." Report of Fray Manuel

focused on the prior governor's decision to move the missions closer to the presidio as the root cause, the composition of the mission populations had also very clearly changed after 1717. The religious environment had been profoundly changed by the emigration of Yamasees and other "heathen" Indians, who not only lived in their own mission towns but also in missions that had formerly been comprised solely of "old Christians."

Second, all of the Indians near St. Augustine lived in an almost unimaginable state of danger and loss. These were refugee communities who had suffered over 20 years of attacks by the Creeks, Yuchis, and Chickasaws, as well as the British—in addition to ongoing labor abuse at the hands of the Spanish. Across the board, Franciscan missionaries identified alcoholism as a major problem and described social breakdown in these mission communities. Much of the behavior was aberrant not only in Spanish terms but more significantly according to Southeastern Indian cultural norms. It was, for example, inviolable for Indian men to physically assault women. While they did not have the language or concepts to reckon with what they witnessed, the Spanish described communities suffering from severe and historic trauma. All of the Indian refugees of St. Augustine had been violently forced out of their homelands and continued to lose family and friends to violent raids, disease, or flight. It was little wonder that they now "waste" in a general state of drunkenness, as one missionary claimed.[42]

Were there Indians in La Florida who thought of themselves as Catholic converts? Undoubtedly yes. But, more often than not when we can glimpse moments of what that conversion meant to Indians who engaged with Catholicism, they emphasized the tangible aspects of that conversion as the Yamasee caciques did when they cast themselves as new converts in order to demand guns or as Luis did when he described himself as an old Christian in order to critique the governor's disconcerting labor abuses.

And then there were the many "heathens" (in this case Yamasees, Creeks, Ais, and others) who engaged in the religious ceremony of baptism only to wipe it away. Bishop San Buenaventura powerfully described this very visceral erasure of Catholicism: "[T]hey make a gesture with the hand on the head, saying go away water, I am not a Christian." Above all what I hope this chapter reveals is that we need to do far more work as scholars of La Florida in understanding, defining, and contextualizing what we mean when we say that Indians converted to Catholicism in Franciscan missions. In part this requires that scholars look at these religious encounters from Indigenous points of

---

Sotomaior, convent of St. Augustine, July 2, 1738, Florida's Friars and Missions in the 1730s, JHC, 19–20.

42. Report of Fray Antonio Fernandez de Mora, July 10, 1738, Florida's Friars and Missions in the 1730s, JHC, 16.

view. And in part this necessitates that scholars more carefully hear the Franciscans themselves.

What is evident from the encounters in the 1720s and 1730s described above is that first, and perhaps most obviously, the Spanish listened attentively to what the Yamasees wanted and went to great lengths to appease them. And second, the presence of hundreds of Yamasees fundamentally changed St. Augustine, especially the methods that Franciscans and Crown officials used as they tried to persuade the Yamasees to stay in the colony and to convert to Catholicism. Over and over again, the Yamasees pushed back against Franciscan demands, in the process fundamentally changing what religious conversion itself meant not only for themselves but also for even those few hundred Indians who self-identified as "old Christians."

Chapter 8

Deconstructing Luis Gerónimo de Oré's Verdadera relación de la Florida

NOBLE DAVID COOK

One of most important sources ethnohistorians have for the original inhabitants of what is now the southeastern United States is Franciscan Friar Luis Gerónimo de Oré's report, printed in Spain in the early seventeenth century and distributed to a limited audience. After church and civil officials read and discussed the *relación* it was set aside in libraries and archives where the vicissitudes of nature and human actions took their toll. Finally, in the early twentieth century a religious historian in Spain discovered a copy of the report and realized its significance, for it provides excellent information on the martyrdom of the early religious who intended to implant Christianity. Oré's report also includes information about inspections of the missions, a brief "history" of La Florida, and an analysis of the foreign threat and relations between church and state as well as recommendations for improvements. In the past quarter century there has been a growing awareness of his long career and the significance of his texts. Yet there is no monographic study of Oré, his life and work, although there are numerous biographical sketches. A primary reason for the lacuna is his disjointed trajectory that carried him to and from the uttermost ends of the Americas and the centers of the Spanish Empire and the Roman Catholic Church.[1]

---

1. Biographical sketches can be found in José Toribio Polo, "Luis Gerónimo de Oré," *Revista Histórica* 2 (1907): 74–91; Manuel de Mendiburu, *Diccionario Histórico Biográfico del Perú* (Lima: Imprenta Gil, 1934), vol. VIII, 247–248; Noble David Cook, "Beyond the Martyrs of Florida: The Versatile Career of Luis Gerónimo de Oré," *The Florida Historical Quarterly* 71 (1992): 169–187; and the "Introduction" in Luis Gerónimo de Oré, *Relación de la vida y milagros de San Francisco Solano*, ed. Noble David Cook (Lima: Pontificia Universidad Católica del Perú, 1998), ix–xxxix; and "Luis Jerónimo de Oré: una aproximación," in Luis Jerónimo de Oré, O.F.M., *Symbolo Catholico Indiano*, ed. Antonine Tibesar O.F.M. (Lima: Australis, 1998 [Lima: Ricardo, 1598]), 35–61; Noble David Cook, "'Tomando posesión,' Luis Gerónimo de Oré y el retorno de los franciscanos a las doctrinas del valle del Colca," in *El hombre y los Andes: Homenaje a Franklin Pease*, ed. Rafael Varón Gabai and Javier Flores Espinosa (Lima: Pontificia Universidad Católica del Perú, 2002), vol. II: 889–903; and Cook, "Viviendo en las

Luis Gerónimo de Oré was born in Peru in Huamanga (modern Ayacucho) in 1554, roughly a decade after Inca Atahualpa's execution. As a young first-generation creole novice, he witnessed Viceroy Francisco de Toledo's execution of Tupac Amaru in Cuzco. He continued his studies in Lima and was ordained by Archbishop Alfonso Toribio de Mogrovejo. Shortly thereafter he participated in Lima's foundational Third Church Council. He was active in several Franciscan *doctrinas* in the Andean highlands and in mixed urban parishes in Cuzco and Potosí. The bishop of Cuzco sent him to Madrid and Rome as solicitor to defend his diocese before the Royal Court and the Papal Consistory. He recruited missionaries in Spain for work in Florida and the Caribbean. Before leaving Spain, he was commissioned by his order to conduct research and compose a biography of Friar Francisco Solano, concentrating on his youth in Andalusia, as part of a Franciscan effort to secure his beatification. From 1614 to 1618, Oré was in Cuba and Florida serving as commissioner of the Franciscans' Santa Elena de la Florida Province. During his final years he served as bishop of Concepción, Chile where he died in 1630. He is best known in the Andes for his linguistic texts with multilingual translations of Church doctrine, and his manual for *doctrineros* in Spanish South America. Those massive and widely used texts helped to instill a standard form for the Quechua and Aymara languages for generations. His actions in Spain and Italy for over a decade are barely known outside his inquiry into Francisco Solano's youth. His years as bishop of the southernmost diocese in America were characterized by efforts to bring peace to the Araucanian frontier as he faced fierce opposition from military officers and civilians over the best method to achieve that goal. That work was largely erased by rebellion, foreign attacks, internal disputes between church and state officials, and periodic natural disasters.

Commissioner Oré's 1618 report on La Florida reappeared in print in 1931 thanks to Atanasio López, O.F.M. It was soon translated into English by Maynard Geiger and published in 1936.[2] A decade ago Michael Francis and Kathleen Kole located a copy of the original in the Hesburgh Libraries of the University of Notre Dame in Indiana and mined it for their excellent study of the Guale revolt published in 2011.[3] Raquel Chang-Rodriguez edited and

---

márgenes del imperio: Luis Jerónimo de Oré y la exploración del *Otro*," *Histórica* (Lima) 32, no. 1 (2008): 11–38.

2. Luis Jerónimo de Oré, *Relación histórica de la Florida, escrito en el siglo XVII*, ed. Atanasio López, 2 vols. (Madrid: Imprenta de Ramona Velasco, 1931–1933); Luis Gerónimo de Oré, *The Martyrs of Florida, 1513–1616*, ed. and trans. Maynard Geiger, O.F.M. (New York: Joseph F. Wagner, 1936).

3. J. Michael Francis and Kathleen M. Kole, *Murder and Martyrdom in Spanish Florida. Don Juan and the Guale Uprising of 1597* (New York: American Museum of Natural History Anthropological Papers, Number 95, 2011).

published the Hesburgh Libraries text in Lima, Peru in 2014, and edited and translated it into English along with Nancy Vogeley in 2017.[4] Both of Chang-Rodriguez's texts include significant biographical information. Her "modernized" Spanish transcription includes supplementary documents.

In the current analysis, I use the original digital copy (on CD) from Notre Dame, and I compare my translations with the abovementioned transcriptions and translations. Most variations are minor, but not all. "Modernized" Spanish transcriptions modify spelling, at times leading to errors. Changed punctuation can result in misinterpretation; the creation of "chapters" may not have been intended by the original author. Almost any modification can lead to differing interpretations. Golden-Age Spanish is rich, with multiple meanings, sometimes dozens, of the same word. Oré's rambling narrative shifts from subject to subject, place to place, and time to time. All such shifts contribute to challenges, confusion, and consternation among specialists. The various titles of modern published versions reflect this. There are different spellings of the author's name. I keep these challenges in mind as I deconstruct the lettered creole friar's text. I also evaluate the nature and verisimilitude of his sources. It is noted that similar flaws were found in Ore's other texts.[5]

Oré's manuscript on Florida was largely complete before he left Cuba, although it may have been modified by last-minute revisions during the voyage to Spain before being hastily set to type. It is unclear where it was printed. Perhaps it was Salamanca, the location of the Franciscan general chapter meeting. This indeed is why 1618 has been considered the most likely publication date, although it may have been printed in Madrid where Oré's 1619 Marianist text appeared.[6] The missing place of publication and printer's name and date, as well as lack of authorizations required for any book that would be distributed or sold to the general public indicates its intended audience. The Florida report was destined only for distribution to Franciscan monasteries, officials in the headquarters of the order, various officials in the

4. Raquel Chang-Rodriguez, ed., *Relación de los mártires de La Florida del P.F. Luis Jerónimo de Oré (c. 1619)* (Lima: Pontificia Universidad Católica del Perú, 2014), 15–62; Luis Jerónimo de Oré, *Account of the Martyrs in the Provinces of La Florida*, ed. and trans. Raquel Chang-Rodriguez and Nancy Vogeley (Albuquerque: University of New Mexico Press, 2017).

5. There are three essential dictionaries in Spanish: Oré's contemporary, Sebastián de Covarrubias Orozco's *Tesoro de la lengua castellana o española* (Madrid: Castalia, [1611] 2013); and the Real Academia Española's *Diccionario de la lengua española*, and the multivolume *Diccionario de autoridades*, accessed on 10/16/2018 at http://web.frl.es/DA.html.

6. Luis Gerónimo de Oré, *Corona de la sacratissima Virgen Maria madre de Dios nuestra señora, En que se contienen ochenta meditaciones, de los principales misterios de la Fé: que corresponden a setenta y tres Ave Maria y ocho vezes el Pater noster, ofrecidas a los felices años que vivio en el mundo. . . .Dedicada a la misma virgen sacrosanta, concebida sin pecado original, en su imagen y Santuario de Copacavana* (Madrid: La Viuda de Cosme Delgado, 1619).

papal bureaucracy, the monarch and members of the Council of the Indies, and probably missionary friars of other orders, perhaps men Oré knew personally. Some copies may have reached secular officials in Cuba and La Florida.

Oré's sources are varied. All are biased in one fashion or another, for his informants, either verbal or written, represent their own point of view and in some cases their memory of previous events. Oré often discusses the motivation of his sources and the accuracy of their testimony. Perhaps due to the variety of sources and lack of time, paper, and ink, the narrative is disjointed, broken into fragments. A series of pagination errors caused by the typesetter occur near the end of the text. A more kindly reviewer might refer to the report as a preliminary draft on the nature of and major issues facing church and state in La Florida, and not a polished historical narrative focusing on a principal theme. The work is neither a "true history," nor a chronicle. There are errors throughout, so many in the initial folios covering the historical background that some readers have tossed the friar's book aside, concluding that it has little value. That negation is not warranted, for seemingly accurate information is found in this work too. Whatever its weaknesses, Oré collected enough material to compile a narrative that has become a standard source on early Spanish Florida.

In initial folios Oré surveys the discovery, exploration, and settlement of La Florida. Oré provided a similar historical background for Andean South America in his 1598 *Symbolo Catholico Indiano*. His purpose then as in Florida was to provide valuable information to future religious who were preparing to travel to the American missions. Although major early figures are noted, Oré often confuses names and his outline of their actions is brief and often flawed. One important source was handed to him by the famous mestizo author Garcilaso de la Vega, "El Inca," in a meeting in Cordova before Oré left Spain for Cuba. *La Florida del Inca* . . . provides the primary foundation for the friar's historical background. Oré briefly, compared to Garcilaso de la Vega's lengthy history, highlights major figures. Juan Ponce de León, the "discoverer," receives a full folio; Luis Vázquez de Ayllón only half, in part as a result of the massacre of two hundred soldiers under his command. Oré misnames explorer [Juan, sic.] Francisco Vázquez de Coronado. Pánfilo de Narvaez's disastrous expedition is noted, partly because of the narrative of Alvar Núñez Cabeza de Vaca who was able to escape and tell the tale accompanied by north-African Morisco slave Estevanico. Oré relates that only "Alvar Núñez Cabeza de Vaca along with three Spaniards escaped. God mercifully granted them the ability to produce miracles among the infidels in the name of Christ, as Father José de Acosta ponders in his book of the *Natura novi orbis*, and other authors."[7]

7. I rely primarily on a CD digitized copy of the original *Relación de los mártires de La Florida*, Hesburgh Libraries, University of Notre Dame (hereafter *Relación de la*

Oré knew Jesuit José de Acosta in Peru in the 1580s. Oré read Acosta's *Natura novi orbis* (Salamanca, 1588) and the comprehensive *Historia natural y moral de las Indias* (Seville, 1590), considered by some to be the foundation of comparative ethnology. Oré briefly mentions Hernando de Soto's "conquest" and journey from the time of his first landing in Florida until his death. Oré recognized that De Soto's infamous mistreatment of the Indigenous lingered in their memories a half-century after his destructive passage.

Who are the other authors, the "*letrados*," Oré mentions as he constructs his text, and where did he access their texts? We know El Inca Garcilaso de la Vega's history was given to Oré, and he promised to take one or more copies to the Franciscans in the Santa Elena Province. Oré had access to Acosta and most of the other authors from the time of his novitiate. He incorporates some of their material in his earlier texts published in Lima in 1598 and Naples in 1607. Does he rely in some cases on memory regarding earlier events and chronology as he writes about Florida? If so it explains some historical inaccuracies. Subsequent inadequate re-examination and correction of typesetting flaws contributed to additional imperfections. As Oré wrote the *Symbolo Catholico Indiano* and the *Rituale, seu manuale peruanum*, he was determined to ensure precision in his translations of Church doctrine, for good reason. Oré may have read various historical treatises in Italy, or in Spain, as he prepared for his Florida tour. Most of these works were available in Franciscan, Jesuit, and Dominican libraries and Oré maintained relationships with members of the latter two, especially the Jesuits. It is equally possible that copies of the texts he mentions existed in Havana. Close examination of the detailed shipping authorizations granted to the religious archived in the Casa de la Contratación reveals a large volume of books transported to America.[8]

Embedded in the historical background, Oré weaves examples of numerous religious who fall victim to the revenge of La Florida's autochthonous people—a native rejection of "outsiders" based on Spanish actions during earlier expeditions. In 1549, Dominicans led by Friar Luis Cáncer offered to plant the Faith in La Florida. Oré relates that on landing ashore and beginning to preach, the Indians, "learning by experience of previous Spanish actions without waiting or wanting to hear them, killed Friar Luis

---

Florida) 2v (recto). There are some printer errors in foliation "Escapando Alvar Nuñez Cabeza de Vaca, con sólo tres Españoles, a los cuales hizo Dios tanta merced, que entre aquellos infieles llegaron a hazer milagros en nombre de Christo, como lo pondera el padre Ioseph de Acosta, en su libro de *Natura novi orbis*, y otros escritores." The reference is to José de Acosta, *Natura novi orbis* (Salamanca, 1588) and the same author's *Historia natural y moral de las Indias* (Seville, 1590) as well as other contemporary authors Oré consulted.

8. An earlier expedition that Oré organized but did not accompany traveled with "en flete de diez toneladas y media de libros y vistuarios a les ha de llevar." Archivo General de Indias [hereafter AGI], Contratación 5538, leg. 2, 225v–226v.

and two other companions."[9] Hatred of the Europeans is a topic Oré returns to frequently in his report. In the next error-laden lines, he shifts to French attempts to establish a settlement along the coast.[10] Oré subsequently writes of the martyrdom of several religious in their attempts to establish a mission in the northern part of La Florida. Here the narrative—based in part on Garcilaso's last chapter in the 1605 edition of *La Florida*—becomes garbled, suggesting that Oré may have been confused by contradictory oral or other accounts that did not coincide with Garcilaso's. Or Oré was simply sloppy.[11] He begins with an early 1570s expedition that set forth from the mission town of Santa Elena. But the actual events Oré presents relate to the 1561 reconnaissance by Angel Villafañe. As they were returning, a group entered and conducted a survey of a large bay they named Madre de Dios, referred to locally as Jacán, and later renamed the Chesapeake Bay by the English.[12] They took back with them a young Indigenous man related to one of the chiefs. Baptized Don Luis and similar to other captured young men, he was expected to serve as a future translator. Oré apparently was not fully appraised of the tragic nature of the Jesuit experience in Florida that Garcilaso briefly narrated. Or Oré chose to ignore it. Their arrival was due in part to the Adelantado Pedro Menéndez de Avilés's actions as he pressed Jesuits in Andalusia to serve in Florida. Michael Gannon provides information based on Jesuit records that Oré lacked, although he could have secured them with more effort.[13]

Once again Oré or the printer errs in chronology when he writes of the Adelantado's transport of fifty settlers in 1577 (sic), and in 1578 (sic) eight Jesuits who sailed to establish a base in Santa Elena.[14] Two of the Jesuits went to Guale territory and another traveled north to the province of Escamacu.

---

9. Oré, *Relación de la Florida*, 2v: "[E]scarmentados de los sucessos pasados con los Españoles, sin aguardar a quererlos oyr, mataron a fray Luis, y a otros dos compañeros. . . ." Paul E. Hoffman, *A New Andalucia and a Way to the Orient: The American Southeast during the Sixteenth Century* (Baton Rouge: Louisiana State University Press, [1990] 2004), 99–101, provides a solid synopsis of Friar Cáncer's actions.

10. These mistakes have been noted many times, most recently by Chang-Rodríguez and Vogeley, *Account of the Martyrs*, 76–77, ft. 76. There are numerous excellent studies of efforts by the French in the Americas during the second half of the sixteenth century.

11. Garcilaso de la Vega, El Inca, *The Florida of the Inca* [1605], ed. and trans. John Grier Varner and Jeannette Johnson Varner (Austin: University of Texas Press, 1951), 637–643.

12. Oré, *Relación de la Florida*, 3r; Chang-Rodríguez, *Relación de los mártires*, 103, ft. 149.

13. Michael Gannon, *The Cross in the Sand: The Early Catholic Church in Florida, 1513–1870* (Gainesville: University of Florida Press, 1965), 32. In *A New Andalucia*, Hoffman pinpointed various errors in Oré's narrative.

14. The events occurred more than a decade earlier; see Chang-Rodríguez and Vogeley, *Account of the Martyrs*, 83–84, ft. 3–4.

Ten-year-old Juan de Lara, son of a Spanish settler came with them to learn the language. Oré wrote that he "now lives in St. Augustine,"[15] indicating possible cooperation as an informant, one who could vividly remember the events but whose recollection of dates was likely to be fuzzy. After eighteen depressing months, the Jesuits returned to Santa Elena and there decided to send Father Alamo to Spain to report. The Jesuits stressed the difficulties and lack of success in baptizing. At the time the Indigenous youth, Don Luis, was studying with the Jesuits in Seville. Aware of the difficulties the Jesuits experienced in Florida, Don Luis suggested to the Jesuit rector that it could be worthwhile to send him along with other religious because "with God's help and his good efforts they would convert the Indians."[16] Encouraged, the Jesuit superiors requested license to send a new group, including Don Luis. The petition was granted and shortly fresh Jesuits with supplies reached Santa Elena. There the Adelantado assigned a ship with provisions to sail north carrying twelve Jesuits and young Alonso de Lara, the older brother of Juan from Santa Elena. Here Garcilaso de la Vega's description of the events weakens and Oré's voice assumes a more authoritative tone thanks to more knowledgeable informants.[17]

Oré writes that the ship reached the Bay of Madre de Dios, known as Jacán and entered one of many rivers and traveled twelve leagues upstream to the villages under the now Cacique Don Luis and his two brothers. According to Hoffman, the ship under Captain Vicente González arrived in September 1570 and the area was broadly called the Bay of Santa Maria, now the Outer Banks of Virginia. The settlement was near the site where Jamestown was later established.[18] Warmly welcomed, the Jesuits found the site attractive and they unloaded their trunks, intending to make it a permanent mission. At this point the ship under Captain González returned to Santa Elena to report on what seemed to be an auspicious beginning. As the fathers worked to build a more suitable "mission settlement," they pressed the Indigenous residents for assistance, assuming that Don Luis would provide all they needed. It was a serious judgment error for the young man soon felt the call of his earlier life. After having lived among Europeans for several years he saw the darker side of "civilization." His own culture continued to pull, a stronger force than his new faith and the Spanish example. The inevitable tension escalated rapidly. Oré explained, as often occurs in efforts to save souls, that "the enemy of the

15. Oré, *Relación de la Florida*, 4r.

16. Oré, *Relación de la Florida*, 4v. "[C]on el ayuda de Dios y su buena diligencia, se co.nvertirian a la Fé los indios della."

17. Garcilaso de la Vega, *Florida of the Inca*, 640, 642; Oré, *Relación de la Florida*, 4v. "Alonso de Lara, hermano mayor del otro que se hizo mención, hijos del poblador de Santa Elena."

18. Hoffman, *A New Andalucia*, 262.

human species always attempts to disrupt similar works."[19] Don Luis, now among his own people, failed to submit to Jesuit mandates. Soon Jesuit Superior Juan Bautista [de Segura] reprimanded him and tried to convince him of the error of reneging on his promises to help bring Christianity to his people. The humiliation was too much for the proud cacique. Don Luis, filled with hatred, desired "to get out of sight the person who reprimanded him,"[20] and left. Oré devotes slightly more than four pages to the incident and provides a vivid and detailed account of what happens to the Jesuits of the ill-fated mission. The pages flow with the ease and grace of Garcilaso de la Vega as the series of events unfold—a tale of anger, hatred, treachery, friendship and enmity, as well as revenge. Oré closes his description of their deaths with scripture from the Book of Job (14:7).[21] The youth Alonso de Lara had been protected by the cacique Don Luis's younger brother from seeing the actual massacre, but he saw the results and shaking, he tearfully convinced the cacique to permit the slain Jesuits' burial in an open area underneath some trees. Oré apologizes for the absence of the names of the martyred "because in the diligent search I have made I have not been able to discover anyone's name, other than their prelate and superior Father Juan Bautista."[22] It was Alonso de Lara, after he was freed, "who later gave a long and true account of the martyrdom of the Fathers as has been told."[23]

The violent Spanish reaction to avenge the deaths of the Jesuits and other Spaniards flows tragically into the first Guale rising that erupted around Santa

---

19. Oré, *Relación de la Florida*, 4v. "[E]l enemigo del genero humano procura estorvar siempre semejantes obras. . . ."

20. Ibid., "[Q]uitar de los ojos de quien lo reprehendia."

21. Oré's references to biblical texts in his report are infrequent, indicating his aim to influence the royal officials.

22. Oré, *Relación de la Florida*, 5v. "[Q]ue en la diligente pesquisa que [h]e hecho, no los [h]e podido descubrir, sino sólo el del padre Juan Bautista su prelado y superior." In *A New Andalucia*, 263–264, Hoffman states that they died in February 1571. As soon as they were aware of the tragedy, the Jesuits made major efforts to secure the names of each victim. An undated handwritten list of the eight was at some point penned in the left margin of the Hesburgh Libraries copy of Oré, *Relación de la Florida*, on f. 5v. In *The Unsettlement of America: Translation, Interpretation, and the Story of Don Luis de Velasco, 1560–1945* (New York: Oxford University Press, 2015), Anna Brickhouse examines the role and nature of Don Luis from a different perspective using literary analysis. Chang-Rodríguez and Vogeley note in their "Introduction," in the *Account of the Martyrs*, 25–26, ft. 40–42, that Brickhouse's use of Oré's and the Franciscan account is secondhand and ignores alternative "Iberian views of settlement" as opposed to the Anglo ones. Indeed, the English-language "archive" is meagre compared to the reams of paper that remain to be encountered in Church and state records, as well as personal ones.

23. Oré, *Relación de la Florida*, 6v. "[E]l cual dio larga y verdadera relacion del martirio de los padres, de la manera que se [h]a referido." It is possible Jesuit Father Juan Rogel also secured a detailed account from Alonso de Lara and with the Jesuit's assistance was able to link names to the events he and perhaps Indigenous informants described.

Elena after the Adelantado departed for Spain in 1572, leaving La Florida's administration in the hands of his son-in-law Don Diego de Velasco.[24] At the time the Guale and the Escamacu to their north were at peace, but as Oré paints it, one of the principal Guale caciques and his wife recently converted to Christianity. Unsurprisingly this rejection of traditional beliefs caused rivals to lose respect for the converted cacique and conspire secretly against him. The plot erupted when a group attacked the latter's village and during the skirmish his nephew killed him. The cacique's wife demanded revenge. Failing to convince other Guale leaders, she approached the governor and demanded justice—her husband was Christian and she expected the Spanish would find and punish the murderer. Governor Velasco was in a difficult position. Hoping to avoid involvement in a local dispute and create enemies he tried to calm tensions and calling the Guale caciques, including the one who had killed the Christian, to Santa Elena to conduct an inquiry. He promised safe conduct and simultaneously did his utmost to placate the widow. But she held firm in the presence of the murderer, and "with greater urgency asked for justice, protesting that if it were not done, there would be among them many deaths."[25] Governor Velasco succumbed to the widow's entreaties and the murderer was judged and executed in front of the other caciques. Their reaction against the Spanish was immediate, as the group returned to their villages and discussed the governor's breach of promise. Filled with indignation and rage, they vowed revenge and organized a confederacy with other chiefdoms. Oré writes that the Escamacu were reputed to be "very valiant, both feared and esteemed as such."[26] Indians who were serving the Spanish fled and reported what was underway, and the Spanish sent twenty-two soldiers from Santa Elena to investigate.

Reaching the village, the soldiers noted the absence of women and children, a sign of impending fighting. Fearing the worst, the soldiers asked why they were not present. The Escamacu replied that they saw the Spanish coming with their guns at the ready and were fearful. In order to convince the Indians that they came in peace, the soldiers disabled their weapons, and were given one of the *bohíos* (native huts) for the night. This was a major error of judgment and the Spaniards paid dearly. At dawn almost all were killed. A soldier named Calderón was one of the few who escaped to speak about his harrowing experience, narrated by Oré. Calderón repeated this story more than once and one must ask how much it was embellished with each retelling.

24. Hoffman, in *A New Andalucia*, 267, places his arrival in Spain in early summer of that year.

25. Oré, *Relación de la Florida*, 7r. "[C]on mayor instancia pedia justicia, protestando que si no la hazía, [h]abria entre ellos muchas muertes."

26. Ibid., 7v. "[M]uy valientes, temidos y estimados por tales."

But the outline as related is clear and Oré's description of the reception of the news in Santa Elena rings true: "The wailing by the brothers, children and wives of those murdered was great." Within days, three other soldiers were ambushed by Guale warriors, "and thus all the land of the Guale rose up in rebellion."[27]

Briefly in 1576, the governor captain-general of Florida was Hernando de Miranda, son-in-law of the Adelantado Pedro Menéndez de Avilés. Increasing internal divisions in the settlement promised greater chaos. Oré, lacking civil records and accurate dates, errs in his chronology. Paul Hoffman, using letters and administrative documents, found that after arriving in Santa Elena in spring 1576, the squabbling reached a point at which Miranda jailed his brother-in-law Diego de Velasco for misappropriation of funds.[28] In Oré's account, Miranda, instead of landing first in Florida went directly to Havana to collect the *situado* (annual royal treasury stipend), traveled to St. Augustine to pay the soldiers and officials, and then continued on three ships to Santa Elena. Hoffman wrote that the events taking place as they were approaching Santa Elena occurred at the same time as the fleet was arriving from Spain. Here there is closer agreement on what happened to the officials setting out for reconnaissance as the ships were moving along the coast. With the weather worsening, ten men, including royal officials were set ashore to give notice. Unfortunately, as the wind rose the ships were driven out to sea. In the meantime, the group began to make their way along the intercoastal waterways toward Santa Elena. It was later discovered, as narrated by Oré, that they were all killed by the Guale. When Governor Hernando de Miranda and his crew reached Santa Elena, they discovered that the Guale had risen against the Spanish. The governor, fearing the worst, dispatched a party to try to save the ten men they had left ashore. That group, reaching a Guale town, saw smoke rising, and within an hour, twelve canoes filled with warriors arrived. In Oré's account they told the men to come ashore and the Guale would provide them with chickens and women. Their opinion of Spanish men, based on prior experience, is unflattering at best. Oré writes that "by now thirty-seven [Spaniards] were dead." When the group reached Santa Elena at night, they saw lights and dancing Indians and realized a siege was underway. When they finally managed to enter the fort, there was "much confusion and lamentations."[29]

By the next day a full assault was underway, and the siege continued twice daily for forty-five days before the governor, assessing the low supply of wicks

27. Oré, *Relación de la Florida*, 7v–8r. "[F]ue grande el llanto de hermanos, hijos y maridos muertos," ". . . y así estaba toda la tierra de Guale amontinada y levantada."

28. Hoffman, *A New Andalucia*, 268–270.

29. Oré, *Relación de la Florida*, 8v. "[C]on este fueron treynta y siete los muertos . . . gran confusión y llanto."

for the harquebuses, decided to send all but seventy soldiers to St. Augustine. But the plan was changed and everyone boarded the ship at night, leaving the fort and everything in it to be sacked by, as Oré said, their enemies. At the end of this section, Oré points out that during the revolt a French galleon, "El Principe," that was damaged by the Spanish armada under Don Cristóbal de Eraso anchored for about three days off St. Augustine's coast. Somehow the French learned that the Spanish had evacuated Santa Elena and the interlopers decided to sail there to repair their ship and scavenge for abandoned armaments. Unfortunately, on approaching they grounded on a sandbar and were unable to break free, leaving themselves vulnerable. The attack came swiftly as a group of Guale fishermen discovered the situation and sounded the notice. The Guale, likely with Escamacu confederates assaulted them and the French survivors were enslaved.[30]

Oré's account of these episodes occurring a quarter century earlier is detailed enough to suggest he was relying on eyewitnesses, long-term settlers who orally shared their knowledge of the events. Were their recollections precise? We know that with the passage of time memory becomes clouded, exaggerations occur, and some seemingly insignificant details are forgotten. But frequently the most impactful actions are embedded sharply in memory. The broad brush strokes are close to the mark more often than not. Oré then highlights the 1577–1595 period and actions of Pedro Menéndez Márquez, nephew of the Adelantado. At the time of his appointment he was admiral of the Indies fleet and treasurer of La Florida.[31] His primary task was to subjugate the Guale and rebuild the settlement and fort of Santa Elena. After a forced stop in St. Augustine due to inclement weather, his ships continued to Santa Elena in October 1578 and established a new fort named San Marcos near the former San Felipe fort that the Guale destroyed. The Spanish revenge was merciless as a hundred well-armed soldiers attacked and burned, according to Oré, all the Guale villages. In one assault alone, the Spanish captured and enslaved 120 Indigenous warriors, forcing them into submission. Oré narrates that "seeing themselves defeated, dead and imprisoned they submitted, confederating in friendship."[32]

Recognizing the superiority of the newcomers' weapons the Guale requested the religious to be sent to Christianize them; "thus they were

30. Ibid., 9r. Based on official documents in *A New Andalucia*, 274–282, Hoffman details French and English actions along the coast north of St. Augustine from the disastrous aftermath of grounding the *Le Prince* in the Santa Elena harbor in early 1577; see also notes in Chang-Rodríguez, *Relación de los mártires*, 120. Pablo E. Pérez-Mallaína, *Spain's Men of the Sea: Daily Life on the Indies Fleets in the Sixteenth Century* (Baltimore: Johns Hopkins University Press, 1998), 30–33, covers the seafaring Eraso family.

31. Oré, *Relación de la Florida*, 9r–14r.

32. Ibid., 9r. "[V]iendose corridos, muertos y presos, vinieron a la obediencia, confederando las amistades."

defeated and subjugated."[33] Oré displays no doubt, guilt, or preoccupation regarding the human and cultural losses suffered by the Indigenous peoples along the Atlantic seaboard. Such an attitude is not surprising among early modern religious figures, more interested in missionary endeavor and saving souls than "pagan" culture. It is equally unlikely that the defeated Guale felt any remorse for their actions.

Oré's narrative of the Franciscan martyrs begins as Father Friar[34] Alonso [de] Reynoso arrives in December 1587 with a sweeping assignment to convert the native peoples in the villages of Nombre de Dios on the north edge of St. Augustine and nearby San Sebastián, and then San Antonio, San Pedro and San Juan. Oré's report becomes more detailed as he relies on informants as well as church and secular reports. Thanks to the request of Pedro Menéndez Márquez, Friar Reynoso and his companions were in Florida, serving among the Guale in Tolomato, Topiqui, Santa Elena, and St. Augustine. Their efforts appeared successful and many accepted baptism. Oré believes those victories were based on peaceful conversion and not force, and were therefore all the more rewarding. Unfortunately, the non-Christians "persecuted the Christians whom they treated as excommunicated, showering on them a thousand outrageous insults."[35] Oré reports that this wound festered about twenty years. The Spaniards suffered too, especially if one erred by entering Indian lands where death was not uncommon. Gradually as more became Christian, the tables were turned and converts began to persecute non-believers. Oré continues, "[T]herefore it is necessary that we the religious become the defenders and protectors of the Hanopiras among the Christian Indians."[36] This is another example of Oré's ethnographic observations. He explains the term "Hanopira" in the Andes meant "a painted man" and that it refers to "infidels for the most part, who go about smeared and painted in a vermilion color, or lacking red lead with a tint or charcoal based ink. In this the infidels and barbarians of La Florida are similar to those on the other [eastern] side of the [Andean] cordillera of Peru. Both are bowmen, but there they go about dressed, or at least less nude than those here, and these have the advantage of being more warlike, and that they lack the vice of drunkenness that all Indians

33. Ibid., "[Y] así se fueron allanando y sujetando."

34. Oré uses the term "*padre fray*" frequently in his report to distinguish friars who as fathers (priests) were consecrated and able to administer the sacraments, especially important in the missions of La Florida that were sparsely populated and distant from each other.

35. Oré, *Relación de la Florida*, 10r. "[P]erseguian a los Christianos y los tenian como por descomulgados entre ellos, diciendoles mil afrentas injuriosas las cuales sufrian." My translation varies significantly from Chang-Rodríguez and Vogely, *Account of the Martyrs*, 99.

36. Oré, *Relación de la Florida*, 10r. "[D]e tal manera que es necessario que los religiosos seamos defensores y amparo de los Hanopiras entre los indios Christianos."

are noted for, both those of New Spain and Peru."[37] José de Acosta's ethnography is intellectually more akin to the modern, yet there were other contemporary *letrados* of the period who contemplated and commented on the cultural characteristics of the newly encountered peoples.

Oré abruptly shifts his narrative of the Franciscan martyrs to the foreign threat, a topic that concerned him deeply from the time of Francis Drake's 1578 passage along the Peruvian coast during his circumnavigation. An English settlement in La Florida as Oré writes in 1616 is a reality and the friar's review and evaluation are important. In May 1588, Captain Vicente González sailed from St. Augustine with Sergeant Major Juan Menéndez Márquez, the pilot Ginés Pinzón and thirty soldiers and seamen. The purpose was reconnaissance of the Bay of Madre de Dios to verify English settlement. Oré provides details that seem to have come from the ship's log. His description begins as they reached Santa Elena where they found the Guale seemingly at peace.[38] They reached the Bay in early June and sailed northwesterly until they encountered a spot recognized by Captain González where the Jesuits were martyred. The bay was carefully probed as they took frequent soundings and measurements of latitude, sailing systematically in a northerly direction. They recorded topography and vegetation, from the pines in the south to the oaks and other hardwoods as the terrain became rougher. Fish were abundant, especially sardines, and in the freshwater tributaries, trout. Deer were plentiful. The relative absence of Indians was notable, although at least one fifteen-year-old boy was taken and another was captured on their return. By June's end they left the bay and sailed southerly for about two days, and then noted another large shallow bay. Upon investigation they discovered a "place assigned for repairing small light vessels, and on land a number of wells made of English clay storage vessels."[39] There was other rubbish, all signs there had been a substantial group of people there. Mission accomplished, they sailed southward, passing today's Charleston and the Guale territory. At the island

37. Ibid., "[I]nfieles, por la mayor parte andan untados y embijados [painted with red lead] con color bermeja, y a falta se embijan con tinze y carbon, en lo cual son semejantes estos de la Florida a los indios infieles y barbaros que [h]ay en la otra vanda de las cordilleras del Piru, y los unos y otros son flecheros, pero alla andan vestidos, o menos desnudos que los de acá, y estos se aventajan en ser mas guerreros, y que carecen del vicio de la embriaguez, [note that the word can mean drunkeness or being in another state as in an hallucigenic state] de que son notados los indios todos, assi de la Nueva España como del Piru." My translation varies significantly from Chang-Rodríguez and Vogely, *Account of the Martyrs*, 100.

38. Oré, *Relación de la Florida*, 10r. Chang-Rodríguez, *Relación de los mártires*, 125, ft. 231, from Geiger, "Introduction," 1936, 58, ft. 15, identifies this as Charleston Bay. Hoffman, *A New Andalucia*, 304, ft. 26 notes that Oré provides the sole account of this reconnaissance effort.

39. Oré, *Relación de la Florida*, 12r. "[V]aradero señalado de chalupas, y en tierra cantidad de poços hechos de pipas Inglesas."

of San Pedro they found Father Friar Baltasar López hard at work with apparently good success. They continued to St. Augustine, anchoring there in July, six weeks from the time they departed.

Fortunately, Oré identifies his source for the description of the reconnaissance. Oré's account was written "according to such an exact and carefully prepared report by Sergeant Major Juan Menéndez, who at present is the Treasurer of His Majesty in the city of St. Augustine."[40] Oré was aware of the value of providing a detailed account of the nature of the English efforts to establish an outpost when he wrote, "Because it is such a true and necessary description of the Bay of La Madre de Dios and ports, with the degrees of latitude and directions for the navigation chart, and for when His Majesty might order the cleaning out of the thieves who have occupied and fortified themselves there during the course of thirty years, it seemed worth including here."[41] As Oré notes, other similar evidence for the English presence was provided by another ship's pilot, Pero Díaz Franco, and by the Irishman David Glavid. Both men separately had been captured by the English and later ended up at the ill-fated Roanoke colony, which at one point held, according to Oré, 300 men and 30 women. Both Díaz Franco and Glavid managed to give Spanish authorities accounts of what they had seen, and Glavid later served as a soldier in St. Augustine from 1595 to 1600.[42]

This critical information needed to reach authorities in Spain quickly. Oré writes that General Pedro Menéndez Márquez set out with his first cousin, Sergeant Major Juan Menéndez Márquez. Their initial attempt failed as foul weather drove them to the coasts of Hispaniola and Cuba. They finally reached Sanlúcar de Barrameda on July 5, 1589. Oré writes with a caveat that "as it was understood," a term Oré rarely used in this section of the report. He writes that the two men reached an agreement with the Crown to return to Florida with a large fleet and to construct a fort housing 300 infantry at around 35.5 degrees. He describes what they planned and details their assignment, all in the subjunctive. Oré's sources probably included soldiers, seamen, and perhaps officers. Hoffman scoured Spanish archives to verify whether the subject was discussed at Court. Finding no evidence of the same, he classified Oré's

---

40. Ibid., "[S]egun esta relacion tan puntual y prolixa, hecha por el dicho sargento mayor Iuan Menendez que al presente es tesorero de su Majestad en la ciudad de San Agustin."

41. Ibid., "Que por ser verdadera y tan necessaria la descripcion de esta bahía de la Madre de Dios, y puertos, con la graduacion y rumbos deste derrotero, para cuando Su Magestad se sirviese de mandar limpiarla de los ladrones que la [h]an ocupado, y se [h]an fortificado en ella tiempo de treinta años, parecio detenerme en ella." The last sentence does not appear in the translation by Chang-Rodríguez and Vogeley, *Account of the Martyrs*, 104.

42. Oré, *Relación de la Florida*, 12r–v. In *Relación de los mártires*, 131, ft. 264–65, Chang-Rodríguez provides the background material based on Geiger, "Introduction," 62, ft. 49.

account a "mistaken story." He further suggests that the Spanish assigned a low priority to what the English were attempting in Roanoke, and went on to detail "documentable" events. But it is possible the report was discussed at the Royal Council or the Casa de la Contratación and is "lost" in the mounds of remaining documents. Spain was fully engaged in reconstructing their armada in the months following the disastrous attempt to invade England.[43] Hoffman, by careful archival research, is able to correct the dating and nature of the two vessels under Pedro Menéndez Márquez in a quick round trip from Spain in 1590 to pick up and deliver part of the critical *situado* to keep the government afloat until the following year. Although unable to stop to verify English settlement inside the Outer Banks, they did secure news in the Caribbean of what the English had in mind, including an armada under Drake.[44]

Commissioner Oré speaks repeatedly of the English threat, explaining its danger and the cost of inaction. He points to their almost yearly arrival along the Atlantic seaboard and their departures from secure ports in Jacán and the island of Bermuda. From there they sailed along the coasts of Cuba, Puerto Rico, Jamaica, and Santo Domingo, and "carry out the robberies they can without anyone being able to punish them." He writes that their ships pillaged all the Spanish cowhides, wine, and other items they wanted, and then returned via the Bahama Canal. He notes the English pilots were as experienced as the Spanish because they regularly crossed the Atlantic for ten or twelve years. Then from their safe havens, the thieves returned rich to England, leaving the owners of merchandise and money stripped of their wealth. Oré points to one item in particular: cowhides—used to fashion diverse leather goods—a principal Cuban export to Spain.

The friar laments that *doncellas* were left without either cash or goods, or a combination of the two, required for dowries. Generally, to secure a "suitable marriage," the larger the dowry, the more prestigious and wealthy the husband. Oré was well aware of the economic and social impact of piracy and war that led to frequent bankruptcies in Spain and the Indies. To drive his point home to the Crown and compel readers into action Oré uses a profound element of the Spanish character: honor. "And above all, *the reputation of the Spanish is shamed* [my italics] by inaction and suffering for so many years of continual attacks by so many corsairs, as they are observing the places without defenses in order to enter them and carry away as much as they can, either by trading [contraband] or by armed force." Oré stresses that the only salvation is a well-armed annual fleet to protect the convoys.[45]

43. Hoffman, *A New Andalucia*, 305.

44. Ibid., 306–307.

45. Oré, *Relación de la Florida*, 14r. "[H]azen los robos que pueden sin poderlos castigar. . . . Y sobre todo muy avergonçada la reputacion de Españoles, en callar a sufrir tantos

Oré, now halfway through his compilation, at last turns to the Franciscan martyrs. His recent completion of the *Relación de la vida y milagros de Francisco Solano* likely contributed to his appointment as commissioner for Florida. That report had been rapidly executed and printed. General Commissioner for the Indies Friar Antonio de Trejo ordered Oré to conduct the inquiry on June 7, 1613, and the friar began recording testimony on July 11! The order to prepare a report on Solano's youth in Spain was related to his Order's broader intentions to preserve the memory of Franciscans martyred during their work in the Indies. The aim was to provide evidence that could lead to beatification and ultimate canonization. Martyrs were prime candidates and details of their lives, work to spread the faith, and the nature of their deaths needed to be recorded. Hagiographies were popular reading for Christians during this period. Books of saints were fostered and neither of Oré's texts on Francisco Solano and the Florida martyrs required authorization by censors. The Franciscans believed the deaths of their brothers during the Guale uprising needed to be documented while there was still evidence. This section begins as Philip II, at the petition of Captain Domingo Martínez Aveño, authorized and helped send to Florida twelve Franciscans. The recruits, largely from Castile, sailed for the Indies on July 14, 1595. Using biographical sketches Oré stresses their spirituality and accomplishments in Spain and Florida.[46]

Their lives and martyrdom have or will receive extensive examination, so I focus primarily on sources and the way Oré integrated them into his narrative. Franciscans among the original group or who were already in La Florida are principal contributors. Father Pedro Bermejo may be one. He served several years in Florida, as the Franciscan guardian in St. Augustine and in 1605 custodian of Santa Elena. In 1616, he was guardian in Bayomo, Cuba, where Oré might have interviewed him. Father Pedro Fernández de Chozas was based at the mission in Latama when the Guale uprising occurred. On learning of the unfolding events, he notified Governor Canzo. After the revolt Friar Chozas returned to Spain and provided a detailed report, and in 1612

años continualmente, tantos corssarios como estan acechando los lugares sin defensa, para entrarse en ellos y llevar quanto pueden, o contratando, o con fuerça de gente y armas." There are several differences in the author's translation and that of Chang-Rodríguez and Vogeley, *Account of the Martyrs*, 108. Part of the variation is due to missing commas in this section of the modern transcription by Chang-Rodríguez, *Relación de los mártires*, 136. Four lines down the transcription is "puertos" rather than "puestos." I recommend reviewing the original.

46. Oré, *Relación de la Florida*, 14r.–23r. For the modern edition of Oré's study of the life of Friar Solano in Andalucia, see "Introduction" in Oré, *Relación de la vida y milagros de San Francisco Solano*, ed. Noble David Cook ([Madrid: 1614] Lima: Pontificia Universidad Católica del Perú, 1998), ix–xxxix. Luis Julian Plandolit, *El Apostol de América San Francisco Solano* (Madrid: Editorial Cisneros, 1963) is the most thorough study of Solano. Early printed texts, including Oré's, provided foundations for Solano's canonization.

he attended the general chapter meeting in Rome. He later was guardian of the Madrid monastery. Friar Chozas and Oré coincided and may have shared concerns prior to Oré's departure for Florida and after his return.[47]

Another Franciscan friar, Father Pedro Ruiz, priest and confessor, was alternately guardian, custodian, and commissioner and at the provincial meeting was named guardian of Havana's Franciscan monastery. One of the most widely known friars chosen for the 1595 Florida mission was Father Francisco de Ávila. Taken captive by the rebels he survived and was able to provide a personal account of his experiences and the deaths of the martyrs. Oré covers both him and Father Veráscola later in the *Relación*. Another on Oré's list, Friar Pedro de Viniegra, quickly mastered the Indigenous language and was very successful in conversion. Oré believed, "It was a shame that he was not a priest to confess and conduct Mass, having competence to be one and to administer the other sacraments." Fortunately, at the request of the Florida friars, the commissioner of New Spain sent an order authorizing them to ordain Viniegra: "In doing so we have produced one of the best ministers for the Indians that we have had during our tenure."[48] The last of the twelve friars assigned to Florida, Father Francisco de Bonilla soon departed to serve in New Spain, but called by Oré he returned to participate in the San Buenaventura de Guadalquini chapter meeting.

Friar Francisco Marrón was one of Oré's best and most experienced sources. He first arrived in Florida around 1574 and served decades as a preacher, custodian, and prelate. His memory was excellent and Oré consulted him regularly prior to his departure for Spain. Writing after the second inspection and provincial chapter meeting, Oré relates that Friar Marrón had preached some eighty years in Spain and the Indies, and was one of the religious who provided a "*relación verdadera*" of the martyrdom of the five Franciscans, and verified Friar Ávila's narrative, the only eyewitness who was left to "tell us how, when and the reason why his companions were martyred."[49]

---

47. For Friar Bermejo, see Chang-Rodríguez, *Relación de los mártires*, 139, ft. 295, provides the background material based on Maynard Geiger, *Biographical Dictionary of the Franciscans in Spanish Florida and Cuba (1528--1841) Franciscan Studies* 21 (Patterson, NJ: Anthony Guild Press, 1940), 34. For Friar Fernández de Chozas, see Chang-Rodríguez, *Relación de los mártires*, 140, ft. 301, and Geiger, *Biographical Dictionary*, 52.

48. Oré, *Relación de la Florida*, 16r. "Era lastima que no fuesse Sacerdote, para confessarlos y dezir Missa, teniendo suficiencia para serlo, y administrar los demas sacramentos. . . . [D]el cual hemos hecho uno de los mejores ministros para los indios, que han pasado en nuestros tiempos."

49. Ibid., 16v. "[C]ontarnos el como y quando, y la causa por que a sus compañeros los martirizaron." Geiger, *Biographical Dictionary*, 35; and López, *Relación histórica*, 5–10, piece together Marrón's presumed initial arrival in La Florida sometime in 1574, in the initial wave of Franciscans. Oré, 16v: "Y fue uno de los religiosos que declararon y dieron relacion verdadera, del martirio de los cinco religiosos que mataron los indios, por la que

Ávila's account was recorded in the Havana Monastery prior to his return to Spain, largely thanks to pressure applied by Guardian Marrón to provide a full account of all he knew about the events from the time the revolt began through his own captivity.

Oré's review of the background of the Guale uprising and his use of Father Ávila's account is analyzed by J. Michael Francis and Kathleen M. Kole. They too argue that Friar Oré likely "consulted native informants, although he does not identify anyone in particular."[50] They also point out that without the original Ávila manuscript, definitive conclusions are compromised. "It is therefore understandable why some scholars might perceive Ávila's captivity narrative with some skepticism."[51] Indeed, caution is required when analyzing all captivity narratives. Francis and Kole point out correctly that Oré's text was compiled twenty years after the events. Yet careful reading and evaluation of Oré's report provides justification for its use. Francis and Kole note and question why among the friars attacked by the Guale, only Ávila was saved. Perhaps he was spared because he was taken to the village of Tulufina where he began work two years earlier and quickly developed an amicable relationship with residents. After initial torment, Ávila was allowed more freedom as the Guale tried to integrate him into their society, according to his narrative, by tempting him with an Indigenous maiden.

Ávila's hope for freedom was ignited when he overheard discussions about his possible ransom or exchange. A young Indian seen as a potential chief had been captured along with others in 1595 and held by Spaniards in St. Augustine. In 1598, the Guale demanded their release in exchange for Ávila. He was released in June and returned to the Franciscan monastery where the governor, needing information on the murderers pressed Ávila for names. The friar refused, citing clerical immunity even after receiving religious authorization. Clearly Ávila was protecting his captors. Francis and Kole point out that memories of events are modified over time. Despite these concerns Oré's almost verbatim copy of Ávila's testimony to Friar Marrón remains the authoritative account of the uprising.[52]

---

compelido de la obedencia dio el padre Avila: la qual irá juntamente en esta relacion, como compañero que fue de los martires, y permitio Dios quedasse el solo, para contarnos el como y quando, y la causa porque a sus compañeros los martirizaron." Chang-Rodríguez and Vogeley provide a different translation of this in *Account of the Martyrs*, 115: "He was one of the religious who gave accurate testimony of the martyrdom of the five religious whom the Indians killed. This testimony he gave compelled by obedience to Father Ávila, and it will be attached to this account, as God spared him to relate the martyrdom of his companions, telling the how, the when, and the cause of the killing."

50. Francis and Kole, *Murder and Martyrdom*, 51.

51. Ibid., 51.

52. Ibid., 51.

At the end of Ávila's testimony, Oré adds another's account. At one point during his captivity, the Indians—intending to attack their enemies—pressed Ávila to make gunpowder and gun balls because they had captured ten harquebuses and planned to use them. Ávila responded that he had no idea how to make them. The captors countered, "Don't make excuses about knowing, because your books speak and tell you how to do it."[53] The friars had done their work well, convincing the Indians that the religious books spoke the words of an all-knowing God, who can even provide instructions on making gunpowder. They brought Ávila the texts, the *Suma*, an oratorio used by the friars, works of Friar Luis de Granada, and a breviary. It seemed Ávila was in a pickle, but clearly pleased to have again his books, and after consulting them he managed to save their "truth." He could not make the gunpowder and balls for lack of the ingredients! Oré points out that his source of information was another religious who knew Ávila before and after his captivity and they communicated frequently with each other. Oré notes he spoke to the other friar at length. Unfortunately for those wishing for more details, Oré confesses that in order to avoid excessive explanations or digressions he left it as it was.[54]

Similar to other sections of Oré's text, his narrative style varies according to the sources he used. Some sections are quite dramatic, but others more measured and somber. His challenge to the Crown to protect the Church and empire against enemies is reminiscent of the Biblical Book of Job. His comments on the elder Friar Marrón are filled with respect and honor. Marrón's success in extracting and making certain the details of the martyrdom of the Franciscans provided by Friar Ávila, as well as his captivity, was critical to the Order's design to archive and distribute the memory of their work in the Indies. A copy was originally archived in Havana's monastery. But it was Commissioner Oré who brought that knowledge to a broader audience thanks to his diligence and persistence. Oré writes that on his deathbed the Friar Marrón told him he was over one hundred. One can almost see a pensive Commissioner Oré dipping his pen into the ink as he composed these words: "He died twenty-two years after [the Guale Revolt] in this Monastery of Havana, and I buried him."[55]

---

53. Oré, *Relación de la Florida,* 21v. "No te excuses que si sabes, que tus libros hablan y dizen como la [h]as de hazer."

54. Ibid., 21v–22r. "Esto de la polvora y balas no lo escribio el padre Avila en su relacion, pero en la que me /22r/ dio un Religioso que fue antes y despues de su cautiverio le trato y comunicó mucho, refiere esto y otras diversas cosas, que por evitar prolixidad se dexan." Chang-Rodríguez and Vogeley, *Account of the Martyrs*, 129, ft. 13, suggest that Friar Marrón or Friar Pareja could be the source, quite correctly although there are other possibilities.

55. Oré, *Relación de la Florida*, 16r. "[M]urio veynte y dos años despues [the Guale revolts] en este Convento de La Habana, y lo enterre yo." This report has not been located.

Oré's most insightful adviser on Florida was Father Francisco Pareja who served many years in the missions. Oré's sketch signals faith in Pareja's judgment as he writes, "By the good example he has always given, he conquered the cruelty and ill temper of the Indians, turning them from wolves into sheep."[56] It was Friar Pareja who at the provincial chapter meeting prepared the synopsis of participants' responses. Oré writes that he was "[o]ne of the religious who most contributed to the conversion of the Indians." The friar devoted more than twenty years, primarily among Timucua speakers in his *doctrina* and others in the province. He was fluent in their language and composed texts for other friars. Pareja's translations of the Christian doctrine, a catechism, a confessional, and other devotional treatises were printed in Mexico in Timucua. Commissioner Oré reports they were so useful that "many Indian men and women have easily learned to read in less than two months and they write letters to one another in their language."[57] Oré writes, "In the inspection that I conducted in order to celebrate the First Provincial Chapter Meeting of this province, he was found to be a saintly man and most deserving of his election."[58] Oré saw in Pareja a fellow spirit who recognized the importance of communicating directly to those they hoped to convert.

With painstaking work, Pareja produced various texts "in the language of the Indians that has superseded the others."[59] Commissioner Oré continues that Pareja had responded in writing to the request for information on the work of the friars in the province to determine whether they believed the Indians were converted to a level of being true Christians and were ready for confession and communion. Pareja's information was so valuable and succinct that Oré essentially includes it verbatim. The questionnaire was similar to the ones used by bishops throughout Spanish America as they conducted their

---

56. Ibid., "[Y] con su buen exemplo que siempre [h]a dado, vencio la crueldad y aspereza de los Indios, volviendolos de lobos corderos."

57. Ibid., 24r.–v. "[U]no de los religiosos que mas se [h]a aventajado en la conversión de los indios." "[C]on facilidad [h]an deprendido muchos indios y indias a leer, en menos de dos meses, y escriben cartas en la lengua los unos a los otros."

58. Ibid., 15v. "Y en la visita que hize para celebrar el primer Capitulo provincial de esta provincia, hallandolo varon santo y dignissimo desta eleccion."

59. Ibid., 15v. "[E]n lengua de los indios, en que [h]a sido aventajado a los demas." See Francisco Pareja, *Confessionario en lengua castellana y timuquana* (Mexico: Viuda de Diego López Davalos, 1613), and his *Cathecismo en lengua castellana y timuquana* (Mexico: Viuda de Pedro Ballii por Adriano Cesar, 1612). See also Jerald T. Milanich, *Laboring in the Fields of the Lord: Spanish Missiones and Southeastern Indians* (Gainesville: University Press of Florida, 1999), and the same author's *The Timucua* (Oxford: Blackwell, 1996); Jerald T. Milanich and William C. Sturtevant, eds., *Francisco Pareja's 1613 Confessionario a documentary source for Timucuan ethnography* (Tallahassee: Florida Division of Archives, History, and Records Management, 1972); John H. Hann, *Apalachee: The Land between the Rivers* (Gainesville: University Press of Florida, 1987), and the same author's *History of the Timucua: Indians and Missions* (Gainesville: University Press of Florida, 1996).

required inspections in their diocese that included large numbers of recent converts. In addition to Father Pareja, many other friars prepared and gave Commissioner Oré their responses. Manuscript copies may still exist, awaiting discovery to illuminate further the efforts of the Franciscans in the frontier missions. Father Pareja's *Relación* as copied by Oré or his secretary provides insight into what the Franciscans were able to accomplish. It is detailed and extensive as Oré records in the closing section of this narrative: "This good religious said many other things in more detail. Because this report is so true and the other religious confirmed Father Pareja's account, for his is the earliest and of such virtue, and they give it such approval that I wanted to avoid redundancies by including others. I dwell only on this one."[60]

Commissioner Oré details his experiences and findings during his inspection of the Florida *doctrinas* and the first provincial chapter meeting in the mission of San Buenaventura de Guadalquini in mid-December 1616 in the final third of the report. Throughout, the narrative shifts from the first and third persons as he includes the reports of others. The inspection of the missions has received special attention by anthropologists and ethnohistorians for obvious reasons. The purpose of Commissioner Oré's mandated inspection of the Florida missions was to evaluate the effectiveness of conversion and catechizing. I expected the results to appear early in his report. But an equivalent first inspection appears near the end of his narrative, followed by the report of his second inspection, then a detailed copy of the actions of the first provincial chapter meeting. Oré notes that he was pressed for time on his first Florida inspection and was unable to conduct the full examination he intended. The reason was based on one item in his original assignment, to deal with numerous challenges for the Order's work in Cuba. For his report on the first inspection of the Florida missions, he was forced to rely on, almost verbatim, the report by Friar Martín de Prieto, the *difinidor* of the province. It may be the closest equivalent to a first inspection that we have other than brief notices scattered elsewhere in Oré's text. Taking an oath in *verbo sacerdotis* administered by Oré, Friar Prieto details his trials and tribulations on the Florida frontier. He arrived in 1605 and he emphasizes successes centering on his 1607–1609 evangelizing efforts from the central Timucua communities westward into Apalachee lands. In one Timucua village Prieto hoped to serve he was jeered and threatened. Santa Ana's shaman informed the friar that the cacique was old and infirm and during his youth he was held captive by Hernando de

60. Oré, *Relación de la Florida*, 26r. "Otras cosas dize mas largamente este buen religioso, que por ser relacion tan verdadera, y que los demas Religiosos contestan con la de este padre Pareja, por ser el mas antiguo, y de tanta virtud y aprobación en las que dan, quise evitar prolixidad en ponerlas, y alargarme en esta sola." Chang-Rodríguez and Vogeley, in *Account of the Martyrs*, 140, do not include this paragraph, although it is in Chang-Rodríguez's *Relación de los mártires*, 174.

Soto. He would never allow his people to be Christians because the Spaniards were terrible. Yet the bold friar entered the cacique's house, whereupon the chief became furious, foaming and spitting. When Prieto began to speak the "word of God," the chief covered his ears and expelled the friar from the village. Miraculously a massive lightning bolt and violent wind gust leveled the structure leaving only a cross and a small chapel that Prieto set up for mass. Prieto reports, "Such was the fear installed in all of them that the next day the cacique sent me a message to catechize him, and within six days I baptized him, and upon completing the baptism he gave his soul to God."[61] Here and elsewhere the Franciscans highlight "divine intervention" to justify and memorialize their work in the missions.

Buoyed by success, Friar Prieto continues to outline his endeavors to win converts. He entered Apalachee territory thanks to Timucua assistance and reached the plaza of Ivitachuco where "there were more than 30,000 Indians."[62] Friar Prieto notes subsequent incursions into the territory by other friars who provided him reports that he delivered to Governor Juan Fernández de Olivera (1609–1612). Prieto relates when the Timucua and Apalachee met in Ivitachuco, he discussed with them the need and value of establishing peace. In spite of a long cultural tradition of skirmishes among southeastern ethnic groups, the friar was surprised that they were amenable to his efforts. Perhaps they recognized that with their rapidly diminishing population their own existence was in jeopardy if they failed to reach an accommodation with the Spanish. Prieto ends his report with a brief geographical description of the fertile land with fields of corn, beans, and squash.[63] Oré closes his transcription verifying that all he wrote derived from Friar Prieto's report, "although I have had a longer and fuller one from Father Friar Alonso Serrano. He arrived later and went about preaching and planting the cross in some of the places of the large population of Apalachee. Later four or five religious entered the territory and all indicated the Indians' desire to become Christian."[64] Oré probably

61. Oré, *Relación de la Florida*, 27r.; after folio 26v. foliation is inaccurate or missing. There are five folios. I use Chang-Rodríguez, *Relación de los mártires*, and replace the incorrect 28r. with 27r. and end with 31v. "Fue tanto el temor que causo a todos, que otro dia me embió a llamar el Cacique para que le catequizasse, y dentro de seys días le bautizé, y acabado de bautizar, dio su alma a Dios." See John E. Worth, *The Timucua Chiefdoms of Spanish Florida*, vol. 1, *Assimilation* (Gainesville: University Press of Florida, 1998), 60–69. The report was also used by Friar Juan de Silva, *Advertencias importantes acerca del buen govierno y administración de las Indias assi en lo espiritual como en lo temporal repartidas en tres memoriales informativos* (Madrid: Por la Viuda de Fernando de Corria Montenegro, 1621).

62. Oré, *Relación de la Florida*, 30r. Chang-Rodriguez, in *Relación de los mártires*, 180, ft. 439, provides alternative names of Vitachuco or Villa Apalache.

63. Oré, *Relación de la Florida*, 28v.

64. Ibid., 28v. "Aunque la [h]e tenido mas larga y copiosa del padre fray Alonso Serrano."

viewed Friar Serrano's report in Spain shortly after his appointment to recruit friars. Once again, we see Oré as a practitioner of early modern oral history, taking systematic testimony from an eyewitness and participant in the events. Veracity depends on a number of variables and Oré often provides readers his informants' names and sometimes assesses verisimilitude.

Oré's personal inspection began on November 16, 1616, as he departed St. Augustine with a full commission by the bishop of Cuba, Alonso Orozco Enríquez de Almendariz, to conduct the equivalent of a diocesan visitation. In that capacity Oré inspected *doctrinas* and parishes, the St. Augustine cathedral, members of the secular clergy, and the military chaplains at the fort. He was able to punish those not fulfilling their duties to maintain a proper Christian example, a frequent problem in military posts. A detailed report of the inspection of each mission and its *doctrineros* was probably prepared, as was the norm. Oré includes here only an outline. He provides geographical descriptions of topography and lists products as well as the distances between missions. He notes the number of Christianized converts, sometimes by age and sex groups. The quality of the outcome of each friar's effort is tested during Oré's inquiry. He also includes the required evaluation of the cleanliness of the house of worship, religious items, availability of religious texts, and adequacy of record keeping.

Oré spent three to four days in each *doctrina*, inspecting, preaching, and confessing in addition to examining the converts to evaluate their knowledge of articles of the faith. He wanted to know the number baptized, and those who died. He also confirmed those who had not been baptized. Oré was familiar with pastoral inspections during his work in the Andes. He knew and perhaps read some of Archbishop Mogrovejo's visitations that in part contributed to his canonization.[65] The mechanics and results are not comparable to those in the Andes, for the topography, settlement densities, and Indigenous cultures are quite different. Most of the information comes from Oré's direct visitation as he traveled, but he could not inspect every mission over this vast territory. His written report of the Florida *doctrinas* is more similar to that of the *doctrinas* and parishes he later inspected in southern Chile. Some of the information comes directly from the *doctrineros* who answered *in verbo sacerdotis* a detailed questionnaire and then brought the completed document to the provincial chapter meeting they were called to attend.[66]

The often-ignored text for the chapter meeting led by Commissioner Oré is vivid enough to feel present, and the discovery of Franciscan democracy is

65. José Antonio Benito, ed., *Libro de visitas de Santo Toribio de Mogrovejo (1593–1605)* (Lima: Pontificia Universidad Católica del Perú, 2006).

66. There are frequent shifts in person when Commissioner Oré and his secretary share observations as they record the chapter meeting.

fascinating. Such freedom and sense of empowerment can be noted in the actions of Oré and the other Franciscans returning to St. Augustine. On January 14, 1617, Commissioner Oré and Franciscan chaplains serving the soldiers and populace of St. Augustine composed a letter to the Crown. In it they expressed gratitude for the years of support they received and pointed out that they had made great strides in converting the Indians and continued to do so. They emphasized that a full report of their undertaking "will be given to Your Majesty by the General Commissioner of the Indies via the *Verdadera relaçion* that the Commissioner [Oré] and Custodio [Friar Lorenzo Martínez] of this province" were carrying to Spain. The report was also to be presented at the general chapter meeting of the Indies scheduled in Salamanca. They also pressed for assistance to secure all needed for Santa Elena Province and their conversion efforts. The friars continued cautiously, entering into the dangerous issue of church-state relations, as they called for a governor who would provide greater assistance to their efforts, rather than impeding them. The Franciscans then requested the monarch to appoint Juan Menéndez Márquez as the new governor. The Royal Treasury official served successfully thirty-six years on land and in the armadas. Their recommendation came regardless of the fact that Governor Treviño y Guillamas remained in office and was not ready to relinquish his post.[67] Three days later, January 17, 1617, the same friars, minus Commissioner Oré composed a more disturbing account of their tenure in Florida and their assessment of the province's needs.[68] Without Oré's voice they were less diplomatic and more direct in their accusations. After years of exertion in Florida, their original hopes were dampened and they now doubted the outcome and were forced to rely on the king's mercy. Their message includes a detailed account of the precarious state they were in and the current governor's lack of support. Their frustration is profound and their grievances are compelling. Part of their disappointment comes from the disappearance of the peoples they hoped to convert. The unfolding demographic catastrophe stands at the top of their list. "We have found that four years ago half of the Indians have perished because of the great plagues and contagious diseases that they suffered." The only silver lining the friars can point to is that, "Your Majesty in large measure deserves recognition that will be given in Glory, for with the help of the twenty-two

67. AGI, Santo Domingo, 235, 71r–v, in Chang-Rodriguez, *Relación de los mártires*, 209–10. Signed in St. Augustine by Commissioner Oré, Chief Minister Friar Francisco Pareja, Friar Pedro Ruiz, Friar Lorenzo Martínez, Friar Alonso Pesquera, Friar Juan de la Cruz, and Friar Francisco Alonso de Jesús.

68. Chang-Rodríguez, *Relación de los mártires*, 203–209, from AGI, Santo Domingo 235, 73–76. Letter signed by Ministro Principal Friar Francisco Pareja, Friar Pedro Ruiz, Friar Lorenzo Martínez, Friar Alonso Pesquera, Friar Juan de la Cruz, Friar Bartolomé Romero, and Friar Francisco Alonso de Jesús, St. Augustine, 17 January 1617.

religious Your Majesty ordered dispatched to these parts, in the five years here, there has been a very large harvest of souls for Heaven during these *mortandades* [die-offs]." The friars end their letter by informing the king that "[t]here remain at least eight thousand, more or less, Christians alive."[69]

With his work in St. Augustine ending, Commissioner Oré and several other Franciscans collected the letters, reports, and papers, and around the third week of January 1617 they boarded a small vessel hoping to return quickly to Cuba. There Commissioner Oré faced several thorny personnel issues postponed during his inspection of Florida. He also had to compile his report of the visitation, at the same time overseeing preparations for the return to Spain. Most of the compiling and contextualization of the report took place in Havana's Franciscan monastery as Oré toiled alongside assistants. The audience for the final compilation included the Crown and royal bureaucracy, the Church in general, and the Franciscans and future missionaries. In that sense it is similar to the way Oré compiled his report on Friar Francisco Solano's early years in Andalusia, as he collected testimony and other information for printing and distribution to authorities in Spain, Peru, and Rome.[70] The timing of the departure from Havana was determined by the availability of a ship sailing for Iberia. By early winter of 1618, Oré had completed all he could do in Cuba, and along with Friar Lorenzo Martínez he sailed from Havana's harbor, passing the fortress of El Moro and entering the Bahama Channel. In spite of potential headwinds, the strong Gulf Stream swept them northward off the Florida coast toward Bermuda and on to Europe. They reached Spain by late spring 1618. Oré's and Custodian Martínez's goal was to reach Salamanca in time to participate in the general chapter meeting.[71]

For distribution the report had to be printed in Spain as quickly as possible. When finally stitched together by Oré, a secretary, or the printer, and

69. AGI, Santo Domingo 235, 73r, "[H]allamos que de quatro años a esta parte an faltado por las grandes pestes y contagiossas enfermedades que had padeçido los indios, la mitad de ellos, en lo qual a tenido vuestra Magestad mui gran parte de merecimiento, que se le dara de gloria, pues con la ayuda de los veinte y dos religiosos que vuestra Magestad mandó despachar a estas partes, a cinco años se an hecho en estas mortandades muy grandes cosechas de almas para el çielo. Quedan asta ocho mil christianos por lo menos vivos, antes más que menos." From Chang-Rodríguez, *Relación de los mártires*, 204, from AGI, Santo Domingo 235, 73–76.

70. Cook, "Introduction," in Oré, *Vida y milagros de San Francisco Solano*, ix–xxxix; and Plandolit, *San Francisco Solano*, 340. Beatification occurred on 25 January 1675 as Pope Clement X issued the brief *Quemadmodum coelestis Imperator*. Celebrations took place in Lima on 22 and 23 April 1679. There were new processes until fifty-one years after beatification when Pope Benedict XIII (27 December 1726) issued the bull of canonization, *Ad fidelium Dei servorum gloriam*. The first fiesta of San Francisco Solano in Lima was on 24 July 1728.

71. Chang-Rodríguez, *Relación de los mártires*, 37, from AGI, Santo Domingo 235, 77r–78v. Friar Martínez was sent subsequently to serve in New Spain.

then hastily set to type and printed, the compilation was ready for distribution. It is doubtful that Oré viewed or even intended his report as a book. The Florida report did reach its various audiences and each extracted what interested them. In initial sections, the friar covered the life and deaths of various martyrs, the Jesuits, Dominicans and others, and then midway through, the Franciscans. Although edifying, it would not have satisfied seventeenth-century hagiographers nor their readers. The report is too filled with errors to satisfy modern historians, although there are sections that cover events not recorded by others. It is not comparable to Garcilaso de la Vega's history, nor did Oré intend it to be.[72] His report stresses the value of the missions and the need for more *doctrineros* and royal support, and here it achieved some success. It may have stimulated some friars to accept the challenge of service in the Indies, even La Florida, for there were still many Indigenous not yet converted but ready for the Franciscan message. The package also included Oré's detailed analysis of the threat of foreign powers and the need to take immediate action to protect Spanish sovereignty over the North American Atlantic seaboard. His voice was not the only one and the challenges were great, but the Crown's ability to counter intervention was limited. Oré also warned the monarch and his councils of tensions between church and state in La Florida, and the need to protect the Amerindians. Church-state conflicts were a constant and tensions pervasive, as Oré soon discovered in Chile as bishop of La Imperial, the southernmost diocese in America.[73]

Perhaps a more accurate title would have been, "True Report on the Status of Florida, circa 1618." The suggestion is based on the variety of subjects covered in Oré's text, not just the martyrs. I use the term "status" because although the early "history" is included, the friar's intent is to present the immediate challenges that demand a response by Spanish authorities. Oré's earlier and later work places him in the Lascasian camp. Here we see him as an "*arbitrista*" as well. Oré is a linguist, musician, *doctrinero* to the masses, solicitor, and administrator—a counterweight to excessive authority. His earlier texts in Quechua and Aymara helped "fix" the lingua franca of much of Andean America. Although under-recognized, he is most certainly a

72. Similar historical errors noted in the *Symbolo catholico indiano* contributed to several twentieth-century Andean historians to set his work aside as unreliable.

73. Cook, "Viviendo en las márgenes del imperio." See Catalina Andrango-Walker, *El 'símbolo católico indiano' (1598): Saberes coloniales y los problemas de la evangelización en la región andina* (Madrid: Iberoamericana-Veruert, Biblioteca Indiana, 2018), 120–127. Andrango-Walker's work, along with Miguel Angel Espinoza Soria, *La Catequesis en Fray Luis Jerónimo de Oré: Aporte a la Nueva Evangelización* (Lima: Convento de los Descalzos, 2012), are the first two monographic studies of Oré's foundational text. Both works should contribute to a new recognition of the lettered creole friar's contribution to the transformation of the Andean world.

"lettered" creole. Friar Oré was exceptionally busy during the next three years. Substantial energy was consumed in advocacy before the royal councils in support of missionary endeavors in Florida and elsewhere. His counsel was now a voice to be respected, given his broad experience in dealing with non-Christians and his understanding of the often contentious relationship between civil and religious authorities. His advocacy seems tempered and designed to convince without alienating, a character trait that served him well. His expertise with the difficult conditions in La Florida, the need to make certain the area was securely defended, well-settled, and secured by amicable relations with its Indigenous population, was sealed with the report's publication. Perhaps it also sealed Oré's appointment as bishop of Concepción, Chile.

Chapter 9

Theodor de Bry and the Tradition of Grand Voyages

HELMUT FLACHENECKER

Cruel Conquistadors—Good Indians

Bartolomé de Las Casas, Dominican and eyewitness in Mexico, made a clear judgment about the role of certain Spanish conquistadors in Florida: they were "tyrants." They organized "carnage and butchery" among "the poor, harmless natives," which was a crime according to God's commandments. The Floridian Indians—de Las Casas mentioned no specific names—were described as "handsome and intelligent and who lived in well-ordered and structured societies." On another occasion the Indians "joyfully" organized a banquet for the foreigners, only to be killed and plundered afterward.[1] Las Casas's crucial consideration rotated around this point: How could these traumatized people be convinced for a new faith in a loving God? He wrote *A Short Account of the Destruction of the Indies* in 1542, fifty years after the arrival of Spaniards in the New World. At this time Las Casas had "the King's ear," because the latter was dissatisfied with the conquistadors, who mostly ignored his will.[2] Was Las Casas right about his general estimation of hospitable Indians and barbarous Spaniards?

Cruel Indians—Peaceful Foreigners

At the core of this paper is the "simple" question: What did Europeans know about America, especially Florida and its population? Roughly speaking there are diverse types of sources: On one side we have a lot of administrative documents by Spanish Church and government authorities (charters, official letters), and on the other side we have documentation. But chronicles from travelers and images, which were produced for a wider audience by engravers to illustrate texts and illustrate certain statements, are the principal focus of

1. Bartolomé de Las Casas, *A Short Account of the Destruction of the Indies*, ed. and trans. Nigel Griffin (London: Penguin, 1992), 102–104.

2. Daniel Castro, *Another Face of Empire: Bartolomé de Las Casas, Indigenous Rights, and Ecclesiastical Imperialism* (Durham and London: Duke University Press, 2007), 104. Widely circulated, the author's intention was "to shock and impress on the reader the horrors."

this paper. The latter category of information was launched in the second half of the sixteenth century. Immediately methodological questions arise: Are they credible? Which degree of accuracy do these sources have? When travelers returned home to Europe, they told stories about what they had seen or experienced. Listeners in their homelands typically had no means of verifying what they had read or heard about the New World.

One of the most popular traveler books, written by German Hans Staden,[3] sharpened "European stereotypes about wild, man-eating savages, fueling popular fantasies about New World peoples that could justify a sense of European superiority," as Eve M. Duffy and Alida C. Metcalf eloquently summarized.[4] Staden, who lived with the Tupinambá in current-day Brazil for months, reported in 1557 in some ways the opposite image of indigenous people compared to Las Casas.

The cannibalism by the Tupinambá, which he said he witnessed, demonstrates also the shocking lust for sensation at home, so that Europeans could act with self-assurance in their beliefs that all pagans are wild, animal-like, and therefore inferior to themselves—and so they have full rights to conquer the New World to change the situation in the name of Christ. And for Staden it was an excellent topic, which was advertised in form of a woodcut on the title page of his book, where a cannibal ate roasted human legs. Sensation was offered in the long title as well: "History and Description of a Land Belonging to a Wild, Naked, Savage, and Man-Eating People, Situated in the New World."[5] Staden insisted on a story that he knew through his own experience, and which was unknown in Germany, and especially in Hesse.

---

3. Staden traveled as a mercenary in the Portuguese military to the northeastern coast of Brazil in 1547. After participating in several battles against Indians and the French, he returned to Europe in late 1548. In 1549 or 1550 he set out for Brazil; after severe thunderstorms he shipwrecked, was rescued, and then lived in a Portuguese trading post in São Vicente for a time where he assisted the Portuguese as a gunner. Staden was captured by the Tupinambá Indians in early 1553. For nine months he lived among them, until he was rescued by the crew of a French ship in 1554. After returning to his Hessian homeland, he worked in a gun powder mill and as a soap boiler. He likely died of the plague. See Eva M. Duffy and Alida C. Metcalf, *The Return of Hans Staden: A Go-between in the Atlantic World* (Baltimore: The Johns Hopkins University Press, 2012).

4. Duffy and Metcalf, *The Return of Hans Staden*, 3.

5. Franz Obermeier and Wolfgang Schiffner, eds., "*1557 Warhaftige Historia vnd beschreibung eyner Landtschafft der Wilden / Nacketen / Grimmigen Menschenfresser Leuthen / in der Newenwelt America gelegen / vor vnd nach Christi geburt im Land zû Hessn vnbekant / biß uff dise ij. nechst vergangene jar / Da sie Hans Staden von Homberg auß Hessen durch sein eygne erfarung erkant / vnd yetzo durch den truck an tag gibt.*" —*Die Wahrhaftige Historia—das erste Brasilienbuch. Akten des Wolfhager Kongresses zu 450 Jahren Hans-Staden-Rezeption*, Fontes Americanae 2 (Kiel: Westensee-Verlag, 2008); Markus Klaus Schäffauer, "Die Vision der Gegessenen: Hans Staden, Autor des Kannibalismus," in *Portugal und das Heilige Römische Reich (16.–18. Jahrhundert)*, ed. Alexandra Curvelo and Madalena Simões (Münster: Aschendorff, 2011), 105–126; Eve M. Duffy and Alida Met-

All of the abovementioned narratives followed already well-known structures. During an expansionist period in twelfth-century Europe, a number of chroniclers, such as Gerald of Wales, realized the social, economic, and religious differences between Spanish readers compared to the Irish and Welsh people, as well as Scandinavians and Slavs (Poles, Hungarians). To provide self-assurance to people (on the socioeconomic level) in Western Europe, the authors worked with stereotypes of wild societies on the margins. For instance, in 1190 Gerald of Wales, described the Irish as uncultivated human beings, as they were nearly naked (and therefore hardly Christians) and had men and women who had immoral relationships.[6]

Cannibalism stories were widespread. Christopher Columbus reported on man-eating Indians in the Caribbean in 1492 and Amerigo Vespucci made assertions about the same phenomenon in South America in 1499. For Vespucci, the Indians were "rational animals" to stress the fact that their moral status was between that of wild animals and human beings. These authors specifically wrote what European readers wanted to read about people who ate their enemies.[7] Staden was also seduced into telling his audience what they wanted to hear, knowing that they never could prove or disprove it.

Jacques Le Moyne, Floridian Indians, and Theodor de Bry: *Les Grands Voyages* (1590–1634)

The English portrait painter John White officially joined the expedition of Sir Richard Grenville to present-day North Carolina. He portrayed many Native people, starting with the Carolina Algonquians, on one of his five or more journeys to the New World.[8] These paintings, but in the case of two

calf, *The Return of Hans Staden: A Go-between in the Atlantic World* (Baltimore: The Johns Hopkins University Pres, 2012), available at http://gutenberg.spiegel.de/buch/ warhaftige-historia-5531/1 (accessed 28 July 2018).

6. Gerald of Wales, *The History and Topography of Ireland*, trans. John J. O'Meara (Harmondsworth: Penguin, 1988), 73–76 ("Intercourse between human beings and animals"), 100–103 ("Nature, customs of the people"), 106 ("Ignorant of the rudiments of the Faith"), 110–112 (Lack of Baptism); Robert Bartlett, *Gerald of Wales: A Voice of the Middle Ages* (Stroud: The History Press, 2006), 36–44, 131–138. For a more general perspective on the trope of "wild men" lacking perhaps an eye or a foot, see Richard Bernheimer, *Wild Men in the Middle Ages* (Cambridge: Harvard University Press, 1952), 31; and David Abulafia, *The Discovery of Mankind: Atlantic Encounters in the Age of Columbus* (New Haven, CT and London: Yale University Press, 2008), 18–20.

7. Abulafia, *Discovery of Mankind*, 155–158, 251–258.

8. White gave his Indians specific bodies and faces, while de Bry changed them to more European faces. Henry Keazor, "Theodor de Bry's Images for America," in *Print Quarterly* 15, no. 2 (1998): 131–149, see 134. De Bry obtained White's picture via Richard Hakluyt, the famous English geographer (ca. 1552–1616). Michiel van Groesen, *The Representations of the Overseas World in the De Bry Collection of Voyages (1590–1634)*, Library

Floridian Indians, he surely took a copy from Jacques Le Moyne de Morgues, because White never visited Florida, as far as is known.

Le Moyne's career is roughly comparable to White's, as he too was the official artist of a colonial expedition of French Huguenots.[9] Jacques Le Moyne de Morgues was born in Dieppe in the Normandy region (ca. 1533), which was a center of cartography and illumination. After surviving Spanish attacks in Florida, he arrived safely at Swansea Bay (Wales) in 1565. He traveled via Bristol to Paris in early 1566. In May 1581 he lived in London because of his religion. One child was born to him and Jeane, his wife. His last will is dated May 16, 1588. He was approximately 55 years old when he died.[10]

Le Moyne also visited Florida in 1564.[11] He described the "official" relationship with the Indians, as well as the internal struggles of the French group of settlers.

In summary, there are three types of sources: a translation of Le Moyne's reports, including his engravings revised by an editor, and short captions under the pictures printed at the end of the reports. The degree of revision to Le Moyne's reports is unknown, as is the identity of the editor.

Las Casas's story,[12] Staden's diary,[13] and drawings by White and Le Moyne were first published by Theodor de Bry (1528–1598). He was a goldsmith and copper-plate engraver in Antwerp and London, and later started a business as a wealthy but "mid-sized" editor, publisher, and bookseller in Frankfurt, a business that was continued by his two sons. De Bry was born in Liège as a Reformed Calvinist, lived in Strasbourg as a refugee, married his first wife there, and then emigrated to Antwerp and London. After choosing to settle

---

of the Written World, 2 (Leiden, Boston: Brill, 2008), 112. See also A. Greve, *Die Konstruktion Amerikas, Bilderpolitik in den "Grand Voyages" aus der Werkstatt de Bry* (Köln, Weimar, Wien: Böhlau, 2004).

9. Paul Hulton, *America 1585: The Complete Drawings of John White*, University of North Carolina Press and British Museum Publications (Milan: University of North Carolina, 1984), 7–9.

10. The will is edited and translated to English in *The Work of Jacques Le Moyne de Morgues: A Huguenot Artist in France, Florida and England*, ed. Paul Hulton, 2 vols. (London: British Museum, 1977), 1:219.

11. "Jacque Le Moyne de Morgues: A Biographical Sketch," in *The Work of Jacques Le Moyne*, vol. 1, 3–12.

12. Van Groesen, *Representations*, appendix one (publications of the de Bry firm), 406: "Narratio regionum indicarum per Hispanos quosdam devastatarum verissima" (1598); 410: "Warhafftiger und gründtlicher Bericht Der Hispanieer grewlichen, und abschewlichen Tyranney, von ihnen in den West Indien, so die Neuwe Welt genennet wirt, begangen" (410); 445: 2nd ed. of German version (1613); 448: 2nd ed. of Latin version (1614).

13. Van Groesen, *Representations*, 393: "Americae tertia pars Memorabile provinciae Brasiliae Historiam continens. . ." (1592); 394: "Drittes Buch Americae, Darinn Brasilia durch Johann Staden. . ." (1593); 424: 2nd ed. of Latin version (1605); 434: 2nd ed. of German version (1610).

in Frankfurt in 1588, where he became a citizen, he married a second time and died there. Father and sons were never in complete agreement about business management; neither son traveled to the New World.[14]

In 1591, de Bry issued the reports by Jacques Le Moyne de Morgues and René de Laudonnière, in Latin and in German,[15] which contained the earliest known European images of Native Americans in what is now Florida.[16] Latin was the common language of European intellectuals, as well as the Catholic Church.[17] The book was never published in Spanish because of de Bry's hostility vis-à-vis the Catholic king.[18] It is striking that the Latin and German translations are not similar; de Bry created "different translations for different readerships."[19]

---

14. Most detailed by van Goesen, *Representations*, 51–78; Margarete Braun-Ronsdorf, "Bry, Theodor," in *Neue Deutsche Bibliographie* 2 (1955), 693; Neil J. Whitehead, "Bry, Theodore de (1528–1598)," in *Literature of Travel and Exploration*, vol. 1, *A to F*, ed. Jennifer Speake and Fitzroy Dearborn (New York: Fitzroy Dearborn Publishers, 2003), 134–136.

15. Van Groesen, *Representations*, 392: "1591 Brevis narration eorum quae in Florida Americae provincia Gallis acciderunt . . . and Der ander Theyl, der Newlich erfundenen Lantschafft Americae, Von dreyen Schiffahrten, so die Frantzosen in Floridam (die gegen Nidergang gelegen) gethan. . ."; 420, 1603, 2nd ed. of German version; 432: 1609, 2nd ed. of Latin version. Ad. Siret, "Bry (Théodore de)," in *Biographie Nationale de l'Académie Royale de Belgique*, vol. 3 (Brussels: Établissements Émile Bruylant, 1872), 127.

16. Hulton, *Work of Jacques Le Moyne*, contains the Latin version of Le Moynes' report (vol. 1, 87–113) and an English translation (117–138), as well as the engravings plus Latin caption texts (vol. 2, pl. 93–134); Michael Alexander, *Discovering the New World Based on the works of Theodor de Bry* (New York: Harper and Row, 1976) (engravings plus legends text in English translation, 17–59); *The New World: The First Pictures of America*, by John White and engravings by Theodore de Bry, ed. and annot. Stefan Lorant (New York: Duell, Sloan & Pearce, 1946; 2nd ed. 1965) (engravings plus English legends text plus Le Moyne report in English). For critical approach to Lorant's book, see review by Samuel E. Morison in *The William and Mary Quarterly* 4, no. 1 (1947): 87–89. See also Charles E. Bennett, *Settlement of Florida* (Jacksonville: University of Florida Press, 1968) (colored engraving, but poor quality, plus English legends text). A German collection of the *Grand Voyage* from 1591 version, and engravings plus legends text, is available at https://www. floridamemory.com/collections/debry/. The figures in this essay are published courtesy of the State Archives of Florida.

17. De Bry hoped for Catholic readers as well: Van Groesen, *Representations*, 243–245; Michiel van Groesen, "Entrepreneurs of Translation: Latin and the Vernacular in the Editorial Strategy of the De Bry Publishing House," in *Translating Knowledge in the Early Modern Low Countries*, ed. Harold J. Cook and Sven Dupré (Wien, Zürich, Berlin: LIT Verlag, 2012), 107–128, see 113. De Bry's sons favored French over Latin for books about fortification techniques (109).

18. Lauren Beck, "Illustrating the Conquest in the Long Eighteenth Century: Theodore de Bry and His Legacy," in *Book Illustration in the Long Eighteenth Century: Reconfiguring the Visual Periphery of the Text*, ed. Christina Ionescu (Cambridge: Cambridge Scholars Publishing, 2011), 501–540, see 504.

19. Van Groesen, "Entrepreneurs of Translation," 123. Therefore, the legend text will be cited in Latin, German, and English in the following annotations.

De Bry was a commercial bookseller who combined religious interests with commercial opportunities. He needed a large group of co-workers to publish his America series: interpreters, who translated the reports from English, French, Dutch, Italian, and other languages into Latin and German, as well as engravers, designers, and printers.[20] Translations as "an instrument to manipulate the image of the non-European world"[21] and engravings were crafted in a parallel fashion, as the latter were constructions combining elements of multiple pictures. Van Groesen summarized: "This technique was common practice in the early modern period, and may have helped readers to understand the illustrations."[22] This means that the content of the engravings cannot be understood as representations of objective reality. These "newly constructed engravings"[23] were combined with captions that summarize engraving contents.[24] The latter were *not* created by the travel narrative writers.

The paintings for the *Grand Voyages* that deal specifically with Florida were originally created by the abovementioned Le Moyne, who was one of the few survivors of the French group who were slaughtered by Pedro Menéndez de Avilés. De Bry bought the paintings from Le Moyne's widow in London in 1588, after Le Moyne passed away, and this shortly after a first face-to-face meeting between the two men.[25] De Bry also modified pictures—Le Moyne's pictures survived only in this form[26]—so that American Indians look generally more like Europeans. Once again, the engravings reflect expectations of European readers.

Twenty-five volumes of *The Great Voyages* were published about the voyages to the "West Indies" (i.e., the Americas, or "Great Voyages," 13 vols.) and the "East Indies" (i.e., India, Japan, and China, or "Small Voyages," 12 vols.) from 1590 through 1634. The books were released first by de Bry, then by his sons Johan Israel and Johan Theodor and, finally, by Matthäus Merian, who married de Bry's granddaughter.[27] The second publication of the series,

20. Van Groesen, *Representations* 47–49, 74–77, 116–122; van Groesen, "Entrepreneurs of Translation" 110 (Names of the five translators).

21. Van Groesen, "Entrepreneurs of Translation," 113.

22. Van Groesen, *Representations*, 124.

23. Ibid., 125 (quotation), 125–129 (on captions).

24. Michèle Duchet, "Le Text grave de Théodore De Bry," in *L'Amérique de Théodore De Bry: Une collection de voyages protestante du XVIe siècle: Quatre études d'iconographie*, ed. Michèle Duchet, Daniel Defert, Frank Lestringant, Jacques Forge (Paris: Centre national de la recherche scientifique, 1987), 18–34.

25. Van Groesen, *Representations*, 113.

26. Except for one showing the French coat of arms and worshipping Indians, which Lorant encountered and published for the first time in 1951, and then in the second of *The New World*, 32. According to Lorant, this painting "had disappeared again." Verification of Lorant's discovery is no longer possible.

27. Van Groesen, *Representations*, 92; Montague Spencer Giuseppi, "The Work of Theodore De Bry and His Sons, Engravers," in *Proceedings of the Huguenot Society of*

dated 1591, was about the Huguenot expedition to Florida. According to Bernadette Bucher, the Great Voyages series comprised "a representation of the New World for the eyes of the Old."[28] Nearly a century after Columbus's encounters across the Atlantic, an oeuvre was published that showed highly distinguished Europeans in the New World and its inhabitants, the Amerindians, in pictures.[29] It is difficult to tell the number of copies printed; van Groesen suggested "up to 1,000."[30]

One reason for the emergence of this type of publication is the introduction and use of a new technique, copperplate engraving, in the late sixteenth century. Copperplate engraving was twice as costly as the older wood-engraving technique. However, the copperplate engravings were more precise and clear-cut and larger print runs were possible.[31] Protestant publishers were the first to take advantage of this new technique for mass production. De Bry and others, for instance, wanted to support Protestant settlement of colonial territories. Thus, the soil of newly discovered lands was praised for its fertility.[32] A typical caption in one such publication glorifies the "beautiful country, well wooded with oak, cedar, and various other trees. The woods abounded in turkeys and deer."[33]

De Bry published adventures, especially struggles against the alleged gruesome and licentious Spaniards. This is the reason why he illustrated the Las Casas report as well.[34] De Bry's abhorrence for Catholicism strengthened his support of the so-called "Black Legend" and led him to create many anti-Spanish engravings.[35] In addition, the interests of big maritime trading companies, such as the English Virginia Company or the Dutch East India Company, were also important.[36] Their financial success depended, at least

London 11/2 (1916), 204–226; Jennifer Speake, "Collections of Literature of Travel and Exploration: Anthologies," in *Literature of Travel and Exploration*, 263–266. Speake suggests (p. 264) that "The de Bry/Merian compilations . . . set a trend for long-running projects in travel publishing."

28. Bernadette Bucher, *Icon and Conquest: A Structural Analysis of the Illustrations of De Bry's Great Voyages* (Chicago, London: University of Chicago Press, 1981), 3; Van Groesen, *Representations*, 10.

29. Bucher, *Icon and Conquest*, 5.

30. Van Groesen, *Representations*, 133.

31. Bucher, *Icon and Conquest*, 4. See also Van Groesen, *Representations*, 80.

32. Van Groesen, *Representations*, 175.

33. Lorant, *The New World*, 45; Hulton, *Work of Jacques Le Moyne*, vol. 2, pl. 97: *[A]moenissimus esse locum compererunt; nam quercubus cedis et aliis arborum generibus consitus erat*; Grand Voyages (German ed.), pl. 5: *[H]aben sie befunden, daß es der allerlustigst Ort war, sintemal es voll Eychen, Cedern vnd allerley anderer Baeume stunde.*

34. Van Groesen, *Representations*, 117; Beck, "Illustrating the Conquest," 506–522; Abulafia, *Discovery of Mankind*, 311–312; Bartolomé de Las Casas, *Der Spiegel der Spanischen Tyrannie*, illustrated by de Bry (Frankfurt: De Bry, 1598).

35. Keazor, "De Bry's Images," 148; Beck, "Illustrating the Conquest," 502.

36. Bucher, *Icon and Conquest*, 6, 10.

indirectly, on the impression Europeans had of world regions that were largely unknown for most people in the "Old World." Also readers' "simple curiosity" and its financial exploitation explain de Bry's engagement and the great popularity of the America series. His publishing policy was determined by "caution and prudence," which was not driven by his Calvinism alone.[37]

De Bry worked with the new technique at his engraving workshops in Frankfurt and Oppenheim,[38] both of which were specialized in mass production. This meant that "De Bry recycled images in whole and in part"[39] so he could reuse them in various other series. The total number of the firm's publications thus far known is over 242.[40]

In conclusion, de Bry took illustrations for the *Great Voyages* from artisans who were in America, and adjusted it to readers' taste. De Bry "borrowed, melded, arranged and adopted" original pictures according to his actual editorial needs.[41] He also used others' pictures for creating his "iconographic models" of the population in the New World.[42] The Indians became Europeanized.[43]

De Bry's Sources of Information

Between 1562 and 1565 France tried to establish French settlers in northern Florida.[44] This was the political background for Le Moyne's journey to the New World. His report includes critiques of the leaders of the settler group, René Goulaine de Laudonnière (1542–1582).[45] Le Moyne received an invitation from French King Charles IX (1560–1574) to join the voyage. In his own words, his task was "to chart the sea coast and to observe the situation of the towns and the depth and course of the rivers, and also the harbours, the people's houses, and anything new . . . in that province."[46]

---

37. Van Groesen, *Representations*, 105. He also looked for Catholic readers, so he accepted a dedication to the prince-bishop of Wuerzburg, Julius Echter, from Mestelbrunn. Ibid., 329, 395.

38. Ibid., 107–112; Siret, "Bry (Théodore de)," 126.

39. Beck, "Illustrating the Conquest," 507.

40. Van Groesen, *Representations*, 389–474 (list of publications of de Bry firm), ibid. 389: "The list contains all works published by the De Bry firm, whether by Theodore, by his widow, by his two sons or by Johan Theodore alone." In "Bry, Theodor," 693, Braun-Ronsdorf writes that she knows of only 173.

41. Keazor, "De Bry's Images," 135.

42. Bucher, *Icon and Conquest*, 16. In total, the *Great Voyages* consist of thirteen parts!

43. Susi Colin, *Das Bild des Indianers im 16: Jahrhundert* (Idstein: Schulz-Kirchner, 1988).

44. D.B. Quinn, "The attempted colonization of Florida by the French, 1562–1565," in Hulton, *Work of Jacques Le Moyne*, vol. 1, 17–44; Lorant, *The New World*, 10–27.

45. The report by Laudonnière is published in an English translation [with the engravings] by W. John Faupel, *A Foothold in Florida* (Sommerset, England: Castle Cary/Antique Atlas, 1992).

Information about the new discoveries was known only by a small group of politically influential people and merchants in Western Europe. They kept it, more or less, as a secret. Consequently, White's and Le Moyne's work had an important influence on the transfer of knowledge across the Atlantic. In the sixteenth century, the great majority of Europeans had little or no news about events on the other side of the great ocean.[47] "Real" Indians could be observed only as a curiosity, and only if you lived in a port city like Seville or Barcelona, Lisbon or Rouen, Bristol or London, and such "sightings" were rare. The few woodcuts that existed before de Bry's publications showed Indians as naked men and women.

De Bry's publications changed this situation a bit, but his audience was very small. Who read the *Great Voyages*? Generally speaking, members of the European aristocracy, mostly Protestants, and German aristocrats in particular,[48] merchants, artisans, and university-educated people. In brief, the great sum of plates in the *Great Voyages* attracted a limited number of wealthy consumers.

The plates and the text are grouped in different ways. Some plates related to different texts and therefore were published more than once. Diverse texts could be preceded by a single plate. Some illustrations, on the other hand, have no direct link to any part of the texts. Certain plates show a precise event (according to Bucher, a "monoscenic method"), perhaps scenes for pleasure and amusement for the Indians, where the Europeans were often only spectators and stood on the sidelines, as discussed later. Or a scene could depict several simultaneous actions, such as a landscape with hunting in the woods and fishing in the river (Bucher calls this the "simultaneous method"). Or several actions linked in the narrative were brought together, mostly in circular order (so-called "rotative method"). Chronology or the passage of time was ignored in such compositions. For example, you can see the birth of a baby, nursing by the mother, and carefree childhood in a single plate. Or de Bry used a "serial method," where events are clearly depicted as occurring over a period time.[49] Some engravings show fantasy elements in ethnography and zoology, such as the crocodiles. In contrast, the legends commenting on or describing the plates relate factual occurrences while the illustrations contain fantastic elements. As a result, writes Bucher, "a mythico-historical amalgam" was constructed, which "intended to introduce America's conquest and colonization to Europeans."[50]

---

46. Hulton, *Work of Jacques Le Moyne*, vol. 1, 119.
47. Bucher, *Icon and Conquest*, 4.
48. For example, rulers of Wuerttemberg, Brandenburg, Saxony. See Van Groesen, *Representations*, 96, 329; Bucher, *Icon and Conquest*, 11.
49. Bucher, *Icon and Conquest*, 24–30, where all these methods are described.
50. Ibid., 22.

French Settlers and Floridian Indians: A Story of Misunderstanding?

In June 22, 1564, when Le Moyne arrived in Florida, which he calls "New France," his party was met by friendly Indians who fed the Frenchmen maize and meat from lizards and other native animals.[51] Without such assistance, foreigners would not survive the always critical starting point of a new settlement. Chief Athore visited the French in their newly built Fort Caroline.[52] The chief was surrounded by counselors, a sorcerer, and flute players whose music was "bad" for European ears. But flautists were an essential part of a chief's arrival or ceremonial event.[53] Then the official negotiations started and ended with the chief becoming an ally of the French king.[54] The Indians also helped the French by constructing the fort.

The engravings simultaneously show the arrival of the French fleet, Frenchmen going ashore, fishing Indians, and a first meeting between the two groups. Then the French erected a stone monument (often called a "column") with the French king's coat of arms to mark the Crown's seizure of land and people. This symbol of political sovereignty was not fully understood by the Indians. So, they interpreted it according to their own cultural ways in which gifts played a an important role by demonstrating relationships with foreigners with whom they wanted an amicable relationship.[55] They offered foodstuffs arranged in an appealing way such as in front of an altar. For the Natives, the foreigners' monument sculpture seemed to be an important place for the French, interpreted as a kind of sacred place, which they "wreathed with flowers and boughs of the choicest trees." The image could also be interpreted as the Indians' veneration of the French king and his omnipresence. Both groups stand apart in the engraving, with only the chief having joined the newcomers. According to the engraving legend, some Indians demanded that the French "kiss the column," and the text suggests that they did so.[56] Saturiba, son of Chief Athore, renewed the treaty with the French, and he agreed to participate in building their fort.[57]

---

51. The Europeans typically disliked the taste of reptiles. See Van Groesen, *Representations*, 180.

52. Hulton, *Work of Jacques Le Moyne*, vol. 1, 120.

53. Jerald T. Milanich, *The Timucua*, The Peoples of America series (Oxford: Malden, 1999), 153.

54. Frank Lestrigant, "L'automne des cannibals ou les outils de la conquête," in *L'Amérique de Théodore De Bry*, 70.

55. Milanich, *Timucua*, 152.

56. Lorant, *The New World*, 51; Hulton, *Work of Jacques Le Moyne*, vol. 2, pl. 100: "Proximi facti, animadverterunt Indos hoc saxum non secus atque idolum colere: nam ipsi Rex eo salutato, et exhibito qualem a suis subditis accipere solet honore, osculum fixit, quem imitate sunt ipsius subditi, ut idem faceremus adhortati." See *Grand Voyages* (German

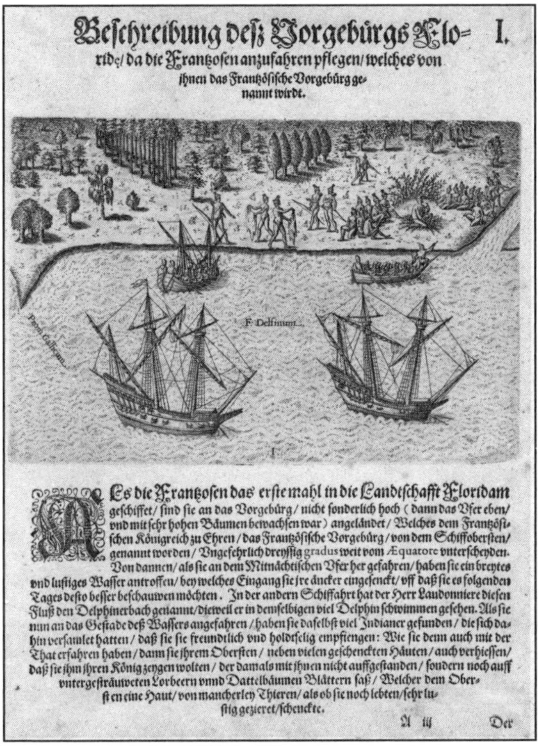
Beschreibung deß Vorgebürgs Flo- I.
ridæ/ da die Frantzosen anzufahren pflegen/ welches von
jhnen das Frantzösische Vorgebürg ge-
nannt wirdt.

ALs die Frantzosen das erste mahl in die Landtschafft Floridam geschiffet/ sind sie an das Vorgebürg/ nicht sonderlich hoch (dann das Vfer eben/ vnd mit sehr hohen Bäumen bewachsen war) angeländet/ Welches dem Frantzösischen Königreich zu Ehren/ das Frantzösische Vorgebürg/ von dem Schiffobersten/ genannt worden/ Vngefehrlich dreyssig gradus weit vom Æquatore vnterscheyden. Von dannen/ als sie an dem Mitnächtischen Vfer her gefahren/ haben sie ein breytes vnd lustiges Wasser antroffen/ bey welches Eingang sie jre ancker eingesenckt/ vff daß sie es folgenden Tages desto besser beschauwen möchten. In der andern Schiffahrt hat der Herr Laudonniere diesen Fluß den Delphinerbach genannt/ dieweil er in demselbigen viel Delphin schwimmen gesehen. Als sie nun an das Gestade deß Wassers angefahren/ haben sie daselbst viel Indianer gefunden/ die sich dahin versamlet hatten/ daß sie sie freundtlich vnd holdtselig empfiengen: Wie sie denn auch mit der That erfahren haben/ dann sie jhrem Obersten/ neben vielen geschenckten Häuten/ auch verhiessen/ daß sie jhm jhren König zeygen wolten/ der damals mit jhnen nicht auffgestanden/ sondern noch auff vntergesträuweten Lorbeern vnnd Dattelbäumen Blättern saß/ Welcher dem Obersten eine Haut/ von mancherley Thieren/ als ob sie noch lebten/ sehr lustig gezieret/ schenckte.

A iij Der

FIGURE 1. Plate I: The Coast of Florida, at Which the French Entered the Country. (All figures published courtesy of the State Archives of Florida)

Body imagery was very important for self-representation on both sides, or at least what we can perceive via European interpretations.[58] Interestingly, the plate shows the Indian chief taller than his European counterpart. When the French arrived, according to the caption, they were welcomed without any "enmity"; the chief was "very handsome, wise, honorable, and strong,

ed.), pl. 8: "Da sie nun nahe hinzu kamen, merckten sie, daß die Indier diesen Stein nicht anderst als ein Goetzen verehrt: Denn in der Koenig selbst mit solchen Geberden (wie im seine Underthanen zu thun pflegen) geehrt vnd darauff gekuesset, welchem alsbald seine Underthanen gefolget, vns auch selbst solchs zu thun vermanet."

57. Lorant, *The New World*, 57: "[T]he French made treaty with Saturiba, the great chief of the adjoining country. They had agreed to erect a fort in his territory. . ."; Hulton, *Work of Jacques Le Moyne*, vol. 2, pl. 103: "Gallos cum Saturioua Rege potente eorum vicino foedus et amicitiam contraxisse, ut arcem in ejus ditione extruere possent. . ."; *Grand Voyages* (German ed.), pl. 11: [W]ie die Frantzosen mit dem Koenig Saturioua, so mechtig vnd ihr Nachbar war, Freundtschafft gemacht haben, daß sie in seinem Landt ein Festung bauwen möchten. . . ."

58. Van Groesen, *Representations*, 205–210.

and at least half a foot taller than the tallest of our men. He was grave and modest, and his bearing was majestic."[59] After this very positive introduction, the image also tells us that he was a pagan: He was nearly naked but his body was covered by tattoos[60] and his hair full of ornaments. He wears some jewelry and, in another illustration, he wears some type of rounded plates, perhaps a gorget made from copper.[61] The chief again dominates the scene as he stands before a group of mourning widows formally making requests for assistance, all of whom were nearly naked and had long hair. Even though Timucua were not cannibals, they were wild, un-Christianized, uncultivated, barbaric. In European eyes, nakedness merited contempt.[62] Long hair on men as well as women was a sign of fertility. When wives became widows, they cut their hair as a sign of grief. Remarriage was allowed only when her hair was (again) long enough, at least, according to what de Bry and co-workers imagined about indigenous customs.[63]

Women as mothers show well-shaped bodies. All Indian bodies are portrayed with ideal European models in common, perhaps in a kind of Greco-Roman style. All male and female Indians have well-proportioned physiques[64] and are well-nourished; no one seems to be even a bit thick in the torso, much less elderly. It may be instructive to compare them with bodies from Albrecht Dürer (1471–1528), the famous painter and engraver, who lived one hundred

---

59. Lorant, *The New World*, 57; Hulton, *Work of Jacques Le Moyne*, vol. 2, pl. 100: "Est vero hic Rex Athore formosus admodum, prudens, honestus, robustus et procerae admodum staturae, nostrorum hominum maximos sesquipeda superans, modesta quadam gravitate praeditus, ut in eo majestas spectabilis reluceat. . ." See also *Grand Voyages* (German ed.), pl. 8: "Dieser Koenig Athore aber ist einschoene Person, klug, zuechtig, starck vnd groß, anderthalben Schuech laenger dann der Groesseste vnter vns."

60. Milanich, *Timucua*, 59: "[T]attooed with designs in azure, red, and black." Tattoos and war paints are, in Christian eyes, an act of self-mutilation. See also Van Groesen, *Representations*, 189–191; Lorant, *The New World*, 57: "[T]he whole force—in war paint and feathers—sat down in a circle. . ."; Hulton, *Work of Jacques Le Moyne*, vol. 2, pl. 100: "[M]ilites pro consuetudine Indica pennis et aliis rebus ornatos in planiciem accersit. . ."; *Grand Voyages* (German ed.), pl. 11: "[S]seine Kriegsknecht (nach Indianischer Gewonheyt mit Ferdern vnd andern dingen gezieret). . . ." According to Abulafia, *Discovery of Mankind*, 164–166, all chiefs Columbus talked to in the Caribbean were naked.

61. Milanich, *Timucua*, 59, 154: The copper came from the Appalachian Mountains, not from the Timucua region itself.

62. Van Groesen, *Representations*, 195–199.

63. Lorant, *The New World*, 73; Hulton, *Work of Jacques Le Moyne*, vol. 2, pl. 111; *Grand Voyages* (German edition), pl. 19.

64. Milanich, *Timucua*, 56: "Timucua were sturdy, muscular, and athletic. Hawk (not flat) noses were frequently mentioned, and the French explorers particularly admired the shapely and well-proportioned physiques of the people. . . . Women were noted to have been lighter body weights than the men." Both men and women had long fingernails, which also could be used as weapons.

FIGURE 2. Plate 21: Mode of Tilling and Planting.

years earlier in Nürnberg.[65] Nudes by European artists always resembled antique statues—they have a "Greek body esthetic."[66] Could de Bry have followed this kind of a scheme?

The story of misunderstanding between Indians and foreigners appeared to start at the very beginning of the relationship. All these problems were mentioned in Le Moyne's report, but would never be visualized in the engravings. Soon there were continual complaints in the French group about bad

65. Dürer knew, by the way, about artifacts from Mexico. He saw them in Brussels (Letter between August 26th and September 3rd 1520): William Martin Conway, *Literary Remains of Albrecht Dürer* (Cambridge: University Press, 1889), 101–102: "I saw the things which have been brought to the King from the new land of gold [Mexico], a sun all of gold a whole fathom broad, and a moon all of silver of the same size. . . . All the days of my life I have seen nothing that rejoiced my heart so much as these things, for I saw amongst them wonderful works of art, and I marveled at the subtle *Ingenia* of men in foreign lands. Indeed I cannot express all that I thought there."

66. Keazor, "De Bry's Images," 146.

food and Laudonnière's defective communications. Le Moyne added, "What is worse, many of these people, who professed that they wanted to live in accordance with the more genuine teaching of the Gospel, were very displeased with him because they were deprived of a minister of the Holy Word."[67] The accusations against Laudonnière increased because of the absence of corn and of Huguenot pastors. A conflict arose[68] between two competing groups in the French community: those who wanted to live a pious and seclusive life in the New World and others who wanted to make a fortune. Despite a friendly beginning, some of the French settlers hoped to become rich quickly by finding gold.

Internal quarrels and intergroup misunderstandings also minimized French support for Satouriwa. The foreigners did not rely exclusively on Satouriwa, and negotiations with other chiefs and groups started as well.[69] Outina, chief of a nearby tribe, sent urgently desired gold to the French settlers to persuade them to support him. The gold was most certainly found in the mountains called Apalatci.[70] The French supported the chief against his enemies, because "the only route to the Appalachian Mountains, where gold and silver were found, passed through Outina's territory."[71] Regardless of this story's veracity, Europeans abroad and at home, wanted to hear such stories—and the Indians delivered them.[72] Gold should also come from Spanish ships that wrecked on the Floridian coast.[73]

The plates depict this critical situation affecting the settlers in only one way. The religious side was not of real interest, and there are no indications of missionary efforts among the Timucua. What really did matter to de Bry, was the search for gold, silver, and copper. The captions mentioned this theme often: One reason for the selected location for Fort Caroline was gold and

---

67. Hulton, *Work of Jacques Le Moyne*, vol. 1, 121; Lorant, *The New World*, 42.

68. Hulton, *Work of Jacques Le Moyne*, vol. 1, 124–125; Lorant, *The New World*, 44–50.

69. Hulton, *Work of Jacques Le Moyne*, vol. 1, 122; Lorant, *The New World*, 48.

70. Hulton, *Work of Jacques Le Moyne*, vol. 1, 123–124; Lorant, *The New World*, 42.

71. Lorant, *The New World*, 59; Hulton, *Work of Jacques Le Moyne*, vol. 2, pl. 104: "Ictum est idfoedus, quia per eius Regis dicionem, et terrestri itinere, et adversis fluminibus aditus solum patebat ad montes Apalatcy, in quibus nascitur aurum, argentum et aes"; *Grand Voyages* (German ed.), pl. 12: "Dieser Bundt aber ward darumb auffgericht, weil durch diß KönigsGebiet allein zu Lande vnd das Wasser vffwarts man den Paß zum Gebuerg Apalatcy, darinn viel Golt, Silber vnd Ertz wechst, haben koendt. . . ."

72. Columbus, for example, believed the story of an island named "Babeque," where incredible quantities of gold could be found. This type of fantasy made Europeans happy. See Abulafia, *Discovery of Mankind*, 155, 166.

73. Hulton, *Work of Jacques Le Moyne*, vol. 1, 127; Lorant, *The New World*, 58. The topic "gold and silver" is mentioned very often, mostly when the settlers had contact with new tribes.

FIGURE 3. Plate 41: Mode of Collecting Gold in Streams Running From the Appalachian Mountains.

silver, which "were more abundant there."[74] Although there were no eyewitnesses, the Europeans wanted to believe the story of minerals in the Appalachian Mountains that were brought over the John's River [River of May] to the coast, which seems impossible given topographical realities. The text ends with a statement that the Spaniards had made use of minerals and infrastructure to "great advantage."[75] Thus far we also have no indication that

74. Lorant, *The New World*, 53; Hulton, *Work of Jacques Le Moyne*, vol. 2, pl. 101: "[P]raeter aurum et argentum quod istic in prima navigatione repertum est"; *Grand Voyages* (German ed.), pl. 9: "[D]ass daselbst am meisen Hirsen vnd Korn wuchse ohne das Golt vnd Silber, so sie in der ersten Schiffahrt daselbst gefunden."

75. Lorant, *The New World*, 117; Hulton, *Work of Jacques Le Moyne*, vol. 2, pl. 133: "Opes quae inde proveniunt, nunc Hispani in suum usum convertere norunt"; *Grand Voyages* (German ed.), pl. 41: "Den Reichthumb, welcher hierauß entstehet, wissen ihnen die Spanier zu dieser zeit wol nuetze zu machen."

FIGURE 4. Plate 13: Outina, with the Help of the French, gains a Victory over his enemy Potanou.

Timucua made metallic devices made for themselves, so there is only one interpretation: this illustration melds European imagination and hopes.

The illustration of battle scenes show a more European understanding of war: exact battle-lines transfer tactics, which were not familiar to the Floridian Indians. Plate and legend explain that French arquebusiers fought on the front line and gave Chief Outina's army a major advantage.[76] The enemy attacked

76. Milanich, *Timucua*, 86; Lorant, *The New World*, 61: "He [Ortina] put the French harquebusiers in the front line, where they very willingly bore the brunt of the fighting, killing many of the enemy and routing Chief Potanou's army. Hulton, *Work of Jacques Le Moyne*, vol. 2, pl. 105: "Gallo stamen in prima acie, ipsis non abnuentibus collocavit: et nisi totum onus pugnae illi sustinuissent, plurimos hostes mactando, et Regis Potanou exercitium in fugam vertendo. . ."; *Grand Voyages* (German ed.), pl. 13: "Doch stellet er die Frantzosen forn an die Spitzen, welches sie sich auch nicht waegerten. Vnd wo ferne sie nicht die gantze Last deß Streitts bestanden, so viel Feinde erleget vnd deß Königes Patanou Heer in die Flucht geschlagen hetten. . . ."

with bows and arrows, all warriors stood in—more or less—correct battle lines as the chief, who makes a majestic gesture like a European war hero "marched his forces in regular ranks like an organized army."[77] This image represents the counterimage to chief Satouriwa, whose name is (unusually) inscribed in the engraving. In the foreground, in a battle detail, French arquebusiers and a single person with shield and sword fought. The military superiority of European weapons is apparent, especially for the European observer. To reassure the latter, all dead warriors were indigenous. But another explanation is also possible: the French were not the first Europeans with whom the Timucua had contact, as the Spanish expeditions of Pánfilo de Narváez (1527/28) and Hernando de Soto (1539) preceded them. Therefore, it could be possible that the Timucuan war strategy had changed to a more European one.[78] If true, then de Bry's plates may illustrate such changes.[79]

A fact, which is demonstrated in only one plate, is a bloody result of the complicated communication with the Indians over the long term. The murder of Pierre Gambié displayed fundamental differences between the two cultures: Gambié earned his money through merchandizing, but he also betrayed the Indians. Indians were increasingly characterized as "treacherous" people. Communication in general—which still was only possible with the help of interpreters—came under general suspicion.[80] The plate shows the assassination of a perfidious Indian and the unaware French merchant. Only Le Moyne's report explains the reasons for this event to the reader.[81]

Le Moyne had an ambivalent picture of the Timucua. At the beginning they were very friendly, as they helped Europeans by building shelters for the settlers and the fort, as well as providing food support. But the Indians were also careful. They observed the settlers' actions, especially during construction of the fort.[82] The situation became complicated because of inadequate translators on both sides.[83] And the Indians were still "savages" because they lost

---

77. Lorant, *The New World*, 63; Hulton, *Work of Jacques Le Moyne*, vol. 2, pl. 106: "[P]rogreditur servatis ordinibus veluti instructa acie, solus in medio agmine, consistens, rubro colare pictus"; *Grand Voyages* (German ed.), pl. 14: "[Z]eucht in gutter Schlachtordnung vnd stellet sich mitten in Hauffen, mit roter Farbe angestrichen."

78. John E. Worth, *The Timucuan Chiefdoms of Spanish Florida*, 2 vols. (Gainesville: University of Florida Press, 1998). In vol. 1, 34, Worth indicates that "new Euro-Indian military alliances . . . shifted the delicate balance of power in the aboriginal landscape of the interior."

79. Milanich, *Timucua*, 150–151; see Worth, *Timucuan Chiefdoms*, vol. 1, 22, 27, 30.

80. Hulton, *Work of Jacques Le Moyne*, vol. 1, 126–128; Lorant, *The New World*, 54; Lestrigant, "L'automne des cannibals," in *L'Amérique de Théodore De Bry*, 71–73.

81. Lorant, *The New World*, 119; Hulton, *Work of Jacques Le Moyne*, vol. 2, pl. 134; *Grand Voyages* (German ed.), pl. 42.

82. Hulton, *Work of Jacques Le Moyne*, vol. 1, 120; Lorant, *The New World*, 36.

83. Hulton, *Work of Jacques Le Moyne*, vol. 1, 121; Lorant, *The New World*, 38.

interest in bringing supplies to the French because through time they received less and less in exchange.[84]

Sometimes the French were surprised by "the organization and wealth" of other Indian tribes they had contact with, but these are rare moments in Le Moyne's report.[85] Mistrust grew, and according to Le Moyne, Laudonnière was warned even by the Spaniards not to trust the Indians.[86] Thus misunderstanding and misjudgment were permanent companions of political and social relationships between Europeans and Indians.

The end of the French settlement is well known. Contacts with the Indians worsened as famine in the French community grew because necessary Indian support was cut off. An English ship captain came to the aid of the French providing foodstuffs. The arrival of naval officer Jean Ribault prevented the French from being forced out of Fort Charlotte. Quickly the fort was reorganized and the waiting for the Spanish attack began. Spaniards came with "a large company of negroes armed with spades and mattocks."[87] Despite promises and contracts, the Spaniards massacred the French because the latter were considered enemies of Catholicism. After a hurricane and the military defeat, Le Moyne, who was wounded in the leg, was able to flee. He returned safely to France.[88]

Religion-related information does not appear in plates nor de Bry's text. Such is also the case with Le Moyne's texts, except for the following: One of the three chiefs in the mountain area "was very devoted to the Christians, . . . he was rich and powerful and had four thousand men permanently under arms."[89] No further information of the devoutness of this tribe is provided. Did these Indians have previous contact with other Europeans? The following information appears only in Le Moyne's text: Two former Spaniards were found, who were Christians, but lived with the Indians after surviving a shipwreck.[90]

To summarize, reading Le Moyne's report shows great discrepancies between his information and the engravings with captions. Le Moyne's report is largely focused on politics—negotiations and wars with the Indians, the French settlers' internal struggle, greed for wealth, and the final battle with the Spaniards. In contrast, the engravings and captions show events within a strong ethnological/cultural background. However, given Le Moyne's

---

84. Hulton, *Work of Jacques Le Moyne*, vol. 1, 123, 131; Lorant, *The New World*, 46, 66.
85. Hulton, *Work of Jacques Le Moyne*, vol. 1, 125; Lorant, *The New World*, 52.
86. Hulton, *Work of Jacques Le Moyne*, vol. 1, 127; Lorant, *The New World*, 56.
87. Hulton, *Work of Jacques Le Moyne*, vol. 1, 131–132; Lorant, *The New World*, 74–78.
88. Hulton, *Work of Jacques Le Moyne*, vol. 1, 133–137; Lorant, *The New World*, 84–86.
89. Hulton, *Work of Jacques Le Moyne*, vol. 1, 126; Lorant, *The New World*, 56.
90. Hulton, *Work of Jacques Le Moyne*, vol. 1, 127; Lorant, *The New World*, 56.

emphases, it is curious that Timucuan musical instruments are described in detail (and in comparison, downplayed in the captioned engravings).[91]

Ethnological Evaluation in Le Moyne–De Bry Illustrations

Archaeological and ethnographical research shows that Floridian Indians farmed maize, beans, squash, and tobacco at a rather low agricultural level (in William C. Sturtevant's words, on a "Neolithic level"). The dog was the only animal they could domesticate.[92] They fished in rivers and the ocean, and their pottery and basketry skills were simple.

The engravings show detailed views of the Timucuans' daily life, such as how they cultivated the soil. A caption reads: "The Indians till the soil very diligently, using a kind of hoe made from fish bone fitted to wooden handles. Since the soil is light, these serve well enough to cultivate it."[93] The connected engraving gives the impression of large and well-cultivated fields. But this view is questionable, given the findings of recent archaeological surveys. There are less indications of farming by the Timucua before the arrival of the Europeans; evidence of fishing and hunting only is certain. First hints of corn production are after the 1450s, but then only small plots are reasonable.[94]

Le Moyne also mentioned Indian games and their deer-hunting skills.[95] They took the head of a deer as a mask (Latin: *Larva*/German: *Larve*) to deceive the "real" deer. However, we must carefully consider how Europeans likely interpreted such impressive hunting techniques. It is likely that Europeans found the same scandalous because it demonstrates a close proximity of humankind to animals—dressing to resemble an animal was despicable

---

91. Hulton, *Work of Jacques Le Moyne*, vol. 1, 120: "Nearer to him [the Chief] were twenty pipers who were playing some primitive thing discordantly and raggedly, merely blowing the pipes as hard as they could. These pipes are no more than extremely thick reeds with two holes, an upper one where they blow and a lower one where the breath comes out, as with the pipes or tubes of organs." See also Lorant, *The New World*, 40.

92. William C. Sturtevant, "The ethnological evaluation of the Le Moyne–De Bry illustrations," in *The Work of Jacques Le Moyne*, ed. Hulton, vol. 1, 69–75.

93. Lorant, *The New World*, 77; Hulton, *Work of Jacques Le Moyne*, vol. 2, pl. 113: "Diligenter colunt terram Indi, eam ob causam ligones e piscium oßibus parare norunt viri, quibus manubrial lignea aptantes, terram fodiunt satis facile, nam mollior est. . ."; *Grand Voyages* (German ed.), pl. 21: "Im Feldtbawen sind sie sehr fleissig, zu nutzen desselbigen, wissen die Männer Hauwen auß Fischknochen zu machen, darein sie hernach hoeltzern Stiel stecken, mit welchen sie die Erde gar leichtlich umgraben koennen, dieweil sie deß orts gar milt ist."

94. See "Before the Churches: Pre-contact Mocama History, Culture, and Religion," by Keith Ashley and Robert L. Thunen in this volume.

95. See also John Anthony Scott, *Settlers on the Eastern Shore: The British Colonies in North America, 1607–1750* (New York, Oxford: Facts on File, 1991), 7; Milanich, *Timucua*, 184.

FIGURE 5. Plate 25: Hunting Deer.

because the unavoidable moral contrast between the two becomes blurred.[96] So in de Bry's caption text, the Indians were not praised for the hunting technique, but rather for their skill in preparing the deerskins (Latin: *pelles cervis*/German: *Hirschhaeute*): "I do not believe any European could do this better."[97]

Wild animals are always an indicator that the people who live in a particular area are not able to dominate the land, whether practically or morally. Thus, alligators (crocodiles) were introduced as "monsters," according to the caption, which could loudly "bellow" when they are hungry.[98] These beasts

96. Van Groesen, *Representations*, 170–172.

97. Lorant, *The New World*, 85; Hulton, *Work of Jacques Le Moyne*, vol. 2, pl. 117; *Grand Voyages* (German ed.), pl. 26.

98. Lorant, *The New World*, 87; Hulton, *Work of Jacques Le Moyne*, vol. 2, pl. 118: [H]uic vasto animali . . . tam horrendum clamorem edunt, ut per dimidii miliaris spatium exaudiri queat." *Grand Voyages* (German ed.), pl. 26: [D]em vngehewren grossen Thier . . . daß man sie wol vber ein halbe Meil wegs hoeren kan."

were "much bigger than the crocodiles of the Nile."[99] It took ten Indians to control the monstrous animal, which demonstrates the difficulties experienced by the Natives in asserting themselves in their natural environment. At the same time, this type of presentation documents European superiority as they no longer have to endure such challenges in their home environment.[100]

Also seen in de Bry's engravings, nature had its specific task as supporter of mankind: the reader viewed an anthropocentric-constructed surrounding where Indians and Europeans acted. Nature, portrayed as constructed scenery, has to be cultivated, adapted to human needs.[101] The purpose of de Bry's engraving was not to show the reader the "real" Florida before Europeans arrived.

The description of the land and its cultivation in the legend contains a few hints about what Christians could learn from the Indians. For example, Indian storehouses for foodstuffs and other material were used and replenished by members of the community as needed with no thoughts of competing with or stealing from others: "Indeed, it would be good if among Christians there were as little greed to torment men's minds and hearts."[102]

Native people's "natural" moderation or temperance (Latin: *sobrietas*) is another topic: "[W]e are so immoderate in both our eating and our drinking habits that we shorten our lives thereby. We might easily learn sobriety and wisdom from these men whom we consider only as savages and beasts."[103] De Bry and his engravers—based on Le Moyne's pictures—created, in some senses, an idyllic world of people without material prosperity, who could live

---

99. Lorant, *The New World*, 49; Hulton, *Work of Jacques Le Moyne*, vol. 2, pl. 99: "[E]t magnum flumen aequae dulcis invenerunt, in quo plurimos Crocodilos Niliacis laonge majores observarunt." *Grand Voyages* (German ed.), pl. 7: "[E]in schoenen vnd grossen bach mit suessem Wasser funden, darinnen sie sehr viel Crocodilen, grosser dann die im Nile sind, gemerckt haben."

100. Van Groesen, *Representations*, 151–153.

101. Ibid., 141–148.

102. Lorant, *The New World*, 79; Hulton, *Work of Jacques Le Moyne*, vol. 2, pl. 114: "Optandum sane esset, ut inter Christianos avaritia non magis regnaret, et hominum animos torqueret"; *Grand Voyages* (German ed.), pl. 22: "Ach wolt Gott daß der Geitz vnter den Christen so wenig Platz hette vnd die Hertzen der Menschen auch so wenig plagte"; Van Groesen, *Representations*, 176.

103. Lorant, *The New World*, 91; Hulton, *Work of Jacques Le Moyne*, vol. 2, pl. 120: "Pudorem sane incutiunt Christianis, qui suis compotationibus et conviviis sine moderamine celebratis, brevitatem vitae sibi accelerantes, merite deberent tradi in disciplinam his barbaris et animantibus brutis ad ediscendam sobrietatem"; *Grand Voyages* (German ed.), pl. 28: "Die Christen sollten sich fuerwar (von wegen dieser Voelcker) billich hoechlich schaemen, dieweil sie in ihren Gastereyen vnd Zechen so gar keyn Maß halten vnd also ihnen selbst ihr Leben verkuertzen. Sollten derhalben billich vnter diesen Barbarischen außlaendischen Leuthen zur Schule gehen vnd von ihnen ja von den vernuenftigen Thieren Mässigkeit lehrnen." The German translation is here more radical—"reasonable animals"—than the Latin and English versions.

in harmony and peace with nature. It is the image of the "noble savage,"[104] which was a literary trope until the end of the nineteenth century, when the German bestselling novelist and adventurer Karl May (1842–1912) created Winnetou, Apache chieftain, a noble savage and crypto-Christian. Tens of thousands of young boys read his books in the twentieth century and were introduced to America's Wild West, as were readers of the *Great Voyages* centuries before to Florida and the Carolinas.

Next, certain legends attached to scenes in *Great Voyages* demonstrate admiration for indigenous people's artistic skills. For instance, the statement, "It is remarkable that these savages should be able to produce such tasteful ornaments," is found at the end of the legend describing the arrival of the new queen and festivities.[105]

Another plate, displaying questionable content, shows Timucuan villages with the palisades around the houses (also shown in other plates but in the background). Archaeological researchers thus far have not found indications of mounds or ditches around excavated Timucuan villages. In addition, extant documents from the sixteenth and seventeenth centuries never mention this kind of fortification.[106] The essential problem was to find enough trees in Florida for the timber to build these palisades.

Every village had its own chief and consisted of dwellings with a ceremonial complex in the center. The complex included "a large council house, a plaza, and probably also a burial mound."[107] The average population of a village was small and communities were typically distant from one another. Chiefs sat on an elevated chair and their clothing and tattoos displayed their status. Village residents worked for the chief and brought foodstuffs to a local storage building. The chief made decisions in consultation with the village council; posts in the council were hereditary. Priests (shamans) and sorcerers (ceremonial leaders, healers) served their communities in diverse areas of life.

The sorcerer is shown to be the only person who represented the religious aspects of life, because the engravings show no scenes of missionary activities. The sorcerer was necessary for ceremonies after a victory or sacrifices to the sun.[108] Because he also appeared to be horrifying to the Europeans, he was

---

104. Daniel Defert, "Collections et nations au XVIe siècle," in *L'Amérique de Théodore De Bry*, 60–63.

105. Lorant, *The New World*, 111; Hulton, *Work of Jacques Le Moyne*, vol. 2, pl. 130: "Mirum homines adeo barbarous tam venustiis inventis praeditos"; *Grand Voyages* (German ed.), pl. 38: "Es ist sich hoechlich zuverwundern, daß diese wilden Leute so schoene Werck erfunden haben."

106. Milanich, *Timucua*, 48, 132.

107. Sturtevant, "The ethnological evaluation," 69.

108. Lorant, *The New World*, 59, 105; Hulton, *Work of Jacques Le Moyne*, vol. 2, pl. 108, 127; *Grand Voyages* (German ed.), pl. 16, 35.

put on a level with the Devil: "After a quarter of an hour his appearance became so frightful that he looked scarcely human."[109] In the next engraving, presumably de Bry himself, caption text referenced a sorcerer, adding, "[H]e must certainly have been possessed of a devil."[110]

The small independent chiefdoms were not generally peaceful, as suggested by most of de Bry's engravings; raiding one another was quite common. The Timucua never created a political entity, and questions about a special "Timucuan ethnic unit" are difficult to answer.[111] They lived in northeastern Florida and southeastern Georgia; depending on time period, the estimated population was between 24,000 and 200,000.[112] Satouriwa and his people, with whom the French had contact, belonged to these groups, but as already suggested, relations were not always peaceful. Together with Utina and Potano, he was one of the leaders connected with a group of villages.[113] The legends accompanying the copper plates contained no precise information about the tribe's structure, as only chiefs or leaders were mentioned. In Le Moyne's report, "Timogua" were mentioned, but it seems the French had no real clue about tribal organization. The name is described by Le Moyne as an expression for "enemy."[114] These villages were, in some cases, also sites for Spanish missions in subsequent years. Reports on archaeological excavations in these locales mention metal artifacts and beads from Europe.[115]

---

109. Lorant, *The New World* 67; Hulton, *Work of Jacques Le Moyne*, vol. 2, pl. 104: "[Q]ua ad quadrantem horae producta, illico tam horrendus apparuit, ut humanam effigiem amplius non exprimeret"; *Grand Voyages* (German ed.), pl. 12: "Welcher, als ers einer viertel stund lang angetrieben, erschroecklich anzusehen war, daß er keim Menschen mehr gleichte."

110. Lorant, *The New World* 61; Hulton, *Work of Jacques Le Moyne*, vol. 2, pl. 105: "[Q]uod Magus praedixerat, quem certum est a daemone fuisse obsessum"; *Grand Voyages* (German ed.), pl. 13: "Dann es sich in der Warheyt befande, was der Zauberer (der gewißlich vom Teuffel besessen war) zuvor gesagt hatt." Van Groesen, *Representations*, 241.

111. Milanich, *Timucua*, 38–56, quote on 45: We know about the language and dialects thanks to Father Francisco Pareja, O.F.M., who was at Mission San Juan del Puerto after 1595.

112. Milanich, *Timucua*, 60. Neighbors of the Timucua were the Guale in the northeast, the Apalachee in the northwest, and the Mayaca in the south. See Worth, *Timucuan Chiefdoms*, especially vol. 1, chapters 1 and 2. Worth (vol. 2, p. 6) has a smaller number for the pre-mission period: 24,000 to 30,000 individuals.

113. Worth, *Timucuan Chiefdoms*, vol. 1, 22–25. According to Worth (vol. 1, 5), a chiefdom consisted "of a number of settlements under the political control of a single hereditary leader, or chief."

114. Hulton, *Work of Jacques Le Moyne*, vol. 1, 125; Lorant, *The New World*, 52; Milanich, *Timucua*, 46, 160. For the Spaniards, the name "Timucua" described all Indians in present-day northern Florida.

115. Milanich, *Timucua*, 47. Also Jerald T. Milanich, *Laboring in the Fields of the Lord. Spanish Missions and Southeastern Indians* (Washington, DC, London: Smithsonian Institution Press, 1999). For Santa Catalina de Guale, see David Hurst Thomas, *The Archeology of Mission Santa Catalina de Guale: 1. Search and Discovery*, Anthropological Papers

The plates also show the dark side of the Natives, as in severe punishment of sentries who fail to fulfill responsibilities. One plate shows the "sacrifice of first-born children." Legend text quotes the author (Le Moyne himself or de Bry's fabrication?) as saying, "I saw this ritual performed once while I was there."[116] The brutality of war is the theme of yet another plate.[117]

These and other renderings of ethnographical information seem to be important for our understanding of Native culture at the time of contact with Europeans, as in some instances they are the only extant documentation. In general, the plates tell us a story of well-organized people. Las Casas also mentioned the excellent organization of the tribal societies. The Timucua were experts "in engineering, agriculture and hunting," their social system was "symbolized in verbal behavior, ceremonies, paraphernalia, the exchange of gifts and mutual respect."[118] They were also known to scalp their enemies[119] and conduct "idolatrous" ceremonies. Regarding documentation, it was de Bry who introduced the scene of Timucuans scalping their enemies.[120] He used European prejudices against foreigners, thus fulfilling his readers' expectations.[121]

The Relationship between Conquerors and Conquered

A closer look at the relationship between the French and the Timucua is worthwhile at this juncture.

---

of the American Museum of Natural History, 63 part 2 (New York: American Museum of Natural History, 1987); David Hurst Thomas, "The Archaeology of Mission Santa Catalina de Guale: Our First 15 Years," in *The Spanish Missions of La Florida*, ed. Bonnie G. McEwan (Gainesville: University Press of Florida, 1993), 1–34; For Santa Maria de Yamassee, see Rebecca Saunders, "Architecture of the Missions Santa María and Santa Catalina de Amelia," in *Spanish Missions*, ed. McEwan, 35–61. For San Pedro y San Pablo de Patale, see Rochelle A. Marrinan, "Archaeological Investigations at Mission Patale, 1984–1992," in *Spanish Missions*, ed. McEwan, 244–294.

116. Lorant, *The New World*, 103; Hulton, *Work of Jacques Le Moyne*, vol. 2, pl. 126: "Nobis praesentibus semel peracta est similis victima"; *Grand Voyages* (German ed.), pl. 3, "Ein solches Opffer ist einmal in vnser Gegenwertigkeyt verrichtet worden."

117. Lorant, *The New World*, 65; Hulton, *Work of Jacques Le Moyne*, vol. 2, pl. 107; *Grand Voyages* (German ed.), pl. 15.

118. Milanich, *Timucua*, 156.

119. Ibid., 160; Tom Conley, *Theatres of Cruelty: Wars of Religion, Violence, and the New World* (Chicago: The Newberry Library, 1990), 18–21.

120. Lorant, *The New World*, 65: "[T]hey cut the skin of the head down to the bone from front to back. . ."; Hulton, *Work of Jacques Le Moyne*, vol. 2, pl. 107: "[E]xactioris quam ullus culter aciei, a fronte in orbem adocciput, capitis cutim ad cranium usque secant. . ."; *Grand Voyages* (German ed.), pl. 15: "[W]elche mit etlichen Rohrstuecken, so schaerpffer dann kein Schermesser sind, inen von der Stirn an rings hervmb die Haut biß auff die Hirnschal abloesen. . . ." Van Groesen, *Representations*, 124, writes from a "de Bry construction through its narrative structure."

121. Van Groesen, *Representations*, 191.

FIGURE 6. Plate 1: The Coastline of Florida.

The French first came ashore in small boats, their ships remaining in deeper water in the distance. Some Indians were fishing, others sat together, the chief in their midst. There is no real interaction between the two groups.

In the next plate the reader sees two Indians who swam to one of the boats to greet the foreigners. Two others hurry to the landing place. One Frenchman points to the group of Indians, an explanation for his gesture is difficult. After a while, the same two ships left the Indian village at the mouth of the river in order to explore the May (St. John) River. The next plate depicts a vacated Indian village—only four Natives observe the arrival in the background. Communication between the two groups is not indicated. The same observation can be made via the engraving that shows the discovery of six more rivers by the French: the only eyewitness is a sea monster. At the next French exploration of a river (Port-Royal), the Indians fled in a hurry (leaving roasting meat behind) when alerted about the French ships.

FIGURE 7. Plate 2: The French sail to the River of May, details of the welcoming scene.

Erection of the column with the French king's coat of arms happened initially in secret: the stone was only a "landmark" in a well-organized cultural landscape.[122] Next, readers are confronted with the settlers' critical situation when their food supply ran out. A talk with the chief of a village and his council with the armed French emissaries ended on a positive note: Two Indians brought food to (unarmed) Frenchmen, who stowed it in a small canoe. According to the attached legend, the friendly chief showed the foreigners

122. Lorant, *The New World*, 47: "[T]he commander gave orders that a landmark, carved in the form of a column and bearing the arms of the King of France, be put into one of the boats and set up at some pleasant and well-chosen spot." See also Hulton, *Work of Jacques Le Moyne*, vol. 2, pl. 98: "Prefectus limitem columnae instar excisum, in quo sculpta errant Regis Galliae insignia, in cymbam exonerari jubet"; *Grand Voyages* (German ed.), pl. 6: "[H]at der Oberste einen grossen Marckstein, wie ein Seul, hauwen lassen, in welchen deß Koeniges auß Franckreich Wapen gegraben vnd denselben in ein Nachen gelegt, damit man ihn an das lustige Ort setzen koendte."

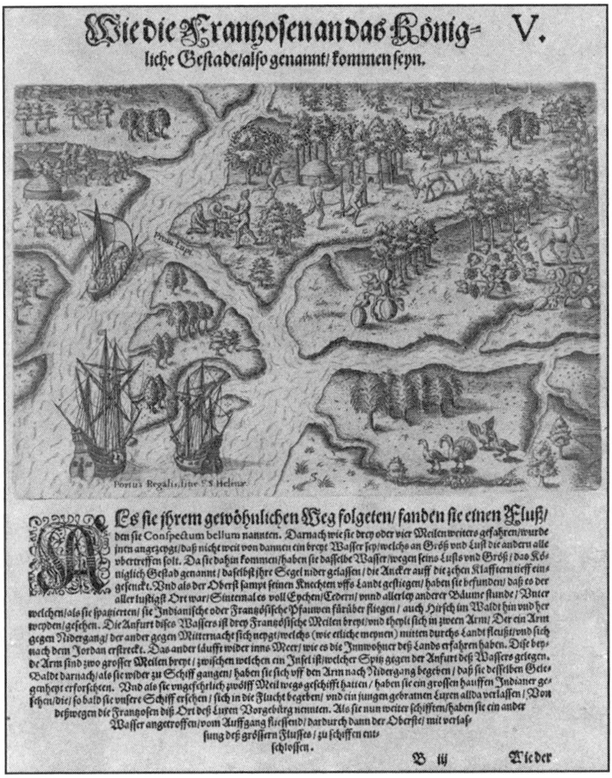

FIGURE 8. Plate 5: The French reach Port Royal, details of fleeing Indians.

his surplus of food.[123] The building of Fort Caroline is the theme of two additional images. In one of them, only Frenchmen are seen working on the fort. Great distrust between the French and Natives prevailed.

The official political relationships between the war chiefs and the French commander are the subject of the next plates. According to the plate legends, extreme caution was observed on both sides, even after they agreed on peaceful interaction. The previously mentioned column with the royal coat of arms shows an impressive Indian chief at the side of a French commander in his formal uniform and three heavily armed guards behind him representing the settlers' protection as well as European power.

123. Lorant, *The New World*, 49: "Chief Ouadé received them in the friendliest manner." Also, Hulton, *Work of Jacques Le Moyne*, vol. 2, pl. 99: "[A]d Regem Ouadé pervenerunt, a quo perhumaniter excepti. . ."; *Grand Voyages* (German ed.), pl. 7: "[S]ind sie zum Koenig Ouade kommen (von welchem sie gantz freundlich empfangen). . . ."

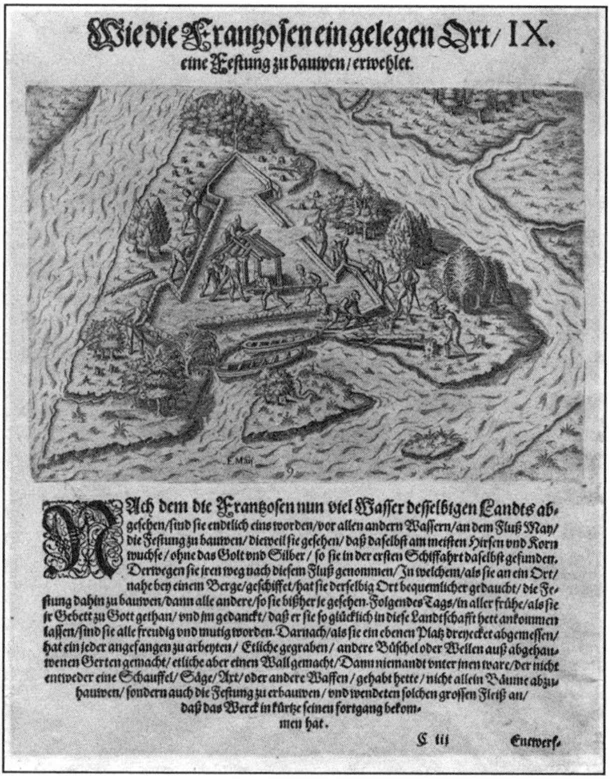

FIGURE 9. Plate 9: The French select a Place for Building a Fort.

The French joined a military expedition with their new ally Outina. In preparation for this event, the Indian chief consulted a sorcerer. The French monitored the scene with harquebuses in hand. Some spoke to one another, but not to the Indians. Involvement of French soldiers in the subsequent battle was discussed above. After the victory, a celebration at the Indian village took place, and again the sorcerer played an important role. The chief spoke only with the French, who again dressed in their best uniforms and carried weapons. Perhaps the Indian leader explained the ceremony to the foreigners—the legend provides no information about the ceremony.

Again, the French, always with their weapons in hand, watched the scene unconcerned, when the warriors' widows proclaimed their losses before the chief. The French talked among themselves; once more, the legend provides not a hint about the involvement of the French at this event. During the official punishment of the careless sentries, the French commander communicates with the Indian chief. The two men are seated on the same bench, which could mean that their ranks in the existing hierarchy were equal—at least in the Euro-

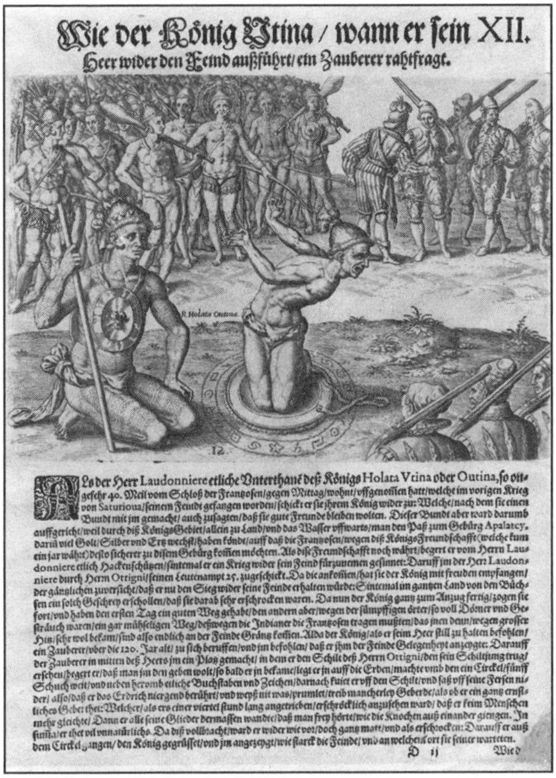

FIGURE 10. Plate 12: Outina, going at the Head of His Army, against the Enemy, consults a Sorcerer on the Event—Detail with the separation of the French group from the Indians.

pean view. The same situation—chief and commander seated together and talking to each other—is repeated in engravings that show the sacrifice of first-born children and the ceremony of sacrificing an animal to the sun.

In summary, the relationship between Indians and French seemed to be very distant; no signs of fraternity were emphasized in the engravings. The closest moment both sides attained (as parsed in the engravings) occurred during the battle. This clear distinction between the two groups seemed to be expected by the European readers, as fraternization between Christians and non-Christians should not happen. Although Indian culture was respected by the artists in many plates, European superiority must be confirmed. Curiosity about the behaviors and ceremonies of the Natives was strong, but this could not be interpreted as acceptance or tolerance. Social hierarchy and barriers were upheld by the French, as this was the only way, in effect, that they could deal with the Indians as Europeans and for Europeans.

FIGURE 11. Plate 18: The Chief applied to by Women whose Husbands have died in the War or by Disease—Detail with the separation of French and Indians.

Summary: Good Savage–Bad Savage

The Le Moyne–de Bry illustrations are the only ones for the Timucua and the oldest depictions of Indian life in Florida. It is worth mentioning again that de Bry changed Le Moyne's originals, so the text by Le Moyne is much more meaningful than the engravings. This text "coincide[s] quite well with the independent documentary evidence on Timucuan culture and with comparative data on other Southeastern Indian cultures."[124]

Text and engravings provide an ambivalent picture of the Timucuans from a European perspective. Only one aspect is clear: the tribes in north-eastern Florida were not cannibals. As mentioned earlier, this characterization of Indians arrived with the storyteller Hans Staden.

124. Sturtevant, "The ethnological evaluation," 70.

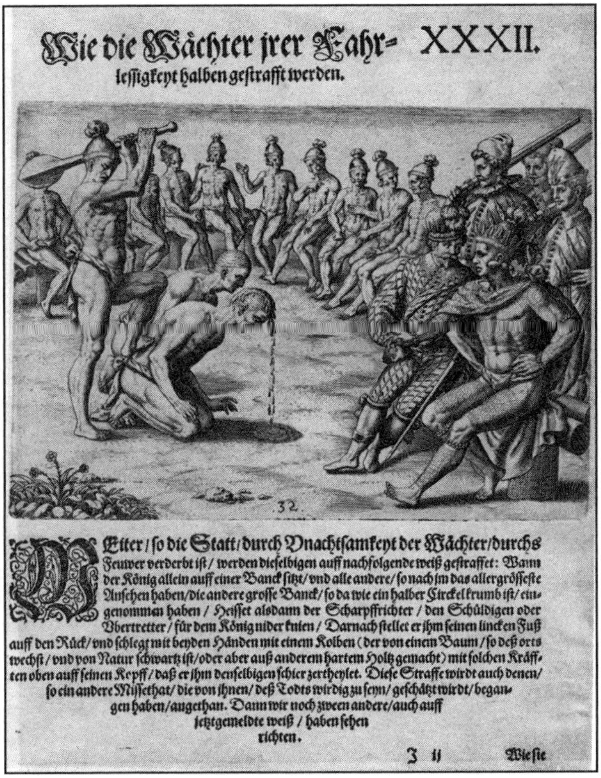

Wie die Wächter jrer Fahrlessigkeyt halben gestrafft werden. XXXII.

WEiter / so die Statt / durch Vnachtsamkeyt der Wächter / durchs Feuwer verderbt ist / werden dieselbigen auff nachfolgende weiß gestraffet: Wann der König allein auff einer Banck sitzt / vnd alle andere / so nach jm das allergrössesste Ansehen haben / die andere grosse Banck / so da wie ein halber Circkel krumb ist / eingenommen haben / Heisset alsdann der Scharpffrichter / den Schüldigen oder Vbertretter / für dem König nider knien / Darnach stellet er jhm seinen lincken Fuß auff den Rück / vnd schlegt mit beyden Händen mit einem Kolben (der von einem Baum / so deß orts wechst / vnd von Natur schwartz ist / oder aber auß anderem hartem Holtz gemacht) mit solchen Kräfften oben auff seinen Kopff / daß er jhm denselbigen schier zertheylet. Diese Straffe wirdt auch denen / so ein andere Missethat / die von jhnen / deß Todts wirdig zu seyn / geschätzt wirdt / begangen haben / angethan. Dann wir noch zween andere / auch auff jetztgemeldte weiß / haben sehen richten.

J ij Wie sie

FIGURE 12. Plate 32: How Sentinels are punished for sleeping on their Posts—Detail about the conversation between the French commander and the Indian chief.

Another image of the Indians was that of wild, naked, fierce people. In contrast to the noble Timucua in Florida with their "majestic and perfect" bodies, who helped the Europeans at least to a limited extent, the Tupinambá, visited by Hans Staden, were the opposite. These Indians were described as aggressive, savage, and hostile by Staden, the first European to visit them. They were bloodthirsty and cannibals, and thus violated a taboo in European culture: cannibalism, a capital (mortal) sin and practically unforgivable, the fierce opposite of charity.[125] According to Whitehead, cannibalism is a "cultural category," and thus caused a strong "ethnological judgement."[126]

125. Lestrigant, "L'automne des cannibals," in *L'Amérique de Théodore De Bry*, 77–88.

126. Neil L. Whitehead, "Hans Staden and the Cultural Politics of Cannibalism," *Hispanic American Historical Review*, 80, no. 4 (2000): 721–751, quote on 721; Van Groesen, *Representations*, 183–188.

The only explanation for Tupinambá actions that Europeans would accept was influence by the Devil. The women, in particular, must be witches, and the men always aggressive. Thus, the women were depicted as old and ugly and the men as beast-like.[127] One does wonder how Staden survived if, in truth, his surroundings among the Tupinambá were as hostile as he described. So, at least two different European impressions of the Indians existed—the good savage, which Las Casas and others stressed, but also the ugly one, which Staden offered. But we must be very careful not to mythologize Las Casas as a "benevolent advocate of human rights."[128]

These images—the good and friendly and the violent and cruel—were already available in the late fifteenth century and shaped Europeans' appraisal of faraway indigenous people literally for centuries. The ideal picture of well-formed bodies continued through many later first-time meetings between Indians and Europeans. For instance, a reverend spoke about the Mohawk people at Albany in 1644 as having "well-formed features, bodies and limbs; they all have black hair and eyes, but their skin is yellow."[129]

In conclusion, the truth or accuracy of the Le Moyne–de Bry engravings must be evaluated with great skepticism. They undeniably reflect a European perspective, but the images are also the *only* ones to have survived the centuries. They do provide some insight, if we analyze them with alongside archaeological and linguistic evidence. These images should be used carefully—they are undeniably impressive—because they still produce an "inner picture," regardless of whether contemporary viewers know or do not know de Bry's intentions.

An Ongoing Story—Missionary Publications in the Eighteenth Century

The direct correlation between a European audience's expectations for exciting adventure stories from completely unknown places, and the decision by authors and painters to adjust their stories and images according to these anticipations, was not limited to the time around 1600. Similar adjustments are found, for instance, in missionary reports during the first half of the eighteenth century as well. These reports are also an excellent ethnographical source, mostly about indigenous religions—the so-called "idolatry"—but also about native cultures and languages. Especially in the New World's Spanish provinces, the missionaries' task was always a decisive legitimation of political

---

127. Bucher, *Icon and Conquest*, 46–48.

128. Castro, *Another Face of Empire*, 178; see the same page about Las Casas's "utopian state of grace."

129. Scott, *Settlers*, 5.

domination.[130] For a European readership, diverse missionary communications meet these expectations. Christian faith and scholarship created a new, global network, in addition to economic and political ones. Public demand for stories from unknown parts of the world, from incomprehensible cultures, beliefs, and behaviors created a huge number of periodicals, which often chose the form of "personal" letters by missionaries. These stories only partially reflected the "truth" of personal experience, as they were very carefully tailored to a specific interest.[131] Such stories also show another side of "truth": the relationship between Europeans and Amerindians was full of misunderstandings, flaws, and distortions, as my example in this paper demonstrated. In Abulafia's words, de Bry's publication was the starting point for this widespread development: "They helped to fix a mental image of the American peoples."[132] The widespread images, used multiple times and sometimes revised and altered, became over many decades emblematic for the Amerindians, confirmed by alleged eyewitnesses whose credibility was determined in part by the religious conflicts of early modern Europe.[133]

---

130. Iris Gareis, "Missionary Reports and Their Relevance as Ethnographic Sources," in *Reporting Christian Missions in the Eighteenth Century: Communication, Culture of Knowledge and Regular Publication in a Cross-Confessional Perspective*, ed. Markus Friedrich and Alexander Schunka, 19–33 (Wiesbaden: Harrassowitz, 2017).

131. Markus Friedrich and Alexander Schunka, "Introduction," in *Reporting Christian Missions in the Eighteenth Century*, ed. Friedrich and Schunka, 7–18.

132. Abulafia, *Discovery of Mankind*, 312.

133. Beck, "Illustrating the Conquest," 531.

Chapter 10

Before the Churches: Precontact Mocama History, Culture, and Religion

KEITH ASHLEY AND ROBERT L. THUNEN

The popular image of the sixteenth century Timucua is one of hierarchically ranked, farming chiefdoms, each consisting of a series of walled villages. Any archaeologist would be hard-pressed to square this depiction of the Timucua with the known archaeological record of northeastern Florida. Current evidence suggests palisades did not exist, corn was grown (but not in large quantities), and traditional material correlates of Southeast chiefdoms are lacking. Focusing on the Mocama-speaking Timucua, we address this discrepancy and explore the social landscape of northeastern Florida by taking a deep historical perspective that integrates archaeological and ethnohistoric data. It is our belief that a genuine grasp of the unique and complex "consequences" of any sixteenth century encounter between natives and newcomers can only be attained through long-term historical research firmly anchored in a rich and nuanced understanding of a region's precontact archaeology.

Mocama Primer

A litany of early to mid-sixteenth century European explorers passed through or skirted the edges of the Timucua territory, including Juan Ponce de León, Lucas Vásquez de Ayllón, Pánfilo de Narváez, Hernando de Soto, Jean Ribault, René de Laudonnière, and Pedro Menéndez de Avilés.[1] Speakers of the Timucua language dwelled in villages distributed across a mosaic of environments between the Atlantic coast and the rolling lacustrine, riverine, and inter-riverine hinterlands of north-central Florida and southeast Georgia. Scholars propose that "as many as 200,000" Timucua speakers occupied a

1. John H. Hann, *A History of the Timucua Indians and Missions* (Gainesville: University Press of Florida, 1996); Jerald T. Milanich, *The Timucua* (Cambridge, MA: Blackwell Publishers, 1996); John E. Worth, *Timucuan Chiefdoms of Spanish Florida*, vol. 1, *Assimilation* (Gainesville: University Press of Florida, 1998a).

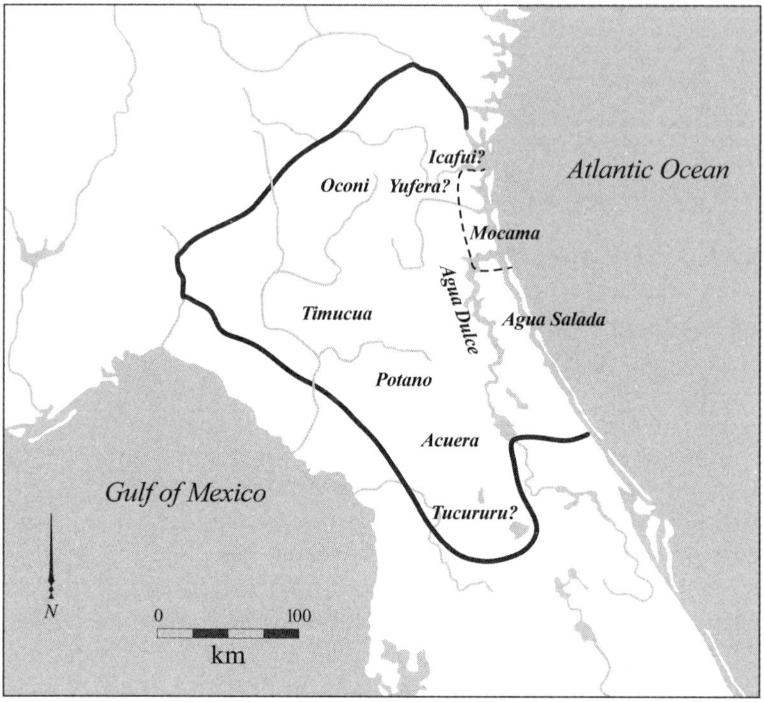

FIGURE 1. Approximate territory associated with Timucuan dialects.

sizeable territory of some 19,000 square miles.[2] Within two centuries, however, disease, warfare, atrocities, and out-migrations devastated Timucuan populations, and the few known to survive purportedly relocated to Cuba with the Spanish in 1763.[3] Perhaps no indigenous group in southeastern North America endured a more protracted entanglement with the French and Spanish than the Timucua.

Mocama was one of a series of Timucuan dialects recorded by a Spanish missionary named Francisco Pareja in the early 1600s (Figure 1).[4] Specifically,

2. Jerald T. Milanich, "Timucua," in *Handbook of North American Indians*, vol. 14, *Southeast*, edited by Raymond D. Fogelson (Washington, DC: Smithsonian Press, 2004a), 219.

3. Milanich, *The Timucua*, xv–xvi.

4. Kathleen Deagan, "Cultures in Transition: Fusion and Assimilation among the Eastern Timucua," in *Tacachale: Essays on the Indians of Florida and Southeastern Georgia during the Historic Period*, ed. Jerald T. Milanich and Samuel Proctor (Gainesville: University Press of Florida, 1978), 91; Julian Granberry, *A Grammar and Dictionary of the Timucua Language* (Gainesville: University Press of Florida, 1993), 6–7; Hann, *A History of the Timucua Indians and Missions*, 4–8; Milanich, *The Timucua*, 41–44; Jerald Milanich and

it was the maritime tongue spoken by tidewater groups along a forty-mile stretch of the Atlantic seaboard, roughly between the St. Johns River, Florida and the Satilla River, Georgia. By the early seventeenth century, the dialect reached as far north as the south end of St. Simons Island (Georgia), and the land was known as the San Pedro or Mocama Province, in reference to the provincial mission capital of San Pedro de Mocama on Cumberland Island, Georgia. The Spanish used the term "Timucua," at this time, exclusively to identify the interior peninsular mission province and its inhabitants.

Brief 500-year History Prior to Contact

Much of what is currently conveyed by scholars about the precontact, early sixteenth century Mocama (Timucua in general) derives from the writings of Spanish and French chroniclers between the 1520s and 1560s in tandem with early Spanish mission-period documents dated to around the turn of the seventeenth century. The conventional view on late pre-Columbian Mocama history takes a page out of the classic "Southeast prehistory" playbook.[5] That is, the Mocama of northeastern Florida started growing corn shortly after 1000 CE which propelled them into a small-scale, chiefdom-level sociopolitical organization. Through long-distance trade, chiefs enjoyed privileged access to foreign valuables, with these exotic markers of high status following them in death, as they were interred in sand mounds built larger than those of earlier generations. Prestige goods flowed into major centers where chiefs resided then down the hierarchy to subordinate villages through elite control.

While we do not deny that contact-era Mocama grew corn, lived in permanent villages, sustained social inequality, and maintained a political hierarchy, we do take exception with the assumption that the five hundred years leading up to contact followed this "Southeast" script. Recent ceramic studies combined with radiocarbon dating enable a better understanding of the cultural history of northeastern Florida.[6] This revised history shows that village

---

William Sturtevant, *Francisco Pareja's 1613 Confessionario: A Documentary Source for Timucuan Ethnography* (Washington, DC: Smithsonian Press, 1972), 1–2.

5. For examples of the classic evolution of Mississippian societies, see Bruce D. Smith, "The Archaeology of the Southeastern United States: From Dalton to de Soto (10,500 B.P.-500 B.P.)," *Advances in World Archaeology* 5 (1986): 1–92; Vincas P. Steponaitis, "Prehistoric Archaeology in the Southeastern United States, 1970–1985," *Annual Review of Anthropology* 14 (1986): 386–393.

6. Keith Ashley, "Refining the Ceramic Chronology of Northeastern Florida," *Florida Anthropologist* 61 (2008): 126–127; Keith Ashley, "Straddling the Florida–Georgia State Line: Ceramic Chronology of the St. Marys Region (ca. A.D. 1400–1700)," in *From Santa Elena to St. Augustine: Indigenous Ceramic Variability (A.D. 1400–1700)*, Anthropological Papers of the American Museum of Natural History, no. 90 (New York: American Museum of Natural History, 2009), 127–138.

aggregation and permanence along with sociopolitical complexity oscillated during the half-millennium prior to the European invasion. While ambiguities and contradictions in details still exist, we can nonetheless outline the basic contours of this revised late pre-Columbian cultural history, based on archaeological data from northeastern Florida.

St. Johns-II (900–1250 CE)

If we were to gaze across the state of Florida one thousand years ago, two civic centers would be prominent in terms of the amount of imported foreign artifacts from the interior Southeast (Figure 2).[7] Both sites occur within the region that becomes the geographical domain of the historic Timucua. One site is Mt. Royal along the middle St. Johns, directly north of Lake George. The second is the Mill Cove Complex situated on the south side of the river, about ten miles from its mouth. Mill Cove incorporates the Shields and Grant mounds, two large sand burial mounds containing hundreds of human burials along with copper plates and beads, galena, mica, quartz crystals, and various non-local stones.[8] Both mounds served as community cemeteries, as each was built up gradually with the addition of burials and soil over a period of more than two centuries. Excavations have shown that the two coeval cemeteries bracketed associated domestic areas, consisting of variable-density refuse scatters and shell middens. One special-event midden (Kinzey's Knoll) near the Shields Mound yielded the remains of ceremonial feasting, ritual artifact production and use, and burial preparation.[9] Radiocarbon assays from a variety of contexts anchor the mound–village complex to ca. 900–1250 CE (a local archaeological phase known as St. Johns-II).

Artifacts from ritual and mortuary contexts evince external exchange relations and connections to interior chiefdoms, including Cahokia near St. Louis. Not only did the residents of Mill Cove acquire exotic raw materials and finished goods from far-flung reaches of the Southeast and Midwest, they also secured ancient stone artifacts with deep histories of hundreds to thousands of years. These objects of great geographic and temporal distances took on sacred value in St. Johns rituals and other acts of social reproduction, as they objectified social connections to far-away people/places and to the society's

---

7. Keith Ashley, "Early St. Johns II Interaction, Exchange, and Politics: A View from Northeastern Florida," in *Late Prehistoric Florida: Archaeology at the Edge of the Mississippian World*, ed. Keith Ashley and Nancy Marie White (Gainesville: University Press of Florida, 2012), 112.

8. Ibid., 104–107.

9. Keith Ashley and Vicki Rolland, "Ritual at the Mill Cove Complex: Realms beyond the River," in *New Histories of pre-Columbian Florida*, ed. Neill J. Wallis and Asa R. Randall (Gainesville: University Press of Florida, 2014), 269–273.

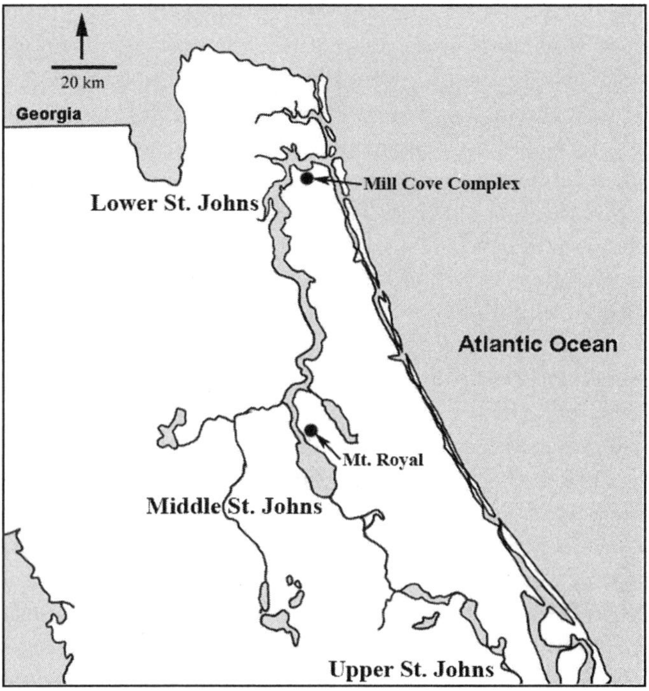

FIGURE 2. Location of Mill Cove Complex and Mt. Royal.

primordial roots.[10] The quantities of nonlocal items at Mill Cove (and Mt. Royal), compared to that of other contemporary Florida and Atlantic coastal sites, underscores the significance of these St. Johns-II communities as major participants in long-distance contacts and interactions that likely included direct procurement, down-the-line trade, intermarriage, diplomacy, questing, and pilgrimage during the eleventh through the thirteenth centuries.[11]

Beyond Mill Cove, we know of at least ten other contemporaneous St. Johns-II communities within the Mocama region, all of which are located in northeastern Florida. Most of these settlements possessed a low, on-site, sand burial mound, much smaller in size and lacking the exotica so conspicuous at Mill Cove.[12] Compared to earlier times, these settlements show more community permanence, with less frequent population movement. Small groups

---

10. Ibid., 276.

11. Ashley, "Early St. Johns II Interaction," 111–115.
Keith Ashley, Neill J. Wallis, and Michael D. Glascock, "Forager Interactions on the Edge of the Early Mississippian World: Neutron Activation Analysis of Ocmulgee and St. Johns Pottery," *American Antiquity* 80, no. 2 (2015), 290–294.

12. Ashley, "Early St. Johns II Interaction," 101–104.

of individuals may have ventured about to some extent to procure certain resources, but apparently never strayed too far from the village burial mound, which served as the locus of community ceremony and interaction. Ritual and mortuary events at Mill Cove likely drew attendees from these villages, and it is possible that some of the dead from these outlying settlements were interred in the Grant or Shields mound.

Although St. Johns-II society at this time interacted with a world of farmers beyond northeastern Florida to the north and west, their diet remained a local fare centered on the exploitation of salt marsh-tidal creek-estuary habitats.[13] A variety of small- to medium-sized fish and shellfish, including mostly oyster and clam, were staples, with deer and other terrestrial animals contributing less to their daily food intake. Wild or encouraged plants were collected, but no evidence of maize farming or consumption exists at this time for these fisher-hunter-gatherers.

As a final point, the period 900–1250 CE is the only time in which groups throughout the entire river valley and parallel Atlantic coast shared the same "St. Johns" ceramic technology. This pottery type has a distinctive chalky feel and microscopic analysis demonstrates the presence of sponge spicules in the pottery paste.[14] Check stamping was the most common exterior surface treatment during St. Johns-II times. This regional ceramic style zone highlights a broad area of frequent interactions between communities of potters that may or may not have involved migrations.

St. Marys-II (1250–1450 CE)

By the mid-thirteenth century, profound changes were underway in the Mocama region. Pottery assemblages, consisting mostly of St. Marys cord-marked and sand-tempered plainwares, replaced ones marked by St. Johns chalky wares.[15] Noticeable alterations in refuse disposal patterns, site locations,

---

13. Ibid., 103–104.

14. Nina Thanz Borremans and Craig D. Shaak, "A Preliminary Report on Investigations of Sponge Spicules in Florida 'Chalky' Paste Pottery," *Ceramic Notes (1986)* 3: 125–132 (Occasional Publications of the Ceramic Technology Laboratory, Florida State Museum, Gainesville); Ann S. Cordell and Steven H. Koski, "Analysis of a Spiculate Clay from Lake Monroe, Volusia County, Florida," *Florida Anthropologist* (2003) 56: 113–125; Vicki L. Rolland and Paulette Bond, "The Search for Spiculate Clays near Aboriginal Sites in the Lower St. Johns River Region, Florida," *Florida Anthropologist* 56 (2003): 91–112.

15. Archaeologists refer to the local phase, dated to 1250–1450 CE, as St. Marys-II. See Michael Russo, "Chronologies and Cultures of the St. Marys Region of Northeast Florida and Southeast Georgia," *Florida Anthropologist* (1992), 116–119; Ashley, "Straddling the Florida–Georgia State Line: Ceramic Chronology of the St. Marys Region (ca. A.D. 1400–1700), 127–130; Keith H. Ashley and Vicki L. Rolland, "St. Marys Cord-marked Pottery (Formerly Savannah Fine Cord Marked of Northeastern Florida and Southeastern Georgia): A Type Description," *Florida Anthropologist* 55, no. 1 (2002): 25–36.

and mortuary contexts accompanied the shift in pottery technology, leading some researchers to infer a southward movement of people from coastal southeastern Georgia.[16] This wave of immigration into northeastern Florida may have coincided with an exodus of many St. Johns peoples, who relocated south as local involvement in interregional exchange faded. Regardless of whether migration was actually responsible for the entire suite of cultural changes that occurred at this time, the zone of interaction marked by a common pottery style now links northeastern Florida to southeastern Georgia, not the St. Johns River to the south.

St. Marys-II habitation sites are remarkably similar and occur as groupings of discrete shell midden heaps, generally assumed to represent the garbage of individual households. Sites containing these household middens occur on all barrier islands and the mainland coast, between the St. Johns and Satilla rivers.[17] The dispersed nature of the more numerous St. Marys-II sites contrasts with the more structured St. Johns-II village-mound settlements, suggesting a higher rate of residential (foraging) mobility during this period. To date, we cannot confidently associate one burial mound in this coastal region with St. Marys-II occupations.[18] In fact, the few known burials attributable to this timeframe occur in non-mound contexts adjacent to shell heaps, suggesting burial in or near residences.

While specifics of the yearly cycle are still not fully understood at this time, there seems little doubt that coastal fishing-hunting-gathering provided the economic foundation, with the rich estuary-salt marsh ecosystem serving as the primary source of sustenance.[19] At present, no St. Marys sites in Florida or Georgia have yielded evidence for growing, eating, or disposing of corn. These coastal groups remained foragers, not farmers, or even part-time horticulturalists.

What is most striking about St. Marys-II sites is their marked similarity in artifact assemblage composition.[20] Utilitarian pottery, displaying few vessel forms, is the predominant artifact category at all sites, followed by small amounts of bone and shell artifacts, rare stone tools/debitage, and no prestige goods of any sort. The paucity of exotic items suggests that social reproduction was predicated on local or regional social relations and did not require long-distance interactions and foreign items, as was the case with earlier "St. Johns-II" groups. The mobilization of labor was likely structured at the

16. Keith H. Ashley, "Interaction, Population Movement, and Political Economy: The Changing Social Landscape of Northeastern Florida (A.D. 900–1500)" (Ph.D. diss., University of Florida), 366–369.

17. Ibid.

18. Ashley, "Early St. Johns II Interaction," 369–370.

19. Ibid., 370–371.

20. Ibid., 373.

household or kin group level, with all households engaged in the same economic tasks. These data suggest that St. Marys groups were more insular than the previous St. Johns-II communities in the region, perhaps a reflection of the more unstable late pre-Columbian landscape of the greater Southeast, in which raiding raged among competing chiefdoms. Therefore, what we have archaeologically for the St. Marys-II period are many structurally and artifactually similar sites, with no hint of any type of regional settlement hierarchy, other than some sites being larger than others due to repeated occupations.

San Pedro (1450–1600+ CE)

Something sparked change during the mid-fifteenth century. Thick grog–tempered San Pedro wares, easily distinguishable from St. Marys vessels, became the dominant pottery series, and its geographical distribution mimics that of St. Marys.[21] Transitional assemblages revealed at a few sites suggest an in situ shift in ceramic technology. More importantly, at this same time, maize makes its first appearance in the archaeological record of northeastern Florida. Within a hundred years of this transition, Spanish and French explorers would encounter a volatile Timucua landscape in which territorial raiding was rampant. Regional networks of interaction appear heightened, as inter-polity alliances and feuds developed among Timucua speakers. In contrast, reduced long-distance exchange activities continued, as few imports from afar appear in Mocama context. Before delving into Mocama archaeology, we now turn our attention to the ethnohistoric record.

From European chroniclers we learn that Mocama social organization was based on ranked matrilineal clans, and village authority was in the hands of a community leader or chief born into the prominent Deer Clan.[22] A chief's power emanated from his/her custody of the esoteric knowledge upon which society

21. Jerald T. Milanich, "Surface Information from the Presumed Site of San Pedro de Mocama Mission," *Conference on Historic Site Archaeology Papers* 5 (1971), 114–121; Keith H. Ashley and Vicki L. Rolland, "Grog-Tempered Pottery in the Mocama Province," *The Florida Anthropologist* 50 (1997), 51–66; Ashley, "Straddling the Florida–Georgia State Line," 130.

22. For information on Mocama sociopolitical organization dating to the 1560s, see, for example, Gonzalo Solis de Meras, *Pedro Menendez de Aviles, Adelantado, Governor and Captain General of Florida, Memorial*, translated by Jeannette Thurber Connor (Gainesville: University Press of Florida, 1964); Bartolome Barrientos, *Pedro Mendez de Aviles, Founder of Florida*, trans. Anthony Kerrigan (Gainesville: University Press of Florida, 1965); Charles Bennett, trans., *Three Voyages: Rene Laudonnière* (Gainesville: University Press of Florida, 1975); Sarah Lawson, trans., *A Foothold in Florida: The Eyewitness Account of Four Voyages Made by the French to that Region and Their Attempt at Colonization, 1562–1568, Based on a New Translation of Laudonnière's L'Histoire Notable de la Florida* (East Grinstead, West Sussex, England: Antique Atlas Publications, 1992). Summaries are found in Hann, *A History of the Timucua Indians and Missions*, 78–82; and Milanich, *The Timucua*, 150–166.

and cosmology rested, enabling him/her and his/her closest kin to perpetuate an ideology that rendered them privileged elites. Higher-ranked chiefs extracted tribute from nearby subordinate villages, as kinship and marriage linked local communities socially and politically. A village council of principal men, however, tempered absolute chiefly power. Throughout the broader territory, multi-community polities or chiefdoms were embroiled in internecine raiding that pitted ever-changing alliances of Timucua against one another.[23] The frequency at which these antagonistic relations are reported in the earliest sixteenth-century Spanish and French accounts points to preexisting intra-Timucua conflicts.

The Mocama at the mouth of the St. Johns River and barrier islands to the north were part of an alliance of as many as thirty chiefs under the sway of a chief known as Saturiwa. A similar coalition characterized the northern Mocama, who were subordinate to Chief Tacatacuru of Cumberland Island. These two Mocama leaders were close allies in the 1560s, as early French documents repeatedly highlight interactions, councils, and general acts of diplomacy involving Saturiwa, Tacatacuru, and other lesser Mocama chiefs.[24] It is still unclear how much actual political authority each chief possessed beyond the local polity level.

Religious practices included first-fruit and death ceremonies, taboos, and other strongly held beliefs.[25] Rituals were performed to create community unity and render the natural and spirit worlds meaningful. Shamanistic practices included healing, curing, divining, and other acts of spiritual contact and intervention. Both men and women filled ritually prized positions, as shaman, curers, herbalists, and midwives, to name a few. Warfare was ritualized with taboo restrictions strictly followed and the sacred black drink consumed. Mocama drank this purifying emetic, concocted of parched and brewed yaupon holly leaves, on a wide range of occasions. Based on the early sixteenth-century writings of Fray Pareja, Tamara Spikes argues that Timucua culture "was structured by their conceptions of purity, impurity, and pollution," which further guided their "interactions with the sacred, structured their social relations, and shaped their worldview."[26]

With this brief documents-based portrait now drawn, what might archaeology have to say about the sixteenth-century Mocama? Archaeological testing

23. See Hann, *A History of the Timucua Indians and Missions*, 80–81.

24. Bennett, trans., *Three Voyages: Rene Laudonnière;* Lawson, trans., *A Foothold in Florida.*

25. Hann, *A History of the Timucua Indians and Missions*, 114–121; Milanich, *The Timucua*, 173–181.

26. Tamara Shircliff Spike, "Death and Death Ritual among the Timucua of Spanish Florida," in *From La Florida to La California: Franciscan Evangelization in the Spanish Borderlands*, ed. Timothy J. Johnson and Gert Melville (Berkeley, CA: Academy of American Franciscan History, 2013), 188.

at four contact-period villages in northeastern Florida by the University of North Florida suggests more dispersed Mocama settlements than the conventional model of a walled village with tightly clustered households.[27] Such sites exhibit mounded, household shell middens peppered broadly over maritime hammocks situated adjacent to rivers or tidal marshes. Site structure is similar to that of the preceding St. Marys-II period, and the two components overlap at some large sites. In terms of village size, a captured mutineer from the French colony at Fort Caroline, near Saturiwa's village, informs Spanish interrogators in Havana that "there are three or four indian places which were settled of 7, 8, 10, and 12 houses, covered with palm, at a half league, and two or three leagues from the fort."[28] A 1565 Spanish document states that Saturiwa's village comprised "twenty-five large dwellings."[29] A community center with a chief's residence and a council house likely tethered these dispersed households together.

With respect to other features of Mocama villages, early French accounts refer to granaries, a ball pole and plaza area, and other vaguely defined buildings. Unfortunately, at this time, the archaeological record is rather silent with specific details regarding contact village layout and actual range of building types, but the sites seem nothing like the major mound centers that existed hundreds of years earlier at Mill Cove and Mt. Royal.

The Mocama encountered by Europeans were the historical product of a long tradition of foraging. Shell midden data from household contexts indicate a continued subsistence economy focused on the exploitation of salt marsh and estuarine resources. The contact-era Mocama also grew corn, although the quantities of preserved cobs, cupules, and kernels recovered to date are not impressive.[30] Stable isotope analyses on human bone from late precontact sites along the Atlantic coast and within the interior of peninsular Florida suggest maize was a minor dietary component.[31] In addition, radiometric assays on corn and soot from cobmarked pottery in northeastern Florida are consistent and indicate that maize appeared no earlier than about

---

27. Ashley, "Straddling the Florida–Georgia State Line, 135–137; Ashley, "Distribution of Contact and Early Mission Period Sites in the Mocama Province," *Florida Anthropologist* 67 (2014): 165–171.

28. Eugene Lyon, Forts Caroline and San Mateo, Vulnerable Outposts. Report submitted to Fort Caroline National Memorial (PX532090219), 1982, Jacksonville, FL.

29. Barrientos, *Pedro Mendez de Aviles, Founder of Florida.*

30. Ashley, "Straddling the Florida–Georgia State Line, 131–132.

31. Dale L. Hutchinson, Clark Spencer Larsen, Margaret J. Schoeninger, and Lynette Norr, "Regional Variation in the Pattern of Maize Adoption and Use in Florida and Georgia," *American Antiquity* (1998); Clark Spencer Larsen, Dale L. Hutchinson, Margaret J. Schoeninger, and Lynette Norr, "Food and Stable Isotopes in La Florida: Diet and Nutrition Before and After Contact," in *Bioarchaeology of Spanish Florida*, ed. Clark Spencer Larsen (Gainesville: University Press of Florida, Gainesville, 2001).

1450 CE in this part of the state.[32] This late date also appears true for the introduction of corn farming among the Guale to the north, and perhaps even the inland Timucua to the west.

It may be that all Timucua speakers were hunter-gatherers for most of their history, only turning to maize production a century or less prior to Juan Ponce de Leon's landfall in Florida. In our opinion, documentary references to the amount of maize grown by the Mocama at first contact are somewhat ambiguous, and, in some instances, possibly exaggerated. Nevertheless, its production was significant and appears related to economic and political shifts among the Mocama. Therefore, from an archaeological perspective, it appears that the Mocama practiced low residential mobility (i.e., year-round site occupations), and their annual subsistence cycle involved a flexible and mixed subsistence strategy of foraging and gardening that likely varied depending on yearly local climatic conditions.

The ethnohistoric pairing of hereditary leadership and centralized decision-making above the village level strongly supports the existence of chiefdoms among the sixteenth-century Mocama. The archaeological record of the Mocama area, however, lacks accepted material correlates for Mississippian chiefdoms such as site size hierarchies, platform mound centers, and until recently exotic elite burials and ritual paraphernalia (discussed below). As both Jerald Milanich and John Worth have noted, "[w]ere it not for the documentary record, we might not ever recognize that the Timucua were organized as simple chiefdoms."[33]

At present, we are still far from understanding the circumstances and processes that brought about the sudden change in Mocama political organization. We strongly agree with claims that agriculture is not a prerequisite for sociopolitical complexity, particularly for groups living along resource-rich coastlines. Take the Calusa of southwestern Florida for example. These fisher-hunter-gatherers maintained a complex chiefdom at the dawn of European arrival.[34] Moreover, in the Guale area, David Hurst Thomas now places the emergence of chiefdoms five hundred or so years before the adoption of corn farming.[35]

---

32. Ashley, "Straddling the Florida–Georgia State Line," 134.

33. Jerald T. Milanich, "Native Chiefdoms and the Exercise of Complexity in Sixteenth-Century Florida," in *Chiefdoms and Chieftaincy in the Americas*, ed. Elsa M. Redmond (Gainesville: University Press of Florida, 1998), 248; John E. Worth, "An Overview of the Suwannee Valley Culture," in *Late Prehistoric Florida: Archaeology at the Edge of the Mississippian World*, ed. Keith Ashley and Nancy Marie White (Gainesville: University Press of Florida, 2012), 169–171.

34. For an excellent assessment of the current state of Calusa archaeology, see William H. Marquardt, "Tracking the Calusa: A Retrospective," *Southeastern Archaeology* (2014), 1–24.

35. David Hurst Thomas, "The "Guale Problem" Revisited: Farming and Foraging on St. Catherines Island (Cal A.D. 1300–1580)," in *Native American Landscapes of St.*

In the Mocama area, however, increased political complexity does seem to coincide with the initial appearance of corn in the archaeological record. In our opinion, however, the growing of corn among the Mocama had less to do with subsistence and more to do with sociopolitical concerns.

As Thomas argues for the Guale, what motivated them to farm was not the energetic or caloric value of corn but the social benefits of farming.[36] Coming up with an answer to why the Mocama decided to grow corn may require us to broaden our geographical scale of analysis and explore external sociohistorical circumstances in which individuals and families attempted to become successful in the highly competitive political climate of the late precontact period. Perhaps to compete with the Guale to the north and with other Timucua speakers to the west (who themselves may have had to exercise complexity due to their neighbors the Apalachee), the Mocama began to emulate them politically.

As part of the process, the Mocama may have incorporated gardening into their economy, with corn initially serving as a form of symbolic capital. Its production, in turn, may have provided certain kin groups or clans the opportunity to increase their social status. Additionally, escalating interregional raiding may have opened avenues to power and status building for successful warriors and diplomats. Guarding villages and establishing successful alliances in the face of low-scale, yet frequent, raiding became a real concern for Timucua communities. Control of esoteric knowledge or ideology may have further bolstered elite demands and enabled them to hold power, even if their grip was tenuous. Perhaps some individuals or groups may have risen up within the structural constraints of Mocama society to secure control over these tangible and intangible resources, enabling them to compel others to turn over surplus and loyalty to gain access to these resources. What eventually resulted were stronger social divides and institutionalized inequalities, which fall more or less in line with the general tenor of contact-era texts. In all likelihood, these factors began to take shape before the material evidence truly manifests itself in the archaeological record.

Mortuary Practices

In terms of precontact religion, the current archaeological record is rather mute. However, one way in which archaeologists often engage the topic of ritual is through the excavation and interpretation of the treatment and burial of the dead. Aspects of mortuary rituals often provide insights into a group's cosmology, since these practices follow culturally specific dictates. At present,

---

Catherines Island, Georgia, vol. 2, *The Data*, ed. David Hurst Thomas, Anthropological Papers of the American Museum of Natural History 88 (New York: American Museum of Natural History, 2008), 1095–1115.

36. Ibid., 1100–1103.

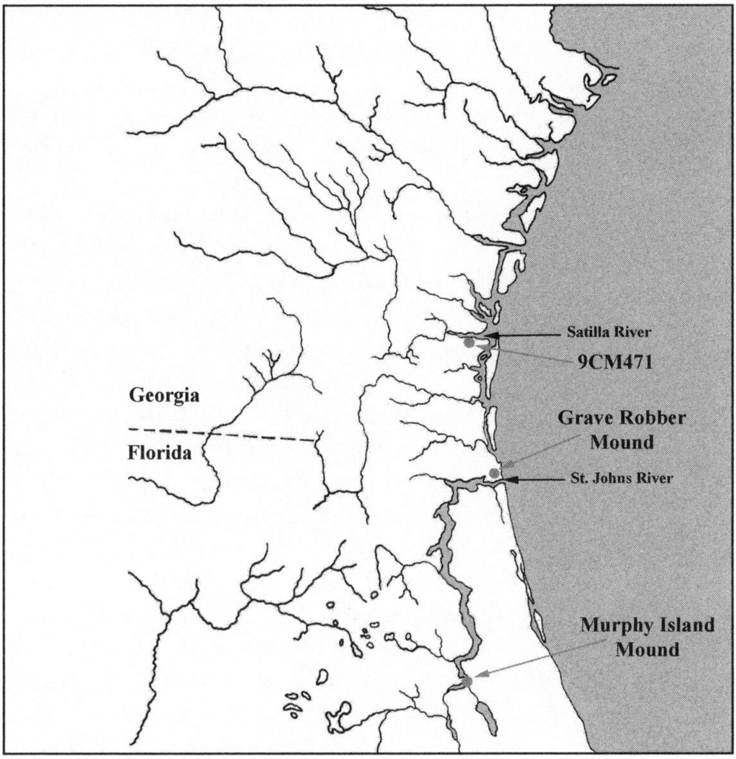

FIGURE 3. Location of three burial mounds: 9CM471, Grave Robber Mound, and Murphy Island Mound.

evidence of mound building in the Mocama region is nonexistent or ambiguous at best. As a final topic of inquiry, we call attention to what we see as an emerging pattern of the reuse or appropriation of preexisting burial mounds by sixteenth-century Timucua people. Our sample is admittedly small and consists of three mounds from the broader Timucua domain: one in the Mocama area, another to the north in the territory of the Yufera dialect, and the third is to the south along the middle St. Johns in lands associated with Outina speakers (Figure 3).

Grave Robber Mound

The Grave Robber Mound is located on the western side of Fort George Island, immediately north of the St. Johns River in northeastern Florida. This mound was extensively looted prior to the 1970s. One reported excavation conducted by locals, in consultation with the State of Florida in the late 1960s, resulted in the discovery of two burials. Details are sketchy since all notes and photographs have been lost, so we must rely on a 2010 interview with one of the excavators and results of a recent analysis of the artifact collection by Vicki Rolland.[37]

At the time of excavation, the mound measured twenty meters in diameter and a little more than two meters in height. A trench dug slightly east of the mound's center came upon two supine burials within a "few feet of the surface." Areas of hematite-colored sand marked the location of each interment. Accompanying Burial A were two stone celts, a large number of small shell beads, two clover-shaped shell ornaments, and eleven variously shaped and sized whelk-shell ear pins. Burial B contained fewer items, although a copper axe laid across his/her chest. Around the individual's neck were massive whelk columella beads. A copper or brass ring was discovered near the burials, but not on a finger. Apparently, these two interments differed from all others purportedly taken from the mound in terms of artifacts, mode of burial, and condition of the bones, suggesting they were intrusive into an earlier mound. In addition, both are among the most lavishly adorned burials known for northeastern Florida.

Dating the mound is a little tricky due to lack of temporally sensitive artifacts. The axe looks to be a classic Mississippian sumptuary artifact, likely postdating 1300 CE. The clover-shaped whelk buttons are interesting, and according to several researchers, they are a lobed variant of a style that is clearly protohistoric, and known for archaeological sites in the Florida panhandle, central Alabama along the Alabama and Tallapoosa rivers, and other adjacent areas.[38] Considering the shell artifact assemblage as a whole, Marvin Smith dates most of this material to the period ca. 1550–1650. If this date is correct, the absence of European artifacts is surprising, based on the location of the site. Perhaps the burials date to the late fifteenth or early sixteenth century. Future compositional analysis of the copper/brass finger ring may provide some temporal clarification.

Shovel test sampling of the area surrounding the burial mound revealed a strong seventeenth-century mission period component and a low-density occurrence of contact-era San Pedro pottery.[39] Dense San Pedro–shell midden

---

37. Vicki Rolland and Keith Ashley, "Two Burials from Grave Robber Mound (8DU141): Unique Evidence of Status and Burial Ritual," paper presented at the 68th annual meeting of the Southeastern Archaeological Conference (Jacksonville, FL, 2011).

38. Marvin Smith, personal communication, 2011; Craig Sheldon, personal communication, 2011; Nancy M. White, "Middle Woodland and Protohistoric Fort Walton at The Lost Chipola Cutoff Mound, Northwest Florida," *Florida Anthropologist* (2011), 255, 257; Nancy M. While, personal communications, 2018.

39. Keith Ashley and Rebecca Gorman, "The Fort George Island Slough Sites Archaeological Survey," report on file with the Florida Division of Historical Resources (Tallahassee: Florida Division of Historical Resources, 2011).

deposits dot the landscape a few hundred meters north of the mound at the suspected location of the Mocama village of Alimacani.

9CM471

Along the Satilla River, Georgia, about twelve miles from Cumberland Island lies site 9CM471. Within its boundaries is a two- to three-meter high sand mound with a basal diameter of twenty-five meters. Units dug into the mound as part of a cultural resource management project in 2007, encountered a human burial at a depth of 70 cm below the surface.[40] All human remains were left in situ, and excavations were performed in strict compliance with the Georgia Council of American Indian concerns. Artifacts included 384 glass beads, an iron halberd, lugged hoe, hatchet, and knife fragment. According to Marvin Smith, the beads suggest a date range of 1550–1600 CE. While uncertain of the mound's origin, the mound excavator Tom Whitley states, "[I]t was clear to us that this is an earlier mound into which the Contact Period burials were intrusive, and not a purposely-built Contact Period mound."[41] Furthermore, it was the only mound recorded in the 1,100-acre survey tract.

Surrounding the mound are a number of discrete surface scatters of shell that form a discontinuous and thin midden. Although testing of this domestic area was limited, no contact-period San Pedro pottery or European artifacts were recovered. Cord-marked pottery believed to date to the period 900–1450 CE dominates, with smaller amounts of grog-tempered and Woodland period pottery (500–900 CE) also present. Moderate amounts of San Pedro pottery occurred hundreds of meters to the east. Unless the site's residents manufactured sand-tempered cord-marked pottery in the sixteenth century, the mound is not directly associated with a contact village. Sites well to the east along Floyd and Shelbine creeks yielded abundant San Pedro pottery.[42] Until more archaeological work is conducted close to the mound, the contemporaneity of the shell heaps and the burial mound remains uncertain. Nevertheless, 9CM471 is believed to represent the village or territory of Yufera, a Timucua dialect spoken on the Georgia mainland, west of Cumberland Island.[43]

---

40. Thomas G. Whitley, Jana Futch, Carolyn Rock, and Dwight Kirkland, "Phase I and II Cultural Resources Survey and Testing of 9400 Acres at Big Pasture, and 1880 Acres at Little Pasture Camden County, Georgia," report on file with Brockington and Associates, Inc. (Savannah: Brockington and Associates, 2012), 82–98.

41. Thomas G. Whitley, personal communication, 2018.

42. Dwight Kirkland, "Preliminary Archaeological Investigations of Floyd Creek, Camden County, Georgia," *Early Georgia* 7 (1979): 1–25.

43. Whitley, et al., "Phase I and II Cultural Resources Survey," 82.

Murphy Island

In 1895, the prolific mound-excavator Clarence B. Moore excavated two sand mounds along the St. Johns River on Murphy Island, Florida.[44] From the northernmost mound, which measured 24.4 meters in diameter and 3.6 meters in height, he encountered artificially colored sands, local and non-local artifacts, and a large number of human burials. An abridged list of these artifacts includes copper gorget and panpipe, tobacco pipes, stone plummets, a tetrapod vessel, and a quartz crystal. These items along with the absence of check-stamped pottery clearly date the burial repository to the Woodland period (ca. 100–500 CE). His excavations, however, also encountered burials with "iron implements and glass beads" in different locations within one meter of the mound surface. Moore considered these "intrusive deposits" that appear to represent at least five historic-period Native American interments.[45]

One burial contained a bone comb, with a scroll decoration on both sides, in association with a stone chisel. A long-bladed iron axe, an unidentified iron tool, and "a number of blue cylindrical beads of glass and spherical polychrome beads of the same material" accompanied a slightly deeper burial. A third interment contained a number of implements of iron described as "a long knife, two chisels, a triangular chisel or tomahawk, and an unidentified tool." Elsewhere an iron hoe and a narrow-bladed iron axe "lay together with fragmentary human remains." Much deeper in the mound he recovered an iron object "resembling the lower portion of a small nail."[46] Unfortunately, the latter unidentified iron object is the only European artifact illustrated in Moore's report. However, photographs of the bone comb, glass beads, and the nail-like iron fragment are part of the National Museum of American Indian's Murphy Island collection. After viewing the photographs, Marvin Smith identified the glass beads as "classic sixteenth-century beads including seven-layer, faceted chevron beads, Nueva Cadiz beads, and long striped, tubular chevron beads."[47] In Spanish areas, an assemblage like this usually dates to about 1560.

Summary

In all three cases, contact-era burials occur in mounds apparently situated away from the center of villages, although we need more testing in areas sur-

---

44. Clarence B. Moore, "Two Sand Mounds on Murphy Island," *Journal of the Academy of Natural Sciences of Philadelphia* 10 (1896): 503–517.

45. Ibid., 513–514.

46. Ibid, 514.

47. Marvin Smith, personal communication, 2011. He further suggests that the unidentified nail-like object looks like a possible cross-bolt tip (arrowhead), but admits that it is difficult to tell from the photograph.

rounding each of the mounds. In addition, ornately garnished burials seem to have been placed in pits dug into preexisting mounds rather than placed on the surface of an extant mound and covered with soil, as part of an ongoing mound building process. In contrast, St. Johns-II mounds built five hundred years earlier appear to have been community cemeteries, with primary and secondary burials added episodically over centuries of time. Perhaps in the Mocama area, mound burial after 1450 was reserved only for elites, with commoners interred in or near their residences.

The intrusive burials are richly furnished with grave goods, some of European origin, suggesting that certain individuals may have been interred in preexisting burial mounds for a reason. Conceivably, interment in these longstanding mortuary facilities was a symbolic act on the part of chiefs and elites to appropriate the past and cement ties to ancestors and the other world. In other words, continued use of a spiritually charged ancient location that held the physical remains of ancestors and potent objects served to connect the present with the sacred past, as chiefly elites were entombed in a place of their ancestors, or at least their perceived ancestors. Ancestor veneration may have played a significant role in the creation and legitimation of elite power, with elites' ancestors closely associated with supernatural forces. Possessing such other worldly connections may have enabled living chiefs to control access to the cosmic realm. Establishing a continuum between the contemporary Mocama world and the deep past further may have reinforced a social group's claim to the land and its resources.

Interestingly, the suspected location of these mound burials in relation to villages does bear a general resemblance to one of the few descriptions of "pre-Christian" burial practices among the Timucua. In 1630, Fray de Jesus states, "In some provinces when the principal cacique died . . . they always kept these [chiefs'] graves separate from the rest and all on the highest hills (montes), distanced from the settlements."[48] Admittedly, it is unclear exactly what province he was alluding to, but it may have been a common practice among Timucua societies.

Conclusion

In this chapter, we have provided a historical backdrop to the Mocama and their biological and cultural ancestors. Unfortunately, we continue to navigate through a fog of uncertainty due to the lack of broad-scale excavations at Mocama villages. Thus, going forward, emphasis needs to be placed on systematically exploring the physical layouts of contact-period archaeological sites

48. Francisco Alonso de Jesús, "1630 Memorial of Francisco Alonso de Jesús on Spanish Florida's Missions and Natives," trans. John H. Hann, *The Americas* 50 (1993), 99.

to better understand village dynamics and social structure. Identifying both sacred spaces such as a council house, plaza, and possibly other buildings would help build on the thin ethnohistoric details relayed by the French and Spanish. Discovering archaeological evidence of family quarters and activity areas would provide both subsistence data and social-context information. Such context-specific data would help raise further questions on the kinds of ritual activities that were part of Mocama life. For the Mocama, ancestors played a vital role in the cosmological character of their worldview. The deliberate interment of elite leaders into older burial mounds suggests how important the past was to the Mocama and how elites used that connection to deep time to their advantage.

Chapter 11

Nombre de Dios: The First and Last Franciscan Mission in Spanish La Florida

KATHLEEN DEAGAN

Mission Nombre de Dios is a place about which a lot is known, but about which surprisingly little is understood. It was the first Franciscan mission in the United States, established at St. Augustine in 1587. It was also the longest-lived mission in Florida, active until the end of the First Spanish Period in 1763. Much of what is known about the location, organization, and operation of the mission and shrine during the colonial period has been revealed through archaeological and related historical projects carried out since 1934 on the present and former grounds of Mission Nombre de Dios. My principal intent in this paper is to summarize what has been learned from that work.

Despite its historical primacy and longevity, Mission Nombre de Dios—in a scholarly sense—has been an uncritically accepted element in the colonial landscape, with little historical or archaeological writing devoted specifically to the mission itself. A number of distinguished modern historians have written about or referred to Mission Nombre de Dios, but the information has usually been included as a comment in a study that was focused on other topics.[1] Archaeological research has been more directly focused on Mission Nombre de Dios itself, largely because archaeological excavation is directly

---

1. Charles Arnade, *Florida on Trial* (Coral Gables, FL: University of Miami Institute of Hispanic Studies Publications, 1959); Amy Bushnell, *Situado and Sabana: Spain's Support System of the Presidio and Mission Provinces of Florida*, Anthropological Papers of the American Museum of Natural History (Athens: University of Georgia Press, 1994); Michael Gannon, *The Cross in the Sand: The Early Catholic Church in Florida, 1513–1870* (Gainesville: University of Florida Press, 1965); Maynard Geiger, *The Franciscan Conquest of Florida*, Studies in Hispanic-American History, vol. 1 (Washington, DC: Catholic University of America, 1937); John Hann, *A History of the Timucua Indians and Their Missions* (Gainesville: University Press of Florida, 1996); John Hann, "St. Augustine's Fallout of the Yamasee War," *Florida Historical Quarterly* 68(2): 180–200 (1989); John Worth, *The Timucuan Chiefdoms of Spanish Florida*, vol. 2, *Resistance and Destruction* (Gainesville: University of Florida Press, 1998).

tied to physical place.[2] However, these studies have usually been concentrated on a single occupation period or aspects of the mission, and most remain unpublished.

Mission and Shrine

Mission Nombre de Dios was established to serve the indigenous Timucua Indians of the St. Augustine area who, by 1620, were considerably diminished in population owing to disease, cultural disruption, and conflict. After that time, the native population of the Mission rarely exceeded fifty souls, making it one of the smallest mission communities in seventeenth-century La Florida. Perhaps at least in part because of this, Mission Nombre de Dios has been inextricably connected with the Shrine of Nuestra Señora de La Leche y Buen Parto (Our Lady of [Mother's] Milk and Safe Delivery), a seventeenth-century devotion that remains active today. Specific details of the shrine's origin are sparse. It is thought that the Franciscans brought a much-venerated statue of Nuestra Señora to Florida sometime in the late sixteenth or early seventeenth century. A shrine was established for Nuestra Señora de La Leche at (it is assumed) Mission Nombre de Dios, and it became the focus of widespread devotion and significant alms contributions.[3]

---

2. James Cusick, Report on the 1993 Excavations at the Nombre de Dios Site (8-SJ-34): The Search for St. Augustine's Early Forts, project report on file, Florida Museum of Natural History, University of Florida, Gainesville, 1993; Kathleen Deagan, *The Nombre de Dios Mission/La Leche Shrine Site, St. Augustine: Summary Report on the 1934–2011 Excavations*, Florida Museum of Natural History Miscellaneous Reports in Archaeology, no. 62 (Gainesville: Florida Museum of Natural History and University of Florida, 2012), available at https://www.academia.edu/8431818/Archaeology_at8SJ34_The_Nombre_de_Dios_Mission_La_Leche_Shrine_Site_St._Augustine; John W. Morris, Excavations at 8-SJ-34, project report on file, Florida Museum of Natural History, University of Florida, Gainesville, 1995; Lillian Seaberg, Report on the Indian Site at the "Fountain of Youth," mss on file, Florida State Museum, University of Florida, Gainesville, 1951, reprinted in *Spanish St. Augustine: A Sourcebook for America's Ancient City*, ed. Kathleen Deagan (New York: Garland Press, 1991), 209–279; Charles Spellman, Communication on archaeological excavations on the grounds of the La Leche Shrine, manuscript on file, Archives of the Catholic Diocese of St. Augustine, October 15, 1952; Gifford Waters, 1997 Excavations at the 8SJ34/Nombre de Dios Site: Florida's First Spanish Fort, project report on file, Florida Museum of Natural History, University of Florida, Gainesville, 1998; Gifford Waters, "Maintenance and Change in 18th-Century Mission Indian Identity: A Multi-Ethnic Contact Situation" (PhD diss., University of Florida, 2005).

3. Focused documentary research on the Shrine of La Leche is also rare. The principal source of our contemporary understanding seems to have derived from the "History of Nuestra Señora de la Leche y Buen Parto and St. Augustine, the Oldest Parish in the United States," Cathedral Parish of St. Augustine, St. Augustine, FL, 1937. Originally printed for distribution, but is long out of print. Copies are in the Cathedral Parish Archives and The University of Florida Library Collections.

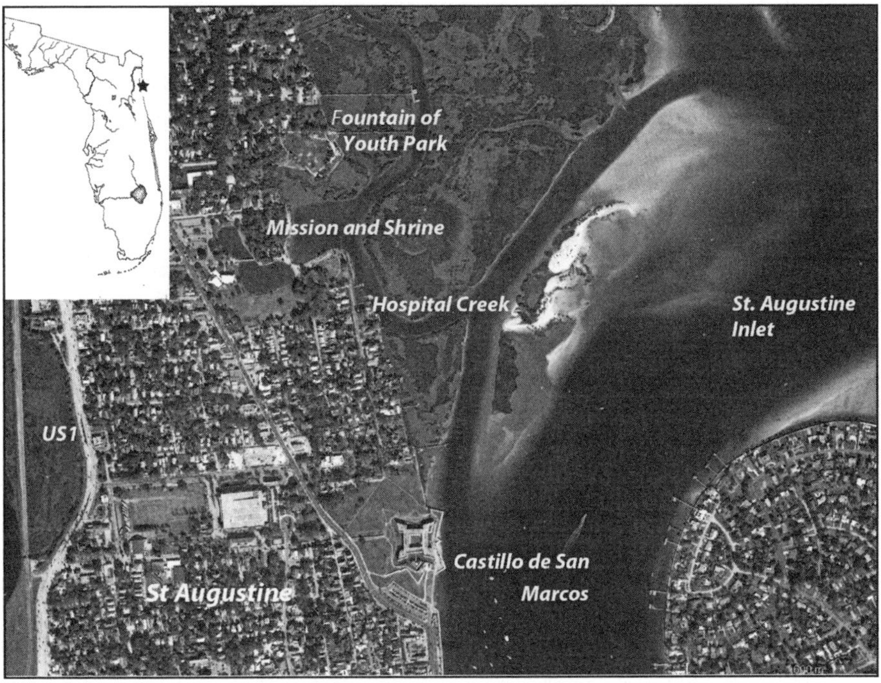

FIGURE 1. Location map.

A key notion that sometimes escapes the contemporary general public is that property boundaries today do not reflect those of the colonial period. When we speak of the Mission Nombre de Dios as a colonial entity, we are talking about a location that—at different times—likely encompassed a large area along the east side of St. Augustine's intracoastal waterway, including the properties today known as the Fountain of Youth Park (8SJ31) and Mission Nombre de Dios (8SJ34) (Figure 1). Much residential development has taken place in this area, and extreme alterations have occurred in the waterways directly east and south of the contemporary Mission and Shrine property. Overall, however, the degree of preservation has been quite remarkable, thanks to the Catholic Church's commitment to sustain a place of pilgrimage and meditation; and that of the Fountain of Youth Park to maintain its property as a historical and educational attraction.

Before the Franciscans

The area was occupied by the Timucuan Indian people prior to arrival of the Spaniards under Pedro Menéndez in 1565. Excavations by the University of Florida and the City of St. Augustine have shown that within and to the north of the Fountain of Youth Park area, a Timucua occupation had existed since at least 800 CE, with earlier, intermittent occupation going back some 3,000 years.[4]

The Menéndez expedition of 1565 made their encampment in the vicinity of today's Hospital Creek, at or close to a village governed by a cacique known as Seloy. Remains of both the Spanish encampment and a Timucua village have been identified in the southeastern quadrant of the Fountain of Youth Park property. Other sixteenth-century Spanish artifacts have been uncovered in the northeast corner of the present Mission Nombre de Dios property, including a section of a ditch or moat, a lime-burning kiln, and a possible blockhouse.[5]

The initial settlement was occupied for less than a year before Timucuan hostility and soldiers' mutiny forced the relocation of the town across the Matanzas River to an as-yet unknown location on Anastasia Island. It remained there until 1572, leaving the previous mainland location unoccupied by Spaniards. In that year the town was moved to the mainland location south of the present-day Plaza de la Constitución.

Although Jesuit missionaries arrived in Florida in late 1566, they were not active in the St. Augustine region, but instead went farther afield to the north and the south (possibly owing at least in part to the intransigence of the Timucua people in the area), and left the mission field in 1572. Very little is known about the dynamics of Timucuan activity in this area between 1566 and 1572, but apparently hostilities had been greatly diminished through pacification, negotiation, and/or the decimation of local populations.

---

4. Kathleen Deagan and Carl Halbirt, "The People Who Met Menéndez," in *The Oldest City*, ed. Susan R. Parker (St. Augustine: St. Augustine Historical Society, 2019).

5. An authoritative source on the Menéndez expeditions is Eugene Lyon, *The Enterprise of Florida* (Gainesville: University Press of Florida, 1976). For summaries of the excavations at the Fountain of Youth Park, see Kathleen Deagan, *Fifty Years of Archaeology at the Fountain of Youth Park site (8-SJ-31), St. Augustine*, Florida Museum of Natural History Miscellaneous Project Report Series, no. 59 (Gainesville: University of Florida, 2008), available at http://www.flmnh.ufl.edu/histarch/foy_site_reports.htm, and *Investigating the Menéndez Defenses: Field Report on the 2011–2015 Excavations at the Fountain of Youth Park Site, St. Augustine*, Florida Museum of Natural History Miscellaneous Project Report Series, no. #62 (Gainesville: University of Florida, 2016), available at https://www.academia.edu/34305249/Investigating_the_1565_Men%C3%A9ndez_Defenses_Florida_Museum_of_Natural_History_Miscellaneous_Papers_in_Archaeology_62. Summaries of the archaeological work at Mission Nombre de Dios can be found in Kathleen Deagan, *The Nombre de Dios Mission/La Leche Shrine Site, St. Augustine: Summary Report on the 1934–2011 Excavations*, Florida Museum of Natural History Miscellaneous Reports in Archaeology, no. #60 (Gainesville: University of Florida, 2012), available at https://www.academia.edu/8431818/Archaeology_at_8SJ34_The_Nombre_de_Dios_Mission_La_Leche_Shrine_Site_St._Augustine.

The First Franciscan Mission

Although at least two Franciscan friars were in La Florida during the 1570s, the first significant group of Franciscan missionaries arrived at St. Augustine in 1587 and immediately set about establishing missions among the native people along the east coast.[6] Fray Alonso Escobedo, author of the famous epic poem *La Florida*, went to the nearby Timucua Indian town of Nombre de Dios, which was about a quarter-league from the Spanish town (1.4 kilometers or about 0.87 miles). Within a few years the church was built and was said to have "statues of many saints."[7]

Brother Escobedo undoubtedly had an easier task than his colleagues farther north, since the town to which he was assigned already had many Christian converts, including its *cacica*, Doña Ana.[8] At least eighty Timucuan converts from the surrounding area attended mass in the town parish before establishment of the mission at Nombre de Dios.

The mission's name seems to have been connected to its location near the original landing site of the Spaniards in 1565. Places of first arrival were frequently given the toponym of Nombre de Dios in sixteenth-century Spanish America. Nombre de Dios, Panamá, for example, was the first settlement in that territory; and when traversing the steep terrain near Durango, Mexico, Cortés wrote that "I went through a pass . . . at the end of this province that we named Nombre de Dios, for being the first in these lands we had passed through."[9]

Such an association is also indicated by St. Augustine native Elixio de la Puente some 200 years later in the key to his 1769 map of St. Augustine. Location 12 is identified as the "Place called Nombre de Dios, which is the same where the first Mass was said on September 8, 1565, when the Spaniards under the command of Pedro Menendez de Avilés set out to conquer these provinces, and afterward an Indian Mission was built there, with a chapel in which was placed an image of María Santísima de la Leche."[10] Once the

---

6. The initial period of mission activity among the Timucua of the St. Augustine area is detailed in Michael Gannon, *The Cross in the Sand* (Gainesville: University Press of Florida, 1965) and John Hann, *A History of the Timucua Indians and Missions* (Gainesville: University Press of Florida, 1996).

7. On Escobedo's poem, see Alonso Gregorio de Escobedo and James Covington, *Pirates, Indians and Spaniards: Father Escobedo's La Florida*, (St. Petersburg, FL: Great Outdoors Pub. Co., 1963). For a description of the church, *see* Charles Arnade, *Florida on Trial, 1593–1602* (Coral Gables, FL: University of Miami Press, 1959).

8. Amy Bushnell, *Situado and Sabana: Spain's Support System for the Presidio and Mission Provinces of Florida* (New York: American Museum of Natural History, 1994).

9. Peter Gerhard, *Geografía histórica de la Nueva España, México* (Mexico City: Universidad Nacional Autónoma de México, 1986), 209–211.

10. Juan Joseph Elixio de la Puente, Plano de la RL: Fuerza Baluartes y Linea de la Plaza de SN. Augustin de Florida (1769), University of Florida Digital Collections

Spaniards returned from their seven-year sojourn on Anastasia Island, they referred to the native town located near the initial settlement as "Nombre de Dios" by virtue of that association.

There is little documentary information about the mission during the first fifteen years of its existence. At the time of its establishment in 1587, the town was governed by Doña Ana, who had assisted the Spanish during the attack of Francis Drake the previous year. In 1595, eighty people were baptized at the mission, and by that date, Doña Ana had been succeeded as *cacica* by her daughter Doña María.[11] Doña María was married to a Spanish soldier and had three children with him; she was also the principal chief of the Saltwater Timucua region. Several other towns were in her jurisdiction that were also served by the friars of Mission Nombre de Dios. Doña María saved St. Augustine from a famine that same year by levying a head tax of one *arroba* (about twenty-five pounds) of maize on each married man in her jurisdiction. This provided forty-eight *fanegas* of corn for the Spaniards (who then numbered fewer than three hundred), indicating that at least forty-eight families were in the region at that time. The Franciscan vicar of Nombre de Dios wrote in 1602 that "I presently serve as the vicar of the head town of Nombre de Dios. It is only two leagues from here, and Capuana is another league, and Palica as well, in addition to other towns, both large and small, at two more leagues, which contain two hundred Christians.[12]

The *cacica* Doña Ana—María's mother and ruler before her—was by then the *cacica* of the San Pedro mission town on Cumberland Island, a Mocama Timucua town. Doña Ana died in 1604, and Doña María became the principal *cacica* of both Nombre de Dios and San Pedro. When Bishop Altamirano visited Nombre de Dios in 1606, his scribe noted that Doña María spent most of her time at San Pedro, and had ten subject villages under her jurisdiction, including the San Pedro mission community on Cumberland Island.[13] This raises some very interesting questions about the dramatic changes that had taken place in Native political organization, territorial concepts, and alliances since the early years of Spanish presence. For example, the earliest missionaries believed that the people of the San Pedro Mission—today's Cumberland Island—spoke the Mocama dialect, and constituted a separate polity from that of the Agua Salada people (who spoke the Agua Salada dialect and lived along the coast to the south and east of the St. Johns River). The Agua Salada polity,

---

(Gainesville), available at https://governorshouselibrary.wordpress.com/2018/01/22/govhouselibrary-on-the-map-colonial-st-augustine/.

11. Antonio de las Alas and Pedro Menéndez de Marques, 1595, in Bushnell, *Situado and Sabana*, 120; Alonso de Alas, 1602, in Charles Arnade, *Florida on Trial*, 57.

12. Fray Bermejo, Needs of the Florida Missions, University of Florida, Stetson Document Collection, AGI 86-5-24, September 14, 1602, trans. Christopher Wooley.

13. John Hann, *History of the Timucua Indians*, 164–165.

led by Cacique Saturiwa, remained violently hostile toward the Spaniards through the 1560s, well after other Timucua *caciques* had treated with Menéndez.[14] This may well have inhibited the relocation of St. Augustine back to the mainland until 1572, and it is plausible that Spanish intervention in Timucua politics and leadership may have expanded the power of the more cooperative Mocama at the expense of the Agua Salada people around St. Augustine.

In any case, the bishop confirmed that 216 people were served by Mission Nombre de Dios, including Doña María and two of her children (her oldest son was in residence at San Pedro when the bishop visited). This number included those in the towns under her jurisdiction, as well as twenty "*españoles*," who may have been Spanish soldiers living with their Indian wives.

In 1654–1655 a smallpox epidemic was reported to have virtually wiped out the population of Nombre de Dios, and then-Governor Rebolledo ordered that a *visita* town on the edge of the Okefenokee swamp should be forcibly moved to St. Augustine to repopulate Nombre de Dios.[15] This apparently did not happen.

The Timucuan population of Nombre de Dios continued to decline through much of the seventeenth century, and did not have a resident friar for much of the century. In 1674, a *visita* conducted by Bishop Gabriel Díaz Vara de Calderón of Cuba noted in St. Augustine that, "Going out of the city at half a league to the north there is a small village of scarcely more than thirty Indian inhabitants, called Nombre de Dios, the mission of which is served by the convent."[16]

The Franciscans established the Shrine of Nuestra Señora de la Leche y Buen Parto in the town of Nombre de Dios at an unknown but earlier date. It was not mentioned by Bishop Calderón, and possibly the earliest documentary note was a statement by Governor Hita y Salazar, written after being elected head of the La Leche confraternity in 1678.[17] The confraternity ded-

---

14. Bartolomé Barrientos, "Vida y Hechos de Pero Menéndez de Aviles," in *Pedro Menéndez de Aviles, Founder of Florida*, trans. A. Kerrigan (Gainesville: University of Florida Press, 1965), 140; Gonzalo Solís de Merás, "La Conquista de La Florida," in *Pedro Menéndez de Aviles and the Conquest of Florida: A New Manuscript*, trans. and ed. David Arbesú (Gainesville: University Press of Florida, 2017), 204–205.

15. John Worth, *The Struggle for the Georgia Coast: An Eighteenth-Century Spanish Retrospective on Guale and Mocama*, Anthropological Papers, no. 75 (New York: American Museum of Natural History, 1995), 47–48; Hann, *A History of the Timucua Indians*, 154–157.

16. Gabriel Díaz Vara Calderon, Lucy L. Wenhold, and John Reed Swanton, "A 17th Century Letter of Gabriel Diaz Vara Calderon, Bishop of Cuba, Describing the Indians and Indian Missions of Florida," *Smithsonian Miscellaneous Collections* 95, no. 16 (1936): 1–14.

17. Pablo de Hita y Salazar, 1688, in Bushnell, *Situado and Sabana*, 131.

icated to Nuestra Señora de la Leche was clearly established by that date. The shrine became the focus of much devotion among Catholics, and women in particular, and drew substantial offerings and alms.

Archaeological work over the past few decades has begun to clarify several aspects of the Nombre de Dios Mission and the Shrine of Nuestra Señora de la Leche, particularly regarding that of place. It seems evident now that the mission's initial church is located on the grounds of what is today the Fountain of Youth Park, and the mission community extended into the area that is today the official Mission Nombre de Dios.

While planting orange trees on the property in 1934, a gardener uncovered human remains. The owner of the park, St. Augustine mayor and former state senator Walter B. Fraser, notified the Smithsonian Institution of the find and financed excavations by archaeologists Matthew Stirling and Ray Dickson to expand and uncover the area.

Dickson eventually opened an east-to-west oriented, 80-by-40–foot block containing more than 112 burials, although mortuary and locational information is available for only 74 of them.[18] The burials were interred in a preexisting, precontact Timucua village midden containing firepits, post molds, a dog burial, food and artifact refuse, and possibly precontact human burials (Figure 2).

The area in which burials were located covered approximately 60 feet east to west and at least 40 feet north to south, but very few deposits suggesting such architectural elements as walls or floors were recorded. The absence of such features may well indicate that the church was larger than the 40-by-80–foot excavated area. Most of the burials documented by Dickson in 1934 were extended, with arms crossed upon the chest, and faces looking eastward. Two extended individuals faced west. Some burials intruded upon others, and in twenty-six cases, two or more individuals were placed in the same burial pit. Six of these group burials included one or two adults and children, perhaps representing family burials, and may reflect epidemic disease eliminating whole families.

Despite the absence of architectural evidence, the compact arrangement of the graves, their highly consistent orientations and burial position, and the intrusion of many burials into earlier burials suggest an interior church burial space used over an extended period of time. The east-facing orientation of

---

18. Ray Dickson, Field notes on excavations at the Fountain of Youth Park, photocopy on file, Fountain of Youth Park (St. Augustine, FL, 1934). Detailed reports of the excavations can be found in Deagan, *Fifty Years of Archaeology at the Fountain of Youth Park*, 38–44; Donald Merritt, "Excavations of a Coastal Eastern Timucuan Village in Northeast Florida" (master's thesis, Florida State University, 1977); Lillian Seaberg, "Report on the Indian Site at the 'Fountain of Youth' (1951), reprinted in *Spanish St. Augustine: A Sourcebook for America's Ancient City*, ed. K. Deagan (New York: Garland Press, 1991), 209–279.

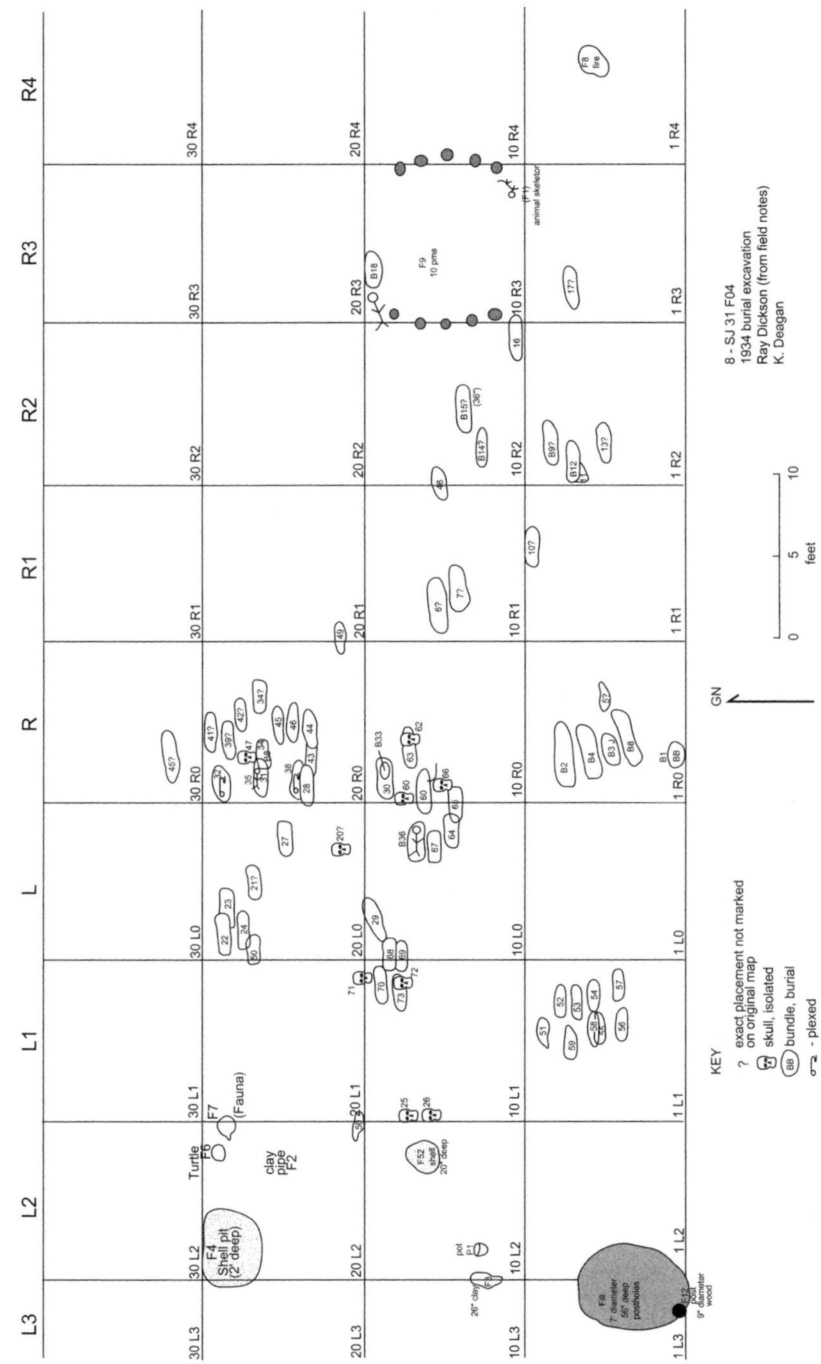

FIGURE 2. 1934 Ray Dickson burial excavation sketch.

the graves suggests that the altar of the church was at the east end, and the entrance at the west.

Possibly the most useful information about the mission activity comes from the features that do not correspond to what is expected of a Catholic burial area. As noted, the burial and church area was established on a village midden containing large amounts of pottery, shell, and animal bone refuse pits and possibly pre-Columbian burials. Three bundle burials and two flexed burials (the traditional patterns used by non-Christian Indians in Florida) were present among the extended remains. Two of the bundle burials were located, respectively, beneath and on the chest of a single female burial, and could possibly have been infants rather than bundles. At least one of the flexed burials intruded into a previous Christian burial. Five burials included an adult accompanied by a single disarticulated human skull. The field notes unfortunately do not provide sufficient detail to offer interpretations.

Grave goods were present, but consisted exclusively of beads, and they only accompanied children and infants, who seem to have been wearing necklaces made of both shell and glass beads. Seed beads accounted for 64.7 percent of the European beads in the burial area. Other than seed beads, three varieties of glass beads dominated the burial assemblage (Table 1). These included gooseberry beads, similar to Cornaline D'Aleppo, but with a core of white glass rather than green glass; and chevron beads. The glass beads had date ranges extending from the second half of the sixteenth century until the eighteenth century, with only a single bead with an initial production date (*terminus post quem*) beginning after about 1630. The full date ranges for the use periods of the beads in the table can extend into the eighteenth century . . . but archaeologists place the most important date as the beginning production date: the terminus post quem, or date after which it has to have been deposited in the ground.

The incorporation of traditional Native American burial practices into early mission burials has been documented at other Florida mission sites, and as David Thomas suggested some time ago,[19] appears to reflect an anthropological sensibility on the part of the Franciscan friars during the early stages of conversion, expressed by their flexibility in accommodating some Native beliefs.[20] This

19. David H. Thomas, "Saints and Soldiers at Santa Catalina: Hispanic Designs for Colonial America," in *The Recovery of Meaning*, ed. Mark Leone and Parker Potter (Washington, DC: Smithsonian Institution Press, 1988), 73–140.

20. Clark Larsen, *On the Frontier of Contact: Mission Bioarchaeology in La Florida*, in *The Spanish Missions of La Florida*, ed. B.G. McEwan (Gainesville: University Press of Florida, 1993), 322–56; Clark Larsen, Mark C. Griffin, Dale L. Hutchinson, et al., "Frontiers of Contact: Bioarchaeology of Spanish Florida," *Journal of World Prehistory* 15, no. 1 (2001), 69–123; Jerald Milanich, *Laboring in the Fields of the Lord* (Washington, DC: Smithsonian Institution Press, 1999), 139.

TABLE 1. Beads Recovered from 1934 Mission Burial Excavations (8SF31)

Native American shell beads	77	14.6%
Glass beads		
Cornaline d'Aleppo, white core	35	6.6%
Gooseberry beads	36	6.8%
Black tumbled with red/white stripes	1	0.2%
Dark blue tumbled with red stripes	1	0.2%
Dark blue spherical	5	0.9%
Dark blue ellipsoid	1	0.2%
Light blue ellipsoid	2	0.4%
Clear ellipsoid	1	0.2%
Small, opaque, white "rice"-like beads	15	2.8%
Seed beads. Unclassified color, predominantly blue	273	51.6%
Glass bead fragments		
Bright blue	16	3.0%
Lavender	16	3.0%
Indeterminate	47	8.9%
Lapidary beads		
Faceted jet rosary bead	1	0.2%
Amber bead	2	0.4%
TOTAL	529	

approach to the initial stage of conversion apparently prevailed for some time, and has also been documented in the much later (predominantly nineteenth-century) missions of California.[21]

Another group of burials was found just 20 feet south of the Dickson church-like group. These were partially excavated in 1955 by Paul Hahn, one of John Goggin's graduate students. Hahn opened an 18-foot square block containing ten burials. Unlike the first group, these burials were all extended, and aligned with heads at the south, facing north. No architectural evidence was located, and this group may mark an external *campo santo* of the mission church. These north-facing burials would still have been facing toward the presumed church altar. None of the accommodative practices noted in the original group—grave goods, flexed burials, or isolated skulls—were present, making it difficult to precisely date the burials. Their absence, however, may indicate a later stage of conversion. A shovel test program at 5-meter intervals carried out by Gifford Waters in 2001 did not any locate any evidence of human skeletal materials between this group of ten internments and the pre-

21. Lee Panich, "Sometimes They Bury the Deceased's Clothing and Trinkets," *Historical Archaeology* 49, no. 4 (2015): 110–129.

viously excavated area presumed to have been the church. Despite the lacunae in records, maps, and artifact materials from those early excavations, they do reveal that this area was the location of an early seventeenth-century mission church, and probably also the Spanish portion of the mission complex at Nombre de Dios during the late sixteenth and early seventeenth centuries.

Other excavations over the years tend to support this understanding of place. Excavations in the area by Gifford Waters in 2001 uncovered a Native American occupation area, including a portion of a circular structure of about five meters in diameter. Associated materials included small amounts of Spanish majolica—predominantly of the Mexico City varieties, and a single sherd of Puebla Blue on White (post-1650). Native ceramics included both St. Johns pottery (36 percent associated generally with the Timucua indigenous to this area) and San Marcos, or Altamaha pottery (49 percent associated with the Guale region).[22]

In 2016, St. Augustine City Archaeologist Carl Halbirt excavated a nearby area prior to garage construction.[23] The most notable feature was a partially excavated barrel well containing San Luis Polychrome and Aucilla Polychrome majolica, and a single sherd of Puebla Polychrome, indicating a date in the first half of the seventeenth century. Barrel wells are almost exclusively associated (thus far) with European presence, and this may indicate the location of living quarters or a kitchen.

The extent to which friars were resident at Nombre de Dios during the seventeenth century is unclear. As mentioned above, the 1654 smallpox epidemic nearly annihilated mission inhabitants; in 1674, Bishop Calderón noted that there were barely thirty Indians at Nombre de Dios and that it was served from the Convento de San Francisco. It seems likely that the importance of the place after that time largely derived from the Shrine of La Leche. Both Spanish soldiers and native residents of the presidio belonged to the *cofradía* of Nuestra Señora de la Leche, and paid the quite substantial sum of four *reales* each.

The next most reliable documentary information thus far available about the mission and shrine comes from Governor Hita y Salazar in a 1678 statement that he had "built a church for Our Lady out of mortar and masonry, the only one like it in the provinces."[24] That structure was severely damaged during the attack on St. Augustine by Carolina Governor James Moore in 1702, but was rebuilt a few years later. Michael Gannon wrote that the recon-

22. Gifford Waters, "Aboriginal Ceramics at Three 18th-Century Mission Sites in St. Augustine, Florida," in *From Santa Elena to St. Augustine: Indigenous Ceramic Variability (A.D. 1400–1700)*, ed. K. Deagan and D.H. Thomas, Anthropological Papers of the American Museum of Natural History, no. 90 (New York: American Museum of Natural History, 2009), 165–176.

23. City of St. Augustine Archaeology Office, St. Augustine, 2016.

24. Pablo de Hita Salazar, 1678, in Bushnell, *Situado and Sabana*, 120–121.

structed shrine was 33-by-15 feet, and could accommodate the forty remaining Indians at the mission.[25] Accounts during the first decades of the eighteenth century indicate that there was a *convento* at the shrine, apparently constructed as part of the post-1702 rebuilding. Fray Josef Bullones described the complex in 1728 as follows:

> Macariz, alias Nombre de Dios, was two musket shots from the presidio, and no more than ten Indians, and a few other women, ever passed through there. The church was always the best because in it was located the image of Nuestra Senora de la Leche, and with the alms from the devout it was constructed of lime and stone [*cal y canto*]. The walls and even the roof were of palm, and they were modestly endowed, and the convent was also made of lime and stone, with the roof being of palm.[26]

We believe that the newly rediscovered buildings at the Mission on the Shrine property are the shrine to Nuestra Señora de la Leche built by Governor Hita y Salazar and the *convento* that was thought to have been added during the post-1702 rebuilding (in effect, a hermitage). These remains were first discovered in 1952 by then-director of the mission and avocational archaeologist Father Charles Spellman. Because there was no circulated report, the presence of the building was never fully appreciated and thus essentially forgotten. In 2010, however, after the diocesan archive was moved to new quarters in St. Augustine, archivist Sr. Cathy Blitzer found some of Father Spellman's notes, and passed them along to our University of Florida team. Using the notes, we were able to relocate the buildings.[27] The footprint of the structures was uncovered in 2014 by Gifford Waters, but it was not until 2018 that the buildings could be studied in detail (Figure 3). That study is still underway.

The building was constructed in two parts (Figure 4). On the east side it was oriented north–south, and built of cut and dressed coquina block. The wall footings are made of coquina rubble and shell, and are very substantial, averaging 27 inches (60 centimeters) in width (Figure 5). This would have been sufficient to support a two-story building on trench footings.[28] In a few areas, remnants of the cut coquina block have survived, and these show the presence of white-painted wall plaster over the coquina.

The coquina section measures 33 feet (10.06 meters) north to south and 23 feet (7.01 meters) east to west, with interior dimensions of 31.5-by-17 feet

25. Gannon, *The Cross in the Sand*, 77.

26. Fray Joseph Bullones to the Crown, 5 October 1728, Stetson Document Collection, 58-2-16/23, bnd. 5242, University of Florida. Translated by Christopher Wooley.

27. See Deagan, *The Nombre de Dios Mission/La Leche Shrine Site*, 37–45.

28. See Albert Manucy, *The Houses of St. Augustine* (St. Augustine: St. Augustine Historical Society, 1962), 67–68.

FIGURE 3. Laser-scanned photogrammetric image of the Nuestra Señora de la Leche Shrine church and *convento.* (University of Florida *En Vision* Lab, 12/18).

(9.6-by-5.2 meters). It is divided into two sections—a northern space with interior dimensions of 18-by-17 feet (5.5-by-5.2 meters), and a southern section 13-by-17 feet (4-by-5.2 meters). Our working assumption has been that at least the exterior coquina footings were the foundation for the shrine built by Governor Hita y Salazar in 1687, and that they served again as the foundation for the chapel rebuilt after the destruction by James Moore in 1702. As of this writing, no evidence to disprove that assumption has been found.

The entrance to the coquina building was on the south side, represented by two levels of what appear to be narrow coquina steps or ledges leading up to the south foundation wall. Several of these blocks retained remnants of exterior painted plaster, indicating that they were above grade and visible. This configuration extended across the entire south façade of the building, and undoubtedly served both as embellishment and as compensation for the ground slope.

Discrete concentrations of coquina rubble along the southern façade may have served as bases or supports for other features, such as columns or bell towers. A 1760 account of the parish church in St. Augustine (originally the Hermitage of Nuestra Señora de la Soledad) described the treatment of that façade: "The old wooden supports have been replaced by building three stone arches, and above them a wall that serves as a tower in which the bells are located."[29]

29. Father Juan Joseph Solana, "Report on the Condition of St. Augustine, 1760," SD 2584 (AGI 86-7-21-41), translated by staff of Historic St. Augustine Preservation Board, 1972. Reprinted in *Spanish St. Augustine*, ed. Kathleen Deagan, 543–576.

FIGURE 4. 2018 excavation.

The western portion of the building is less robust in construction, and appears to have consisted largely of tabby (a cement-like conglomerate of oyster shell, lime, water, and sand poured into forms and allowed to dry) (Figure 6). Above-ground tabby wall fragments survive in only a few places, and the building footprint is represented by narrow (9 inches or 23 centimeters wide) packed shell footings.

Our current interpretation of the tabby construction is that it was added in two stages. The easternmost tabby wall was attached directly to the west wall of the coquina building, evidenced by notching cut into the coquina to hold the wooden forms into which the tabby was poured. This easternmost tabby wall paralleled the westernmost wall of the coquina building, forming an area of 11-by-33.4 feet (3.4-by-10.2 meters) with two unequally sized rooms. It is divided into two rooms along the same line as the coquina building division, and this is the only portion of the entire complex with a poured tabby floor. It is also the only tabby construction with preserved segments of the above-grade tabby walls. These segments are very regular and well consolidated, with plastered interior and exterior surfaces. The connection to and alignment with the coquina building, and the very well-made tabby construction suggests that this was part of the coquina chapel building rather than part of the building represented by the shell footings to the west, thought to have been the location of the *convento*. It may have been an addition that predated the rest of the tabby construction.

FIGURE 5. Coquina wall foundation detail.

The tabby construction to the west of the wall and floor described above are believed to be the remains of a *convento* or living quarters for the friar who tended to the shrine. The structure measures 33.2-by-11.4 feet (10.3-by-3.6 meters) and is divided into at least three rooms. Because the first documented mention of a convent at the La Leche shrine occurs during the eighteenth century, and because tabby was generally not in use until after 1700 in St. Augustine, it is presumed that the *cal y canto* convento was added after the Moore raid of 1702.

The walls of the convento are represented only by packed shell footings, and a few areas of rubble and shell concentration. Construction methods seem to have been somewhat haphazard, with irregularly aligned walls and very shallow footings. The north and south walls of the western tabby building extend eastward to the coquina building, connecting to the well-made tabby rooms to the east. This created a wall surrounding the entire complex.

The area between the presumed convent remains and the tabby room associated with the coquina chapel was an open, unfloored area apparently serving as a patio. Work done this summer explored that area, and revealed that it was in fact an open patio. There are considerably more artifacts in the

FIGURE 6. Tabby wall foundations.

western tabby section than in the coquina section, supporting the notion that the tabby building served as living quarters. The 1951 excavation by Father Spellman, for example, recovered 2,553 artifacts (1,759 from the convent structure and 794 from the Church structure). In the presumed convento section, there were 4.7 artifacts per square foot (.44 artifacts per square meter) of excavated soil. In contrast, the coquina, presumably the chapel section, contained only 2.5 artifacts per square foot (.23 artifacts per square meter).

The artifact assemblage is dominated by Native American ceramics, which is not unexpected at an Indian mission site. European-origin pottery, however, is proportionally much more frequent at this site than it is at other Spanish-identified households in St. Augustine. The friars made particular use of a majolica type known as San Agustín Blue on White, which dates from about 1650 to 1750 (Figure 7). This type is relatively uncommon in the Spanish town and seems to have been a provision supplied particularly to this *convento.* Other artifacts including nails, glass bottle fragments, glass beads, kaolin pipestem fragments, and red-painted plaster were also recovered and are currently under study.

The mission and shrine area is unique as a site of religious pilgrimage and shrine dedicated to a devotion important to colonial women and children, which is still the case for women and families at present. The persistent longevity of physical place and spiritual purpose for more than three hundred years is perhaps the most remarkable aspect of the Shrine of Nuestra Señora de la Leche.

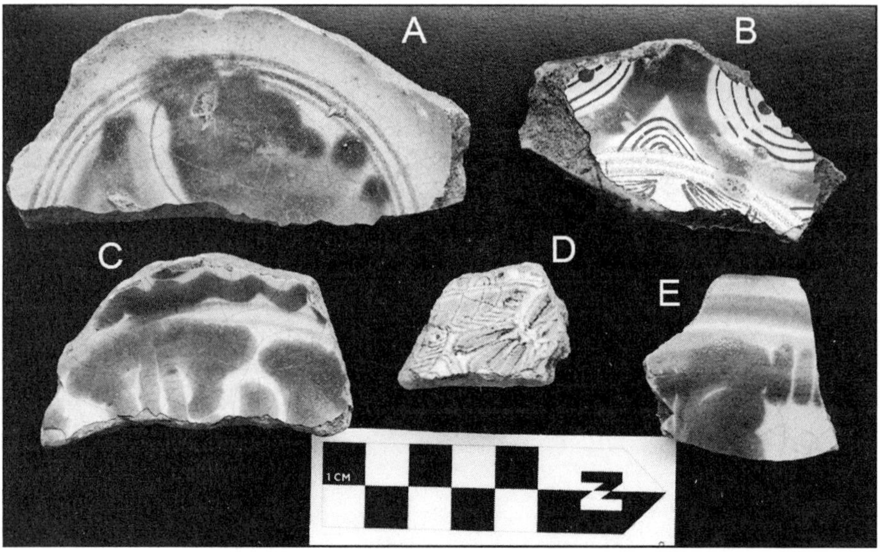

FIGURE 7. San Agustín Blue on White majolica.

As the field, archival, and laboratory work on this project continues, research will expand beyond the shrine structure itself to investigate its social context in Spanish St. Augustine.

Nombre de Dios is unique among Franciscan sites in colonial La Florida, as it offers a fascinating counterpoint to the frontier mission experience. The native people of Mission Nombre de Dios undoubtedly had a very different experience from that of their frontier counterparts in engaging with Spanish town residents, not only in the longevity of interactions, but also in their intensity and diversity. Intercultural relationships were based not just on a shared religious practice, but also on labor organization, domestic servitude, intermarriage, and probably market commerce. The consequences of these exchanges and comparisons to the lives of native people in the mission frontiers are only now starting to be addressed.

Chapter 12

Signaling Jesuit, Franciscan, and Mississippian Agendas along the Georgia Bight

David Hurst Thomas[1]

Pedro Menéndez de Avilés founded the colony of La Florida in 1565 to create a strategic Spanish coastal foothold safeguarding the treasure-laden fleets of the Indies passing through the Bahama channel and sailing back to Spain. Not only did King Philip II need to prevent the French and British from capturing the cargoes of silver, gold, and other valuables, but La Florida would provide a base to shelter shipwrecked mariners, to rescue survivors, and to salvage goods that sank offshore. This permanent base would also provide a center for launching further expeditions to explore the interior. The overarching strategic significance of La Florida ensured a relatively stable source of royal funding, but also required that Spanish colonists rely heavily on coastal Native American populations to buffer against interruptions in external supply lines. When granting Pedro Menéndez de Avilés the rights to establish the towns of St. Augustine and Santa Elena, Spanish King Philip II stipulated a number of conditions, including assurances that the Adelantado would attend to the spiritual welfare of not only Florida's European colonists, but of the indigenous people already living there.[2]

Governor Menéndez de Avilés initially entrusted the evangelization of La Florida to the upstart Jesuit Order (founded only three decades earlier), but before long, responsibility shifted to the Franciscans. These two religious orders shared identical apostolic objectives—to salvage souls and to convert indigenous people—but the Jesuits and Franciscans followed a wholly different asceticism. And although missionizing the same coastal Mississippian populations, these missionizing strategies and ultimate results could not have differed more.

1. I am grateful to Diana Rosenthal Roberson and Lorann Pendleton Thomas for assistance in preparing this manuscript.

2. J. Michael Francis, *St. Augustine, America's First City: A Story of Unbroken History and Enduring Spirit* (St. Augustine: City of St. Augustine, 2015).

The Jesuit Missions of La Florida

The king's contract mandated involvement of the newly formed Society of Jesus, making Spanish Florida the very first Jesuit missionary endeavor anywhere in the Americas.[3] Juan Rogel, among the first Jesuit priests to arrive in St. Augustine in September of 1566, was assigned to work among the Calusa Indians at Charlotte Harbor. His companion, Francisco Villarreal, was sent to mission among the Tequesta Indians (located near Miami). Both soon complained about the futility of attempting to apply Jesuit principles to the wide-ranging hunter-gatherers of southern Florida.[4]

Convinced that Jesuit missionization stood a better chance of success among coastal tribes farther north, Rogel arrived at Santa Elena on 3 July 1568. Having chosen to work among the Orista in part because there was less linguistic diversity along the Georgia Bight, Rogel established a church and convent. He felt "very secure" in his new surroundings, assigning three Spanish boys to learn the language, noting that "the soldiers go two by two without a hand being laid on them by the Indians. They even feed them all the time . . . and I do not doubt that of the Indians' natural inclination and disposition, a missionary could reap great fruit if placed among them."[5] By late 1569, Rogel still found little to criticize and maintained that comparing the Calusa of South Florida to the Guale and Orista was like comparing barbarians to a politic people living orderly lives.

The Jesuit tide turned quickly and reports from La Florida soon took on a far more discouraging tone. Rogel now complained that "for nine out of the twelve months they wander without any fixed abode . . . each goes his own way. . . . [T]hey have been accustomed to live in this way for many thousands of years." When he tried to follow, his presence was resented. Rogel then learned, to his dismay, that food scarcities at Santa Elena had convinced the deputy governor to order forty soldiers to Orista to live off the stored maize supplies of the Indians. Knowing that he would be unable

3. Paul E. Hoffman, *Florida's Frontiers* (Bloomington: Indiana University Press, 2002), 53–60; Nicholas P. Cushner, *Why Have You Come Here? The Jesuits and the First Evangelization of Native America* (New York: Oxford University Press, 2006), 31; J. Michael Francis and Kathleen M. Kole, *Murder and Martyrdom in Spanish Florida: Don Juan and the Guale Uprising of 1597*, Anthropological Papers of the American Museum of Natural History 95 (New York: American Museum of Natural History, 2011), 30–34; James M. Woods, *A History of the Catholic Church in the American South, 1513–1900* (Gainesville: University Press of Florida, 2011), 9–10.

4. Charles Hudson, *The Juan Pardo Expeditions: Exploration of the Carolinas and Tennessee, 1566–1568*, rev. ed. (Tuscaloosa: University of Alabama Press, 2005), 155.

5. Jesuit quotes as cited in Cushner, *Why Have You Come Here*, 47.

to protect the Indians from the soldiers, Rogel left Orista and returned to Santa Elena.[6]

Soon after the arrival of Juan Baptista de Segura, the new superior, Jesuit letters from Havana to Rome condemned the Florida missions as "a waste of time"—the Indians were single-minded and uncompromising, the priests were becoming ill, and the general scarcity of religious personnel required that missionaries arriving in La Florida act as chaplains in the forts. Segura concluded that "Florida, or the 300 leagues that I have seen of it is one long pile of sand: That's why there are so few Indians living here. Everyone goes nude unless they have a little piece of deerskin to cover themselves. The great variety of languages take a lifetime to learn. . . . For nine months of the year the Indians are hunting or scavenging for roots which makes it impossible to preach the gospel to them. They live like beasts and are given to the most heinous sins among themselves." Segura concluded that "Florida is not for the Society of Jesus."

In 1571, Jesuit General Francisco de Borja informed Menéndez de Avilés that he was pulling all Jesuits out of coastal Georgia and the rest of La Florida, admitting that "one can count on the fingers of the hand the number of converts made." The first Jesuit attempt to missionize the New World thus ended in utter failure.

Enter the Franciscans

The Jesuit departure left La Florida shorthanded of religious personnel, both sacred and secular. When Pedro Menéndez de Avilés returned to Spain in 1572, he left the garrison at La Florida without a church or clergyman. There were subsequent accusations that, lacking a priest to administer the sacraments, mass was not celebrated for two years. When a parish priest did finally arrive in 1574, there still was no church and he was forced to celebrate mass in the fortress. Santa Elena fared little better, with one parishioner forced to wait eight months until a priest materialized to baptize his daughter. Lent was apparently celebrated two weeks prematurely and the aging friar in attendance forgot much of the liturgy.[7]

With the Jesuits' declaration that La Florida "is not for the Society of Jesus," Menéndez de Avilés turned to the Franciscan Order to reignite missionary work. Despite the deplorable religious conditions in St. Augustine and Santa Elena, the missionary effort plodded along. Archival records doc-

6. Grant D. Jones, *The Ethnohistory of the Guale Coast through 1684*, Anthropological Papers of the American Museum of Natural History, vol. 55, no. 2 (New York: American Museum of Natural History, 1978), 179–210.

7. These dire conditions are chronicled by Francis and Kole, *Murder and Martyrdom*, 30–34.

ument a secular priest named Fromonte (accompanied by several soldiers) dispatched by Menéndez de Avilés in 1572 to minister to the local Guale residents of St. Catherines Island. But Fromonte was soon pulled away from the Georgia coast to serve the soldiers stationed at Santa Elena. Sometime in the early 1570s, a handful of Theatine friars lived in the villages of Orista and St. Catherines Island.[8]

Following two decades of low-level missionary efforts, ten Franciscan friars arrived in 1587 and their numbers increased to nearly three dozen by 1595. These Franciscans established a chain of multiple missions along the Georgia–Florida coastline and, at its peak, some seventy Franciscan friars served in La Florida, with roughly 25,000 Indian converts living in thirty-eight missions—considerably larger than their southwestern or California counterparts.[9] By 1595, missions on St. Catherines and Cumberland islands provided a combined tribute of 447 bushels (*arrobas*) of maize, weighing more than five tons. The next year, the combined maize tribute from Guale, San Pedro, and Nombre de Dios increased to nearly seven tons.

Why did the Franciscan missions prosper where the Jesuits had failed so miserably? How could the Jesuits write off coastal Georgia as "the most miserable thing ever discovered," and, just two decades later, Franciscan friars called the cornfields of St. Catherines Island "the breadbasket" of Spanish Florida?[10] Did the Jesuits get it wrong? Or were the Jesuit priests deliberately scapegoating the Indians of La Florida to cover up their own failures?[11]

Probably not. The Jesuit missionaries toiling along the Georgia coast had no earthly way of knowing they were caught in the most severe drought of the sixteenth century. The bald cypress tree-ring record dramatically documents the prolonged drought that struck the Georgia Bight between 1562 and 1571—with the most disastrous conditions concentrated during the brief Jesuit interval (1565 to 1569).[12] So when Frs. Rogel and Sedeño complained

8. Ibid., 31.

9. Ibid., tables 1, 2, and 3; David Hurst Thomas, "The Life and Times of Junípero Serra: A Pan-Borderlands Perspective [A Tibesar Distinguished Lecture]," *The Americas* 71, no. 2 (2014): 185–225.

10. Amy Turner Bushnell, *Situado and Sabana: Spain's Support System of the Presidio and Mission Provinces of Florida*, Anthropological Papers of the American Museum of Natural History, no. 74 (New York: American Museum of Natural History, 1994), 147; see also Cushner, *Why Have You Come Here*, 47.

11. Jones, *Ethnohistory of the Guale Coast*, 191; Sarah M.S. Pearsall, "'Having Many Wives' in Two American Rebellions: The Politics of Households and the Radically Conservative," *The American Historical Review* 118, no. 4 (October 2013): 1001–1028.

12. David W. Stahle, Malcolm K. Cleaveland, Dennis B. Blanton, Matthew D. Therrell, and David A. Gay, "The Lost Colony and Jamestown Droughts," *Science* 280 (1998): 564–567; Dennis Blanton and David Hurst Thomas, "Paleoclimates and Human Responses along the Central Georgia Coast: A Tree-Ring Perspective," in *Native American Land-*

of extremely poor harvests, little stored foodstuffs, rampant hunger, native rebellions, and local unrest, they were recording exactly what they saw. Although rarely addressed by environmental historians, the early mission days along the Georgia shoreline underscore both the productivity and fragility of such coastal landscapes. While the Franciscans had short-term climate change on their side, the Jesuits decidedly did not.

European Theo-Visions for La Florida

Dramatic short-term climatic change cannot itself explain the vastly different experiences of the two religious orders along the Georgia coast. Jesuits and Franciscans missionized the same sixteenth-century landscape, evangelized the same indigenous peoples, and shared the same apostolic goals of the greater Roman Catholic Church. For each, their primary objective was the salvation of souls, with a secondary obligation to the conversion and acculturation of indigenous peoples. Yet despite these overarching commonalities, the two competing religious orders arrived in Spanish Florida steeped in vastly different "theo-visions" of asceticism, administrative regulation, and the practicalities of mission life—leading to vastly different outcomes.[13]

A Jesuit Theo-vision

Ignatius Loyola founded a then-secret Catholic congregation on August 15, 1534, called the Society of Jesus, soon to be known as the Jesuit Order. This time of extraordinary religious strife in Europe pitted Roman Catholic Church orthodoxy against revisionist doctrines of Martin Luther and John Calvin. At the Council of Trent (1545–1563), the Vatican assigned the Jesuits the specific task of bringing Protestant dissidents back to the Mother Church, and the aggressive Council's decrees left no room for interpretation or compromise. The Spanish Inquisition would play a large role in this strategy, as would reforms of practice and rephrasing of theology within the Roman Catholic Church, particularly with regard to the sacramental system: baptism, confession, penance, and the eucharist. From the outset, the Jesuit Order emphasized this doctrinal purity and conformity to Roman Catholic tradi-

scapes of St. Catherines Island, ed. David Hurst Thomas, Anthropological Papers of the American Museum of Natural History, no. 88 (New York: American Museum of Natural History, 2008), 799–806.

13. The concept of theo-vision has been elaborated on by Fr. Joseph P. Chinnici, O.F.M., "Theo-history and the California Frontier," *Boletín: The Journal of the California Missions Studies Association* 21, no. 2 (2004): 55–62; see also Charles W. Polzer, *Rules and Precepts of the Jesuit Missions of Northwest New Spain* (Tucson: University of Arizona Press, 1976); David Hurst Thomas, "The Life and Times of Junípero Serra," 213–214.

tion—the absolute and total acceptance of Christian dogma and Greco-Roman culture, with ultimate goal of ensuring that Christians would be exactly the same everywhere in the world.[14]

Fledgling Jesuits took the three vows common to religious orders of the day—namely poverty, chastity, and obedience. But reflective of the Ignatian "Letter of Obedience," Jesuits took a fourth vow of obedience, specifically with regard to worldwide missions. This vow reflects a broader dedication to the universal Church, meaning that a Jesuit must be ready to accept whatever mission the Pope requires, serving the greater good of all people from all faiths and cultures. This philosophical tone can be traced directly to Ignatius's famous "Letter of Obedience" (issued on 26 March 1533) and the follow-up papal bull from Paul III (17 September 1540), which stipulated unquestioned "obedience" to the Holy Father. The theoretical rules and precepts of the Jesuit Order spelled out precisely how priests were to behave in practice. "Corrective pastoral discipline became the spearhead for order and deference to civil and ecclesiastical rules. Religious unity was equated with uniformity. These were the ingredients of a successful authoritarian state."[15]

Jesuit efforts in La Florida were deeply rooted in the struggles of their founder, reflecting what Nicholas Cushner terms "an almost new spirit of Catholicism, at once truculent and uncompromising."[16] Such "truculence" assumed a dominant role in the emerging Jesuit theo-vision as exported to America. The theoretical rules and precepts of the Order spelled out exactly how Jesuit priests were to behave in practice and Ignatius quite literally wanted his "letter of obedience" read monthly in all Jesuit houses and churches.

Although both religious orders promoted missionary evangelization, the theo-vision of the two orders translated into a very different set of administrative regulations. Believing that missionization was mostly a spiritual activity, the Jesuits thought it sufficient to hone their own spirituality. This meant that early Jesuits were mandated to operate as individuals, not as members of an overarching Jesuit community. Although Jesuit missionaries were to experience only occasional contact with their fellow Blackrobes, each missionary was expected to consult with a superior, in writing, prior to every important move, then submit a full report afterward. All were required to attend a semi-annual *junta*, where they filed the required reports, requested supplies, and renewed their Jesuit vows.[17]

---

14. Polzer, *Rules and Precepts*, 40; Cushner, *Why Have You Come Here*, 18–19.

15. Cushner, *Why Have You Come Here*, 19, 65; see also Polzer, *Rules and Precepts*, 13.

16. Cushner, *Why Have You Come Here*, 1.

17. Polzer, *Rules and Precepts*, 15.

Unlike their Franciscan counterparts, Jesuit priests bound for New World service received no special training for their evangelical work, and those arriving in La Florida harbored some serious misconceptions about those already living there. The contemporary imagery throughout Europe of non-Christian American Indian populations was one of "nakedness, passion, cruelty, and incivility, a person locked into the chains of Satan's wiles." Cushner notes that "all Indians whether Christian or pagan were distinguished from the '*gente de razón,*' 'the people of reason,' the Spaniard. Once baptized, the Indian might have been the spiritual equal of the Spaniard, but never his social equal."[18] So viewed, the Christian Indian could emerge from such paganism, but it would be a struggle—ever poised on the brink of retrogression and requiring constant monitoring to remain authentically Christian.

Jesuit priests arriving in La Florida were handicapped by the widespread European Renaissance belief that social stability and settled village life were essential prerequisites for effective evangelization—tacitly viewed as the only "civilized" way to live. The underlying Western suspicion was that anyone who deviated from a stable agricultural lifeway is to be viewed as primitive, backward, savage, and underdeveloped—explaining the Jesuits reluctance to missionize to Native Americans who refused to settle down. Beyond the obvious logistical issues of required attendance at mass, residential mobility created problems for Jesuits employing an immersion-type indoctrination throughout the year, when residence changed with the seasons.

Like most Europeans of their day, Jesuit missionaries were steeped in a Ptolemaic geography holding that lands situated at the same distance from the pole must share similar flora, fauna, and climate. Perceiving apparent shortcomings of the Georgia Bight, Segura concluded that Jesuits moving northward should find more fertile and temperate landscapes that would ripen into a "new Andalusia" blessed with the agricultural, sylvan, and mineral riches of the Hispanic homeland. In a last-ditch effort to salvage their first New World enterprise, eight Jesuits departed Santa Elena for modern Virginia, founding missions on the York River, not far from where the British would later encounter Powhatan's village. The gamble failed and within months, all eight Jesuit missionaries were martyred by the Algonquin people.[19]

First encounters with the American Indian shocked the Jesuit Order. The brief experience in La Florida thoroughly eroded the European myth of the ennobled savage, exposing instead a land of "desolate beaches and a people who lived by a subsistence economy. The Indian languages were incompre-

18. Cushner, *Why Have You Come Here*, 65.

19. Paul E. Hoffman, *A New Andalucía and a Way to the Orient: The American Southeast during the Sixteenth Century* (Baton Rouge: Louisiana State University Press, 1990), 34–36; Hudson, *The Juan Pardo Expeditions*, 156.

hensible and their customs and religion reprehensible. Conversion was difficult and immediate success unattainable. . . . [This] inhospitable land . . . proved to be a mirage: from a distance attractive and full of promise but up close, insubstantial."[20]

A Franciscan Theo-vision

The Franciscan Order had already logged a long history in the Americas when Pedro Menéndez de Avilés defined Spanish Florida in 1565. Founded in 1209, Franciscan membership had skyrocketed to 22,000 friars only two centuries later. Two Franciscans accompanied Christopher Columbus in 1493, specifically charged by the Spanish Crown with bringing Catholicism to the indigenous New World. At the request of Hernán Cortés, King Carlos V sent the first Franciscan monks (known as the Twelve Apostles of Mexico) in May 1524 with a specific mandate of establishing missions throughout the country; three years later, seventy Franciscan *conventos* had been constructed throughout Mexico. In 1531, Franciscans set up missions in Peru in large numbers, with at least one friar having accompanied Francisco Pizarro on an earlier expedition.

By the mid-sixteenth century, the Franciscan Order had amassed, quite literally, a world of missionary experience, refining their early persuasive strategies in Peru, Mexico, and even a fourteenth-century Franciscan mission to the Mongols. Their emergent theo-vision stressed the value of flexibility, adaptability, and heterogeneity in their administration of Christian doctrine. During their first half-century in the Andes, Franciscans relied on the ancient Catholic principle of *accomodatio* to new cultures, sometimes deliberately adapting local Quechua terminology for the Christian God and his worship. They also interpreted local Quechua narratives and artifacts as pointing to pre-Hispanic visitations to Peru by Christian gods, leaving behind miraculous crosses and saintly footprints.[21]

The Franciscans promoted "creative architectural provisions," including the construction of sixteenth-century "Franciscan mosques" in Mexico and "convento kivas"[22] in the American Southwest that provided familiar-yet-Fran-

20. Cushner, *Why Have You Come Here*, 47.

21. Jaime Lara, *Birdman of Assisi: Art and the Apocalyptic in the Colonial Andesi* (Tucson: Center for Medieval and Renaissance Studies and Bilingual Press, Arizona State University, 2016), 82–83, 85.

22. James E. Ivey, "Convento Kivas in the Missions of New Mexico," *New Mexico Historical Review* 73, no. 2 (1998): 121–152; David Hurst Thomas, "Social Agency in the Spanish Mission Borderlands," in *Franciscans and American Indians in Pan-Borderlands Perspective: Adaptation, Negotiation, and Resistance*, ed. Jeffrey M. Burns and Timothy J. Johnson (Oceanside: Academy of American Franciscan History, 2018), 17–34.

ciscan spaces where children and others could be taught the basics of Christianity, the catechism, and Spanish culture.[23] Franciscans arriving in Spanish Florida drew upon long-established architectural and ecclesiastical conventions, adapted to the specifics of coastal Mississippian culture and customs. The entire mission complex—not just the church and friary, but also the offices, storerooms, workshops, sheds, barns, pens, herds, and fields—became a virtually self-contained Franciscan community. This utopian plan reflected deliberate designs derived from more than eight hundred years of monastic tradition and four centuries of Franciscan development. The missions of La Florida deliberately embodied elements of local Mississippian architecture in the form of council houses capable of sheltering thousands inside; several missions also sported ball courts, where *pelota* games pitted traditional rivals in sometimes-violent combat. The ritualized architecture of La Florida thus reflected the material consequences of a hybrid blend of Franciscan ideals played out in the context of continuing Mississippian beliefs and motivations.

Unlike its emerging Jesuit counterpart, Franciscan theo-vision downplayed "individualistic" evangelization to embrace instead a group (or team) approach to missionization. In the seventeenth century, Franciscans would create multiple apostolic colleges that wholly distinguished their missionary efforts from the Jesuit manner of recruitment, training, and support. Even in its sixteenth-century iteration, Franciscan missionary practice typically established a *custodia* to oversee a series of *conventos* (mission residences), helping to foster a sense of Franciscan collegiality (wholly distinct from the Jesuit theo-vision holding that missionaries avoid living inside a religious community).[24]

Franciscan friars arrived in La Florida knowing the earliest Spanish explorers throughout the deep American South had encountered indigenous hierarchical and authoritarian structures not so different from their own, with social status defined along a complex system of racial gradients and classifications. Mississippian governance maintained relatively short-term chiefdoms characterized by long-distance trade networks and centralized leadership.[25] For centuries before European arrival, Mississippian societies defined their own hereditary birthrights grounded in genealogical descent from a single

23. David J. Weber, *The Spanish Frontier in North America* (New Haven, CT: Yale University Press, 1992), 10–11.

24. Polzer, *Rules and Precepts*, 11.

25. John E. Worth, "Spanish Missions and the Persistence of Chiefly Power," in *The Transformation of the Southeastern Indians, 1540–1760*, ed. Robbie Ethridge and Charles Hudson (Jackson: University Press of Mississippi, 2002), 39–64; John E. Worth, "Catalysts of Assimilation: The Role of Franciscan Missionaries in the Colonial System of Spanish Florida," in *From La Florida to La California: Franciscan Evangelization in the Spanish Borderlands*, ed. Timothy J. Johnson and Gert Melville (Berkeley, CA: Academy of American Franciscan History, 2013), 131–142.

noble ancestor. The privileged chiefly class was accorded considerable status and wealth. Mississippian subordinates supplied the labor and material resources underwriting this hereditary inequality, sometimes risking their lives in chiefly warfare.[26] The Spanish newcomers insisted on direct negotiations with paramounts, and the subordinates were expected to fall in line. Individual chiefdoms identified closely with their *micos* and were protective of chiefly authority. When disputes arose between towns and lineages, they sometimes split to acquire distinctive social identities, each maintaining its own ceremonial center and suite of ritual practices.

Jesuit priests were spectacularly unsuccessful in their push to convert and baptize the Indians of La Florida. But a few years later, Franciscan friars missionized these very same Indians using *conquest by compact* that promised mutual defense and exclusive trade in return for commitment to obedience to Spanish officials—and a promise to join the missionary effort.[27] Explicitly recognizing the top-down dynamics of stratified Mississippian society, Franciscans' early efforts among the Timucua and Guale concentrated on converting the hereditary caciques to Christianity. If successful, the paramount facilitated the conversion of the community. By doing so, Franciscan missionaries adjusted and modified their own approach to Christian baptism, working squarely within the context of chiefly authority—several pledged allegiance and obedience to Spanish officials, but others refused the gospel and all that went with it. Those paramounts siding with the Spanish not only enjoyed a powerful military ally, but they also gained access to new tools, technologies, and prestige items that reinforced their chiefly authority.[28]

In stark contrast to the "truculent and uncompromising" individualistic strategy of Jesuit thinking,[29] Franciscan friars were empowered with a degree of social agency in constructing their generation of mission architecture and the way in which the Catholic rituals would be conducted. They based the missions on their own personal experiences in the churches they attended as

26. David Hurst Thomas, "Honor and Hierarchies: Long-term Trajectory in the Pueblo and Mississippian Worlds," in *Native and Spanish New Worlds: Sixteenth-Century Entradas in the American Southwest and Southeast*, ed. Clay Mathers, Jeffrey M. Mitchem, and Charles M. Haecker (Tucson: University of Arizona Press), 251–273; David Hurst Thomas, "War and Peace on the Franciscan Frontier," in *From La Florida to La California: The Genesis and Realization of Franciscan Evangelization in the Spanish Borderlands*, ed. Timothy J. Johnson and Gert Melville (Berkeley: Academy of American Franciscan History, 2013), 105–130.

27. Amy Turner Bushnell, "'These people are not conquered like those of New Spain': Florida's Reciprocal Colonial Compact," in *500 Years of Florida History—The Seventeenth Century*, ed. Jane Landers, special issue of the *Florida Historical Quarterly* 92 (2014): 530; Thomas, "Social Agency," 17–34.

28. Francis and Kole, *Murder and Martyrdom*, 91.

29. Cushner, *Why Have You Come Here*, 19.

children, the mission colleges, and the other missions visited—all of which molded idealized plans in the minds of friars and influenced what was built at the new missions. Modern Franciscan friars sometimes speak of their self-perception as "amiable anarchists," willing to modify established rules and protocols to achieve the ultimate goal of salvation. Perhaps reflecting this contemporary sense of "inculturation," the Franciscan plan varied considerably across medieval Europe and in Renaissance Mexico, where individual friars traveling into the Spanish Borderlands carried with them accumulated monastic experiences.[30] Ethnohistorian and archaeologist John Worth took this perspective a step further to argue that Franciscan friars stationed in La Florida functioned like the modern Peace Corps, being granted voluntary admittance into indigenous communities to assist in the transition to a new order.[31]

Paramount chiefs of La Florida competed with one another—sometimes violently—to enter into the Franciscan mission system; by courting the Spanish newcomers, they defined novel ways to maintain and continue their Mississippian practices and employ ostentatious displays of wealth and status items to reinforce their hereditary status. Oddly enough, the Franciscan mission system provided Mississippian polities a way of projecting past practices into an uncertain future.

Plural Marriage, Multiple Problems

As sixteenth-century Christians, Jesuit and Franciscan missionaries shared common ground when it came to marriage. Preserving "correct" marriage practices remained the backbone of the Reformation, whether Catholic or Protestant. The Catholic Church frowned upon premarital sex and marriage between cousins or between consanguineous adults. Polygyny—the practice permitting males to marry two or more women—was outright forbidden. This implicit sense of masculine privilege over nature and the household bespoke "a Christian religious fundamentalism that alleged certainty in everything."[32] Throughout the expanding Spanish sphere, insistence on Christian-style monogamy came to signal power, authority, and empire.

Such androcentric worldviews clashed with indigenous beliefs along the Georgia Bight, where marriage was not a religious issue at all, but rather a fundamental socioeconomic relationship shaped by descent. Guale and Mocama communities traced their kinship and social identities through the female line—and because matrilineages typically controlled housing, land, and

30. Contemporary Franciscan usages of "amiable anarchists" and "inculturation" are discussed in Thomas, "The Life and Times of Junípero Serra," 223.

31. Worth, "Catalysts of Assimilation."

32. Cushner, *Why Have You Come Here*, 15; see also Pearsall, "'Having Many Wives.'"

property, indigenous women occupied the most honored places. Women from elite matrilineages typically delegated outright political power to their male "blood" relatives because "for the most part [Mississippian] women were influential rather than powerful, and they were more inclined to sway opinion behind the scenes rather than out in the open."[33]

Marriage practices followed suit. Guale and Mocama individuals were born into specific matrilineages, and the associated kinship affinities carried specific marital protocols including exogamy, arranged marriages, and lineage preferences. But whereas lineages might strongly encourage a young woman about whom to marry, her consent was always necessary. Marriages could be brittle, and unsuccessful unions were typically dissolved. Premarital sex was tacitly accepted and Mississippian communities typically distinguished between marriage *per se* and the privilege of men to buy concubines. Only the wealthy could afford plural wives, which often took the form of sororal polygyny (marriage of two or more sisters).[34]

Keenly aware of such conflicting practices, Jesuit priests targeted their earliest New World missions toward the monogamous Orista, deliberately skipping over the polygamous Guale of the Georgia Bight. Matrimony was a relatively recent Catholic sacrament; the Council of Trent declared it so only in the mid-sixteenth century and some of the canonical intricacies had yet to be ironed out. In Florida, the Jesuits and then the Franciscans struggled manfully with the complicated cases of conscience created by a polygamous society, trying to differentiate "natural marriage," an inviolable contract, from concubinage, and to determine which of a man's consorts was his "rightful" wife.[35] Given the remarkably brief Jesuit tenure in La Florida, such struggles regarding proper Christian marriage among the native populations remained largely irrelevant. Once Fr. Sedeño dismissed the Florida Indians as "beasts wallowing in sin," who cared who they married?[36]

The Franciscan friars of Spanish Florida did not enjoy the luxury of dismissal. In fifteenth-century Spain, the Franciscan Order earned a "most confrontational" reputation in promoting their "true Christian" beliefs over those of Jews, Muslims, and other infidels.[37] Whereas Franciscans were instrumental in passing the first laws in the New World against polygyny and divorce,[38] in sixteenth-century Mexico, friars condoned continued polygyny for selected

33. Charles Hudson, *The Southeastern Indians* (Knoxville: University of Tennessee Press, 1976), 185–187.

34. Hudson, *The Southeastern Indians*, 96, 199.

35. Bushnell, *Situado and Sabana*, 99.

36. Cushner, *Why Have You Come Here*, 47.

37. Pearsall, "'Having Many Wives,'" 1010.

38. Woodrow Borah and Sherburne F. Cook, "Marriage and Legitimacy in Mexican Culture: Mexico and California," *California Law Review* 54, no. 2 (May 1966): 955.

baptized and powerful natives, where "having several wives was an index of status for men and was still standard in some communities in the early post-conquest period."[39]

The Franciscan Order tacitly sanctioned similar contradictions in La Florida, where the missionizing strategy reinforced traditional chiefly power by channeling access to indigenous land and labor through long-term hierarchies. As cultural brokers, friars enjoyed a measure of respect within the St. Augustine community, but also remained fully capable of lobbying for Indian interests when necessary vis-à-vis military and secular authorities. Notwithstanding their role as a sixteenth-century Peace Corps, the consequences of built-in contradictions would soon spill Franciscan blood along the Georgia coast.

Consistent with their *conquest-by-contract* missionizing strategy, consenting Guale leaders began with the first three sacraments that conveyed grace to a Christian—baptism, penance, and the eucharist. After completing these three sacraments, males and females were eligible to complete their transition into responsible adulthood through Christian matrimony.[40] In the mid-1570s, the first Franciscan missionaries presided over several such marriages, including those of the Guale *cacique* and his wife.[41]

In September 1597, the Spanish province of Guale violently erupted. Five Franciscans stationed in the province were martyred and most of the *doctrinas* along the coast were razed.[42] Subsequent accounts of this rebellion derive exclusively from a single, non-eyewitness account of the Franciscan friar Luis Gerónimo de Oré. Oré concluded that the friars were attacked because they attempted to end polygamous marriage, thereby subverting the right of don Juanillo, a *mico* (chieftain) of Tolomato (capital of the Guale Province at the time), to inherit the title of *mico mayor* from his uncle who held it.[43] In response, Spanish soldiers burned the remaining Guale and

39. Sarah Cline, "The Spiritual Conquest Reexamined: Baptism and Christian Marriage in Early Sixteenth-Century Mexico," *Hispanic American Historical Review* 73, no. 3 (August 1993): 479–480; see also Pearsall, "'Having Many Wives,'" 1010.

40. Bushnell, *Situado and Sabana*, 97–99.

41. Jones, *Ethnohistory of the Guale Coast*, 182.

42. John Tate Lanning, *The Spanish Missions of Georgia* (Chapel Hill: University of North Carolina Press, 1935); Michael V. Gannon, *The Cross in the Sand: The Early Catholic Church in Florida, 1513–1870* (Gainesville: University Press of Florida, 1965); Jones, *Ethnohistory of the Guale Coast*, 183–85; Elliot H. Blair and David Hurst Thomas, "The Guale Uprising of 1597: An Archaeological Perspective from Mission Santa Catalina de Guale (Georgia)," in *Indigenous Landscapes and Spanish Missions: New Perspectives from Archaeology and Ethnohistory*, ed. Lee M. Panich and Tsim D. Schneider (Tucson: University of Arizona Press, 2014), 25–40.

43. Luis Gerónimo de Oré, *The Martyrs of Florida (1513–1616)*, trans. with biographical introduction and notes by Maynard Geiger, Franciscan Studies, no. 18 (New York: Joseph W. Wagner, 1936).

Mocama settlements and forced the Indians inland. The 1597 rebellion was "resolved" when most of the principal Guale and Mocama leaders again rendered obedience to the Spanish Crown, and an indigenous force killed don Juanillo during an inland battle in 1601.[44] Franciscan missions returned to the Georgia coast in 1604.

Oré's enduring narrative has been significantly amplified. In 1723, Andrés González de Barcía Carballido y Zúñiga fabricated a speech from Juanillo urging the Guale to overthrow the Franciscans:

> They take from us our women, allowing us to one, and that, in perpetuity, forbidding us to exchange them for others. They prohibit us from our dancing, banquets, feasts, celebrations, games, and warfare, and in order that, being deprived of these, we might lose our ancient valor and skill, which we inherited from our ancestors. . . . All they do is to reprimand us, treat us in an injurious manner, oppress us, preach to us, and call us bad Christians. They deprive us of every vestige of happiness which our ancestors obtained for us. . . . In this deceitful manner they subject us, holding us bound to their wills. What have we to hope for except to become slaves?[45]

Although scholars universally acknowledge don Juanillo's speech to be an eighteenth-century fabrication, the basic tone and message remains widely accepted.[46] Twentieth-century Franciscan historian Maynard Geiger, for instance, while admitting that Barcía's narrative was a fake, still argued that it be accepted as "poetically true"—an accurate reflection of the anti-Christian, anti-Spanish sentiment that correctly casts the 1597 Guale uprising as a "desperate attempt to wipe out the Christian culture that had just taken root. Christian morality faced a hand-to-hand conflict with inveterate pagan custom. . . . If the heir to the caciquedom was to go on in open defiance of a fundamental Christian law, he would nullify to a great extent whatever efforts the missionaries made on behalf of Christianity."[47]

This foundational premise must now be seriously questioned.

44. Francis and Kole, *Murder and Martyrdom*, 137–138, table 8.

45. Andrés González de Barcía Carballido y Zúñiga and Anthony Kerrigan, *Barcía's Chronological History of the Continent of Florida . . . from the Year 1512, in which Juan Ponce de Leon discovered Florida, until the Year 1722* (Gainesville: University of Florida Press, 1973); Maynard Geiger, *The Franciscan Conquest of Florida, 1573–1618* (Washington, DC: Catholic University of America, 1937).

46. Francis and Kole, *Murder and Martyrdom*, 42.

47. Geiger, *The Franciscan Conquest of Florida*, 88.

The Guale and Mocama: People without History?[48]

> The perceived timelessness of indigenous people, as encapsulated by Don Juan's speech, is a trope that has itself become practically timeless . . . casting indigenous people and their institutions as unchanging, as old as the hills, even incapable of change.
>
> —Sarah M.S. Pearsall[49]

Conventional historiography of the 1597 Guale uprising privileges the Spanish perspectives as reflected in the surviving documents and is rooted in the mistaken assumption that indigenous people are somehow timeless—as Eric Wolf put it: "people without history."[50] Anthropologists and historians today are increasingly critical of the long-held and widely shared view of non-European peoples as isolated and static entities before the advent of European colonialism. Arguing for more consideration of societies in both "civilized" and "uncivilized" worlds, such alternative perspectives hold that, prior to European contact, Native American and other indigenous populations were as perpetually changing and intertwined with the processes of large-scale pre-Columbian interaction spheres as their European counterparts. Transcending these biases requires that we critically re-read extant documentary evidence while also seeking out other records about the past created by indigenous people themselves.

This is exactly what has happened with the 1597 Guale uprising. In a critical re-reading of the documentary evidence, J. Michael Francis and Kathleen M. Kole revisited the nature and implications of the so-called "Juanillo Revolt." They identified several ambiguities and paradoxes in the standard interpretation of the rebellion and convincingly demonstrated that the importance of mission-period Guale sociopolitical structure had been underestimated. Francis and Kole question the simplistic juxtapositions of supposed indigenous and Hispanic interests to argue instead that the Guale uprising of 1597 was not a wholesale indigenous rebellion against Spanish authority at all. The violence reflected instead long-standing tensions among indigenous chiefdoms of the Georgia Bight.

Nothing in the Francis and Kole research disputes the baseline contention that the 1597 unpleasantness stemmed from Franciscans' effort to abolish the Guale practice of plural wives. But the near-obsessive overemphasis on Christian marriage and indigenous polygamy by Oré, Barcía, Geiger, and many others effectively created a universal symbol of Spanish imperialism and empire

48. Subtitle from Eric R. Wolf, *Europe and the People without History* (Berkeley: University of California Press, 1982).

49. Pearsall, "'Having Many Wives,'" 1027.

50. Wolf, *Europe and the People without History.*

reflecting Reformation-era European agendas informed by androcentric views of the timeless Other.

The Guale and Mocama were not a people without history. Their ancestry began millennia ago with tribal-level societies living in economically self-sufficient, virtually sedentary, and politically autonomous villages in coastal Georgia. They practiced a seasonal mix of terrestrial foraging, shellfishing, and estuarine fishing subsistence, made the earliest pottery in North America, and practiced matrilineal descent at least 3,500 years ago. These ancient coastal Georgians reckoned social status along egalitarian principles, meaning that they were born with equal rights, with social status accrued in direct proportion to life accomplishments.[51] They were the healthiest Georgians ever (including today).[52]

This all changed about 800 CE with the advent of hereditary inequality. No longer did personal accomplishments or the wealth accumulated in life determine an individual's standing in society.[53] Social status and political power were instead assigned at birth to selected elites, reflecting their definable genealogical affinities to noble matrilineages. Although indigenous coastal Georgians likely descended from the same roots, sharp divisions would come to separate their outlook, their interests, and their respective fitness benefits.

The dominants, a small and privileged chiefly class, probably flaunted a certifiable genealogical relationship to the reigning matrilineage. But over the generations, a cultural fiction arose that the distinguished ancestors and their immediate elite offspring literally descended from supernatural forces. Lesser positions within the dominant elite likely varied with the genealogical distance to the elite leader. Certain members of the emerging elite acquired greater status and wealth by manipulating social, economic, and political relationships

---

51. David Hurst Thomas and Clark Spencer Larsen, *The Anthropology of St. Catherines Island*, vol. 2, *The Refuge-Deptford Mortuary Complex*, Anthropological Papers of the American Museum of Natural History 56, no. 1 (New York: American Museum of Natural History, 1979); David Hurst Thomas, "Population Growth, Intensification, and the Emergence of Social Inequity on St. Catherines Island," in *Native American Landscapes of St. Catherines Island, Georgia*, ed. David Hurst Thomas, Anthropological Papers of the American Museum of Natural History, no. 88 (New York: American Museum of Natural History, 2008), 1046–1079.

52. Clark Spencer Larsen, *The Archaeology of Santa Catalina de Guale*, vol. 2, *Biocultural Interpretations of a Population in Transition*, Anthropological Papers of the American Museum of Natural History, no. 68 (New York: American Museum of Natural History, 1990); Clark Spencer Larsen and Christopher B. Ruff, "The Stresses of Conquest in Spanish Florida: Structural Adaptation and Change Before and After Contact," in *In the Wake of Contact: Biological Response to Conquest*, ed. Clark Spencer Larsen and George R. Milner (New York: John Wiley & Sons, 1994), 31–34.

53. Thomas, "Population Growth," 1046–1079; see also Kent Flannery and Joyce Marcus, *The Creation of Inequality: How Our Prehistoric Ancestors Set the Stage for Monarchy, Slavery, and Empire* (Cambridge: Harvard University Press, 2012).

to their benefit. Subordinates, supporting themselves as best they could, generated virtually all the subsistence and luxury goods for the elite. Commoners supplied the labor, produced the chiefly wealth, and in the case of drafted conscripts, risked dying in chiefly warfare.

The transition to heritable social inequity took place entirely within the context of a shellfishing economy, predating maize farming on the island by several centuries on the Georgia coast.[54]

Tensions on the New Mississippian Frontier

Something dramatic happened in the fifteenth century, magnifying tensions and the potential for violence as these local foraging communities were propelled into intensified political competition with rival chiefdoms of the inland Mississippian world. Bald cypress tree rings document a remarkably severe drought circa 1359–1377 CE that destroyed the maize crops and crippled the large farming Mississippian populations living along the Savannah River. A combination of extreme environmental stress and shifting political landscapes triggered the abandonment of the Savannah River Valley, which became a "wilderness" by the time of Hernando de Soto's arrival in 1540 CE.[55]

Some Mississippian refugees moved southward, pressuring the shellfishing chiefdoms along the Georgia coastline who were suddenly propelled into an intense regional political competition between rival chiefdoms of the Mississippian world. Immersion in this new Mississippian frontier precipitated massive changes in the subsistence, lifeways, iconography, and flows of tribute among coastal Georgians.

These in-migrating Mississippian populations were maize farmers, introducing corn for the first time to the Georgia Bight.[56] Terrestrial farming might have seemed to offer another way to intensify provisioning strategies, depending on specific year-to-year conditions. Slash-and-burn farming (the only kind

---

54. Clark Spencer Larsen, Margaret J. Schoeninger, Nikolaas J. van der Merwe, Katherine M. Moore, and Julia A. Lee-Thorp, "Carbon and Nitrogen Stable Isotopic Signatures of Human Dietary Change in the Georgia Bight," *American Journal of Physical Anthropology* 89 (1992): 197–214; Thomas, *Native American Landscapes*, 1046–1079.

55. David G. Anderson, *The Savannah River Chiefdoms: Political Change in the Late Prehistoric Southeast* (Tuscaloosa: University of Alabama Press, 1994), 327; Hudson, *The Juan Pardo Expeditions*, 60–61; Charles M. Hudson, Marvin T. Smith, and Chester B. DePratter, "The Hernando de Soto Expedition: From Apalachee to Chiaha," *Southeastern Archaeology* 3 (1984): 71–72.

56. David Hurst Thomas, "The 'Guale Problem' Revisited: Farming and Foraging on St. Catherines Island (cal A.D. 1300–1580)," in *Native American Landscapes of St. Catherines Island, Georgia*, ed. David Hurst Thomas, Anthropological Papers of the American Museum of Natural History, no. 88 (New York: American Museum of Natural History, 2008), 1095–1115.

feasible on the Georgia coast) generated lower caloric returns than most shellfishing and wild plant food collecting options—about the same as collecting oysters and ribbed mussels, spearing small fish, hunting gray squirrels, and preparing acorn meal.[57] Hunting rabbits and ducks, collecting clams, and preparing hickory nut oil generated more food energy than corn farming; only a few shellfish taxa and small seed harvesting ranked lower. This means that if a Mississippian woman cared only about feeding her own family, she would do better by walking away from the cornfields and gathering hickory nuts and acorns (in the fall) or collecting hard clams (all year round).

But this did not happen. Solid archaeological and documentary evidence makes it clear that significant maize cultivation and consumption did indeed take place two centuries before European arrival, begging the obvious question:[58] If growing corn is less energy efficient than harvesting most marsh resources—and it certainly seems to be—why did late precontact indigenous communities of the Georgia coastline invest so heavily in maize cultivation?

The answer is tribute. To be sure, growing corn was less efficient and more expensive than shellfishing, with the heightened risk of droughts, torrential rains, insect infestations, and other factors that destroyed crops. But because maize was easy to store, transport, and quantify, corn tribute was the primary currency that fueled the Mississippian world, and regional geopolitics transferred this practice to the shellfishers of the Georgia coast. Prehistoric maize cultivation on the Georgia Bight can only be understood in light of Late Mississippian sociopolitical structure.[59]

Guale and Mocama communities developed at least two administrative levels in which lesser elites paid tribute to higher-ups, defining and formalizing power relationships among chiefdoms "obsessed with status positions, alliances, and trade."[60] The most productive terrestrial and estuarine

---

57. K. Renee Barlow, "A Formal Model for Predicting Agriculture among the Fremont," in *Foraging Theory and the Transition to Agriculture*, ed. Douglas J. Kennett and Bruce Winterhalder (Berkeley: University of California Press, 2006), 87–102; see also Thomas, *Native American Landscapes*, 1095–1115.

58. Thomas, *Native American Landscapes*, 1095–1115; John E. Worth, "Guale," in *Handbook of North American Indians*, vol. 14, *Southeast*, ed. Raymond D. Fogelson (Washington, DC: Smithsonian Institution Press, 2004), 238–244.

59. David G. Anderson, "Chiefly Cycling and Large-scale Abandonment Viewed from the Savannah River Basin," in *Political Structure and Change in the Prehistoric Southeastern United States*, ed. John F. Scarry (Gainesville: University Press of Florida, 1996), 150–191; John H. Blitz, "Mississippian Chiefdoms and the Fusion–Fission Process," *American Antiquity* 64 (1999): 577–592; Thomas, *Native American Landscapes*, 1070–1077; David Hurst Thomas, "The Shellfishers of St. Catherines Island: Hardscrabble Foragers or Farming Beachcombers?" *Journal of Island and Coastal Archaeology* 9 (2014): 169–182.

60. David G. Anderson, *The Savannah River Chiefdoms: Political Change in the Late Prehistoric Southeast* (Tuscaloosa: University of Alabama Press, 1994), 77; see also Worth, "Guale," 238–244.

resource patches were owned by the most powerful chiefly matrilineages, which required subordinates to pay tributary obligations for farming and foraging rights.[61]

This meant that most coastal Georgians now had to balance concerns about feeding their families against the demands of tribute, offerings, and taxes. At least two centuries before the first Europeans arrived, the foraging farmers of the Georgia Bight were sowing and cultivating designated *sabana* corn fields for their elites—the caciques, the *principales*, the medicine men/women, the interpreters, the ballplayers, and others demanding tribute. Subordinates maintained a large, communal *sabana* to feed widows, orphans, and travelers, to finance public feasts, and to provide rations for those working on construction projects, long-distance trade, or military campaigns.

Why would the non-elite majority submit to the wishes of the few who sought to subordinate and exploit them? Why would subordinates agree to build the council houses and granaries, collect and render hickory nut oil, tend the chiefly fish weirs, harvest and process the chiefly oysters, build and paddle the chiefly canoes, and wage war against the chiefly enemies?

Violence and tension were always significant factors in pre-Columbian Mississippian chiefdoms—notoriously unstable and characterized by a chiefly cycling of communities that rose in power, declined, and sometimes collapsed altogether allowing new power centers to crop up elsewhere.[62] While some commoners likely elected to bud off and live elsewhere, they faced high costs in relocating and, with the increasing population density, eventually came to realize the lack of unoccupied territories. Most subordinates apparently stayed put, taking advantage of sufficient food and increased security—despite the rake-off pocketed by dominants.

Even self-interested, disadvantaged subordinates might have felt they benefited from such heritable inequality—with the social costs and benefits of belonging to the greater Mississippian community outweighing concerns of provisioning for the Guale elite.[63] The collection of tribute, offerings, and taxes represented the social payment for the costs of performing rituals and conducting warfare for the polity as a whole—basically, the cost of protecting the group within their (culturally defined) global world system, as they then knew it.

---

61. John E. Worth, *The Timucuan Chiefdoms of Spanish Florida*, vol. 1, *Assimilation* (Gainesville: University Press of Florida, 1998).

62. Anderson, "Chiefly Cycling"; Blitz, "Mississippian Chiefdoms and the Fusion–Fission Process."

63. Jean E. Arnold, *The Origins of a Pacific Coast Chiefdom: The Chumash of the Channel Islands* (Salt Lake City: University of Utah Press, 2001).

Tensions on the New Franciscan Frontier

Franciscan missionaries reinforced and transformed long-term Guale practices of tribute and labor by empowering hereditary chiefs to help control and enforce new trade alliances among Spanish and indigenous communities. The friars were also to experience the long-standing conflicts and tensions surrounding tribute, labor, plural marriage, territorial defense, and chiefly power politics that characterized the Georgia Bight for hundreds of years before the French and Spanish arrived in the mid-1560s.

The 1597 uprising underscored the vulnerability of the Spanish mission strategy of accommodating indigenous hierarchies and long-term chiefly dynamics, underestimating the remarkable extent to which the sixteenth-century Guale world was changing. In Mississippian times, such chiefly status had been reinforced by exotics including conch shells, polished greenstones, and native copper wire. The shift to a market-based economy introduced new trappings of chiefly power including Spanish clothing (such as fine woolen friar's cloth, pressed linen, stockings, silk buttons, and Chinese taffeta), multicolored glass beads, and knives with special handles.[64]

Because chiefly power and status relied heavily on the labor of the women of the community, *micos* were sometimes pushed to violence to retain access. When Juanillo turned to violence in 1597, for instance, he was responding to perceived threats to define and regulate his own household. Although these violent actions obviously targeted the friars, Juanillo was also playing to his Guale community, encouraging them to join the rebellion and continue to support his status and power. The Franciscan mission tribute system might even (ironically) have promoted an increase in plural unions, as elite men sought to enhance and reinforce their power and influence through more wives and children.[65]

During the early Franciscan period, some high-profile Guale women married Spaniards in Catholic ceremonies to cement alliances per the *conversion-by-compact* protocols. Pearsall has inquired whether the increase in Franciscan-style marriage was a threat to elite-leading Guale men: "Were Spanish men seen as rivals for Guale women, as well as meddling controllers of households and heavy-handed demanders of tribute?"[66] Oré recorded the simultaneous tensions that arose between converts and non-converts, with some holdouts "persecuting" the converts. Noting that Guale married in pre-1597 Franciscan-style ceremonies abandoned their proper Christian spouses during

64. Joseph M. Hall, Jr., *Zumano's Gifts: Indian-European Exchange in the Southeast* (Pittsburgh: University of Pittsburgh Press, 2012); Worth, *Timucuan Chiefdoms,* 24; Thomas, "Social Agency," 29–31.

65. Pearsall, "'Having Many Wives,'" 1015.

66. Ibid.

the uprising, some favoring unions with "infidels," bearing "two or three children" in the period from 1597 to 1601, Oré dryly noted that the difficulties in getting the Guale men to return to their proper Christian wives required "more work than if they had to be newly converted."[67]

The Mississippian and Franciscan frontiers likewise extracted a huge physical cost. Human health began to deteriorate on the Mississippian frontier due to the significant changes in diet, settlement, work practices, and other consequences of exploitation and colonization. Maize is hazardous to human health, a carbohydrate with high sugar content contributing to dental disease and preventing absorption of iron. Overdependence on maize can also disrupt bodily growth due to the poor quality of its protein. The decision to grow corn carried huge consequences for health and well-being. When coastal Georgians began eating more maize and less seafood, they upset their long-term subsistence balance, and the impacts were immediate. Guale people living on the Mississippian frontier became shorter, weaker, suffered from chronic malnutrition and anemia, and were more likely to contract infectious diseases.[68]

In Mississippian villages and Franciscan missions alike, increased production of food (especially maize) increased workload and changed levels of physical activity. Mississippian communities were subject to increased tribute demands, and the Spanish practice of *repartimiento* required heavy physical work, including agricultural labor, travel, and carrying of heavy burdens (pack animals were rare until the late mission period).[69]

The congregation of Guale and Mocama populations into a limited number of settlements contributed to the maintenance and spread of infectious disease, with Mississippian villages and Franciscan missions becoming reservoirs for epidemic diseases, resulting in increased mortality, decreased fertility, and, ultimately, population decline. Poor sanitary conditions in these settled communities created conditions for more localized soft-tissue infections that spread to adjacent bone. Throughout the seventeenth century, more than half a dozen epidemics swept through La Florida, resulting in the deaths of thousands.[70] Conflict increased among competing Mississippian chiefdoms and other tribes now allied with British interests and displaced tribes from the

67. Oré, *Relación Histórica de la Florida*, 106, as cited in Pearsall, "'Having Many Wives,'" 1016.

68. Clark Spencer Larsen, *Bioarchaeology: Interpreting Behavior from the Human Skeleton*, 2nd ed. (Cambridge: Cambridge University Press, 2015), 16–18, 70–71, 313–315.

69. John H. Hann, *Apalachee: The Land between the Rivers* (Gainesville: University of Florida Press, 1988); David J. Weber, *The Spanish Frontier in North America* (New Haven, CT: Yale University Press, 1992), 126–129.

70. John H. Hann, "Demographic Patterns and Changes in Mid-seventh Century Timucua and Apalachee," *Florida Historical Quarterly* 63, no. 4 (1986): 265–285.

north. The dietary change, disease epidemics, and the social change that characterized both the Mississippian and Franciscan frontiers doubtless inflamed long-standing chiefly rivalries. Tensions increased as Spanish demands for maize tribute impacted Guale and Mocama labor arrangements, marriage practices, and gender roles.[71]

Conclusions and Implications

The contrasts between competing European religious orders are obvious. A handful of drought-plagued years and a "truculent and uncompromising" theo-vision rendered the Jesuit enterprise a nonstarter in Spanish Florida.[72] The succeeding Franciscan theo-vision—grounded in flexibility, adaptability, and heterogeneity—helped foster a Spanish colonial–Mississippian hybrid that introduced the external support attempting to maintain the authority of hereditary chiefs by reinforcing elements of traditional rank and privilege.

The articulation of these competing theo-visions with indigenous Mississippian cosmology is more difficult to assess. The Guale and Mocama people were not "people without history." We can today trace their complex trajectory back more than 5,000 years, and this record clearly demonstrates that the tensions and violence surrounding ascribed social status, frontier life, taxation and tribute, hierarchical disputes over inherited leadership titles, discontent over tribute paid and received, political problems involving plural marriage, labor tensions between elites and commoners, degrading landscapes, children dying from disease, malnutrition, droughts, and crop failure were all factors in coastal Georgia long before Columbus blundered into the Caribbean. Violence and conflict are endemic in chiefdom-level societies.[73] This was true of the Mississippian chiefdoms throughout the American Southeast, and the Franciscans unwittingly involved themselves in these tensions by perpetuating local chiefly hierarchies to provision their enterprise in Spanish Florida.

Indigenous polygamy played a prominent role in the 1597 rebellion and continued to color engagements afterward. The continuing polygamous practices in the Franciscan missions underscores the enduring significance in rank and power among Guale communities and power of their leadership to negotiate some flexibility in mandated Christian monogamy with the Franciscans. As a consequence of *conversion by contract*, friars were required to tolerate situations they could not condone—simultaneously standing by their unflinching

71. Pearsall, "'Having Many Wives,'" 1015.

72. Cushner, *Why Have You Come Here*, 17.

73. Thomas, *Native American Landscapes*, 1052–1063, 1080–1094; Thomas, "Shellfishers of St. Catherines Island," 169–182.

commitment to lifelong Christian-style marriage and mediating what they perceived as an equally committed disdain for sacramental marriage by the Guale.

Spanish colonialism in general has been characterized as an "emasculating experience" for indigenous males—with polygamy (whether Muslim or Native American) perceived as an overt sign of sexual and political subversion among populations that were only nominally Christian.[74] This often-overlooked power of gender politics played a key role in the ethnogenesis of these hybrid Mississippian–Spanish mission communities, with both Spanish and Guale perceiving access to women as a means of maintaining and stimulating further power and status among other males. Sarah Pearsall has emphasized the symbolic and practical roles of plural unions in such competing agendas: When Franciscans vigorously prosecuted polygyny, they were interpreting native actions as "anti-Christianity, apostasy, desecration, political subversion, and violence among indigenous populations. When many Native Americans did so, they were flagging masculine status, authority, labor organization, hierarchy, and political confederation."[75] In the case of the 1597 uprising, when some Guale men responded with an "aggressive hypermasculinity," the audience may not necessarily have been Spanish at all, but rather an effort to unite the local indigenous community for military support and to reassert chiefly authority in times of political stress.

The near-total demographic collapse, coupled with English-sponsored slave raids from the north, would ultimately drive surviving Franciscan missions southward into the shadow of St. Augustine. But the Franciscan theo-vision in La Florida helped facilitate the survival of ancient chiefly lineages and Mississippian-style social systems long after the total collapse of indigenous polities in the interior, which became the "Mississippian shatter zone."[76] In the end, of course, the demographic and political realities of Spanish colonial existence ultimately doomed the Franciscan/Mississippian missions of La Florida.

---

74. Ann Twinam, "Women and Gender in Colonial Latin America," in *Women's History in Global Perspective*, vol. 2, ed. Bonnie G. Smith (Urbana: University of Illinois Press, American Historical Association, 2005), 196.

75. Pearsall, "'Having Many Wives,'" 1002.

76. Robbie Ethridge, "Creating the Shatter Zone: The Indian Slave Trader and the Collapse of the Mississippian World," in *Light on the Path: The Anthropology and History of the Southeastern Indians*, ed. Thomas J. Pluckhahn and Robbie Ethridge (Tuscaloosa: University of Alabama Press, 2006), 207–218.

About the Authors

Keith Ashley is assistant professor of anthropology in the Department of Sociology, Anthropology, and Social Work at the University of North Florida. His research interests center on indigenous northeastern Florida, before and after the European invasion.

Dr. Denise I. Bossy is associate professor of History at the University of North Florida, where she specializes in local Indigenous history. She is the editor of *Yamasee Indians: From Florida to South Carolina*, the prize-winning author of articles and book chapters on the Native and colonial South, and also works with local museums to improve their Indigenous content.

George Aaron Broadwell is Elling Eide Professor of Anthropology at University of Florida. His research focuses on Native languages of the United States and Mexico, with a particular emphasis on Choctaw, Timucua, and Seminole Creek.

Noble David Cook, Professor Emeritus of Florida International University, has authored numerous books and articles on historical demography, ethnohistory, migration, microhistory, and social history. His work is interdisciplinary, covering topics in the early modern Hispanic Atlantic World. Cook has published several articles on the friar and later Bishop Luis Gerónimo de Oré (1554–1630) and has completed a book-length study of him.

Alejandra Dubcovsky is an associate professor of history at the University of California, Riverside. Her first book, *Informed Power: Communication in the Early American South* (HUP 2016), won the 2016 Michael V. R. Thomason Book Award from the Gulf South Historical Association. Her work has been featured in *Ethnohistory*, *Early America Studies*, *The Journal of Southern History*, *Native South*, and the *William and Mary Quarterly*, among others.

Leonardo Falcón (Ph.D. Florida International University, 2019) is an Instructor of History and Latin American Studies at Nassau Community College in Garden City, New York. He is currently working on revising and expanding his dissertation on the subject published in this volume.

Helmut Flachenecker, Professor for Franconian History of the Middle Ages (Regional History), University of Wuerzburg; 2012 Visiting Professor at Kent State University, and 2015 and 2018 at Flagler College, St. Augustine; Head of the Research Center of the Teutonic Order at the University of Wuerzburg.

Timothy J. Johnson is the Craig and Audrey Thorn Distinguished Professor of Religion at Flagler College. He is a member of the Historical Commission for the Canonization of Antonio Cuipa and Companions. He has published extensively in the areas of Franciscan history and theology

Lisa Marie Noetzel's research interest is the language contact between Spanish Franciscans and the Timucua, an extinct tribe from Northeast and North-central Florida. She has taught at Washington University and the College of Coastal Georgia.

David Hurst Thomas (Senior Curator in Residence at the American Museum of Natural History) was captivated by Spanish missions since high school, when his mother took him to all 21 California missions. This fascination with mission archaeology sparked a career in American anthropology and led to four decades of fieldwork on the missions of Spanish Florida and the American Southwest. Thomas was elected in 1989 to the National Academy of Sciences, received the Franciscan Institute Medal three years later, and became a Fellow of the Academy of American Franciscan History in 2014.

Robert L. Thunen is currently a Research Associate for the Center for Community Initiatives and the Archaeology Laboratory at the University of North Florida. Current research interests: applied use of LiDAR to Landscape Archaeology, the contact period concerning the Mocama and Forts Caroline, and Mateo.

John E. Worth is professor of historical archaeology in the Department of Anthropology at the University of West Florida in Pensacola. He has conducted archaeological and ethnohistorical research for more than three decades in the Southeastern U.S., primarily focusing on interactions between Native Americans and Spaniards during the colonial era in Florida and Georgia. He is author of *Discovering Florida: First-Contact Narratives of Spanish Expeditions along the Lower Gulf Coast* (2014), *The Timucuan Chiefdoms of Spanish Florida* (1998), *The Struggle for the Georgia Coast* (1995 and 2007), and more than one hundred-fifty other professional and lay publications and presented papers.

Index

Note: Page numbers in *italics* refer to illustrative matter.